Frommer's®

Santa Fe, Taos & Albuquerque

11th Edition

D0980992

by Lesley S_____

Here's what the critics say about Frommer's:

"Amazingly easy to use. Very portable, very complete."

—*Booklist*

"Detailed, accurate, and easy-to-read information for all price ranges."
—*Glamour Magazine*

"Hotel information is close to encyclopedic."

—*Des Moines Sunday Register*

"Frommer's Guides have a way of giving you a real feel for a place."
—*Knight Ridder Newspapers*

BICENTENNIAL
1807
WILEY
2007
BICENTENNIAL

Wiley Publishing, Inc.

About the Author

Lesley S. King grew up on a ranch in northern New Mexico. She's a freelance writer and photographer, and a columnist for *New Mexico* magazine. Formerly managing editor for *The Santa Fean,* she has written for *The New York Times,* United Airline's *Hemispheres* magazine, and *Audubon,* among other publications. She is the author of *Frommer's New Mexico, Frommer's Great Outdoor Guide to Arizona & New Mexico,* and *New Mexico For Dummies.* She's also the coauthor of *Frommer's American Southwest.* Due for release in 2007 are two new books, *King of the Road* and *The Santa Fe Farmers Market Cookbook.* Kathleen Raphael helped research this book.

Published by:

Wiley Publishing, Inc.

111 River St.
Hoboken, NJ 07030-5774

ISBN-13: 978-0-470-04826-9
ISBN-10: 0-470-04826-3

Editor: Jennifer Anmuth
Production Editor: Ian Skinnari
Cartographer: Andrew Murphy
Photo Editor: Richard Fox
Anniversary Logo Design: Richard Pacifico
Production by Wiley Indianapolis Composition Services

For information on our other products and services or to obtain technical support, please contact our Customer Care Department within the U.S. at 800/762-2974, outside the U.S. at 317/572-3993 or fax 317/572-4002.

Wiley also publishes its books in a variety of electronic formats. Some content that appears in print may not be available in electronic formats.

Manufactured in the United States of America

5   4   3   2   1

Contents

(11) Getting to Know Taos

(12) Where to Stay in Taos

(13) Where to Dine in Taos

(14) What to See & Do in Taos

(15) Albuquerque

Appendix: Northern New Mexico in Depth   281

Index   298

List of Maps

An Invitation to the Reader

In researching this book, we discovered many wonderful places—hotels, restaurants, shops, and more. We're sure you'll find others. Please tell us about them, so we can share the information with your fellow travelers in upcoming editions. If you were disappointed with a recommendation, we'd love to know that, too. Please write to:

Frommer's Santa Fe, Taos & Albuquerque, 11th Edition
Wiley Publishing, Inc. • 111 River St. • Hoboken, NJ 07030-5774

An Additional Note

Please be advised that travel information is subject to change at any time—and this is especially true of prices. We therefore suggest that you write or call ahead for confirmation when making your travel plans. The authors, editors, and publisher cannot be held responsible for the experiences of readers while traveling. Your safety is important to us, however, so we encourage you to stay alert and be aware of your surroundings. Keep a close eye on cameras, purses, and wallets, all favorite targets of thieves and pickpockets.

Other Great Guides for Your Trip:

Frommer's New Mexico
Frommer's American Southwest
Frommer's National Parks of the American West

Frommer's Star Ratings, Icons & Abbreviations

Every hotel, restaurant, and attraction listing in this guide has been ranked for quality, value, service, amenities, and special features using a **star-rating system.** In country, state, and regional guides, we also rate towns and regions to help you narrow down your choices and budget your time accordingly. Hotels and restaurants are rated on a scale of zero (recommended) to three stars (exceptional). Attractions, shopping, nightlife, towns, and regions are rated according to the following scale: zero stars (recommended), one star (highly recommended), two stars (very highly recommended), and three stars (must-see).

In addition to the star-rating system, we also use **seven feature icons** that point you to the great deals, in-the-know advice, and unique experiences that separate travelers from tourists. Throughout the book, look for:

Finds	Special finds—those places only insiders know about
Fun Fact	Fun facts—details that make travelers more informed and their trips more fun
Kids	Best bets for kids and advice for the whole family
Moments	Special moments—those experiences that memories are made of
Overrated	Places or experiences not worth your time or money
Tips	Insider tips—great ways to save time and money
Value	Great values—where to get the best deals

The following **abbreviations** are used for credit cards:

AE	American Express	DISC	Discover	V	Visa
DC	Diners Club	MC	MasterCard		

Frommers.com

Now that you have this guidebook to help you plan a great trip, visit our website at **www.frommers.com** for additional travel information on more than 3,500 destinations. We update the site regularly, to give you instant access to the most current trip-planning information available. At Frommers.com, you'll find scoops on the best airfares, lodging rates, and car rental bargains. You can even book your travel online through our reliable travel booking partners. Other popular features include:

- Online updates of our most popular guidebooks
- Vacation sweepstakes and contest giveaways
- Newsletters highlighting the hottest travel trends
- Online travel message boards with featured travel discussions

What's New in Northern New Mexico

Northern New Mexico has come by its *"mañana"* reputation honestly. Usually change happens . . . tomorrow. But there are some lively additions in the region well worth exploring.

GETTING TO KNOW SANTA FE At this writing, one of the "City Different"'s landmarks, the Sweeney Convention Center, has been razed, with construction beginning soon on a larger, more refined space, to be completed in 2007.

WHERE TO STAY IN SANTA FE In 2006, one of Santa Fe's most notable addresses received a major remodel including addition of a spa. The newly named **Eldorado Hotel & Spa**, 309 W. San Francisco St. (© 800/286-6755 or 505/988-4455; www.eldoradohotel.com) has new furnishings, bedding, and decor in the rooms, and the Nidah Spa offers a full range of treatments including their signature turquoise gemstone therapy. Meanwhile, Santa Fe Budget Inn has also received a makeover and name change. Now called **Santa Fe Sage Inn**, 725 Cerrillos Rd. (© 866/433-0335 or 505/982-5952; www.santafesageinn.com), the rooms have Southwest furnishings, with Aztec-style bedding and whimsical art on the walls. And to announce yet another moniker update: the Spencer House B&B has become **AdobeStar Inn**, 222 McKenzie St. © 800/647-0350 or 505/988-3024; www.adobestarinn.com). Under new ownership, the rooms have taken on Southwestern themes such as an O'Keeffe room—decorated in bright primary colors—and the Abiquiu room, which showcases photos of that crimson-rock country. See chapter 5.

WHERE TO DINE IN SANTA FE Many Santa Feans' favorite new spot is **Aquasanta**, 451 W. Alameda (© 505/982-6297). In a cozy hacienda-like atmosphere complete with kiva fireplace, diners feast on fresh, often organic, inventively prepared food. At lunch, the lamb burger rates as one of the city's best lunches. Santa Fe's famed restaurant **Coyote Café**, 132 Water St. (© 505/983-1615; www.coyotecafe.com/santafe. htm), has received a makeover, bringing the elegance of warm earth tones to the space, complimenting its stellar creative Southwestern menu. Another Santa Fe favorite receiving a makeover is **Ristra**, 548 Agua Fria St. (© 505/982-8608; www.ristrarestaurant.com). Now more contemporary in its ambience, the food still has an elegant blend of French and Southwestern flavors. And, the biggest change to an existing restaurant is the transformation of The Palace to **Señor Lucky's at the Palace**, 142 W. Palace Ave. (© 505/982-9891; www.senor luckys.com). It now has a festive patio and elegant Western interior and serves delectably complex foods by the same chef as the famed Geronimo. Try the tacos! If you're looking for a bit of Italy, head to **Trattoria Nostrani**, 304 Johnson St. (© 505/983-3800; www.trattoria nostrani.com), a Northern Italian cafe not far from the plaza. The chefs there visit Italy each year to enhance their offerings such as roasted quail with sweet Italian sausage or rack of lamb. Meanwhile, the chef at notable 315 has opened an American food restaurant that has locals talking. **The Railyard Restaurant & Saloon,** 530 S. Guadalupe St. (② 505/989-3300; www.railyardrestaurantandsaloon.com), offers tasty steaks and other types of fare as well. The sesame-and-panko-crusted tuna is dynamite. On Canyon Road, the new spot to sip beer and watch the world pass by is **Sol Café,** 802 Canyon Rd. (② 505/989-1949; www.solcafesantafe.com). While you're there, have an Asian chicken salad or the wild mahimahi with a macadamia crust. See chapter 6.

WHAT TO SEE & DO IN SANTA FE The "City Different"'s newest way to relax is with an Indo-Asian spa treatment at **Absolute Nirvana Spa, Tea Room & Gardens,** 106 Faithway St. (② 505/983-7942; www.absolutenirvana.com). The spa has master-level therapists who use plants, herbs, and spices in their treatments. See p. 133.

EXCURSIONS FROM SANTA FE The **High Road Marketplace,** a co-op gallery off the Santuario de Chimayo plaza (② 866/343-5381 or 505/351-1078; www.highroadnewmexico.com), offers art and crafts from all over northern New Mexico, with an excellent collection of devotional crosses. Also along the High Road to Taos, in a vintage theater in the village of Peñasco, the **Sugar Nymphs Bistro,** 15046 NM 75 (② 505/587-0311), serves inventive food such as a pork tenderloin with chipotle cream sauce. See chapter 10.

WHERE TO STAY IN TAOS For better or worse, the Taos Ski Valley seems to be condo-izing. Last year the Edelweiss made the move. This year the Snakedance has become **Snakedance Condominiums & Spa,** 110 Sutton Place (② 800/332-9815 or 505/776-2277; www.snakedancecondos.com). These upscale

condos at the very base of the mountain offer all the luxuries of home. See chapter 12.

WHERE TO DINE IN TAOS The Taos dining scene, always imaginative, has a few new notches on its hostess stand. First, **La Folie,** 106-B Paseo del Pueblo Norte (② 505/751-7549), offers elegant French food in a relaxed urban environment. Lunch has soups, salads, and sandwiches, while dinner offers stacked creations with delectable accoutrements such as tenderloin with saffron polenta. Though it has been in town for seven years, **Caffé Renato,** 133 Paseo del Pueblo Norte (② 505/758-0244; www.johnfarnsworth.com/cafferenato.htm), has moved to a stellar location just steps from the plaza. The restaurant offers American and Italian fare in a gallery setting. The front and back patios are the place to be in summer, eating salads or panini sandwiches or salmon with lemon tarragon aioli. Taoseños are bowled over by **Gutiz,** 812-B Paseo del Pueblo Norte (② 505/758-1226), a French-Latin fusion spot in a modest space north of town. Some come for the fresh baked bread with brie at breakfast or the pork tenderloin with onion confit at lunch. Ice cream lovers congregate at **Taos Cow,** 485 NM 150, Arroyo Seco (② 505/776-5640; www.taoscow.com). Breakfast tacos and sandwiches are a prelude to ice cream made with natural ingredients in flavors such as cherry ristra or simply good old chocolate. See chapter 13.

WHAT TO SEE & DO IN TAOS The **Kit Carson Home and Museum,** 113 Kit Carson Rd. (② 505/758-4613), has become a whole different museum from its predecessor, which closed in 2004. It now offers a glimpse of the sparseness of 19th-century frontier-town life.

WHERE TO STAY IN ALBUQUERQUE The Sheraton Old Town has come under new management and received a major makeover. With it has come a name change. Now **Hotel Albuquerque of Old Town,** 800 Rio Grande Blvd., NW (✆ **800/237-2133;** www.hotelabq.com), offers colonial elegance near the city's best attractions. Those who like the bustle of a city but have a tight budget can now opt for **Hotel Blue,** 717 Central Ave., NW (✆ **877/878-4868** or 505/924-2400; www.thehotelblue.com). A renovation has turned this 1960s property into an Art Deco "boutique hotel" within walking distance of clubs and restaurants. See chapter 15.

WHERE TO DINE IN ALBUQUERQUE   Those who befriend complex flavors will enjoy **AmbroZia Café & Wine Bar,** 108 Rio Grande Blvd., NE (✆ **505/242-6560;** www.ambroziacafe.com), in Old Town. In an intimate setting, this restaurant serves contemporary global food. The duck burger with polenta fries is especially memorable. In a relaxed urban atmosphere, with wood floors and red brick walls, **Gold Street Caffè,** 218 Gold Ave., SW (✆ **505/765-1633**), offers contemporary American cuisine with a focus on quality ingredients. Try the seafood stew. If a sandwich craving hits you, head to **Oak Tree Café,** 5504 Menaul Ave., NE, Suite G (✆ **505/830-2233**), for New York–style deli creations. Strike up a conversation with the owner and he'll help you feel at home.

WHAT TO SEE & DO IN ALBUQUERQUE   The city's new **Balloon Museum,** 9201 Balloon Museum Dr., NE (✆ **505/768-6020;** www.balloonmuseum.com), tells the history of ballooning from its first flight in 1783 to the present, with authentic air-crafts displayed. Albuquerque's brightest new district—Gold Avenue—offers fun shopping and dining. As well as the Gold Street Caffè (see above) it offers many shopping options, topped off with handmade ice cream from **Cold Stone Creamery,** 101 Gold Ave., SW (✆ **505/843-9456;** www.coldstonecreamery.com). See chapter 15.

EXPLORING NEARBY PUEBLOS & MONUMENTS   At **Acoma Pueblo** (✆ **800/747-0181** or 505/552-6604), visitors now have more than the Sky City to see. A 40,000-square-foot museum below the pueblo offers a glimpse into this culture's past and present. And the mining village of Madrid along the Turquoise Trail has become a booming arts town. At **Al Leedom Studio,** 2485 NM 14 (✆ **505/473-2054;** www.alleedom.com), visitors can watch the artist blow glass on weekends. Meanwhile, **Indigo Gallery,** 2584 NM 14 (✆ **505/438-6202**), represents 20 New Mexico artists working in a broad range of mediums. See chapter 15.

1

The Best of Northern New Mexico

New Mexico's Pueblo tribes have one character who stands out among many as a symbol of the spirit of this state: the fun-maker, called by a variety of names, most notably Koshare. Within the Native American dances, this black-and-white-striped character has many powers. He can cure some diseases, make rain fall, and increase fertility. Above all, the irreverent joker exposes our deepest foibles.

As you travel throughout northern New Mexico, you may see evidence of the Koshare-like powers in the land's magical beauty and in the tender relationships between cultures. This place has witnessed immense geologic upheavals, from volcanic explosions to cataclysmic ground shifts. It has seen tragedy in the clash among Spanish, Native American, and Anglo cultures. And yet, with its Koshare nature, it has transformed those experiences into immeasurable richness. Today, it is a land of stunning expanses, immense cultural diversity, and creativity—a place where people very much pursue their own paths.

The center of the region is Santa Fe, a hip, artsy city that wears its 400-year-old mores on its sleeve. Not far away is upstart **Taos,** the little arts town and ski center of just 5,000 people that lies wedged between the 13,000-foot **Sangre de Cristo Mountains** and the 700-foot-deep **Rio Grande Gorge. Albuquerque** is the big city, New Mexico style, where people from all over the state come to trade. Not far from these three cities are the 19 settlements and numerous ruins of the Native American Pueblo culture, an incredible testament to the resilience of a proud people. And through it all weave the **Manzano, Sandia, Sangre de Cristo,** and **Jemez mountains,** multimillion-year-old reminders of the recent arrival of humans in this vast and unique landscape.

From skiing to art galleries, you have a wealth of choices in front of you when planning a trip to northern New Mexico. To help you get started, here are some of my favorite things to do, places to stay, and places to eat in and around Santa Fe, Taos, and Albuquerque.

1 The Most Unforgettable Northern New Mexico Experiences

- **Northern New Mexican Enchiladas:** There are few things more New Mexican than the enchilada. You can order red or green chile, or "Christmas"—half and half. Sauces are rich, seasoned with *ajo* (garlic) and oregano. New Mexican cuisine isn't smothered in cheese and sour cream, so the flavors of the chiles, corn, and meats can really be savored. Enchiladas are often served with *frijoles* (beans), *posole* (hominy), and *sopaipillas* (fried bread). See "Chiles, Sopaipillas & Other New Mexican Specialties" in the appendix.

Northern New Mexico

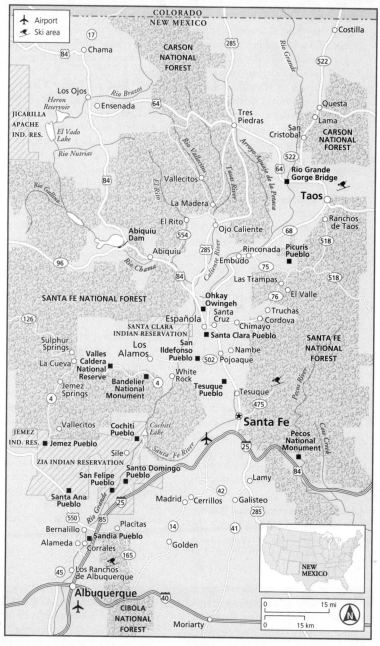

COLORADO
NEW MEXICO

✈ Airport
⛷ Ski area

17

84 ○ Chama

CARSON
NATIONAL
FOREST

285

Rio Grande

○ Costilla

522

Los Ojos ○
Heron
Reservoir

Rio Brazos

○ Ensenada

64

Tres
Piedras

Questa ○

San
Cristobal

Lama ○

522

CARSON
NATIONAL
FOREST

JICARILLA
APACHE
IND. RES.

El Vado
Lake

Rio Nutrias

Rio Gallina

Rio Vallecito

Tusas River

Arroyo-Aguaje de la Petaca

64

Rio Grande
Gorge Bridge ■

Taos ●

84

Vallecitos ○

La Madera ○

El Rito ○

El Rito

Abiquiu
Dam

554

285

Ojo Caliente ○

68

Ranchos
de Taos ○

518

Rinconada ○

Picuris
Pueblo ■

96

Abiquiu ○

Rio Chama

84

Embudo ○

Caliente River

75

Las Trampas ○

518

SANTA FE NATIONAL FOREST

126

Ohkay
Owingeh ■

El Valle ○

76

Santa
Cruz ○

Truchas ○
Cordova ○

Española ○

Chimayo ○

SANTA CLARA
INDIAN RESERVATION

■ Santa Clara Pueblo

SANTA FE
NATIONAL
FOREST

Sulphur
Springs ○

Valles
Caldera
National
Reserve

Los
Alamos ●

San
Ildefonso
Pueblo ■

Nambe ○

Pecos River

La Cueva ○

502

Pojoaque ○

Jemez ○
Springs

4

Bandelier
National
Monument ■

White ○
Rock

4

Tesuque
Pueblo ■

Tesuque ○

475

★ Santa Fe

Vallecitos ○

Cochiti
Pueblo ■

Cochiti
Lake

Santa Fe River

Pecos
National
Monument ■

Cow Creek

JEMEZ
IND. RES.

■ Jemez Pueblo

Sile ○

ZIA INDIAN RESERVATION

25

84

San Felipe
Pueblo ■

Santo Domingo
Pueblo ■

Lamy ○

Santa Ana
Pueblo ■

42

550

Rio Grande

25

Madrid ○ Cerrillos ○

Galisteo ○

285

Bernalillo ○

85

Placitas ○

14

41

Alameda ○

Sandia Pueblo ■

Corrales ○

Golden ○

165

45

Los Ranchos
de Albuquerque ○

NEW
MEXICO

Albuquerque ●

40

0   15 mi

CIBOLA
NATIONAL
FOREST

Moriarty ○

0   15 km

N

- **High Road to Taos:** This spectacular 80-mile route into the mountains between Santa Fe and Taos takes you through red painted deserts, villages bordered by apple and peach orchards, and the foothills of 13,000-foot peaks. You can stop in Cordova, known for its woodcarvers, or Chimayo, known for its weavers. At the fabled **Santuario de Chimayo,** you can rub healing dust between your fingers. See "Along the High Road to Taos" in chapter 10.

- **Santa Fe Opera** (© 800/280-4654 or 505/986-5900; www.santafeopera. org): One of the finest opera companies in the United States has called Santa Fe home for nearly 50 years. Performances are held during the summer months in a hilltop, open-air amphitheater. The big highlight for 2007 is a Santa Fe Opera–commissioned world premiere by Chinese-American composer Tan Dun—who won an Oscar for scoring *Crouching Tiger, Hidden Dragon*—titled *Tea: A Mirror of Soul.* See p. 144.

- **Museum of International Folk Art** (706 Camino Lejo; © 505/476-1200): Santa Fe's perpetually expanding collection of folk art is the largest in the world, with thousands of objects from more than 100 countries. You'll find an amazing array of imaginative works, ranging from Hispanic folk art *santos* (carved saints) to Indonesian textiles and African sculptures. See p. 113.

- **Albuquerque International Balloon Fiesta** (© 800/733-9918): The world's largest balloon rally assembles some 750 colorful balloons and includes races and contests. High-lights are the mass ascension at sunrise and the special shapes rodeo, in which balloons in all sorts of whimsical forms, from liquor bottles to cows, rise into the sky. See "Northern New Mexico Calendar of Events" in chapter 2.

- **María Benitez Teatro Flamenco** (Institute for Spanish Arts; © 888/435-2636): Flamenco dancing originated in Spain, strongly influenced by the Moors; it's a cultural expression held sacred by Spanish gypsies. Intricate toe and heel clicking, sinuous arm and hand gestures, expressive guitar solos, and *cante hondo,* or "deep song," characterize the passionate dance. A native New Mexican, María Benitez was trained in Spain, to which she returns each year to find dancers and prepare her show. This world-class dancer and her troupe perform at the Lodge at Santa Fe from late June to early September. See p. 146.

- **Taos Pueblo** (Veterans Hwy., Taos Pueblo; © 505/758-1028): Possibly the original home of pueblo-style architecture, this bold structure where 200 residents still live much as their ancestors did a thousand years ago is awe-inspiring. Rooms built of mud are poetically stacked to echo the shape of Taos Mountain behind them. As you explore the pueblo, you can visit the residents' studios, munch on bread baked in an *horno* (a beehive-shaped oven), and wander past the fascinating ruins of the old church and cemetery. See p. 208.

2 The Best Splurge Hotels

- **Bishop's Lodge Ranch Resort & Spa** (Bishop's Lodge Rd., Santa Fe; © 505/983-6377): More than a century ago, Bishop Jean-Baptiste Lamy often escaped clerical politics by hiking into a valley north of town called Little Tesuque. He built a retreat and chapel that years later have become

The Bishop's Lodge. All rooms are spacious and feature handcrafted furniture and local artwork. Activities include horseback riding, hiking, tennis, and swimming. See p. 75.

- **Inn of the Anasazi** (113 Washington Ave., Santa Fe; ✆ **800/688-8100** or 505/988-3030): Just steps from the plaza, this elegant hotel offers a taste of Anasazi architecture. The interior utilizes stacked sandstone with touches of Navajo artwork to create a warm ambience. Add to that excellent amenities and stellar service. See p. 68.

- **La Posada de Santa Fe Resort and Spa** (330 E. Palace Ave., Santa Fe; ✆ **800/727-5276** or 505/986-0000): With the feel of a meandering adobe village but the service of a fine hotel, this has become one of New Mexico's premier resorts. It has a Zen-Southwestern-style spa and pool and spacious spa rooms. Most rooms don't have views but have outdoor patios, and most are tucked back into the quiet compound. See p. 70.

- **Rancho de San Juan** (US 285 near Española; ✆ **505/753-6818**): Just 38 miles from Santa Fe, in the enchanting country near Ojo Caliente, this award-winning inn offers complete luxury and the quiet of the country.

The recently renovated rooms in the inn, as well as the casitas set among the hills, are all decorated with impressive art and antiques, and have spectacular views. See p. 165.

- **El Monte Sagrado** (317 Kit Carson Rd., Taos; ✆ **800/828-TAOS** or 505/758-3502): With guest rooms and casitas set around a grassy "Sacred Circle," this new eco-resort is the quintessence of luxury. Every detail, from the waterfalls and chemical-free pool and hot tubs to the authentic theme decor in the rooms, has been created with conscious care. See p. 181.

- **Hyatt Regency Tamaya Resort and Spa** (1300 Tuyuna Trail, Santa Ana Pueblo; ✆ **800/55-HYATT** or 505/867-1234): Situated on Santa Ana Pueblo land, this grand resort has all a human might need to get away from the world. Three swimming pools, a 16,000-square-foot, full-service spa and fitness center, the 18-hole Twin Warriors Championship Golf Course designed by Gary Panks, and views of the Sandia Mountains make for plenty to do. Meanwhile, spacious rooms offer quiet for those who'd rather do nothing. It's only 25 minutes from Albuquerque and 45 minutes from Santa Fe. See p. 242.

3 The Best Moderately Priced Hotels

- **Santa Fe Motel and Inn** (510 Cerrillos Rd., Santa Fe; ✆ **800/930-5002** or 505/982-1039): Rooms at this inn, walking distance from the plaza, combine the ambience of the Southwest—bold colors and some handmade furniture—with a standard motel price tag. See p. 74.

- **El Rey Inn** (1862 Cerrillos Rd., Santa Fe; ✆ **800/521-1349** or 505/982-1931): If old-style court motels awaken the road warrior in you, this is your place. Built in the 1930s and

added onto over the years, the King provides a variety of types of rooms, all nicely appointed. See p. 77.

- **Best Western Kachina Lodge & Meeting Center** (413 Paseo del Pueblo Norte, Taos; ✆ **800/522-4462** or 505/758-2275): A mainstay since the 1950s, when it was built, this hotel offers clean and efficient rooms set around a grassy courtyard studded with blue spruce trees. On the north end of town, it's close to most attractions. See p. 185.

- **Wyndham Albuquerque Hotel** (2910 Yale Blvd., SE, Albuquerque; ✆ **800/227-1117** or 505/843-7000): Even though this hotel is near the airport, Albuquerque's attractions are just minutes away (thanks to its easy access to freeways). The spacious rooms have a warm Anasazi feel, and the views are spectacular. See p. 238.

4 The Most Unforgettable Dining Experiences

- **The Compound** (653 Canyon Rd., Santa Fe; ✆ **505/982-4353**): This reincarnation of one of Santa Fe's classic restaurants serves daring contemporary American food in a soulful setting. Such delicacies as monkfish chorizo with watercress or grilled beef tenderloin with Italian potatoes will please sophisticated palates—and probably simpler ones too. See p. 88.

- **Santacafé** (231 Washington Ave., Santa Fe; ✆ **505/984-1788**): The food here borrows from an international menu of preparations and offerings. The minimalist decor accentuates the beautiful architecture of the 18th-century Padre Gallegos House. One of my favorite dishes is the Alaskan halibut with English peas and saffron couscous. See p. 93.

- **Geronimo** (724 Canyon Rd., Santa Fe; ✆ **505/982-1500**): Set in the 1756 Borrego House on Canyon Road, this restaurant offers brilliant flavors in a serene adobe atmosphere. The elk tenderloin here is Santa Fe's most prized entree. Come for lunch and sit on the patio to watch the action on Canyon Road. See p. 90.

- **The Shed** (113½ E. Palace Ave., Santa Fe; ✆ **505/982-9030**): The Shed, a Santa Fe luncheon institution since 1953, occupies several rooms in part of a rambling hacienda that was built in 1692. The sauces here have been refined over the years, creating amazing flavors in basic dishes like enchiladas, burritos, and stuffed *sopaipillas*. The mocha cake is renowned. See p. 100. Sister restaurant **La Choza** is just as good, with a similar menu. See p. 99.

- **De La Tierra** (317 Kit Carson Rd., Taos; ✆ **800/828-TAOS** or 505/758-3502): Located at the new eco-resort El Monte Sagrado, this elegant restaurant serves imaginative regional American food and other delights such as wild game. The pan roasted rack of lamb with sage bread pudding and grilled asparagus is excellent. An expansive wine list completes the experience. See p. 196.

- **Joseph's Table** (108-A South Taos Plaza, Taos; ✆ **505/751-4512**): Now in new digs on Taos Plaza, this font of creativity serves delightful dishes with plenty of flair. Try the steak au poivre over mashed potatoes with a Madeira mushroom sauce. Delectable. See p. 196.

- **AmbroZia Café & Wine Bar** (108 Rio Grande Blvd., NE, Albuquerque; ✆ **505/242-6560**): This new restaurant claims it makes "Food for the Gods," and I have to agree. The offerings might even give Apollo pause, so complex do they seem, but when they hit the palate, the sensation is pure heaven. See p. 244.

5 The Best Things to Do for Free

- **The Galleries along Canyon Road:** Originally a Pueblo Indian route over the mountains and later an artists' community, Santa Fe's Canyon Road is now gallery central—the arts capital of the Southwest. The narrow one-way street is lined with more than 100 galleries, in addition to restaurants and private residences. Artwork ranges from the beautiful to the bizarre. You can step into artists' simple studio galleries as well as refined galleries showing world-renowned artists' works, such as paintings by Georgia O'Keeffe and sculptures by Frederic Remington. Be sure to stop for lunch at one of the street-side cafes. See "Walking Tour 2: Barrio de Analco & Canyon Road" in chapter 7.

- **Pueblo dances:** These native dances, related to the changing cycles of the earth, offer a unique chance to see how an indigenous culture worships and rejoices. Throughout the year, the pueblos' people participate in ceremonies ranging from harvest and deer dances to those commemorating the feast days of their particular saints—all in the mystical light of the northern New Mexico sun. See chapter 10 for more information on visiting pueblos.

- **Rio Grande Gorge:** A hike into this dramatic gorge is unforgettable. You'll first see it as you come over a rise heading toward Taos, a colossal slice in the earth formed 130 million years ago. Drive about 35 miles north of Taos, near the village of Cerro, to the Rio Grande Wild River Area. From the lip of the canyon, you descend through millions of years of geologic history on land inhabited by Indians since 16,000 B.C. When you reach the river, you can dip your toes in the fabled *rio*. If you're not a hiker, you can get a sense of the canyon by walking across the Rio Grande Gorge Bridge. See chapter 14.

- **Old Town:** Albuquerque's commercial center until about 1880, Old Town still gives a remarkable sense of what life was once like in a Southwestern village. You can meander down crooked streets and narrow alleys and rest in the cottonwood-shaded plaza. Though many of the shops are now very touristy, you can still happen upon some interesting shopping and dining finds here. Native Americans sell jewelry, pottery, and weavings under a portal on the plaza. See p. 254.

6 The Best Outdoor Activities

- **Taos Ski Valley:** World renowned for its difficult runs and the ridge where skiers hike for up to 2 hours to ski fresh powder, Taos has long been a pilgrimage site for extreme skiers. Over the years, the ski area has opened up new bowls to accommodate intermediate and beginning skiers, too. See p. 212.

- **Sandia Peak Tramway:** The world's longest tramway ferries passengers 2¾ miles, from Albuquerque's city limits to the summit of the 10,378-foot Sandia Peak. On the way, you'll likely see rare Rocky Mountain bighorn sheep and birds of prey. Go in the evening to watch the sun set, and then enjoy the glimmering city lights on your way down. See p. 256.

- **Bandelier National Monument:** These ruins provide a spectacular peek into the lives of the ancestral Puebloan culture, which reached its peak in this area around 1100 A.D. Less than 15 miles south of Los Alamos, the ruins spread across a peaceful canyon. You'll probably see deer and rabbits as you make your way through the canyon to the most dramatic site, a kiva and dwelling in a cave 140 feet above the canyon floor. See p. 157.

- **Whitewater Rafting on the Rio Grande:** In spring and early summer, the region's most notorious white-water trip, the Taos Box, takes rafters on an 18-mile jaunt through the Rio Grande Gorge. Less extreme types can enjoy a trip down Pilar and still get plenty wet. See p. 218.

- **Llama Trekking:** Also in the Taos area, two outfitters take hikers on day or multiday trips. You get to enjoy the scenery while the stout and docile creatures do the work. The trips come with gourmet food. See p. 217.

- **Hot Air Ballooning:** One of the biggest treats about being in Albuquerque is waking each day and looking at the sky. Unless it's very windy or extremely cold, you'll likely see some colorful globes floating serenely on the horizon. You might even be startled with the sound of flames blasting as one flies over your head! The experience of riding in one is indescribable. You're literally floating, being carried along by nothing but the wind. Try it! See p. 261.

- **Bosque del Apache National Wildlife Refuge** (San Antonio; ✆ 505/835-1828): About 80 miles south of Albuquerque, this is one of the nation's finest refuges. In winter, visitors come to see volumes of birds. In early December, the refuge may harbor as many as 45,000 snow geese, 57,000 ducks of many different species, and 18,000 sandhill cranes. Seeing them "fly out" to the fields in the morning, or "fly in" to the lakes in the evening is a life-altering experience. See p. 262.

7 The Best Offbeat Experiences

- **Watching Zozobra Burn** (Santa Fe; ✆ 505/988-7575): Part of Las Fiestas de Santa Fe held in early September, this ritual draws crowds to the core of the city to cheer as "Old Man Gloom," a giant marionette, moans and struggles as he burns. The Fiestas also include Masses, parades, dances, food, and arts. See p. 18.

- **Theater Grottesco** (551 W. Cordova Rd. #8400, Santa Fe; ✆ 505/474-8400): This theater troupe likes to shock, confuse, confound, and tickle its audience's funny bones. Their original works—presented for about a month each spring or summer, and sometimes in the winter as well—combine adept movement with sound, story, and, well . . . complete brilliance. See p. 146.

- **Black Hole** (4015 Arkansas, Los Alamos; ✆ 505/662-5053): Oddball history buffs will love wandering among this shrine to the nuclear age. Packed to the ceiling with the remains of the nuclear age, from Geiger counters to a giant Waring blender, it's peace activist Edward Grothus' statement about the proliferation of war and the materials that make it happen. See p. 156.

- **D.H. Lawrence Ranch** (NM 522, San Cristobal; ✆ 505/776-2245): North of Taos, this memorial offers a look into the oddly touching devotion for this controversial author, who lived and wrote in the area in the early 1920s. The guest book reveals a wellspring of stories of pilgrimages to the site. See p. 209.

- **American International Rattlesnake Museum** (202 San Felipe St., NW; ✆ 505/242-6569): This Albuquerque museum offers a glimpse of reptilian life. You'll see living specimens of common, uncommon, and very rare rattlesnakes of North, Central, and South America in naturally landscaped habitats. More than 30 species are included, along with oddities such as albino and patternless rattlesnakes. See p. 260.

2

Planning Your Trip to Northern New Mexico

As with any trip, a little preparation is essential before you start your journey to northern New Mexico. This chapter provides a variety of planning tools, including information on when to go and how to get there.

1 Visitor Information

Numerous agencies can assist you with planning your trip. The Visitors Information Center for the **New Mexico Department of Tourism** is located at 491 Old Santa Fe Trail, Santa Fe, NM 87501 (© **800/545-2070** or 505/827-7336). You can also find general New Mexico information on the Department of Tourism's website at **www.newmexico.org**. Santa Fe, Taos, and Albuquerque each have their own information service for visitors (see the "Orientation" sections in chapters 4, 11, and 15, respectively).

Northern New Mexico: Pre-Departure Checklist

- To check in at a kiosk with an e-ticket, do you have the credit card you bought your ticket with or a frequent-flier card?
- Did you find out your daily ATM withdrawal limit?
- If you purchased traveler's checks, have you recorded the check numbers, and stored the documentation separately from the checks?
- Did you bring your ID cards that could entitle you to discounts, such as AAA and AARP cards, student IDs, etc.?
- Did you leave a copy of your itinerary with someone at home?
- Did you make advance reservations? Depending on when you travel, you'll want to make a few. If you plan to attend the Santa Fe Indian Market in August or the Albuquerque International Balloon Fiesta in October be sure to make hotel reservations long in advance. Up to a year is recommended.
- Did you make sure your favorite attraction is open? This is only of real concern in relation to visiting the pueblos, which operate on their own schedules dictated by holy days and nature's seasons.
- Do you have sunscreen and a water bottle? In New Mexico, you should carry these things with you at all times.

A valuable resource for information on outdoor recreation is the **Public Lands Information Center,** on the south side of town at 1474 Rodeo Rd., Santa Fe, NM 87505 (© **877/276-9404** or 505/438-7542). Here, adventurers can find out what's available on lands administered by the National Forest Service, the Bureau of Land Management, the Fish and Wildlife Service, the National Park Service, the New Mexico Department of Game and Fish (which sells hunting and fishing licenses), and the New Mexico State Parks Division. The Information Center collaborates with the New Mexico Department of Tourism. Log on to the website at **www.publiclands.org**, and you'll also be able to access links to 261 separate sites, which can be found by looking up either a particular activity or agency.

For Internet addresses of individual cities' visitor centers, see chapters 4, 11, and 15.

2 Entry Requirements & Customs

ENTRY REQUIREMENTS
PASSPORTS

For information on how to get a passport, go to "**Passports**" in the "**Fast Facts**" section of this chapter—the websites listed provide downloadable passport applications as well as the current fees for processing passport applications. For an up-to-date, country-by-country listing of passport requirements around the world, go to the "Foreign Entry Requirement" Web page of the U.S. State Department at **http://travel.state.gov**. International visitors can obtain a visa application at the same website.

VISAS

For information on how to get a visa, go to "**Visas**" in the "**Fast Facts**" section of this chapter.

The U.S. State Department has a **Visa Waiver Program** allowing citizens of the following countries (at press time) to enter the United States without a visa for stays of up to 90 days: Andorra, Australia, Austria, Belgium, Brunei, Denmark, Finland, France, Germany, Iceland, Ireland, Italy, Japan, Liechtenstein, Luxembourg, Monaco, the Netherlands, New Zealand, Norway, Portugal, San Marino, Singapore, Slovenia, Spain, Sweden, Switzerland, and the United Kingdom. Citizens of these nations need only a valid passport and a round-trip air or cruise ticket upon arrival. If they first enter the United States, they may also visit Mexico, Canada, Bermuda, and/or the Caribbean islands and return to the United States without a visa. Further information is available from any U.S. embassy or consulate. Canadian citizens may enter the United States without visas; they need only proof of residence.

Citizens of all other countries must have (1) a valid passport that expires at least 6 months later than the scheduled end of their visit to the United States, and (2) a tourist visa, which may be obtained without charge from any U.S. consulate.

MEDICAL REQUIREMENTS

Unless you're arriving from an area known to be suffering from an epidemic (particularly cholera or yellow fever), inoculations or vaccinations are not required for entry into the United States. If you have a medical condition that requires **syringe-administered medications,** carry a valid signed prescription from your physician—the Federal Aviation Administration (FAA) no longer allows airline passengers to pack syringes in their carry-on baggage without documented proof of medical need. If you have a disease that requires treatment with **narcotics,** you should also carry documented proof with you—smuggling narcotics aboard a plane is a serious offense that carries severe penalties in the U.S.

For **HIV-positive visitors,** requirements for entering the United States are somewhat vague and change frequently. For up-to-the-minute information, contact **AIDSinfo** (☏ **800/448-0440** or 301/519-6616 outside the U.S.; www.aidsinfo.nih.gov) or the **Gay Men's Health Crisis** (☏ **212/367-1000;** www.gmhc.org).

CUSTOMS
WHAT YOU CAN BRING INTO NORTHERN NEW MEXICO

Every visitor more than 21 years of age may bring in, free of duty, the following: (1) 1 liter of wine or hard liquor; (2) 200 cigarettes, 100 cigars (but not from Cuba), or 3 pounds of smoking tobacco; and (3) $100 worth of gifts. These exemptions are offered to travelers who spend at least 72 hours in the United States and who have not claimed them within the preceding 6 months. It is altogether forbidden to bring into the country foodstuffs (particularly fruit, cooked meats, and canned goods) and plants (vegetables, seeds, tropical plants, and the like). Foreign tourists may carry in or out up to $10,000 in U.S. or foreign currency with no formalities; larger sums must be declared to U.S. Customs on entering or leaving, which includes filing form CM 4790. For details regarding U.S. Customs and Border Protection, consult your nearest U.S. embassy or consulate, or **U.S. Customs** (☏ **202/927-1770;** www.customs.ustreas.gov).

WHAT YOU CAN TAKE HOME FROM NORTHERN NEW MEXICO
Canadian Citizens

For a clear summary of Canadian rules, write for the booklet *I Declare,* issued by the **Canada Border Services Agency** (☏ **800/461-9999** in Canada, or 204/983-3500; www.cbsa-asfc.gc.ca).

U.K. Citizens

For information, contact **HM Customs & Excise** at ☏ **0845/010-9000** (from outside the U.K., 020/8929-0152), or consult their website at **www.hmce.gov.uk**.

Australian Citizens

A helpful brochure available from Australian consulates or Customs offices is *Know Before You Go.* For more information, call the **Australian Customs Service** at ☏ **1300/363-263,** or log on to **www.customs.gov.au**.

New Zealand Citizens

Most questions are answered in a free pamphlet available at New Zealand consulates and Customs offices: *New Zealand Customs Guide for Travellers, Notice no. 4.* For more information, contact **New Zealand Customs,** The Customhouse, 17–21 Whitmore St., Box 2218, Wellington (☏ **04/473-6099** or 0800/428-786; www.customs.govt.nz).

3 Money

If you come from a major city, such as New York or London, you may find northern New Mexico overall fairly inexpensive, although Santa Fe will be closer in price to what you're accustomed to. In Taos and Albuquerque, you can still get good accommodations and meals without wincing. Santa Fe, however, may hurt a bit, especially if you hit the hottest spots in town, which cater to sophisticated tastes.

ATMS

Nationwide, the easiest and best way to get cash away from home is from an ATM (automated teller machine), sometimes referred to as a "cash machine," or "cashpoint." The **Cirrus** (☏ **800/424-7787;** www.mastercard.com) and **PLUS** (☏ **800/843-7587;** www.visa.com) networks span the country; you can find them even in remote regions. Look at the

What Things Cost in Santa Fe	US$	Euro€	UK£
Double room in high season at La Posada de Santa Fe Resort & Spa	299	235	160
Double room in high season at Santa Fe Motel and Inn	119	93	64
Dinner for two at Geronimo, without drinks, tax, or tip	115	90	61
Dinner for two at La Choza, without drinks, tax, or tip	25	19	13
An imported Mexican beer at the Dragon Room	4	3	2
One-hour massage at Ten Thousand Waves Japanese Health Spa	92	72	49
Adult admission to the Museum of International Folk Art	8	6	4

back of your bank card to see which network you're on, and then call or check online for ATM locations at your destination. Be sure you know your personal identification number (PIN) and daily withdrawal limit before you depart. *Note:* Remember that many banks impose a fee every time you use a card at another bank's ATM, and that fee can be higher for international transactions (up to $5 or more) than for domestic ones (where they're rarely more than $2). In addition, the bank from which you withdraw cash may charge its own fee. To compare banks' ATM fees within the United States, use **www.bankrate.com**. For international withdrawal fees, ask your bank.

CREDIT CARDS & DEBIT CARDS

Credit cards are the most widely used form of payment in the United States: **Visa** (Barclaycard in Britain), **MasterCard** (EuroCard in Europe, Access in Britain, Chargex in Canada), **American Express, Diners Club,** and **Discover.** They also provide a convenient record of all your expenses, and they generally offer relatively good exchange rates. You can withdraw cash advances from your credit cards at banks or ATMs, provided you know your PIN.

Visitors from outside the U.S. should inquire whether their bank assesses a 1% to 3% fee on charges incurred abroad.

It's highly recommended that you travel with at least one major credit card. You must have one to rent a car, and hotels and airlines usually require a credit card imprint as a deposit against expenses.

ATM cards with major credit card backing, known as "**debit cards**," are now a commonly acceptable form of payment in most stores and restaurants. Debit cards draw money directly from your checking account. Some stores enable you to receive "cash back" on your debit-card purchases as well. The same is true at most U.S. post offices.

TRAVELER'S CHECKS

Traveler's checks are widely accepted in the U.S., but foreign visitors should make sure that they're denominated in U.S. dollars; foreign-currency checks are often difficult to exchange.

You can buy traveler's checks at most banks. Most are offered in denominations of $20, $50, $100, $500, and sometimes $1,000. Generally, you'll pay a service charge ranging from 1% to 4%.

The most popular traveler's checks are offered by **American Express** (☎ 800/807-6233; ☎ 800/221-7282 for card holders—this number accepts collect calls, offers service in several foreign languages, and exempts Amex gold and platinum cardholders from the 1% fee.); **Visa** (☎ 800/732-1322)—AAA members can obtain Visa checks for a $9.95 fee (for checks up to $1,500) at most AAA offices or by calling ☎ 866/339-3378; and **MasterCard** (☎ 800/223-9920).

If you do choose to carry traveler's checks, keep a record of their serial numbers separate from your checks in the event that they are stolen or lost. You'll get a refund faster if you know the numbers.

4 When to Go

Forget any preconceptions you may have about the New Mexico "desert." The high desert climate of this part of the world is generally dry but not always warm. Santa Fe and Taos, at 7,000 feet above sea level, have midsummer highs in the 90s (30s Celsius) and lows in the 50s (teens Celsius). This is the busiest time of year in New Mexico, when most cultural activities are in full swing and prices and temperatures rise. You'll want to make hotel reservations in advance.

Spring and fall are some of New Mexico's most pleasant seasons, with highs in the 60s (teens Celsius), and lows in the 30s (−1°C and below). Spring can be windy, but the skiing can be excellent, with sunny days and the season's accumulated deep snow. Fall is a particularly big draw because the aspens turn golden in the mountains. In both spring and fall, tourist traffic is sparse and room rates are lower.

Winter can be delightful in northern New Mexico, when typical daytime temperatures are in the low 40s (single digits Celsius), and overnight lows are in the teens (−8°C and below). The snowy days here are some of the prettiest you'll ever see, and during a good snow year (as much as 300 in. at Taos Ski Valley), skiers can really enjoy the region. However, during holidays, the slopes can get crowded. During all the seasons, temperatures in Albuquerque, at 5,300 feet, often run about 10° warmer than elsewhere in the northern region.

Average Temperatures (High/Low) and Annual Rainfall (Inches)

		Jan	Apr	July	Oct	Rainfall
Albuquerque	Temp (°F)	46/28	69/42	91/66	71/45	8.9
	Temp (°C)	8/−2	21/6	33/19	22/7	
Santa Fe	Temp (°F)	42/18	62/33	85/56	65/38	14.0
	Temp (°C)	6/−8	17/1	29/13	18/3	
Taos	Temp (°F)	40/10	64/29	87/50	67/32	12.1
	Temp (°C)	4/−12	18/−2	31/10	19/0	

NORTHERN NEW MEXICO CALENDAR OF EVENTS

January

New Year's Day. Transfer of canes to new officials and various dances at most pueblos. Turtle Dance at Taos Pueblo (no photography allowed). Call ☎ 505/758-1028 for more information. January 1.

Winter Wine Festival. A variety of wine offerings and food tastings prepared by local chefs take place in the Taos Ski Valley. Call ☎ 505/776-2291 for details. Mid-January.

February

Candelaria Day Celebration, Picuris Pueblo. Traditional dances. Call ℂ **505/ 587-2519** for more information. February 2.

Mt. Taylor Winter Quadrathlon. Hundreds of athletes come from all over the West to bicycle, run, cross-country ski, and snowshoe up and down this mountain. For information, call ℂ **800/748-2142.** Mid-February.

Just Desserts Eat and Ski. Cross-country skiers ski from point to point on the Enchanted Forest course near Red River, tasting decadent desserts supplied by area restaurants. Call ℂ **505/754-2374.** Late February.

March

National Fiery Foods/Barbecue Show. Here's your chance to taste the hottest of the hot and plenty of milder flavors, too. Some 10,000 general public attendees show up to taste sauces, salsas, candies, and more, and to see cooking demonstrations at the Albuquerque Convention Center. For information, call ℂ **505/873-8680** or go to **www.fiery-foods.com**. Early March.

Rio Grande Arts and Crafts Festival. A juried show featuring 200 artists and craftspeople from around the country takes place at the State Fairgrounds in Albuquerque. Call ℂ **505/292-7457** for more information, or visit **www.rio grandefestivals.com**. Second week of March.

Chimayo Pilgrimage. On Good Friday, thousands of pilgrims trek on foot to the Santuario de Chimayo, a small church north of Santa Fe that's believed to aid in miracles. For information, call ℂ **505/351-4889.**

April

Easter Weekend Celebration. Celebrations include Masses, parades, corn dances, and other dances, such as the bow and arrow dance at Nambe. Call ℂ **505/793-2036** for information.

American Indian Week, Indian Pueblo Cultural Center, Albuquerque. A celebration of Native American traditions and culture. For dates and information, call ℂ **505/843-7270.**

Gathering of Nations Powwow, University Arena, Albuquerque. Dance competitions, arts-and-crafts exhibitions, and Miss Indian World contest. Call ℂ **505/836-2810,** or visit **www. gatheringofnations.com**. Late April.

May

Taste of Santa Fe. Sample Santa Fe's best chefs' recipes, including appetizers, entrees, and desserts at Santa Fe's La Fonda Hotel. For information, held ℂ **505/982-6366,** ext. 112. Held in May or June.

Taos Spring Arts Festival. Contemporary visual, performing, and literary arts are highlighted during 2 weeks of gallery openings, studio tours, performances by visiting theatrical and dance troupes, live musical events, traditional ethnic entertainment, literary readings, and more.

Events are held at venues throughout Taos and Taos County. For dates and ticket info, contact the Taos County Chamber of Commerce, P.O. Drawer I, Taos, NM 87571 (ℂ **800/ 732-TAOS** or 505/758-3873; www. taoschamber.com). All month.

June

San Antonio Feast Day. Corn dances at many of the pueblos. For information, call ℂ **505/843-7270.** June 13.

Rodeo de Santa Fe. This 4-day event features a Western parade, a rodeo dance, and five rodeo performances. It attracts hundreds of cowboys and cowgirls from all over the Southwest who compete for sizable purses in such events as Brahma bull and bronco riding, calf roping, steer wrestling, barrel racing, trick riding, and clown and animal acts.

The rodeo grounds are at 3237 Rodeo Rd., off Cerrillos Road, 5½ miles south of the plaza. Performances are in the evening Wednesday to Saturday; and on Saturday afternoon. For tickets and information, call (C) **505/471-4300** or visit **www.rodeodesantafe.org**. It takes place sometime around the third weekend in June.

Rodeo de Taos, County Fairgrounds, Taos. A fun event featuring local and regional participants. For information, call (C) **505/758-5700** or, in mid- to late June call (C) **505/758-3974**. Third or fourth weekend in June.

Taos Solar Music Festival, Kit Carson Municipal Park, Taos. Sit out on the grass, under the sun, and listen to major players at this event celebrating the summer solstice. A tribute to solar energy, the event has a stage powered by a solar generator and educational displays within a "Solar Village." For information, call (C) **505/758-9191.** Late June.

New Mexico Arts and Crafts Fair. A tradition for 43 years, this juried show offers work from more than 200 New Mexico artisans, accompanied by nonstop entertainment for the whole family. This can be a good place to find Hispanic arts and crafts.

The fair is held at the State Fairgrounds in Albuquerque. Admission cost varies. For information, call (C) **505/884-9043** or check online at **www.nmartsandcraftsfair.org**. Last full weekend in June.

July

Fourth of July celebrations (including fireworks displays) are held all over New Mexico. Call the chambers of commerce in specific towns and cities for information.

Pancake Breakfast on the Plaza. Rub elbows with Santa Fe residents at this locals' event on the plaza. For information, call (C) **505/982-2002.** July 4.

Taos Pueblo Powwow. Intertribal competition in traditional and contemporary dances. Call (C) **505/758-1028** for more information or visit **www.taospueblopowwow.com.** Second weekend in July.

Eight Northern Pueblos Artist and Craftsman Show. More than 600 Native American artists exhibit their work at the eight northern pueblos. Traditional dances and food booths; location varies. Call (C) **505/747-1593** for location and exact dates. Third weekend in July.

Fiestas de Santiago y Santa Ana. The celebration begins with a Friday-night Mass at one of the three Taos-area parishes, where the fiesta queen is crowned. During the weekend there are candlelight processions, special Masses, music, dancing, parades, crafts, and food booths.

Taos Plaza hosts many events and most are free. For information, contact the Taos Fiesta Council, P.O. Box 3300, Taos, NM 87571 ((C) **800/732-8267;** www.fiestasdetaos.com). Third weekend in July.

Spanish Market. More than 300 Hispanic artists from New Mexico and southern Colorado exhibit and sell their work in this lively community event. Artists are featured in special demonstrations, while an entertaining mix of traditional Hispanic music, dance, foods, and pageantry creates the ambience of a village celebration. Artwork for sale includes *santos* (painted and carved saints), textiles, tinwork, furniture, straw appliqué, and metalwork.

The markets are found at Santa Fe Plaza in Santa Fe. For information, contact the Spanish Colonial Arts Society, P.O. Box 5378, Santa Fe, NM 87502 (✆ **505/982-2226;** www.spanishcolonial.org). Last full weekend in July.

August

San Lorenzo Feast Day, Picuris Pueblo. Traditional dances and foot races. Call ✆ **505/587-2519** or visit **www.santaana.org/calendar.htm** for details. August 10.

Pueblo Independence Day, Jemez Pueblo. Participants from many of the Pueblos convene to celebrate the Pueblo Revolt of 1680. Food, art booths, dances, and live music fill the sunny plaza. Call ✆ **505/829-3530.** Mid-August.

The Indian Market. This is the largest all–Native American market in the country. About 1,000 artisans display their baskets and blankets, jewelry, pottery, woodcarvings, rugs, sand paintings, and sculptures at rows of booths around Santa Fe Plaza, surrounding streets, and de Vargas Mall. Sales are brisk. Costumed tribal dancing and crafts demonstrations are scheduled in the afternoon.

The market is free, but hotels are booked months in advance. For information, contact the **Southwestern Association for Indian Arts,** P.O. Box 969, Santa Fe, NM 87504-0969 (✆ **505/983-5220;** www.swaia.org). Third weekend in August.

Music from Angel Fire. World-class musicians gather in Angel Fire to perform classical and chamber music. For information and schedules, call ✆ **505/377-3233** or go to **www.angelfirenm.com**. Mid-August to the first week in September.

September

New Mexico Wine Festival. New Mexico wines are showcased at this annual event in Bernalillo, near Albuquerque, which features wine tastings, an art show, and live entertainment. For a schedule of events, call ✆ **505/867-3311.** Labor Day weekend.

Las Fiestas de Santa Fe. An exuberant combination of spirit, history, and general merrymaking, Las Fiestas is the oldest community celebration in the United States. The first fiesta was celebrated in 1712, 20 years after the peaceful resettlement of New Mexico by Spanish conquistadors in 1692. La Conquistadora, a carved Madonna credited with the victory, is the focus of the celebration, which includes Masses, a parade for children and their pets, a historical/hysterical parade, mariachi concerts, dances, food, and arts, as well as local entertainment on the plaza. Zozobra, "Old Man Gloom," a 40-foot-tall effigy made of wood, canvas, and paper, is burned at dusk on Thursday to revitalize the community.

Zozobra kicks off Las Fiestas. For information, call ✆ **505/988-7575.** Weekend following Labor Day.

Enchanted Circle Century Bike Tour. About 500 cyclists turn out to ride 100 miles of scenic mountain roads, starting and ending in Red River. All levels of riders are welcome, though not everyone completes this test of endurance. Call ✆ **505/754-2366.** Weekend following Labor Day.

New Mexico State Fair and Rodeo. This is one of America's top state fairs; it features parimutuel horse racing, a nationally acclaimed rodeo, entertainment by top country artists, Native American and Spanish villages, the requisite midway, livestock shows, and arts and crafts.

The fair and rodeo, which last 17 days, are held at the State Fairgrounds in Albuquerque. Advance tickets can be ordered by calling ✆ **505/265-1791** or visiting **www.nmstatefair.com**. Early September.

Taos Trade Fair, La Hacienda de los Martinez, Lower Ranchitos Road, Taos. This 2-day affair reenacts Spanish colonial life of the mid-1820s and features Hispanic and Native American music, weaving and crafts demonstrations, traditional foods, dancing, and visits by mountain men. Call © **505/758-0505.** Last full weekend in September.

San Geronimo Vespers Sundown Dance and Trade Fair, Taos Pueblo. This event features a Mass and procession; traditional corn, buffalo, and Comanche dances; an arts-and-crafts fair; foot races; and pole climbs by clowns. Call © **505/758-0505** for details. Last weekend in September.

Santa Fe Wine & Chile Fiesta. This lively celebration boasts 5 days of wine and food events, including seminars, guest chef demonstrations and luncheons, tours, a grand tasting and reserve tasting, an auction, and a golf tournament. It takes place at many venues in downtown Santa Fe with the big event on the last Saturday. Tickets go on sale in early July and sell out quickly. For information, call © **505/438-8060** or visit **www.santafewineandchile.org**. Last Wednesday through Sunday in September.

Taos Fall Arts Festival. Highlights include arts-and-crafts exhibitions and competitions, studio tours, gallery openings, lectures, concerts, dances, and stage plays. Simultaneous events include the **Old Taos Trade Fair,** the **Wool Festival,** and **San Geronimo Day** at Taos Pueblo.

The festival is held throughout Taos and Taos County. Events, schedules, and tickets (where required) can be obtained from the **Taos County Chamber of Commerce,** P.O. Drawer I,

Taos, NM 87571 (© **800/732-8267** or 505/758-3873; www.taoschamber.com). Mid-September (or the third weekend) to the first week in October.

October

Albuquerque International Balloon Fiesta. The world's largest balloon rally, this 9-day festival brings together more than 750 colorful balloons and includes races and contests. There are mass ascensions at sunrise, "balloon glows" in the evening, and balloon rides for those desiring a little lift. Various special events are staged all week.

Balloons lift off at Balloon Fiesta Park (at I-25 and Alameda NE) on Albuquerque's northern city limits. For information, call © **800/733-9918** or visit **www.balloonfiesta.com**. Second week in October.

Taos Mountain Balloon Rally. The Albuquerque fiesta's "little brother" offers mass dawn ascensions, tethered balloon rides for the public, and a Saturday parade of balloon baskets (in pickup trucks) from Kit Carson Park around the plaza. Call © **800/732-8267** for more information. Last weekend of October.

November

Weems Artfest. Approximately 260 artisans, who work in a variety of media, come from throughout the world to attend this 3-day fair, held at the State Fairgrounds in Albuquerque. It's one of the top 100 arts-and-crafts fairs in the country. For details, call © **505/293-6133.** Early November.

Festival of the Cranes. People come from all over the world to attend this bird-watching event just an hour and a half south of Albuquerque at Bosque del Apache National Wildlife Refuge, near Socorro. Call © **505/835-1828.** Weekend before Thanksgiving.

Yuletide in Taos. This holiday event emphasizes northern New Mexican

> **Tips   Quick ID**
>
> Tie a colorful ribbon or piece of yarn around your luggage handle, or slap a distinctive sticker on the side of your bag. This makes it less likely that someone will mistakenly appropriate it. And if your luggage gets lost, it will be easier to find.

traditions, cultures, and arts, with carols, festive classical music, Hispanic and Native American songs and dances, historic walking tours, art exhibitions, dance performances, candlelight dinners, and more.

Events are staged by the **Taos County Chamber of Commerce,** P.O. Drawer I, Taos, NM 87571 (© **800/ 732-8267;** www.taoschamber.com). From Thanksgiving through New Year's Day.

December

Winter Spanish Market, El Museo Cultural, Santa Fe. Approximately 150 artists show their wares at this little sister to July's major event. See the Spanish Market in July (above) for more information. Call © **505/982-2226.** First full weekend in December.

Christmas in Madrid Open House. Even if you never get out of your car, it's worth going to see the spectacular lights display in this village between Albuquerque and Santa Fe on the Turquoise Trail. You'll also find entertainment, refreshments in shops, and Santa Claus. For additional information, call © **505/471-1054.** First two weekends in December.

Canyon Road Farolito Walk, Santa Fe. Locals and visitors bundle up and stroll Canyon Road, where streets and rooftops are lined with *farolitos* (candle lamps). Musicians play and carolers sing around *luminarias* (little fires). Though it's not responsible for the event, the **Santa Fe Convention and Visitors Bureau** (© 505/955-6200) can help direct you there; or ask your hotel concierge. Christmas Eve at dusk.

Dance of the Matachines and Other Dances. Many pueblos celebrate the Christmas holiday with dances. The Dance of the Matachines takes place at Picuris and San Juan pueblos on Christmas Day. Contact © **505/587-2519** for dance schedules for these and other pueblos. Christmas Eve through Christmas Day.

Torchlight Procession, Taos Ski Valley. Bold skiers carve down a steep run named Snakedance in the dark while carrying golden fire. For information, call © **800/992-7669** or 505/ 776-2291, or visit **www.skitaos.org**. December 31.

5 Travel Insurance

The cost of travel insurance varies widely, depending on the cost and length of your trip, your age and health, and the type of trip you're taking, but expect to pay between 5% and 8% of the vacation itself. You can get estimates from various providers through **InsureMyTrip.com**. Enter your trip cost and dates, your age,

and other information for prices from more than a dozen companies.

TRIP-CANCELLATION INSURANCE

Trip-cancellation insurance will help retrieve your money if you have to back out of a trip or depart early, or if your travel supplier goes bankrupt. Permissable reasons for trip cancellation can range from sickness to natural disasters to the State Department declaring a destination unsafe for travel.

For more information, contact one of the following recommended insurers: **Access America** (☏ 866/807-3982; www.accessamerica.com); **Travel Guard International** (☏ 800/826-4919; www.travelguard.com); **Travel Insured International** (☏ 800/243-3174; www.travelinsured.com); and **Travelex Insurance Services** (☏ 888/457-4602; www.travelexinsurance.com).

MEDICAL INSURANCE

Although it's not required of travelers, health insurance is highly recommended. Most health insurance policies cover you if you get sick away from home—but verify that you're covered before you depart, particularly if you're insured by an HMO.

International visitors should note that unlike many European countries, the United States does not usually offer free or low-cost medical care to its citizens or visitors. Doctors and hospitals are expensive, and in most cases will require advance payment or proof of coverage before they render their services. Good policies will cover the costs of an accident, repatriation, or death. Packages such as **Europ Assistance's "Worldwide Healthcare Plan"** are sold by European automobile clubs and travel agencies at attractive rates. **Worldwide Assistance Services, Inc.** (☏ 800/777-8710; www.worldwideassistance.com) is the agent for Europ Assistance in the United States.

Though lack of health insurance may prevent you from being admitted to a hospital in nonemergencies, don't worry about being left on a street corner to die: The American way is to fix you now and bill the living daylights out of you later.

INSURANCE FOR BRITISH TRAVELERS Most big travel agents offer their own insurance and will probably try to sell you their package when you book a holiday. Think before you sign. **Britain's Consumers' Association** recommends that you insist on seeing the policy and reading the fine print before buying travel insurance. **The Association of British Insurers** (☏ 020/7600-3333;www.abi.org.uk) gives advice by phone and publishes *Holiday Insurance,* a free guide to policy provisions and prices. You might also shop around for better deals: Try **Columbus Direct** (☏ 0870/033-9988; www.columbusdirect.net).

INSURANCE FOR CANADIAN TRAVELERS Canadians should check with their provincial health plan offices or call **Health Canada** (☏ 866/225-0709; www.hc-sc.gc.ca) to find out the extent of their coverage and what documentation and receipts they must take home in case they are treated in the United States.

Travel in the Age of Bankruptcy

Airlines go bankrupt, so protect yourself by **buying your tickets with a credit card.** The Fair Credit Billing Act guarantees that you can get your money back from the credit card company if a travel supplier goes under (and if you request the refund within 60 days of the bankruptcy). **Travel insurance** can also help, but make sure it covers against "carrier default" for your specific travel provider. And be aware that if a U.S. airline goes bust mid-trip, a 2001 federal law requires other carriers to take you to your destination (albeit on a space-available basis) for a fee of no more than $25, provided you rebook within 60 days of the cancellation.

LOST-LUGGAGE INSURANCE

On flights within the United States, checked baggage is covered up to $2,500 per ticketed passenger. On flights outside the United States (and on U.S. portions of international trips), baggage coverage is limited to approximately $9.07 per pound, up to approximately $635 per checked bag. If you plan to check items more valuable than what's covered by the standard liability, see if your homeowner's policy covers your valuables, get baggage insurance as part of your comprehensive travel-insurance package, or buy Travel Guard's "BagTrak" product.

If your luggage is lost, immediately file a lost-luggage claim at the airport, detailing the luggage contents. Most airlines require that you report delayed, damaged, or lost baggage within 4 hours of arrival. The airlines are required to deliver luggage, once found, directly to your house or destination free of charge.

6 Health & Safety

STAYING HEALTHY

One thing that sets New Mexico apart from most other states is its elevation. Santa Fe and Taos are about 7,000 feet above sea level; Albuquerque is more than 5,000 feet above sea level. The reduced oxygen and humidity can precipitate some unique problems, not the least of which is acute mountain sickness. In its early stages, you might experience headaches, shortness of breath, loss of appetite and/or nausea, tingling in the fingers or toes, lethargy, and insomnia. The condition can usually be treated by taking aspirin as well as getting plenty of rest, avoiding large meals, and drinking lots of nonalcoholic fluids (especially water). If it persists or worsens, you must return to a lower altitude. Other dangers of higher elevations include hypothermia and sun exposure, and these should be taken seriously. To avoid dehydration, drink water as often as possible.

Limit your exposure to the sun, especially during the first few days of your trip and, thereafter, between 11am and 2pm. Liberally apply sunscreen with a high protection factor. Remember that children need more protection than adults do.

It's important to monitor your children's health while in New Mexico. They are just as susceptible to mountain sickness, hypothermia, sunburn, and dehydration as you are.

Avoiding "Economy Class Syndrome"

Deep vein thrombosis, or as it's know in the world of flying, "economy-class syndrome," is a blood clot that develops in a deep vein. It's a potentially deadly condition that can be caused by sitting in cramped conditions—such as an airplane cabin—for too long. During a flight (especially a long-haul flight), get up, walk around, and stretch your legs every 60 to 90 minutes to keep your blood flowing. Other preventative measures include frequent flexing of the legs while sitting, drinking lots of water, and avoiding alcohol and sleeping pills. If you have a history of deep vein thrombosis, heart disease, or another condition that puts you at high risk, some experts recommend wearing compression stockings or taking anticoagulants when you fly; always ask your physician about the best course for you. Symptoms of deep vein thrombosis include leg pain or swelling, or even shortness of breath.

Healthy Travels to You
The following government websites offer up-to-date health-related travel advice.
- **Australia:** www.dfat.gov.au/travel
- **Canada:** www.hc-sc.gc.ca/index_e.html
- **U.K.:** www.dh.gov.uk/PolicyAndGuidance/HealthAdviceForTravellers/fs/en
- **U.S.:** www.cdc.gov/travel

Other things to be wary of are arroyos, or creek beds in the desert where flash floods can occur without warning. If water is flowing across a road, *do not* try to drive through it because chances are the water is deeper and flowing faster than you think. Just wait it out. Arroyo floods don't last long.

Visitors to the state should also be careful of contracting the plague and hantavirus, a few cases of each reported annually in the state. Both diseases can be fatal, and both are transmitted through exposure to infected rodent droppings. Though it's unlikely that you'll be exposed to such things while traveling, be careful anytime you note the presence of mice or other rodents.

Finally, if you're an outdoorsperson, be on the lookout for snakes—particularly rattlers. Avoid them. Don't even get close enough to take a picture (unless you have a very good zoom lens).

GENERAL AVAILABILITY OF HEALTH CARE
The most reliable hospitals in the area are **St. Vincent's Hospital,** 455 St. Michaels Dr. in Santa Fe (© **505/820-5250**), and **Presbyterian Hospital,** 1100 Central Ave. SE in Albuquerque (© **505/841-1234,** or 505/841-1111 for emergency service).

Contact the **International Association for Medical Assistance to Travelers** (IAMAT) (© **716/754-4883** or, in Canada, 416/652-0137; www.iamat.org) for tips on travel and health concerns in the countries you're visiting, and for lists of local, English-speaking doctors. The

United States **Centers for Disease Control and Prevention** (© **800/311-3435;** www.cdc.gov) provides up-to-date information on health hazards by region or country and offers tips on food safety. The website **www.tripprep.com**, sponsored by a consortium of travel medicine practitioners, may also offer helpful advice on traveling abroad. You can find listings of reliable clinics overseas at the **International Society of Travel Medicine** (www.istm.org).

WHAT TO DO IF YOU GET SICK AWAY FROM HOME
We list **hospitals** and **emergency numbers** under "Fast Facts" for each city in chapters 4, 11, and 15.

If you suffer from a chronic illness, consult your doctor before your departure. Pack **prescription medications** in your carry-on luggage, and carry them in their original containers, with pharmacy labels—otherwise they won't make it through airport security. Visitors from outside the United States should carry generic names of prescription drugs. For U.S. travelers, most reliable health-care plans provide coverage if you get sick away from home. Foreign visitors may have to pay all medical costs upfront and be reimbursed later. See "Medical Insurance," under "Travel Insurance," above.

STAYING SAFE
Tourist areas as a rule are safe, but, despite recent reports of decreases in violent crime in Santa Fe, it would be wise to check with the tourist offices in Santa Fe, Taos, and Albuquerque if you are in doubt about which neighborhoods are

Fire, Water, and Golf

Over the past few years, national news programs have run vivid stories with the banner headline "New Mexico is Burning." Though the state has witnessed some major wildfires, including the Cerro Grande in Los Alamos in 2000, which trespassed into the city leveling some 400 dwellings, New Mexico has never been "on fire." Forests in the West will always burn—it's a natural part of their cycles. However, the state's forests are drier than they've been in many years, which may be leading to more fires.

A more apt headline for the state's recent problems is "New Mexico is Drying Up." Blame global warming or simply weather cycles; the state has received scant rain and snowfall in recent years. For a few years running, Santa Fe residents have been forced to abide by water-use restrictions, limiting how much they can water their gardens and wash their cars.

The drought has led to a focused assessment of water use throughout the region, and golf courses have emerged as the big black hat. And yet, more continue to be built. Area pueblos are scrambling to take advantage of the income golf can bring in. Santa Ana Pueblo has installed two 18-hole courses, and Pojoaque and Santa Clara have each installed 18 holes.

With longstanding water rights in hand, the pueblos believe they are entitled to use the water. All this presupposes a well that can't run dry, but with Rio Grande flows at their lowest in years, the future looks grim. How does this affect the traveler? You can be relatively sure you won't burn up during your visit, you may have to *ask* for a glass of water when you dine at a restaurant, and, well, you might want to bring along your clubs—while the water lasts.

safe. (See the "Orientation" sections in chapters 4, 11, and 15 for the names and addresses of the specific tourist bureaus.)

Remember that hotels are open to the public, and in a large hotel, security may not be able to screen everyone who enters. Always lock your room door; don't assume that once inside your hotel you are automatically safe and no longer need to be aware of your surroundings.

Be aware that New Mexico has a higher-than-average reported incidence of rape. Women should not walk alone in isolated places, particularly at night.

ECOTOURISM

New Mexico hasn't become a big ecotourism destination but there are a few options. In Taos, **El Monte Sagrado,** a resort near the center of town, offers luxurious surroundings totally in tune with nature, utilizing sustainable technologies throughout. Contact ℂ **800/828-TAOS;** www.elmontesagrado.com. (See chapter 12) In Santa Fe, **Santa Fe Mountain Adventures** (ℂ **800/965-4010** or 505/988-4000; www.santafemountainadventures.com) leads programs that combine outdoor adventures with arts and cultural experiences, and spa treatments. A collaborative effort in conjunction with *Outside* magazine, the business is eco-conscious. See chapter 7 for more details.

You can find eco-friendly travel tips, statistics, and touring companies and associations—listed by destination under "Travel Choice"—at the TIES website, www.ecotourism.org. **Ecotravel.com** is part online magazine and part eco-directory that lets you search for touring companies in several categories (water-based, land-based, spiritually oriented, and so on). Also checkout **Conservation International** (www.conservation.org)—which, with *National Geographic Traveler,* annually presents **World Legacy Awards** (www. wlaward.org) to those travel tour operators, businesses, organizations, and places that have made a significant contribution to sustainable tourism.

7 Specialized Travel Resources

TRAVELERS WITH DISABILITIES

Most disabilities shouldn't stop anyone from traveling in the United States. There are more options and resources out there than ever before. Throughout the state of New Mexico, measures have been taken to provide access for travelers with disabilities. Several bed-and-breakfasts have made one or more of their rooms completely wheelchair accessible. The **Information Center for New Mexicans with Disabilities** (© 800/552-8195 in New Mexico, or 505/272-8549 outside the state) accesses a database with lists of services ranging from restaurants and hotels to wheelchair rentals. It's a service of the **Developmental Disabilities Planning Council** (© 800/311-2229). The *Access New Mexico* guide lists accessible hotels, attractions, and restaurants throughout the state. For more information, contact the **Governor's Commission on Disabilities,** 491 Old Santa Fe Trail, Lamy Building Room 117, Santa Fe, NM 87503 (© 505/827-6465; www.state. nm.us/gcch/accessnm.htm).

The chambers of commerce in Santa Fe and Taos will answer questions regarding accessibility in their areas. It is advisable to call hotels, restaurants, and attractions in advance to be sure that they are fully accessible.

The **Golden Access Passport** gives visually impaired or permanently disabled persons (regardless of age) free lifetime entrance to all properties administered by the National Park Service, the U.S. Fish and Wildlife Service, the U.S. Forest Service, the U.S. Army Corps of Engineers, the Bureau of Land Management, and the Tennessee Valley Authority. This may include national parks, monuments, historic sites, recreation areas, and national wildlife refuges.

You may pick up a Golden Access Passport at any NPS entrance fee area by showing proof of medically determined disability and eligibility for benefits under federal law. Besides free entry, the Golden Access Passport also offers a 50% discount on federal-use fees charged for such facilities as camping, swimming, parking, boat launching, and tours. For more information, go to www.nps.gov/ fees_passes.htm or call © **888/467-2757.**

Many travel agencies offer customized tours and itineraries for travelers with disabilities. Among them are **Flying Wheels Travel** (© **507/451-5005;** www.flying wheelstravel.com), **Access-Able Travel Source** (© **303/232-2979;** www.access-able.com), and **Accessible Journeys** (© **800/846-4537** or 610/521-0339; www.disabilitytravel.com). **Avis Rent a Car** has an "Avis Access" program that offers such services as a dedicated 24-hour toll-free number (© **888/879-4273**) for customers with special travel needs; special car features such as swivel seats, spinner knobs, and hand controls; and accessible bus service.

Organizations that offer assistance to disabled travelers include **MossRehab** (www.mossresourcenet.org), the **American Foundation for the Blind (AFB)** (© **800/232-5463;** www.afb.org), and **SATH (Society for Accessible Travel & Hospitality)** (© **212/447-7284;** www. sath.org).

The community website **iCan** (www. icanonline.net/channels/travel) has destination guides and several regular columns on accessible travel. Also check out the quarterly magazine *Emerging Horizons* (www.emerginghorizons.com.); and *Open World* magazine, published by SATH.

GAY & LESBIAN TRAVELERS

New Mexico is a pretty gay-friendly place in general, especially in Santa Fe, with its cosmopolitan attitude. Only in the smaller villages will locals look askance.

Common Bond (© 505/891-3647) provides information and outreach services for Albuquerque's gay and lesbian community as well as referrals for other New Mexico cities. A recorded message on this phone line gives lists of bars and clubs, businesses, and publications, as well as health and crisis information and a calendar of events. Volunteers are on hand (generally in the evenings) to answer questions. Another good resource is **www.gaynm.com**, a website that provides news, resources, and lists of events.

The International Gay and Lesbian Travel Association (IGLTA) (© 800/ 448-8550 or 954/776-2626; www.iglta. org) is the trade association for the gay and lesbian travel industry, and offers an online directory of gay- and lesbian-friendly travel businesses; go to their website and click on "Members."

Many agencies offer tours and travel itineraries specifically for gay and lesbian travelers. Among them are **Now, Voyager** (© 800/255-6951; www.nowvoyager. com) and **Olivia Cruises & Resorts** (© 800/631-6277; www.olivia.com).

Gay.com Travel (© 800/929-2268 or 415/644-8044; www.gay.com/travel or www.outandabout.com) is an excellent online successor to the popular *Out & About* print magazine. It provides regularly updated information about gay-owned, gay-oriented, and gay-friendly lodging, dining, sightseeing, nightlife,

and shopping establishments in every important destination worldwide.

The following travel guides are available at many bookstores, or you can order them from any online bookseller: *Spartacus International Gay Guide* (Bruno Gmünder Verlag; www.spartacusworld. com/gayguide), *Odysseus: The International Gay Travel Planner* (Odysseus Enterprises Ltd.), and the *Damron* guides (www.damron.com), with separate, annual books for gay men and lesbians.

SENIOR TRAVEL

Members of **AARP** (formerly known as the American Association of Retired Persons), 601 E St. NW, Washington, DC 20049 (© 888/687-2277; www.aarp. org), get discounts on hotels, airfares, and car rentals. AARP offers members a wide range of benefits, including *AARP: The Magazine* and a monthly newsletter. Anyone over 50 can join.

The **U.S. National Park Service** offers a **Golden Age Passport** that gives seniors 62 years or older lifetime entrance to all properties administered by the National Park Service—national parks, monuments, historic sites, recreation areas, and national wildlife refuges—for a one-time processing fee of $10, which must be purchased in person at any NPS facility that charges an entrance fee. Besides free entry, a Golden Age Passport also offers a 50% discount on federal-use fees charged for such facilities as camping, swimming, parking, boat launching, and tours. For more information, go to **www.nps.gov/ fees_passes.htm** or call © 888/467-2757.

Many reliable agencies and organizations target the 50-plus market. **Elderhostel** (© 877/426-8056; www.elder hostel.org) arranges study programs for those aged 55 and over. **ElderTreks** (© 800/741-7956; www.eldertreks.com) offers small-group tours to off-the-beaten-path or adventure-travel locations, restricted to travelers 50 and older.

INTRAV (© **800/456-8100**; www.intrav. com) is a high-end tour operator that caters to the mature, discerning traveler (not specifically seniors), with trips around the world that include guided safaris, polar expeditions, private-jet adventures, and small-boat cruises down jungle rivers.

Recommended publications offering travel resources and discounts for seniors include the Albuquerque-based monthly tabloid *Prime Time* (© **505/880-0470**), which publishes a variety of articles aimed at New Mexicans 50 years and older; the quarterly magazine *Travel 50 & Beyond* (www.travel50andbeyond. com); *Travel Unlimited: Uncommon Adventures for the Mature Traveler* (Avalon); *101 Tips for Mature Travelers,* available from Grand Circle Travel (© **800/221-2610** or 617/350-7500; www.gct.com); and *Unbelievably Good Deals and Great Adventures That You Absolutely Can't Get Unless You're Over 50* (McGraw-Hill), by Joann Rattner Heilman.

FAMILY TRAVEL

If you have enough trouble getting your kids out of the house in the morning, dragging them thousands of miles away may seem like an insurmountable challenge. But family travel can be immensely rewarding, giving you new ways of seeing the world through smaller pairs of eyes.

Be aware that family travel in northern New Mexico may be a little different from what you're accustomed to. You'll find few huge Disney-like attractions here. Instead, the draws are culture and the outdoors. Rather than spending time in theme parks, you may go white-water rafting down the Rio Grande, skiing at one of the many family-friendly areas, climbing a wooden ladder up to a cliff dwelling, or trekking through the wilderness with a llama.

If your brood is not very adventurous, don't worry. Some of the hotels and resorts listed in this book have inviting pools to laze around or on-site activities planned especially for kids. Whatever your choice, northern New Mexico will definitely offer your children a new perspective on the United States by exposing them to ancient ruins, Southwestern cuisine, and Hispanic and Native American cultures that they may not experience elsewhere.

To locate accommodations, restaurants, and attractions that are particularly kid-friendly, refer to the "Kids" icon throughout this guide.

Recommended family travel reading includes:

- The Santa Fe quarterly *Tumbleweeds* (© **505/984-3171**) offers useful articles on family-oriented subjects in the Santa Fe area and a quarterly day-by-day calendar of family events. Free in locations all over Santa Fe or by mail for $15.
- Lynnell Diamond's *New Mexico for Kids* (Otter Be Reading Books), a learning activity guidebook for young people, is available online at **Amazon. com**.
- *How to Take Great Trips with Your Kids* (The Harvard Common Press) is full of good general advice that can apply to travel anywhere.

Familyhostel (© **800/733-9753**; www. learn.unh.edu/familyhostel) takes the whole family, including kids ages 8 to 15, on moderately priced U.S. and international learning vacations. Lectures, field trips, and sightseeing are guided by a team of academics.

Recommended family travel websites include **Family Travel Forum** (www. familytravelforum.com), a comprehensive site that offers customized trip planning; **Family Travel Network** (www. familytravelnetwork.com), an award-winning site that offers travel features, deals, and tips; **Traveling Internationally with Your Kids** (www.travelwithyourkids. com), a comprehensive site offering sound advice for long-distance and international travel with children; and **Family Travel Files** (www.thefamilytravelfiles. com), which offers an online magazine and a directory of off-the-beaten-path tours and tour operators for families.

TRAVELING WITH PETS

Traveling with pets can be a real joy, or a danger to them, especially here in the high desert where interior car temperatures can be deceptively high—or low. It's best not to leave your pet unattended for more than a few minutes.

More and more hotels in the region are becoming pet friendly. Look in the service information of the accommodation chapters for the ones that welcome them. In a pinch, you can always rely on Motel 6 for accepting pets. Websites worth checking out include www.pets welcome.com, www.pettravel.com, and www.travelpets.com.

8 Planning Your Trip Online

SURFING FOR AIRFARE

The most popular online travel agencies are **Travelocity** (**www.travelocity.com**, or www.travelocity.co.uk); **Expedia** (**www. expedia.com**, www.expedia.co.uk, or www.expedia.ca); and **Orbitz** (**www. orbitz.com**).

In addition, most airlines now offer online-only fares that even their phone agents know nothing about. For the websites of airlines that fly to and from your destination, go to "Getting There," p. 30.

Other helpful websites for booking airline tickets online include:

- www.biddingfortravel.com
- www.cheapflights.com
- www.hotwire.com
- www.kayak.com
- www.lastminutetravel.com
- www.opodo.co.uk
- www.priceline.com
- www.sidestep.com
- www.site59.com
- www.smartertravel.com

SURFING FOR HOTELS

In addition to **Travelocity, Expedia, Orbitz, Priceline,** and **Hotwire** (see

Frommers.com: The Complete Travel Resource

For an excellent travel-planning resource, we highly recommend **Frommers. com** (www.frommers.com), voted Best Travel Site by *PC Magazine*. We're a little biased, of course, but we guarantee that you'll find the travel tips, reviews, monthly vacation giveaways, bookstore, and online-booking capabilities thoroughly indispensable. Among the special features are our popular **Destinations** section, where you'll get expert travel tips, hotel and dining recommendations, and advice on the sights to see for more than 3,500 destinations around the globe; the **Frommers.com Newsletter,** with the latest deals, travel trends, and money-saving secrets; our **Community** area featuring **Message Boards,** where Frommer's readers post queries and share advice (sometimes even our authors show up to answer questions); and our **Photo Center.** When your research is finished, the **Online Reservations System** (www.frommers.com/book_a_trip) takes you to Frommer's preferred online partners for booking your vacation at affordable prices.

above), the following websites will help you with booking hotel rooms online:

- www.hotels.com
- www.quickbook.com
- www.travelaxe.net
- www.travelweb.com
- www.tripadvisor.com

It's a good idea to **get a confirmation number** and **make a printout** of any online booking transaction.

SURFING FOR RENTAL CARS

For booking rental cars online, the best deals are usually found at rental-car company websites, although all the major online travel agencies also offer rental-car reservations services. Priceline and Hotwire work well for rental cars, too; the only "mystery" is which major rental company you get, and for most travelers the difference between Hertz, Avis, and Budget is negligible.

9 The 21st-Century Traveler

INTERNET ACCESS AWAY FROM HOME
WITHOUT YOUR OWN COMPUTER

To find cybercafes in your destination check **www.cybercaptive.com** and **www. cybercafe.com**.

Aside from formal cybercafes, most **youth hostels** and **public libraries** offer Internet access. Avoid **hotel business centers** unless you're willing to pay exorbitant rates.

Most major airports now have **Internet kiosks** scattered throughout their gates. These give you basic Web access for a per-minute fee that's usually higher than cybercafe prices.

WITH YOUR OWN COMPUTER

More and more hotels, cafes, and retailers are signing on as Wi-Fi (wireless fidelity) "hotspots." Mac owners have their own networking technology, Apple AirPort. **T-Mobile Hotspot** (www.t-mobile.com/hotspot) serves up wireless connections at more than 1,000 Starbucks coffee shops nationwide. **Boingo** (www.boingo.com) and **Wayport** (www.wayport.com) have set up networks in airports and high-class hotel lobbies. IPass providers (see below) also give you access to a few hundred wireless hotel lobby setups. To locate other hotspots that provide **free wireless networks** in cities around the world, go to

www.personaltelco.net/index.cgi/WirelessCommunities.

For dial-up access, most business-class hotels in the United States offer dataports for laptop modems, and a few thousand hotels in the United States and Europe now offer free high-speed Internet access. In addition, major Internet Service Providers (ISPs) have **local access numbers** around the world, allowing you to go online by placing a local call. The **iPass** network also has dial-up numbers around the world. You'll have to sign up with an iPass provider, who will then tell you how to set up your computer for your destination(s). For a list of iPass providers, go to **www.ipass.com** and click on "Individuals Buy Now." One solid provider is **i2roam** (© **866/811-6209** or 920/235-0475; www.i2roam.com).

Wherever you go, bring a **connection kit** of the right power and phone adapters, a spare phone cord, and a spare Ethernet network cable—or find out whether your hotel supplies them to guests.

For information on electrical currency conversions, see "Electricity," in the "Fast Facts" section at the end of this chapter.

CELLPHONE USE IN THE UNITED STATES

Just because your cellphone works at home doesn't mean it'll work everywhere

Online Traveler's Toolbox

Veteran travelers usually carry some essential items to make their trips easier. Following is a selection of handy online tools to bookmark and use. You'll also find helpful sites listing weekly events, restaurant reviews, and other travel tidbits in the introduction to each northern New Mexico city in chapters 4, 11, and 15.

- **Airplane Food** (www.airlinemeals.net)
- **Airplane Seating** (www.seatguru.com; and www.airlinequality.com)
- **Foreign Languages for Travelers** (www.travlang.com)
- **Maps** (www.mapquest.com)
- **Time and Date** (www.timeanddate.com)
- **Travel Warnings** (http://travel.state.gov; www.fco.gov.uk/travel; www.voyage.gc.ca; and www.dfat.gov.au/consular/advice)
- **Universal Currency Converter** (www.xe.com/ucc)
- **Visa ATM Locator** (www.visa.com), **MasterCard ATM Locator** (www.mastercard.com)
- **Weather** (www.intellicast.com; and www.weather.com)

in the U.S. (thanks to our nation's fragmented cellphone system). It's a good bet that your phone will work in major cities, but take a look at your wireless company's coverage map on its website before heading out; T-Mobile, Sprint, and Nextel are particularly weak in rural areas. If you need to stay in touch at a destination where you know your phone won't work, **rent** a phone that does from **InTouch USA** (✆ **800/872-7626;** www.intouchglobal.com) or a rental car location, but beware that you'll pay $1 a minute or more for airtime.

If you're venturing deep into national parks, you may want to consider renting a **satellite phone ("satphone").** It's different from a cellphone in that it connects to satellites rather than ground-based towers. Unfortunately, you'll pay at least $2 per minute to use the phone, and it only works where you can see the horizon (i.e., usually not indoors). In North America, you can rent Iridium satellite phones from **Road-Post** (✆ **888/290-1606** or 905/272-5665; www.roadpost.com). InTouch USA (see above) offers a wider range of satphones but at higher rates.

If you're not from the United States, you'll be appalled at the poor reach of our **GSM (Global System for Mobiles) wireless network,** which is used by much of the rest of the world. Your phone will probably work in most major U.S. cities; it definitely won't work in many rural areas. (To see where GSM phones work in the U.S., check out www.t-mobile.com/coverage/national_popup.asp.) And you may or may not be able to send SMS (text messaging) home.

10 Getting There

BY PLANE

The gateway to Santa Fe, Taos, and other northern New Mexico communities is the **Albuquerque International Sunport**

(✆ **505/842-4366** for the administrative offices; www.cabq.gov/airport; call the individual airlines for flight information).

Tips Prepare to Be Fingerprinted

As of January 2004, many international visitors traveling on visas to the United States will be photographed and fingerprinted at Customs in a new program created by the Department of Homeland Security called **US-VISIT.** Non–U.S. citizens arriving at airports and on cruise ships must undergo an instant background check as part of the government's efforts to deter terrorism by verifying the identity of incoming and outgoing visitors. Exempt from the extra scrutiny are visitors entering by land or those (mostly in Europe; see p. 12) who don't require a visa for short-term visits. For more information, go to the Homeland Security website at **www.dhs.gov/dhspublic**.

Airlines serving Albuquerque include **American** (© 800/433-7300), **US Airways** (© 800/235-9292), **Continental** (© 800/523-3273), **Delta** (© 800/221-1212), **Frontier** (© 800/432-1359), **Mesa** (© 800/637-2247), **Northwest** (© 800/225-2525), **Southwest** (© 800/435-9792), **TWA** (© 800/221-2000), and **United** (© 800/241-6522).

In conjunction with United Airlines, **Great Lakes** (© 505/473-4118) offers commuter flights to and from **Santa Fe Municipal Airport** (© 505/955-2900) via Denver. Flying into Santa Fe will save you time but will cost more than flying into Albuquerque.

IMMIGRATION & CUSTOMS CLEARANCE Foreign visitors arriving by air, no matter what the port of entry, should cultivate patience and resignation before setting foot on U.S. soil. Clearing immigration control can take as long as 2 hours. This is especially true in the aftermath of the September 11, 2001, terrorist attacks, when U.S. airports considerably beefed up security clearances. People traveling by air from Canada, Bermuda, and certain Caribbean countries can sometimes clear Customs and Immigration at the point of departure, which is much faster.

GETTING INTO TOWN FROM THE AIRPORT

Most hotels have courtesy vans to meet their guests and take them to their respective destinations. In addition, **Checker Airport Express** (© 505/765-1234) in Albuquerque runs vans to and from city hotels. Find Checker's booth near the baggage claim area. In Santa Fe, **Roadrunner Shuttle** (© 505/424-3367) meets every flight and takes visitors anywhere in Santa Fe.

FLYING FOR LESS: TIPS FOR GETTING THE BEST AIRFARE

- Passengers who can book their ticket either **long in advance** or **at the last minute,** or who **fly midweek** or **at less-trafficked hours** may pay a fraction of the full fare. If your schedule is flexible, ask if you can secure a cheaper fare by changing your flight plans.
- Search the **Internet** for cheap fares (see "Planning Your Trip Online").
- Keep an eye on local newspapers for **promotional specials** or **fare wars,** when airlines lower prices on their most popular routes.
- Join **frequent-flier clubs.** Membership entitles you to better seats, faster response to phone inquiries, and prompter service if your luggage is stolen or your flight is canceled or delayed, or if you want to change your seat. And you don't have to fly to earn points; **frequent-flier credit cards** can earn you thousands of miles for doing your everyday shopping. To play the frequent-flier game

Tips Getting through the Airport

- Arrive at the airport 1 hour before a domestic flight and 2 hours before an international flight; if you show up late, tell an airline employee and he or she will probably whisk you to the front of the line.
- Beat the ticket-counter lines by using airport electronic kiosks or even online check-in from your home computer, from where you can print out boarding passes in advance. Curbside check-in is also a good way to avoid lines.
- Bring a current, government-issued photo ID such as a driver's license or passport. Children under 18 do not need government-issued photo IDs for flights within the U.S., but they do for international flights to most countries.
- Speed up security by removing your jacket and shoes before you're screened. In addition, remove metal objects such as big belt buckles. If you've got metallic body parts, a note from your doctor can prevent a long chat with the security screeners.
- Use a TSA-approved lock for your checked luggage. Look for Travel Sentry certified locks at luggage or travel shops and Brookstone stores (or online at www.brookstone.com).

to your best advantage, consult Randy Petersen's **Inside Flyer** (www.insideflyer.com). Petersen and friends review all the programs in detail and post regular updates on changes in policies and trends.

BY CAR

Driving is the best way to see northern New Mexico, so you'll want to either drive here or rent a car (see the "Getting Around Northern New Mexico" section below for a listing of rental car agencies that service the region).

Albuquerque is at the crossroads of two major interstate highways. I-40 runs from Wilmington, North Carolina (1,870 miles east), to Barstow, California (580 miles west). I-25 extends from Buffalo, Wyoming (850 miles north), to El Paso, Texas (265 miles south). I-25 skims past Santa Fe's southern city limits. To reach Taos, you have to leave I-25 at Santa Fe and travel north 74 miles via US 84/285 and NM 68, or exit I-25 9 miles south of

Raton, near the Colorado border, and proceed 100 miles west on US 64.

Parking is quite available and reasonably priced throughout the region both at meters and in city parking garages.

The following table shows the approximate mileage to Santa Fe from various cities around the United States.

BY BUS

Because Santa Fe is only about 58 miles northeast of Albuquerque via I-40, most visitors to Santa Fe take the bus directly from the Albuquerque airport, at a cost of about $20 to $25 one-way. **Sandia Shuttle Express** buses (© 888/775-5696) make the 70-minute run between the airport and Santa Fe hotels 10 times daily each way (from Albuquerque to Santa Fe 6:30am–6pm; from Santa Fe to Albuquerque 8:45am–8:20pm). Reservations are required, ideally 48 hours in advance. **Santa Fe Shuttle** (© 888/833-2300) offers eight trips daily (from Albuquerque to Santa Fe 6:30am–10:45pm; from

Distances to Santa Fe (in Miles)

From	Distance	From	Distance
Atlanta	1,417	Minneapolis	1,199
Boston	2,190	New Orleans	1,181
Chicago	1,293	New York	1,971
Cleveland	1,558	Oklahoma City	533
Dallas	663	Phoenix	595
Denver	391	St. Louis	993
Detroit	1,514	Salt Lake City	634
Houston	900	San Francisco	1,149
Los Angeles	860	Seattle	1,477
Miami	2,011	Washington, D.C.	1,825

Santa Fe to Albuquerque 5:05am–8pm). Reservations are required. Two other bus services shuttle between Albuquerque and Taos (via Santa Fe) for $20 to $35 one-way: **Faust's Transportation** (© **888/830-3410** or 505/758-3410) and **Twin Heart Express & Transportation** (© **800/654-9456** or 505/751-1201).

The **public bus depot** in Albuquerque is located on 2nd Street at Lead (300 2nd St. SW). Contact **Texas, New Mexico, and Oklahoma** (TNM&O; © **505/242-4998**) for information and schedules. Fares run about $11 to Santa Fe and $22 to Taos. However, the **bus stations** in Santa Fe (858 St. Michael's Dr.; © **505/471-0008**) and Taos (5 miles south of the plaza at 1386 Paseo del Pueblo Sur; © **505/758-1144**) are several miles south of each city center. Because additional taxi or shuttle service is needed to reach most accommodations, travelers usually find it more convenient to pay a few extra dollars for an airport-to-hotel shuttle.

BY TRAIN

Amtrak (© **800/USA-RAIL** or 505/842-9650; www.amtrak.com) passes through northern New Mexico twice daily. The *Southwest Chief*, which runs between Chicago and Los Angeles, stops once eastbound and once westbound in Gallup, Albuquerque, Lamy (for Santa Fe), Las Vegas, and Raton. The Albuquerque train station is in the center of downtown, with easy access to hotels. A spur runs on a limited schedule from Lamy approximately 20 miles to downtown Santa Fe, within walking distance to the plaza.

You can get a copy of Amtrak's National Timetable from any Amtrak station, from travel agents, or by writing Amtrak, 400 N. Capitol St. NW, Washington, DC 20001. You can also check Amtrak timetables online, at **www.amtrak.com**. A photo ID is required for check-in.

11 Packages for the Independent Traveler

Package tours are simply a way to buy the airfare, accommodations, and other elements of your trip (such as car rentals, airport transfers, and sometimes even activities) at the same time and often at discounted prices.

One good source of package deals is the airlines and train companies themselves. Most major airlines offer air/land packages, including **Southwest Airlines Vacations** (© **800/243-8372;** www.swavacations.com), **American Airlines**

Vacations (© 800/321-2121; www.aa vacations.com), **Delta Vacations** (© 800/221-6666; www.deltavacations.com), **Continental Airlines Vacations** (© 800/301-3800; www.covacations.com), and **United Vacations** (© 888/854-3899; www.unitedvacations.com). Several big **online travel agencies**—Expedia, Travelocity, Orbitz, Site59, and Lastminute.com—also do a brisk business in packages.

Amtrak Vacations (© **800/268-7252;** www.amtrakvacations.com) offers train packages.

Travel packages are also listed in the travel section of your local Sunday newspaper. Or check ads in the national travel magazines such as *Arthur Frommer's Budget Travel Magazine, Travel + Leisure, National Geographic Traveler,* and *Condé Nast Traveler.*

12 Escorted General-Interest Tours

Escorted tours are structured group tours, with a group leader. The price usually includes everything from airfare to hotels, meals, tours, admission costs, and local transportation.

Despite the fact that escorted tours require big deposits and predetermine hotels, restaurants, and itineraries, many people derive security and peace of mind from the structure they offer. Escorted tours—whether they're navigated by bus, motor coach, train, or boat—let travelers sit back and enjoy the trip without having to drive or worry about details. They take you to the maximum number of sights in the minimum amount of time with the least amount of hassle. They're particularly convenient for people with limited mobility and they can be a great way to make new friends.

On the downside, you'll have little opportunity for serendipitous interactions with locals. The tours can be jam-packed with activities, leaving little room for individual sightseeing, whim, or adventure—plus they often focus on the heavily touristed sites, so you miss out on many a lesser-known gem.

Not many escorted tours are offered in New Mexico. The tour companies I spoke to said most visitors to New Mexico have such disparate interests it's difficult to create packages to please them. Still, a few tour companies can help you arrange a variety of day trips during your visit and can also secure lodging. **Tauck World Discovery,** 10 Norden Place, Norwalk, CT 06855 (© **800/788-7885;** www.tauck.com), offers weeklong cultural trips to northern New Mexico. **Destination Southwest, Inc.,** 20 First Plaza Galeria, Suite 212, Albuquerque, NM 87102 (© **800/999-3109** or 505/766-9068; www.destinationsouthwest.com), offers an escorted tour to the Albuquerque International Balloon Fiesta. **Rojotours & Services,** P.O. Box 15744, Santa Fe, NM 87506-5744 (© **505/474-8333**), can help with a variety of day trips during your visit.

13 Special-Interest Trips

New Mexico is in the process of developing a network of special-interest trips that I'm certain will expand even more in upcoming years. One useful website to follow, offered by the **New Mexico Department of Tourism**, is www.nmtourism.org/siteseeing/index.php. Click on tour operators and you'll find a variety of offerings covering almost any interest.

My favorite operator is **Santa Fe Mountain Adventures** (© **800/965-4010** or 505/988-4000; www.santafemountainadventures.com), which combines outdoor adventures such as hiking and river running with cultural activities such as visits to pueblos or museums, with more relaxing ones such as spa treatments and meditation practices. A collaborative effort in conjunction with *Outside* magazine, the business is eco-conscious. See chapter 7 for more details.

Jane Butel Cooking School, 2655 Pan American NE, Suite F (℗ **800/473-8226** or 505/243-2622; www.janebutel.com) offers week-long and weekend packages with a hotel stay and full-participation classes. The weekend classes are held in noted chef and television personality Jane Butel's home kitchen in Corrales, a village along the Rio Grande on the edge of Albuquerque. The week-long classes are in Santa Fe.

Some of the world's most outstanding photographers convene in Santa Fe at various times during the year for the **Santa Fe Photography & Digital Workshops,** P.O. Box 9916, Santa Fe, NM 87504, at a delightful campus in the hills on the east side of town (℗ **505/983-1400;** www.santafeworkshops.com). Most courses are full time, lasting a week. Food and lodging packages are available.

Bicycle Adventures, P.O. Box 11219, Olympia, WA 98508 (℗ **800/443-6060** or 360/786-0989) offers tours to northern New Mexico. Riders get to experience some of the region's most lovely routes such as the High Road to Taos and the Enchanted Circle. Participants visit major sights such as Santa Fe's Canyon Road and Taos Pueblo and can even opt for a river trip. In business for 23 years, this company knows how to put together a good tour.

If you'd like to pursue an artistic adventure, check out the week-long classes in such media as painting, Native American pottery making, and weaving offered by **Taos Art School** (℗ **505/758-0350;** www.taosartschool.org). This organization is especially known for its weaving and horseback-riding creative "odyssey." Open since 1989, the school is a virtual campus in which classes go where they need to be. For instance, a painting class on Georgia O'Keeffe is held in Abiquiu, a Pueblo pottery class at Taos Pueblo, and a class on the churches in New Mexico is held at five different churches in the region. The fees vary from class to class and include lodging and meals.

14 Getting Around Northern New Mexico

BY PLANE

Overseas visitors can take advantage of the APEX (Advance Purchase Excursion) reductions offered by all major U.S. and European carriers. In addition, some large airlines offer transatlantic or transpacific passengers special discount tickets under the name **Visit USA,** which allows mostly one-way travel from one U.S. destination to another at very low prices. Unavailable in the U.S., these discount tickets must be purchased abroad in conjunction with your international fare. This system is the easiest, fastest, cheapest way to see the country.

Northern New Mexico doesn't have carriers flying between its cities, which is just as well. The best parts of the region happen *between* the major destinations.

BY CAR

The most convenient way to get around northern New Mexico is by private car. Auto and RV rentals are widely available for those who arrive without their own transportation, either at the Albuquerque airport or at locations around each city.

I have received good rates and service from **Avis** at the Albuquerque airport (℗ 800/831-2847, 505/842-4080, or 505/471-5892 in Santa Fe; www.avis.com); **Thrifty,** 2039 Yale Blvd. SE, Albuquerque (℗ 800/367-2277 or 505/842-8733; www.thrifty.com); **Hertz,** Albuquerque International Airport (℗ 800/654-3131 or 505/842-4235; www.hertz.com); **Dollar,** Albuquerque International Airport (℗ 800/369-4226; www.dollar.com); **Budget,** Albuquerque International

Airport (℗ 505/247-3443; www.budget. com); **Alamo,** 2601 Yale Blvd. SE, Albuquerque (℗ 800/327-9633; www.alamo. com); and **Rent-A-Wreck** of Albuquerque, 2001 Ridgecrest (℗ 800/247-9556 or 505/232-7552; www.rentawreck. com/nm.htm).

Drivers who need wheelchair-accessible transportation should call **Wheelchair Getaways of New Mexico,** 1015 Tramway Lane NE, Albuquerque (℗ 800/408-2626 or 505/247-2626; www.wheelchair getaways.com); the company rents vans by the day, week, or month.

If you're visiting from abroad and plan to rent a car in the United States, you probably won't need the services of an additional automobile organization. If you're planning to buy or borrow a car, automobile-association membership is recommended. **AAA, American Automobile Association** (℗ 800/222-4357; http:// travel.aaa.com), is the country's largest auto club and supplies its members with maps, insurance, and, most important, emergency road service. *Note:* Foreign driver's licenses are usually recognized in the U.S., but you should get an international one if your home license is not in English.

BY BUS

For information about getting to the region's major cities by bus, see the "Getting There," section of this chapter above.

BY TRAIN

International visitors can buy a USA Rail Pass, good for 15 or 30 days of unlimited travel on **Amtrak** (℗ 800/USA-RAIL; www.amtrak.com). The pass is available through many overseas travel agents. See Amtrak's website for the cost of travel within the western, eastern, or northwestern United States. With a foreign passport, you can also buy passes direct from some Amtrak locations, including San Francisco, Los Angeles, Chicago, New York, Miami, Boston, and Washington, D.C. Reservations are generally required and should be made as early as possible. Regional rail passes are also available.

Railway routes are extremely limited around northern New Mexico. **Amtrak** (℗ 800/USA-RAIL or 505/842-9650; www.amtrak.com) runs from Albuquerque to Lamy, with a small spur railroad running to Santa Fe.

15 Tips on Accommodations

No two travelers are alike; fortunately, New Mexico has a broad-enough range of accommodations to satisfy even the most eccentric adventurer. If you long to be pampered, you'll find a few swanky resorts within the region, with a variety of luxury options such as pool and exercise facilities, golf, tennis, horseback riding, and spa treatments. Of course, none of it comes cheap.

If you're looking to really savor the flavor of New Mexico, you may want to opt for one of its historic hotels. This may include a hacienda-style inn—an adobe one- or two-story structure often built around a courtyard. You'll also find some Victorian inns that have a frontier flavor.

Within this variety of architecture, the amenities vary, from places with antique but workable plumbing and no television, to those with hot tubs and dataports in rooms.

In recent years, bed-and-breakfast inns (B&Bs) have proliferated in New Mexico. Though you can find traditional Victorian-style B&Bs here (and some lovely ones at that), complete with lacy bedding and elaborately carved accents, you can also choose from old hacienda-style homes or tiered adobe structures. All are comfortable and a few luxurious, with prices in the moderate to expensive range.

We all have those nights when only predictability will do. That's when a chain hotel comes in handy. You'll find all the major ones in New Mexico, though not quite everywhere. The small villages still shun such cookie-cutter establishments, but most everywhere else you can find them along the highways or in the town centers.

LANDING THE BEST ROOM

Somebody has to get the best room in the house. It might as well be you. You can start by joining the hotel's frequent-guest program, which may make you eligible for upgrades. A hotel-branded credit card usually gives its owner "silver" or "gold" status in frequent-guest programs for free. Always ask about a corner room. They're often larger and quieter, with more windows and light, and they often cost the same as standard rooms. When you make your reservation, ask if the hotel is renovating; if it is, request a room away from the construction. Ask about nonsmoking rooms, rooms with views, rooms with twin, queen-, or king-size beds. If you're a light sleeper, request a quiet room away from vending machines, elevators, restaurants, bars, and discos. Ask for a room that has been most recently renovated or redecorated.

If you aren't happy with your room when you arrive, ask for another one. Most lodgings will be willing to accommodate you.

16 Tips on Dining

You know you're in a food-conscious place when the local newspaper uses chiles (and onions) to rate movies, as does Santa Fe's *New Mexican*. A large part of that city's cachet as a chic destination derives from its famous cuisine, while Taos and Albuquerque are developing notable reputations themselves. The competition among restaurants is fierce, which means that locals are spoiled rotten by the selection of good food on hand, and visitors have plenty of options from which to choose. Aside from establishments serving the northern New Mexican and New Southwestern cuisine that the region is famed for, you can also find French, Italian, Asian, Indian, and interesting hybrids of those. Luckily, not all the top restaurants are high-end; several hidden gems satisfy your taste buds without emptying your wallet.

Note that reservations are always recommended at the higher-end restaurants and are essential during peak seasons. Throughout the region, only a few restaurants serve late, so be sure to plan dinner before 8pm. Most restaurants are casual, so almost any attire is fine, though for the more expensive ones, jeans and flip-flops might not be your best choice.

At the beginning of each city's dining section I give more details about the dining scene there. Also, for a full run-down on northern New Mexico's own special cuisine see the appendix.

17 Recommended Books & Films

BOOKS

Many well-known writers made their homes in northern New Mexico in the 20th century. In the 1920s, the most celebrated were **D. H. Lawrence** and **Willa Cather,** both short-term Taos residents. Lawrence, the romantic and controversial English novelist, spent time here between 1922 and 1925; he reflected on his sojourn in *Mornings in Mexico* and *Etruscan Places.* Lawrence's Taos period is described in *Lorenzo in Taos,* which his patron, Mabel Dodge Luhan, wrote. Cather, a Pulitzer-prize winner famous for her depictions of the pioneer spirit, penned *Death Comes for the Archbishop,* among other works. This fictionalized account of the 19th-century Santa Fe

King of the Road

If you like road trip stories to small New Mexico towns, check out my new book *King of the Road* (New Mexico Magazine Press, 2007). It's a compilation of articles from my monthly column in *New Mexico Magazine,* in which locals tell the stories of their hometowns. It's illustrated with my photos too. Available on www.nmmagazine.com.

bishop, Jean-Baptiste Lamy, grew out of her stay in the region.

Many contemporary authors also live in and write about New Mexico. John Nichols, of Taos, whose *Milagro Beanfield War* was made into a Robert Redford movie in 1987, writes insightfully about the problems of poor Hispanic farming communities. Albuquerque's Tony Hillerman has for 2 decades woven mysteries around Navajo tribal police in books such as *Listening Woman* and *A Thief of Time.* (Robert Redford, this time as director, has made movie versions of many of Hillerman's novels that feature the character Jim Chee for PBS.) In more recent years, Sarah Lovett has joined his ranks with a series of gripping mysteries, most notably *Dangerous Attachments.* The Hispanic novelist Rudolfo Anaya's *Bless Me, Ultima* and Pueblo writer Leslie Marmon Silko's *Ceremony* capture the lifestyles of their respective peoples. A coming-of-age story, Richard Bradford's *Red Sky at Morning* juxtaposes the various cultures of New Mexico. Edward Abbey wrote of the desert environment and politics; his *Fire on the Mountain,* set in New Mexico, was one of his most powerful works.

Excellent works about Native Americans of New Mexico include *The Pueblo Indians of North America* (Holt, Rinehart & Winston, 1970) by Edward P. Dozier and *Living the Sky: The Cosmos of the American Indian* (University of Oklahoma Press, 1987) by Ray A. Williamson. Also look for *American Indian Literature 1979–1994* (Ballantine, 1996), an anthology edited by Paula Gunn Allen.

For general histories of the state, try Myra Ellen Jenkins and Albert H. Schroeder's *A Brief History of New Mexico* (University of New Mexico Press, 1974) and Marc Simmons's *New Mexico: An Interpretive History* (University of New Mexico Press, 1988). In addition, Claire Morrill's *A Taos Mosaic: Portrait of a New Mexico Village* (University of New Mexico Press, 1973) does an excellent job of portraying the history of that small New Mexican town. I have also enjoyed Tony Hillerman's (ed.) *The Spell of New Mexico* (University of New Mexico Press, 1976) and John Nichols and William Davis's *If Mountains Die: A New Mexico Memoir* (Alfred A. Knopf, 1979). *Talking Ground* (University of New Mexico Press, 1996), by Santa Fe author Douglas Preston, tells of a contemporary horseback trip through Navajoland, exploring the native mythology. One of my favorite texts is *Enchantment and Exploitation* (University of New Mexico Press, 1985) by William deBuys. A new, very extensive book that attempts to capture the multiplicity of the region is *Legends of the American Southwest* (Alfred A. Knopf, 1997) by Alex Shoumatoff.

Enduring Visions: 1,000 Years of Southwestern Indian Art by the Aspen Center for the Visual Arts (Publishing Center for Cultural Resources, 1969) and Roland F. Dickey's *New Mexico Village Arts* (University of New Mexico Press, 1990) are both excellent resources for those interested in Native American art. If you become intrigued with Spanish art during your visit to New Mexico, you'll find E. Boyd's *Popular Arts of Spanish New Mexico*

(Museum of New Mexico Press, 1974) to be quite informative.

If you like to cook, look for the *Santa Fe Farmer's Market Cookbook*, with recipes from vendors and chefs, to be released in spring 2007.

FILMS

If you like to start traveling before you climb on the plane or into the car, you can do so easily by watching any number of movies filmed in the state. Over the years so many have been filmed that I won't list them all. Instead, I'll give the ones that provide a glimpse into the true nature of New Mexico. *Silverado* (1985), a light-hearted western, and the heartfelt mini-series *Lonesome Dove (1989),* based on a Larry McMurtry novel, start my list. Billy Bob Thorton's film adaptation (2000) of the novel *All the Pretty Horses,* Ron Howard's film version of *The Missing*

(2003), and Billy Crystal in *City Slickers,* are also some of my favorite westerns.

Favorite classics include *Butch Cassidy and the Sundance Kid* (1969), filmed in Taos and Chama; *The Cowboys* (1972), with John Wayne; Clint Eastwood's *Every Which Way But Loose* (1978); and Dennis Hopper in the 1960s classic *Easy Rider* (1969).

More contemporary themes are explored in *Contact* (1997), which features the National Radio Astronomy Very Large Array in western New Mexico, as did *Independence Day* (1996). Also exploring alien themes, *The Man Who Fell to Earth* (1976), with David Bowie, was filmed in southern New Mexico.

In recent years, New Mexico modified its tax laws to encourage filming here, so keep your eyes open for film crews taking over small villages or blocking off city streets. You may even get a part as an extra!

FAST FACTS: Northern New Mexico

Area Code The telephone area code for all of New Mexico is **505,** though at press time plans were rumbling to add new ones in the state. No matter where you are in the state, if you're placing a call outside city limits, it's usually considered long distance, and you must use the 505 area code.

ATM Networks See "Money," p. 13.

Automobile Organizations Auto clubs will supply maps, suggested routes, guidebooks, accident and bail-bond insurance, and emergency road service. The **American Automobile Association (AAA)** is the major auto club in the United States. If you belong to an auto club in your home country, inquire about AAA reciprocity before you leave. You may be able to join AAA even if you're not a member of a reciprocal club; to inquire, call AAA (© **800/222-4357**). AAA is actually an organization of regional auto clubs, so look under "AAA Automobile Club" in the White Pages of the telephone directory. AAA has a nationwide emergency road service telephone number (© 800/AAA-HELP).

Business Hours **Offices** and **stores** are generally open Monday to Friday, 9am to 5pm, with many stores also open Friday night, Saturday, and Sunday in the summer season. Most **banks** are open Monday to Thursday, 9am to 5pm, and Friday, 9am to 6pm. Some may also be open Saturday morning. Most branches have ATMs available 24 hours. Call establishments for specific hours.

Car Rentals See "Getting Around Northern New Mexico," p. 35.

Cashpoints See "ATM Networks," above.

Currency The most common bills are the $1 (a "buck"), $5, $10, and $20 denominations. There are also $2 bills (seldom encountered), $50 bills, and $100 bills (the last two are usually not welcome as payment for small purchases).

Coins come in seven denominations: 1¢ (1 cent, or a penny); 5¢ (5 cents, or a nickel); 10¢ (10 cents, or a dime); 25¢ (25 cents, or a quarter); 50¢ (50 cents, or a half dollar); the gold-colored Sacagawea coin, worth $1; and the rare silver dollar.

For additional information see "Money," p. 13.

Drinking Laws The legal age for purchase and consumption of alcoholic beverages is 21; proof of age is required and often requested at bars, nightclubs, and restaurants, so it's always a good idea to bring ID when you go out. In New Mexico, major supermarkets and liquor stores sell beer, wine, and liquor.

Do not carry open containers of alcohol in your car or any public area that isn't zoned for alcohol consumption. The police can fine you on the spot. And nothing will ruin your trip faster than getting a citation for DUI ("driving under the influence"), so don't even think about driving while intoxicated.

Driving Rules See "Getting Around Northern New Mexico," p. 35.

Electricity Like Canada, the United States uses 110 to 120 volts AC (60 cycles), compared to 220 to 240 volts AC (50 cycles) in most of Europe, Australia, and New Zealand. Downward converters that change 220–240 volts to 110–120 volts are difficult to find in the United States, so bring one with you.

Embassies & Consulates All embassies are located in the nation's capital, Washington, D.C. Some consulates are located in major U.S. cities, and most nations have a mission to the United Nations in New York City. If your country isn't listed below, call for directory information in Washington, D.C. (© **202/555-1212**) or log on to **www.embassy.org/embassies**.

The embassy of **Australia** is at 1601 Massachusetts Ave. NW, Washington, DC 20036 (© **202/797-3000**; www.austemb.org). There are consulates in New York, Honolulu, Houston, Los Angeles, and San Francisco.

The embassy of **Canada** is at 501 Pennsylvania Ave. NW, Washington, DC 20001 (© **202/682-1740**; www.canadianembassy.org). Other Canadian consulates are in Buffalo (New York), Detroit, Los Angeles, New York, and Seattle.

The embassy of **Ireland** is at 2234 Massachusetts Ave. NW, Washington, DC 20008 (© **202/462-3939**; www.irelandemb.org). Irish consulates are in Boston, Chicago, New York, San Francisco, and other cities. See website for complete listing.

The embassy of **New Zealand** is at 37 Observatory Circle NW, Washington, DC 20008 (© **202/328-4800**; www.nzemb.org). New Zealand consulates are in Los Angeles, Salt Lake City, San Francisco, and Seattle.

The embassy of the **United Kingdom** is at 3100 Massachusetts Ave. NW, Washington, DC 20008 (© **202/588-7800**; www.britainusa.com). Other British consulates are in Atlanta, Boston, Chicago, Cleveland, Houston, Los Angeles, New York, San Francisco, and Seattle.

Emergencies In case of emergency, dial 911. For more specific information, see chapters 4, 11, and 15.

Gasoline (Petrol) At press time, in the U.S., the cost of gasoline (also known as gas, but never petrol), is abnormally high. Taxes are already included in the printed price. One U.S. gallon equals 3.8 liters or .85 imperial gallons. Fill-up locations are known as gas or service stations.

Holidays Banks, government offices, post offices, and many stores, restaurants, and museums are closed on the following legal national holidays: January 1 (New Year's Day), the third Monday in January (Martin Luther King, Jr., Day), the third Monday in February (Presidents' Day), the last Monday in May (Memorial Day), July 4 (Independence Day), the first Monday in September (Labor Day), the second Monday in October (Columbus Day), November 11 (Veterans' Day/Armistice Day), the fourth Thursday in November (Thanksgiving Day), and December 25 (Christmas). The Tuesday after the first Monday in November is Election Day, a federal government holiday in presidential-election years (held every 4 years, and next in 2008).

For more information on holidays see "Northern New Mexico Calendar of Events," earlier in this chapter.

Hospitals See chapters 4, 11, and 15.

Hotlines See chapters 4, 11, and 15.

Internet Access See chapters 4, 11, and 15. Also take a look at the "Online Traveler's Toolbox," and "The 21st-Century Traveler" for more options.

Legal Aid If you are "pulled over" for a minor infraction (such as speeding), never attempt to pay the fine directly to a police officer; this could be construed as attempted bribery, a much more serious crime. Pay fines by mail, or directly into the hands of the clerk of the court. If accused of a more serious offense, say and do nothing before consulting a lawyer. Here the burden is on the state to prove a person's guilt beyond a reasonable doubt, and everyone has the right to remain silent, whether he or she is suspected of a crime or actually arrested. Once arrested, a person can make one telephone call to a party of his or her choice. International visitors should call your embassy or consulate.

Lost & Found Be sure to tell all of your credit card companies the minute you discover your wallet has been lost or stolen and file a report at the nearest police precinct. Your credit card company or insurer may require a police report number or record of the loss. Most credit card companies have an emergency toll-free number to call if your card is lost or stolen; they may be able to wire you a cash advance immediately or deliver an emergency credit card in a day or two. Visa's U.S. emergency number is © **800/847-2911** or 410/581-9994. American Express cardholders and traveler's check holders should call © **800/221-7282.** MasterCard holders should call © **800/307-7309** or 636/722-7111. For other credit cards, call the toll-free number directory at © **800/555-1212.**

If you need emergency cash over the weekend when all banks and American Express offices are closed, you can have money wired to you via **Western Union** (© **800/325-6000;** www.westernunion.com).

Mail At press time, domestic postage rates were 24¢ for a postcard and 39¢ for a letter. For international mail, a first-class letter of up to 1 ounce costs 84¢ (63¢ to Canada and Mexico); a first-class postcard costs 75¢ (55¢ to Canada and Mexico); and a preprinted postal aerogramme costs 75¢. For more information go to **www.usps.com** and click on "Calculate Postage."

If you aren't sure what your address will be in the United States, mail can be sent to you, in your name, c/o General Delivery at the main post office of the city or region where you expect to be. (Call ✆ **800/275-8777** for information on the nearest post office.) The addressee must pick up mail in person and must produce proof of identity (driver's license, passport, etc.). Most post offices will hold your mail for up to 1 month, and are open Monday to Friday from 8am to 6pm, and Saturday from 9am to 3pm.

Always include zip codes when mailing items in the U.S. If you don't know your zip code, visit www.usps.com/zip4.

Maps The New Mexico Department of Tourism will send you a free state map. Call **800/545-2070** or 505/827-7336.

Measurements See the chart on the inside front cover of this book for details on converting metric measurements to U.S. equivalents.

Newspapers & Magazines National newspapers include the *New York Times, USA Today,* and the *Wall Street Journal*. National news weeklies include *Newsweek, Time,* and *U.S. News and World Report*. In large cities, most newsstands offer a small selection of the most popular foreign periodicals and newspapers, such as *The Economist* and *Le Monde*. For information on local publications, see the "Fast Facts" sections in chapters 4, 11, and 15.

Passports For Residents of Australia: You can pick up an application from your local post office or any branch of Passports Australia, but you must schedule an interview at the passport office to present your application materials. Call the **Australian Passport Information Service** at ✆ **131-232,** or visit the government website at www.passports.gov.au.

For Residents of Canada: Passport applications are available at travel agencies throughout Canada or from the central **Passport Office,** Department of Foreign Affairs and International Trade, Ottawa, ON K1A 0G3 (✆ **800/567-6868;** www.ppt.gc.ca). *Note:* Canadian children who travel must have their own passport. However, if you hold a valid Canadian passport issued before December 11, 2001, that bears the name of your child, the passport remains valid for you and your child until it expires.

For Residents of Ireland: You can apply for a 10-year passport at the **Passport Office,** Setanta Centre, Molesworth Street, Dublin 2 (✆ **01/671-1633;** www.irlgov.ie/iveagh). Those under age 18 and over 65 must apply for a 3-year passport. You can also apply at 1A South Mall, Cork (✆ **021/272-525**) or at most main post offices.

For Residents of New Zealand: You can pick up a passport application at any New Zealand Passports Office or download it from their website. Contact the **Passports Office** at ✆ **0800/225-050** in New Zealand or 04/474-8100, or log on to www.passports.govt.nz.

For Residents of the United Kingdom: To pick up an application for a standard 10-year passport (5-yr. passport for children under 16), visit your nearest passport office, major post office, or travel agency or contact the **United Kingdom Passport Service** at ☎ **0870/521-0410** or search its website at www.ukpa.gov.uk.

Police In case of emergencies, dial ☎ 911. For local police stations, see chapters 4, 11, and 15.

Safety See "Health & Safety," earlier in this chapter.

Smoking Santa Fe recently outlawed smoking at indoor public places, including restaurants and nightclubs. Most Albuquerque and Taos restaurants also ban smoking, though a few do have smoking sections. Some hotels offer rooms which allow smoking, though the number of these is dwindling.

Taxes Please see chapters 4, 11, and 15 for specifics about city taxes. The United States has no value-added tax (VAT) or other indirect tax at the national level. Every state, county, and city may levy its own local tax on all purchases, including hotel and restaurant checks and airline tickets. These taxes will not appear on price tags.

Telephone, Telegraph, Telex & Fax Generally, hotel surcharges on long-distance and local calls are astronomical, so you're better off using your **cellphone** or a **public pay telephone.** Many convenience groceries and packaging services sell **prepaid calling cards** in denominations up to $50; for international visitors these can be the least expensive way to call home. Many public phones at airports now accept American Express, MasterCard, and Visa credit cards. **Local calls** made from public pay phones in most locales cost either 25¢ or 35¢. Pay phones do not accept pennies, and few will take anything larger than a quarter.

Most long-distance and international calls can be dialed directly from any phone. **For calls within the United States and to Canada,** dial 1 followed by the area code and the seven-digit number. **For other international calls,** dial 011 followed by the country code, city code, and the number you are calling.

Calls to area codes **800, 888, 877,** and **866** are toll-free. However, calls to area codes **700** and **900** (chat lines, bulletin boards, "dating" services, and so on) can be very expensive—usually a charge of 95¢ to $3 or more per minute, and they sometimes have minimum charges that can run as high as $15 or more.

For **reversed-charge or collect calls,** and for person-to-person calls, dial the number 0 then the area code and number; an operator will come on the line, and you should specify whether you are calling collect, person-to-person, or both. If your operator-assisted call is international, ask for the overseas operator.

For **local directory assistance** ("information"), dial 411; for long-distance information, dial 1, then the appropriate area code and 555-1212.

Telegraph and telex services are provided primarily by Western Union. You can telegraph money, or have it telegraphed to you, very quickly over the Western Union system, but this service can cost as much as 15% to 20% of the amount sent.

Most hotels have **fax machines** available for guest use (be sure to ask about the charge to use it). Many hotel rooms are even wired for guests' fax machines. A less expensive way to send and receive faxes may be at stores such as **The UPS Store** (formerly Mail Boxes Etc.).

Time The continental United States is divided into **four time zones:** Eastern Standard Time (EST), Central Standard Time (CST), Mountain Standard Time (MST), and Pacific Standard Time (PST). Alaska and Hawaii have their own zones. For example, when it's 9am in Los Angeles (PST), it's 7am in Honolulu (HST),10am in Denver (MST), 11am in Chicago (CST), noon in New York City (EST), 5pm in London (GMT), and 2am the next day in Sydney.

New Mexico is on Mountain Standard Time (MST), 7 hours behind Greenwich Mean Time. **Daylight saving time** takes effect at 2am the first Sunday in April until 2am the last Sunday in October, except in Arizona, Hawaii, the U.S. Virgin Islands, and Puerto Rico. Daylight saving moves the clock 1 hour ahead of standard time. (A new law will extend daylight saving in 2007; clocks will change the second Sunday in March and the first Sunday in November.)

Tipping Tips are a very important part of certain workers' income, and gratuities are the standard way of showing appreciation for services provided. (Tipping is certainly not compulsory if the service is poor!) In hotels, tip **bellhops** at least $1 per bag ($2–$3 if you have a lot of luggage) and tip the **chamber staff** $1 to $2 per day (more if you've left a disaster area for him or her to clean up). Tip the **doorman** or **concierge** only if he or she has provided you with some specific service (for example, calling a cab for you or obtaining difficult-to-get theater tickets). Tip the **valet-parking attendant** $1 every time you get your car.

In restaurants, bars, and nightclubs, tip **service staff** 15% to 20% of the check, tip **bartenders** 10% to 15%, tip **checkroom attendants** $1 per garment, and tip **valet-parking attendants** $1 per vehicle.

As for other service personnel, tip **cab drivers** 15% of the fare, tip **skycaps** at airports at least $1 per bag ($2–$3 if you have a lot of luggage), and tip **hairdressers** and **barbers** 15% to 20%.

Toilets You won't find public toilets or "restrooms" on the streets in most U.S. cities but they can be found in hotel lobbies, bars, restaurants, museums, department stores, railway and bus stations, and service stations. Large hotels and fast-food restaurants are often the best bet for clean facilities. If possible, avoid the toilets at parks and beaches, which tend to be dirty; some may be unsafe. Restaurants and bars in resorts or heavily visited areas may reserve their restrooms for patrons.

Useful Phone Numbers

   U.S. Dept. of State Travel Advisory: ℂ 202/647-5225 (manned 24 hrs.)

   U.S. Passport Agency: ℂ 202/647-0518

   U.S. Centers for Disease Control International Traveler's Hotline: ℂ 404/332-4559

Visas For information about U.S. visas go to **http://travel.state.gov** and click on "Visas." Or go to one of the following websites:

Australian citizens can obtain up-to-date visa information from the **U.S. Embassy Canberra,** Moonah Place, Yarralumla, ACT 2600 (ℂ **02/6214-5600**), or by checking the U.S. Diplomatic Mission's website at **http://usembassy-australia.state.gov/consular**.

British subjects can obtain up-to-date visa information by calling the **U.S. Embassy Visa Information Line** (ℂ **0891/200-290**) or by visiting the "Visas to the U.S." section of the American Embassy London's website at **www.us embassy.org.uk**.

Irish citizens can obtain up-to-date visa information through the **Embassy of the USA Dublin,** 42 Elgin Rd., Dublin 4 (✆ **353/1-668-8777**), or by checking the "Consular Services" section of the website at **http://dublin.usembassy.gov**.

Citizens of **New Zealand** can obtain up-to-date visa information by contacting the **U.S. Embassy New Zealand,** 29 Fitzherbert Terrace, Thorndon, Wellington (✆ **644/472-2068**), or get the information directly from the "For New Zealanders" section of the website at **http://usembassy.org.nz**.

3

Suggested Northern New Mexico Itineraries

You may already have an idea of how you want to spend your time in New Mexico—power shopping, perhaps, or time-traveling through ancient culture. But if you're not sure what to do, here are four suggested itineraries, outlined in 1-week and 2-week segments. For each one, I assume that you're starting in Albuquerque, either by driving in your own car or flying into the Albuquerque International Sunport, the air transportation hub of the state, and then renting a car.

Northern New Mexico has a mix of museums and indoor activities, but the real attractions here are the living culture and spectacular scenery en route. With this in mind, I've combined scenic drives with city stays in these tours. In order to get a true sense of this place, take your time—linger at a country cafe or wander a plaza for an hour. You might be surprised at how easily you get enveloped in the experience of being a New Mexican.

1 Culture Cruising: Northern New Mexico in a Week

A week in Northern New Mexico isn't quite long enough to do justice to the area's rich and varied landscape, but if that's all the time you have, you can definitely hit the highlights. You can gaze at the ancient petroglyphs etched on stone at Petroglyph National Monument, shop one of the world's top art markets on Canyon Road in Santa Fe, marvel at the play of light on the Rio Grande Gorge in Taos—and maybe even take a white-water rafting trip through it. See map on p. 47.

Day ❶: Albuquerque
If you have some energy left after traveling, head to **Old Town** (p. 254), where you can wander through the **plaza** and peruse some shops. Be sure to duck into some of the back alleyways and little nooks—you'll uncover some of the city's most inventive shops in these areas. Next, head over to the **Albuquerque Museum of Art and History** (p. 253) to get a good sense of the story of this land. Finish the day with one of New Mexico's premier treats—an enchilada—at **Sadie's** (p. 248). Wash it down with one of their margaritas.

Day ❷: Albuquerque
Start out at the **Indian Pueblo Cultural Center** (p. 254), where you'll get a sense of the cultures you'll encounter up north, and then head to the **Albuquerque Biological Park** (p. 259), both in the vicinity of **Old Town Plaza.** From here, go west of town to visit the **Petroglyph National Monument** (p. 257). (If it's summer, you may want to go during the cooler early morning.) In the late afternoon, find your way to Central Avenue, just south of Old Town, and drive east on **Route 66.** This takes you right through

Airport ✈

Ski area ⛷

COLORADO
NEW MEXICO

CARSON
NATIONAL
FOREST

Chama

Los Ojos

Heron
Reservoir

Ensenada

Rio Brazos

El Vado
Lake

Rio Nutrias

Rio Gallina

Abiquiu
Dam

Abiquiu

Rio Chama

SANTA FE NATIONAL FOREST

Sulphur
Springs

La Cueva

Valles
Caldera
National
Reserve

Jemez
Springs

Vallecitos

Jemez Pueblo

ZIA INDIAN RESERVATION

Santo Domingo
Pueblo

San Felipe
Pueblo

Santa Ana
Pueblo

Bernalillo

Alameda

Los Ranchos
de Albuquerque

Albuquerque

Rio Grande

Costilla

Questa

Lama

San
Cristobal

CARSON
NATIONAL
FOREST

Rio Grande
Gorge Bridge

Taos

Ranchos
de Taos

Picuris
Pueblo

Las
Trampas

El Valle

SANTA FE
NATIONAL
FOREST

Tres Piedras

Rio Vallecitos

Taos River

Arroyo Aguaje de la Petaca

Vallecitos

La Madera

El Rito

Ojo Caliente

Rinconada

Embudo

Ohkay
Owingeh

Santa
Cruz

Española

Chimayo

Truchas

Cordova

Santa Clara Pueblo

Nambe

Los
Alamos

San Ildefonso
Pueblo

Bandelier
National
Monument

White
Rock

Tesuque
Pueblo

Tesuque

Santa Fe

Pecos River

Pecos
National
Monument

SANTA CLARA
INDIAN RESERVATION

Cochiti
Pueblo

Cochiti
Lake

Sile

Placitas

Sandia Pueblo

Corrales

Golden

Cerrillos

Madrid

Lamy

Galisteo

Cow Creek

Moriarty

NEW
MEXICO

0   15 mi

0   15 km

downtown, to the Nob Hill district and the Sandia Mountains foothills, respectively. Finish your day with a ride up the **Sandia Peak Tramway** (p. 256). After you reach the top, you may want to hike along the crest, though this isn't safe for young kids. Ideally, you should ride up during daylight and back down at night for a view of the city lights. You may even want to dine at **High Finance Restaurant and Tavern** on the top (p. 248).

Day ❸: The Turquoise Trail 🐾🐾 and Santa Fe

Today, strike out for the ghost towns and other sights along the **Turquoise Trail** (p. 278) to Santa Fe, stopping to peruse some of the galleries in **Madrid** (p. 279). This will put you in Santa Fe in time to do some sightseeing. Head straight to the **plaza** (p. 109), the **Palace of the Governors** (p. 106), and **St. Francis Cathedral** (p. 108). If you shop from the Native Americans selling under the portal, be sure to ask about the art you buy; the symbols on it may have interesting significance. Next, make your way over to the **Georgia O'Keeffe Museum** (p. 109). Finish your day with an enchilada at **The Shed** (p. 100). In the evening, depending on the season, you may want to check out Santa Fe's excellent arts' scene; try the **Santa Fe Opera** (p. 144) or the **Santa Fe Chamber Music Festival** (p. 145).

Day ❹: Santa Fe Arts

In the morning, head up to Museum Hill, where you can take your pick from four very unique museums: the **Museum of International Folk Art** (p. 113), the **Museum of Indian Arts & Culture** (p. 113), the **Wheelwright Museum of the American Indian** (p. 114), and the **Museum of Spanish Colonial Art** (p. 114). You can have lunch at the **Museum Hill Café** (p. 112). On your way back to the plaza, take a stroll and do some shopping on **Canyon Road** (p. 9). At sunset during the warmer months, you can enjoy a cocktail at the bell tower of the historic **La Fonda Hotel** (p. 69). Eat dinner at **Coyote Café** (p. 88) or **Santacafé** (p. 93)—or if you lingered over your shopping, stop in at **Geronimo** (p. 90) or **The Compound** (p. 88) on Canyon Road.

Day ❺: Bandelier National Monument 🐾🐾🐾 and North to Taos

Head out of town today to **Bandelier National Monument** (p. 157). Linger among the ruins and be sure to climb the ladders to see the kiva set high above the canyon floor. Then continue north to Taos. On your way into the city, stop at the **San Francisco de Asis church** (p. 205). And if you like music, head out to the **Sagebrush Inn** (p. 185) for some country-and-western tunes.

Day ❻: Taos 🐾🐾🐾

Spend your morning exploring **Taos Pueblo** (p. 208), the **Millicent Rogers Museum** (p. 205), and the **Rio Grande Gorge Bridge** (p. 211). You can then ditch your car for the afternoon and step out on foot. Do some shopping around **Taos Plaza.** At cocktail hour, head to the **Adobe Bar** (p. 224) at The Historic Taos Inn or the **Anaconda Bar** (p. 224) at the new El Monte Sagrado.

Day ❼: The High Road 🐾🐾

On your last day, enjoy a leisurely morning and then head south on the **High Road to Taos** (see chapter 10). Be sure to spend some time at the **Santuario de Chimayo** (p. 159), where you can rub healing dust between your fingers. You may want to spend the night at a bed-and-breakfast in **Chimayo** (p. 158) along the way. Depending on your flight time the next morning, stay the night in Santa Fe or Albuquerque.

2 Northern New Mexico in 2 Weeks

If you have two weeks to spend exploring the region, consider yourself fortunate. In addition to hitting the highlights, you'll be able to spend time getting to know such places as Chama and Chaco National Cultural Park. See map on p. 50.

Day ❶ to ❹: Albuquerque and Santa Fe

For days one through four, follow the previous itinerary, "Culture Cruising: Northern New Mexico in a Week."

Day ❺: Santa Fe

In the morning, take **The Plaza Area** (p. 109) walking tour, spending time at the **Museum of Fine Arts** (p. 106) and the **Loretto Chapel** (p. 116). If you're visiting during the warm seasons, have lunch in the Sena Plaza at **La Casa Sena** (p. 90). In the afternoon, take the **Barrio de Analco** walking tour up Canyon Road, allowing you more time for shopping that lovely street. Be sure to stop in at **El Zaguan** (p. 126) to see an old New Mexico hacienda.

Day ❻: High Road to Taos ✦✦

On day six, travel the **High Road to Taos** (see chapter 10), stopping to rub healing dust between your fingers at the **Santuario de Chimayo** (p. 159). On the way into Taos, stop at the **San Francisco de Asis church** (p. 205). While there, take note of the thickness of the structure's walls. If you like music, head out to the **Sagebrush Inn** (p. 185) for some country-and-western music or to the **Anaconda Bar** (p. 224) to hear some jazz or other live music.

Day ❼: Taos ✦✦✦

Spend your morning at **Taos Pueblo** (p. 208), where you may want to sample some fry bread. Next head to the **Millicent Rogers Museum** (p. 205) and the **Rio Grande Gorge Bridge** (p. 211). During the afternoon, do some shopping

around the **Taos Plaza,** and then visit the **Taos Art Museum** (p. 206). Don't just look at the art there. The Fechin Home where the museum is housed is a work of art itself. At cocktail hour, head to the **Adobe Bar** (p. 224) at The Historic Taos Inn or the **Anaconda Bar** (p. 224) at El Monte Sagrado to hear live music.

Day ❽: The Enchanted Circle ✦✦

Take the 90-mile loop north of Taos through old Hispanic villages and mining towns to see some of the region's most picturesque landscapes. If you're a literary type, be sure to stop at the **D.H. Lawrence Ranch** (p. 209), and if you're a hiker, stretch your legs at the **Wild Rivers Recreation Area** (p. 226).

Day ❾: West to Chama

If you're traveling in the spring, summer, or fall, take a scenic drive west to Chama. En route, stop in at **Tierra Wools** (p. 172) to see the weaving. Then wander around Chama to learn about the area's train history. In the afternoon you'll prepare for tomorrow's train ride on the **Cumbres & Toltec Scenic Railroad** (p. 169). Be sure to make your train reservations well in advance. As well as offering a great ride, the Cumbres & Toltec is a living train museum, so take some time to wander the grounds. Often volunteers will tell fun stories about the train and its history. Spend the night in Chama. If it's wintertime, the train won't be running, so you'll want to stay in Taos and head to **Taos Ski Valley** (p. 212) for a day of skiing. Or, if you're not a train buff, and it's spring, take a white-water raft trip down the **Taos Box** (p. 218) or **Pilar** (p. 218).

Northern New Mexico in 2 Weeks

Day ⑩: Cumbres & Toltec Scenic Railroad ☆☆

Spend the day riding the **Cumbres & Toltec Scenic Railroad** (p. 169). Your best bet is to ride the train to the halfway point and turn around and come back. Spend the night in Chama. If you don't ride the train and have stayed in Taos, take a **Llama trek** (p. 216), with a gourmet lunch.

Day ⑪: Head South to Bandelier National Monument ☆☆☆

This will be a day of pure scenery. You'll drive through **Abiquiu** and see the crimson-and-white hills that Georgia O'Keeffe painted, and then head into the Jemez Mountains. Stop at **Bandelier National Monument** (p. 157). Here you'll hike among ancient ruins. Follow the Frijoles Trail as far up as you'd like, making sure you stop to climb the ladders to the kiva perched high on the canyon wall. From Bandelier, you'll make your way west past the **Valles Caldera National Preserve** (p. 158), pausing to look out across this amazing collapsed volcano. From here, head south on the **Jemez Mountain Trail** (p. 276). Spend the night at the **Cañon del Rio** (p. 167) in Jemez Springs.

Day ⑫: Chaco Culture National Historic Park ☆☆☆

Though it's a long, dusty drive to **Chaco Culture National Historic Park** (p. 166), its combination of a stunning setting and expansive ruins makes it worthwhile. In fact, Chaco is the Holy Grail for Southwest history buffs. Be sure to hike up the **Pueblo Alto Trail** (p. 168) to get a full view of the grand kivas and amazing network of dwellings. If you have camping equipment, spend the night at Chaco. If not, you can spend the night at one of the many chain hotels in Grants or head back to Albuquerque.

Day ⑬: Acoma Pueblo ☆☆☆

Today, depending on whether you spent the night camping at Chaco or returned to Albuquerque the night before, you can either drive to I-40 from Chaco and then head east or head west from Albuquerque to **Acoma Pueblo** (p. 272). Tour the village with the requisite bus and walking tour, but then be sure to hike down on your own in order to get a good sense of this mesa-top village, where people still live as their ancestors did hundreds of years ago. Spend the night in Albuquerque.

Day ⑭: Albuquerque

Today—your last day in Albuquerque—take a **balloon ride** (p. 261) in the early morning. (And if you want to do this, be sure to make your reservations in advance.) Then head to the new **Balloon Museum** (p. 253) to learn more about the sport. Finish the afternoon cooling off at your hotel pool, or if you're energetic, visit the **National Hispanic Cultural Center** (p. 254). Have dinner at **Seasons Grill** (p. 246) or **AmbroZia Café and Wine Bar** (p. 244).

3 Family Time: Northern New Mexico in a Week for Kids— and the Young of Heart

Although New Mexico lacks the major theme park variety of attractions, it makes up for it by offering experiences that have a deeper impact. This trip takes families to the region's most notable sights—including Petroglyph National Monument and Bandelier National Monument—but it's not too jam-packed; it also fits in some time for poolside lounging. When planning this trip, keep in mind that the climate in this region is fairly mild, but summers in Albuquerque can be scorching and winters in Santa Fe and Taos can be cold. See map on p. 53.

Day ❶: Albuquerque

If you have some energy after traveling, head to **Old Town** (p. 254), where you can wander the **plaza,** peruse some shops, and, if you have time, head over to the **Explora Science Center** (p. 260). Finish the day with one of New Mexico's premier treats—an enchilada—at **Sadie's** (p. 248).

Day ❷: Albuquerque

Start out at the **Indian Pueblo Cultural Center** (p. 254), and then head to the **Albuquerque Biological Park** (p. 259). Be sure to visit the Biological Park's butterfly exhibit. Alternatively, you may want to visit the **Rio Grande Zoo** (p. 261). Don't miss the polar bears there. Both are in the vicinity of **Old Town Plaza.** Then head out to **Petroglyph National Monument** (p. 257), west of town. (If it's summer, you may want to go first thing in the morning while the air is cool.) In the late afternoon, find your way to Central Avenue, just south of Old Town, and drive east on **Route 66** (p. 251). This takes you right through downtown, to the Nob Hill district and the Sandia Mountains foothills, respectively. Finish your day with a ride up the **Sandia Peak Tramway** (p. 256). After you reach the top, you may want to hike along the crest, though this isn't safe for young kids. Ideally, you should ride up during daylight and ride down at night for a view of the city lights. You may even want to dine at **High Finance Restaurant and Tavern** (p. 248) at the top.

Day ❸: The Turquoise Trail 🐾🐾 and Santa Fe

In the morning, strike out for the ghost towns and other sights along the **Turquoise Trail** to Santa Fe. Stop in **Madrid** to peruse the **Old Coal Mine Museum** (p. 278). You'll arrive in Santa Fe in time to do some sightseeing. Head straight to the **plaza,** the **Palace of the Governors** (p. 106), and **St. Francis Cathedral** (p. 108). Next, make your way over to the **Santa Fe Children's Museum** (p. 120), where the kids can do some rock climbing or other fun activities. Finish your day with an enchilada at **The Shed** (p. 100). In the evening, depending on the season, you may want to get a sitter and take in some of Santa Fe's excellent arts, such as the **Santa Fe Opera** (p. 144) or the **Santa Fe Chamber Music Festival** (p. 145). Alternatively, if you'd like to take the kids along, head to **La Casa Sena** (p. 90) to hear some show tunes.

Day ❹: Santa Fe Arts

Head up to **Museum Hill,** and visit the **Museum of International Folk Art** (p. 113) so your kids can see the excellent toy collection. Also noteworthy are the **Museum of Indian Arts & Culture** (p. 113) and the **Wheelwright Museum** (p. 114), which often have kids-oriented activities such as craft-making and storytelling. Check their schedules in advance. Have lunch at **Sol Café** (p. 100) on Canyon Road so your kids can get a burger and you can peruse the arts scene for a bit. In the afternoon, head out to the living history site **El Rancho de las Golondrinas** (p. 117).

Day ❺: The High Road to Taos 🐾🐾

Travel the High Road to Taos, following the directions in chapter 10. Stop for lunch at **Leona's** and visit the **Santuario de Chimayo** (p. 158). On the way into Taos, stop at the **San Francisco de Asis church** (p. 159). If you like music, get a sitter and head to the **Sagebrush Inn** (p. 185) for some country-and-western tunes or to the **Anaconda Bar** (p. 224) to hear some jazz or other live performance.

Day ❻: Taos 🐾🐾🐾

Spend the morning of day six at **Taos Pueblo** (p. 208) and the **Rio Grande Gorge Bridge** (p. 211). On the west side of the Gorge, the **West Rim Trail** (p. 217) offers a fun hike with stunning views over the canyon, though you'll want to watch

Northern New Mexico in a Week for Kids

the kids carefully. During the afternoon, do some shopping around the **Taos Plaza,** and then visit the **Kit Carson Home and Museum** (p. 211). For a fun dinner, head to **Taos Pizza Out Back** (p. 201).

Day ❼: Enjoying the Outdoors

Head west and spend the day riding the **Cumbres & Toltec Scenic Railroad** (p. 169). Be sure to check departure times for the train and make reservations in advance. Alternatively, depending on the season, you might want to go skiing at **Taos Ski Valley** (p. 212) or white-water rafting at **Pilar** (p. 218) on the Rio Grande. Spend the night either in Chama or Taos and then drive south to Albuquerque to catch your plane.

4 Pack Your Gear: An Active Tour of Northern New Mexico

Anyone who skis, hikes, mountain bikes, or rafts knows that the Southwest is unsurpassed in its offerings for outdoors enthusiasts. New Mexico is no exception, and the highest concentration of sports lies in the north. You can ski world-class terrain at Taos Ski Valley, bike the edge of the Rio Grande Gorge, and hike the mountains among ancient Anasazi ruins at Bandelier National Monument. Be aware that the region is known for its mercurial weather conditions—always be prepared for extremes. Also, northern New Mexico is over 6,000 feet in elevation, so it may take you time to catch your breath. Be patient on the long upward hills. The sports you do will, of course, depend a lot on the season. For the full benefit of this trip, take it in late March or early April. With a little advance preparation, you might be able to ski and river raft on the same trip! See map on p. 55.

Day ❶: Albuquerque

When you arrive in Albuquerque, you may want to get acclimated to the city by strolling through **Old Town** (p. 254) and visiting the **Albuquerque Biological Park** (p. 259) to get a sense of the nature in the area and the **Pueblo Cultural Center** (p. 254) to get acquainted with the culture you'll encounter as you head north.

Day ❷: Albuquerque

For a truly unique experience, you may want to schedule a **balloon ride** (p. 261) first thing in the morning. Just be sure to make advance reservations for this exhilarating activity. If you're a bike rider or hiker, head to **Petroglyph National Monument** (p. 257) to see thousands of symbols etched on stone. In the evening, ride the **Sandia Peak Tramway** (p. 256) and go hiking along the crest. If you'd like, you can have dinner at the **High Finance Restaurant** (p. 248) and view the city lights as you come down.

Day ❸: The Turquoise Trail 🎿🎿 to Santa Fe

Head for the ghost towns and other sights along the **Turquoise Trail** (p. 278) to Santa Fe. If you like to ride horses, schedule a ride in Cerrillos with **Broken Saddle Riding Company** (p. 280). This will put you in Santa Fe in time to do some late-afternoon sightseeing. Head straight to the **plaza** (p. 109), the **Palace of the Governors** (p. 106), and **St. Francis Cathedral** (p. 108). When you've had enough touring for one day, and you've worked up an appetite, treat yourself to an enchilada at **The Shed** (p. 100).

Day ❹: Santa Fe

Use your own bike or rent a cruiser in town to ride around the plaza and up **Canyon Road** (p. 9). Stop at the top of Canyon at the **Randall Davey Audubon Center** (p. 117) to do some bird-watching. Alternatively, you may want to head to the mountains to do some hiking on the **Borrego Trail** (p. 131) or, if it's

An Active Tour of Northern New Mexico

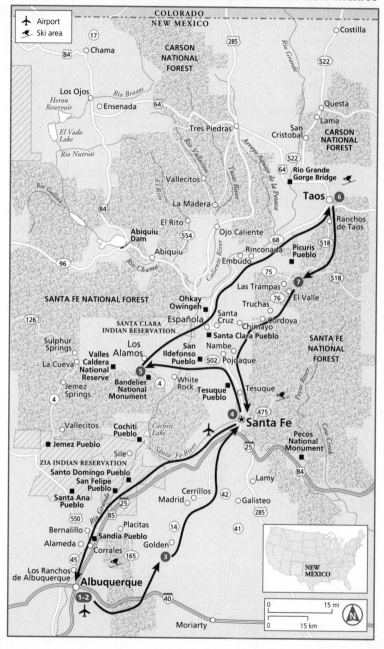

winter, some skiing at **Ski Santa Fe** (p. 132). Finish your day at one of the fun restaurants or cafes on **Canyon Road** (p. 9). In the evening, depending on the season, you may want to take in some of Santa Fe's excellent arts, such as the **Santa Fe Opera** (p. 144) or the **Santa Fe Chamber Music Festival** (p. 145).

Day ❺: Bandelier National Monument ☆☆☆

Head out from Santa Fe to **Bandelier National Monument** (p. 157) and hike among ancient ruins. Follow the Frijoles Trail as far up as you'd like, making sure you stop to climb the ladders to the kiva perched high on the canyon wall. Trail runners like to jog the Frijoles Trail, with its easy descent back to the start. Follow the Rio Grande River north and you'll come to Taos. Spend the evening strolling around the **plaza** (p. 109) to get a feel of the city.

Day ❻: Taos

Sports lovers have many options in this town. If you like to ride horses, take a ride on Taos Pueblo land. Alternatively, you may want to take a **llama trek** (p. 216) into the Rio Grande Gorge, or hike up to the top of **Wheeler Peak** (p. 217), New Mexico's highest, a full-day trek. If it's ski season, you'll definitely want to spend the day at **Taos Ski Valley** (p. 212). If you're visiting in the spring and the rivers are running, take the full-day heart-throbbing romp through the **Taos Box** (p. 218) or a half-day trip at **Pilar** (p. 218).

Day ❼: The High Road ☆☆

The last day, take a leisurely drive south toward Santa Fe. You'll want to take the **High Road** (p. 158), through the art villages of **Cordova** (p. 160) and **Chimayo** (p. 158). Stop at the **Santuario de Chimayo** (p. 159) and have lunch on the patio at **Rancho de Chimayo** (p. 160). Depending on your plane reservations, you can spend the night in Santa Fe or Albuquerque.

4

Getting to Know Santa Fe

After visiting Santa Fe, Will Rogers reportedly once said, "Whoever designed this town did so while riding on a jackass backwards and drunk." You, too, may find yourself perplexed when maneuvering through the meandering lanes and one-way streets in this, the oldest capital city in the United States.

But Santa Fe's crooked streets, combined with its Pueblo-style architecture and setting at the base of elegantly sloping mountains, provide a sense of exotic sophistication. Just remember to pack your walking shoes, because exploring the city by foot is the best way to get a feel for its idiosyncrasies. And if you do get lost, ask one of the 70,000 inhabitants living here—7,000 feet above sea level—for directions.

Native Americans enlighten the area with viewpoints and lifestyles deeply tied to nature and completely contrary to the American norm. Many of the Hispanics in this area still live within extended families and practice a devout Catholicism; they bring a slower pace to the city and an appreciation for deep-rooted ties. Meanwhile, a strong cosmopolitan element contributes cutting-edge cuisine, world-class opera, first-run films, and some of the finest artwork in the world.

Like most cities of Hispanic origin, Santa Fe contains a **plaza** in its center. Here, you'll find tall shade trees and lots of grass. The area is full of restaurants, shops, art galleries, and museums, many within centuries-old buildings, and is dominated by the beautiful **St. Francis Cathedral,** a French Romanesque structure.

On the plaza, you'll see Native Americans selling jewelry under the portal of the **Palace of the Governors,** teenagers in souped-up low-riders cruising along, and people young and old hanging out in the ice cream parlor. Such diversity, coupled with the variety of architecture—which ranges from Pueblo-style to Romanesque to Gothic—prompted the tourism department here to begin calling this city the "City Different."

Not far away is **Canyon Road,** a narrow, mostly one-way street packed with galleries and shops. Once it was the home of many artists, and today you'll still find some who work within gallery studios. There are a number of fine restaurants in this district as well.

Farther to the east slopes the rugged **Sangre de Cristo** range. Locals spend a lot of time in these mountains—picnicking, hiking, and skiing. When you look up at the mountains, you see the peak of **Santa Fe Baldy** (with an elevation of over 12,600 ft.). Back in town, to the south of the plaza, is the **Santa Fe River,** a tiny tributary of the Rio Grande that is little more than a trickle for much of the year.

North is the **Española Valley,** and beyond that, the village of Taos, about 66 miles away. South of the city are ancient Native American **turquoise mines** in the Cerrillos Hills, and to the southwest is metropolitan Albuquerque, some 58 miles away. To the west, across the Caja del Rio

Plateau, is the **Rio Grande,** and beyond that, the 11,000-foot **Jemez Mountains** and **Valle Grande**—an ancient and massive volcanic caldera. Pueblos dot the entire Rio Grande Valley, within an hour's drive in any direction.

1 Orientation

ARRIVING

BY PLANE   Many people choose to fly into the Albuquerque International Sunport. However, if you want to save time and don't mind paying a bit more, you can fly into the **Santa Fe Municipal Airport** (© 505/955-2900), just outside the southwestern city limits on Airport Road. In conjunction with United Airlines, commuter flights are offered via Denver, Colorado, by **United Express** (© 800/241-6522; www.united.com), which is operated by **Great Lakes Aviation** (© 800/473-4118; www.greatlakesav.com).

If you do fly into Albuquerque, you can rent a car or take one of the bus services. See "Getting There," in chapter 2, for details.

From the Santa Fe Municipal Airport, **Roadrunner Shuttle** (© 505/424-3367) meets every flight and takes visitors anywhere in Santa Fe. From the Albuquerque Sunport to Santa Fe, **Santa Fe Shuttle** (© 888/833-2300 or 505-466-8500; www. shuttlesantafe.com) runs shuttles 8 am to 8pm.

BY TRAIN & BUS   For detailed information about train and bus service to Santa Fe, see "Getting There," in chapter 2.

BY CAR   I-25 skims past Santa Fe's southern city limits, connecting it along one continuous highway from Billings, Montana, to El Paso, Texas. I-40, the state's major east–west thoroughfare, which bisects Albuquerque, affords coast-to-coast access to Santa Fe. (From the west, motorists leave I-40 in Albuquerque and take I-25 north; from the east, travelers exit I-40 at Clines Corners and continue 52 miles to Santa Fe on US 285. *Note:* Diesel is scarce on US 285, so be sure to fill up before you leave Clines Corners.) For those coming from the northwest, the most direct route is via Durango, Colorado, on US 160, entering Santa Fe on US 84.

For information on car rentals in Albuquerque, see "Getting Around Northern New Mexico," in chapter 2; for agencies in Santa Fe, see "Getting Around," later in this chapter.

VISITOR INFORMATION

The **Santa Fe Convention and Visitors Bureau** is at 125 Lincoln Ave. downtown (P.O. Box 909), Santa Fe, NM 87504-0909 (© 800/777-CITY or 505/955-6200). You can also log on to the bureau's website, at **www.santafe.org**. You might also try **www.visitsantafe.com** for more information.

CITY LAYOUT

MAIN ARTERIES & STREETS   The limits of downtown Santa Fe are demarcated on three sides by the horseshoe-shaped Paseo de Peralta and on the west by St. Francis Drive, otherwise known as US 84/285. Alameda Street follows the north side of the Santa Fe River through downtown, with the State Capitol and other government buildings on the south side of the river, and most buildings of historic and tourist interest on the north, east of Guadalupe Street.

The plaza is Santa Fe's universally accepted point of orientation. Its four diagonal walkways meet at a central fountain, around which a strange and wonderful assortment of people of all ages, nationalities, and lifestyles can be found at nearly any hour of the day or night.

If you stand in the center of the plaza looking north, you'll be gazing directly at the Palace of the Governors. In front of you is Palace Avenue; behind you, San Francisco Street. To your left is Lincoln Avenue, and to your right is Washington Avenue, which divides the downtown avenues into east and west. St. Francis Cathedral is the massive Romanesque structure a block east, down San Francisco Street. Alameda Street is 2 full blocks behind you.

Near the intersection of Alameda Street and Paseo de Peralta, you'll find Canyon Road running east toward the mountains. Much of this street is one-way. The best way to see it is to walk up or down, taking time to explore shops and galleries and even have lunch or dinner.

Running to the southwest from the downtown area, beginning opposite the state office buildings on Galisteo Avenue, is Cerrillos Road. Once the main north–south highway connecting New Mexico's state capital with its largest city, it is now a 6-mile-long motel and fast-food strip. St. Francis Drive, which crosses Cerrillos Road 3 blocks south of Guadalupe Street, is a far less tawdry byway, linking Santa Fe with I-25, 4 miles southwest of downtown. The Old Pecos Trail, on the east side of the city, also joins downtown and the freeway. St. Michael's Drive connects the three arteries.

FINDING AN ADDRESS   The city's layout makes it difficult to know exactly where to look for a particular address. It's best to call ahead for directions.

MAPS   Free city and state maps can be obtained at tourist information offices. An excellent state highway map is published by the **New Mexico Department of Tourism,** 491 Old Santa Fe Trail, Lamy Building, Santa Fe, NM 87503 (✆ **800/733-6396** or 505/827-7307; to receive a tourism guide call ✆ **800/777-CITY**). There's also a Santa Fe visitor center in the same building. More specific county and city maps are available from the **State Highway and Transportation Department,** 1120 Cerrillos Rd., Santa Fe, NM 87504 (✆ **505/827-5100**). Members of the **American Automobile Association,** 1644 St. Michael's Dr. (✆ **505/471-6620**), can obtain free maps from the AAA office. Other good regional maps can be purchased at area bookstores.

2 Getting Around

The best way to see downtown Santa Fe is on foot. Free **walking-tour maps** are available at the **tourist information center,** 125 Lincoln Ave. (✆ **800/777-CITY** or 505/984-6760), and several guided walking tours, as well as two self-guided tours, are included in chapter 7.

BY BUS

In 1993, Santa Fe opened **Santa Fe Trails** (✆ **505/955-2001**), its first public bus system. There are seven routes, and visitors can pick up a map from the Convention and Visitors Bureau. Some buses operate Monday to Friday 6am to 11pm and Saturday 8am to 8pm. There is some service on Sunday, and there is some service on holidays. Call for a current schedule and fare information.

BY CAR

Cars can be rented from any of the following firms in Santa Fe: **Avis,** Santa Fe Airport (✆ **505/471-5892**); **Budget,** 1946 Cerrillos Rd. (✆ **505/984-1596**); **Enterprise,**

Santa Fe Orientation

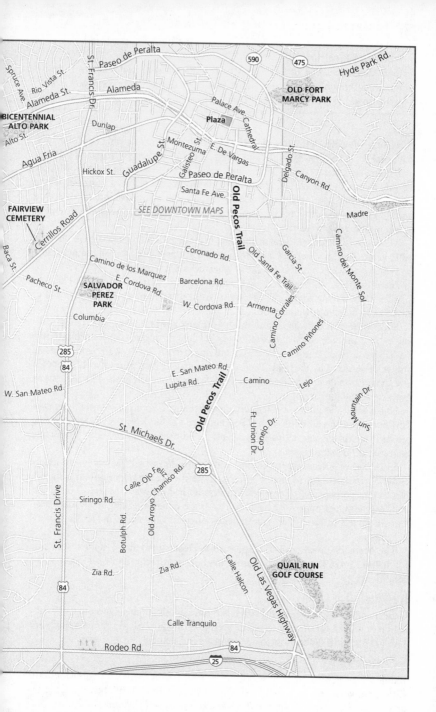

Driving Warning

New Mexico has one of the highest per-capita rates of traffic deaths in the nation; although the number has actually been dropping in recent years, it's still a good idea to drive extra carefully!

2641A Cerrillos Rd., 4450 Cerrillos Rd. (at the Auto Park), and Santa Fe Hilton, 100 Sandoval St. (© **505/473-3600**); and **Hertz,** Santa Fe Airport (© **505/471-7189**).

If Santa Fe is merely your base for an extended driving exploration of New Mexico, be sure to give the vehicle you rent a thorough road check before starting out. There are a lot of wide-open desert and wilderness spaces here, so if you break down, you could be stranded for hours before someone passes by, and cellphones don't tend to work in these remote areas.

Make sure your driver's license and auto club membership (if you have one) are valid before you leave home. Check with your auto-insurance company to make sure you're covered when out of state and/or when driving a rental car.

Note: In 2002, the Santa Fe City Council imposed a law prohibiting use of cell-phones while driving within the city limits, with strict fines imposed. If you need to make a call, be sure to pull off the road.

Street parking is difficult to find during summer months. There's a metered parking lot near the federal courthouse, 2 blocks north of the plaza; a city lot behind Santa Fe Village, a block south of the plaza; and another city lot at Water and Sandoval streets. If you stop by the Santa Fe Convention and Visitors Bureau, at 125 Lincoln Ave., you can pick up a wallet-size guide to Santa Fe parking areas. The map shows both street and lot parking.

Unless otherwise posted, the speed limit on freeways is 75 mph; on most other two-lane open roads it's 60 to 65 mph. The minimum age for drivers is 16. Seat belts are required for drivers and all passengers ages 5 and over; children under 5 must use approved child seats.

Since Native American reservations enjoy a measure of self-rule, they can legally enforce certain designated laws. For instance, on the Navajo reservation, it is forbidden to transport alcoholic beverages, leave established roadways, or go without a seat belt. Motorcyclists must wear helmets. If you are caught breaking reservation laws, you are subject to reservation punishment—often stiff fines and, in some instances, detainment.

The **State Highway and Transportation Department** has a toll-free hot line (© **800/432-4269**) that provides up-to-the-hour information on road closures and conditions.

BY TAXI

Cabs are difficult to flag from the street, but you can call for one. Expect to pay a standard fee of $3.88 for the service and an average of about $2.50 per mile. **Capital City Cab** (© **505/438-0000**) is the main company in Santa Fe.

BY BICYCLE

Riding a bicycle is an excellent way to get around town. Check with **Sun Mountain Bike Company,** 102 E. Water St. (inside El Centro) (© **505/982-8986**); **Bike-N-Sport,** 524 Cordova Rd. (© **505/820-0809**), or **Santa Fe Mountain Sports,** 607 Cerrillos Rd. (© **505/988-3337**), for rentals.

FAST FACTS: Santa Fe

Airport See "Orientation," above.

Area Code All of New Mexico is in area code **505**. However, at press time the state was initiating moves to add another area code, which may affect Santa Fe.

ATM Networks As in most U.S. destinations, ATMs are ubiquitous in the cities of northern New Mexico. However, in the small mountain towns, they're scarce. ATMs are linked to a network that most likely includes your bank at home. **Cirrus** (✆ 800/424-7787; www.mastercard.com) and **PLUS** (✆ 800/843-7587; www.visa.com) are the two most popular networks in the United States and in this region.

Babysitters Most hotels can arrange for sitters on request. Alternatively, call professional, licensed sitters **Ida Rajotte** (✆ 505/471-6875) or **Linda Iverson** (✆ 505/982-9327).

Business Hours **Offices** and **stores** are generally open Monday to Friday, 9am to 5pm, with many stores also open Friday night, Saturday, and Sunday in the summer season. Most **banks** are open Monday to Thursday, 9am to 5pm, and Friday, 9am to 6pm. Some may also be open Saturday morning. Most branches have ATMs available 24 hours. Call establishments for specific hours.

Car Rentals See "Getting Around Northern New Mexico," in chapter 2, or "Getting Around," above.

Climate See "When to Go," in chapter 2.

Currency Exchange You can exchange foreign currency at **Bank of America,** 1234 St. Michael's Dr. (✆ 505/473-8211).

Dentists **Dr. Gilman Stenzhorn** (✆ 505/982-4317 or 505/983-4491) offers emergency service. He's located at 1496 St. Francis Dr., in the St. Francis Professional Center.

Doctors **The Lovelace Clinic,** 440 St. Michaels Dr. (✆ 505/995-2400), is open Monday to Thursday 8am to 6pm; Friday 8am to 5pm; and Saturday 8am to 3pm. For physician and surgeon referral and information services, call the **American Board of Medical Specialties** (✆ 866/275-2267).

Embassies & Consulates See "Fast Facts" in chapter 2.

Emergencies For police, fire, or ambulance emergencies, dial ✆ **911.**

Etiquette & Customs Certain rules of etiquette should be observed when visiting the pueblos. See chapter 10 for details.

Hospitals **St. Vincent Hospital,** 455 St. Michaels Dr. (✆ **505/983-3361,** or 505/995-3934 for emergency services), is a 248-bed regional health center. Patient services include urgent and emergency-room care and ambulatory surgery. Health services are also available at the **Women's Health Services Family Care and Counseling Center** (✆ 505/988-8869). **Ultimed,** 707 Paseo de Peralta (✆ 505/989-8707), a new urgent-care facility near the plaza, offers comprehensive health care.

Hot Lines The following hot lines are available in Santa Fe: **battered families** (✆ 505/473-5200), **poison control** (✆ 800/432-6866), **psychiatric emergencies** (✆ 888/920-6333 or 505/820-6333), and **sexual assault** (✆ 505/986-9111).

Information See "Visitor Information," under "Orientation," above.

Internet Access Head to the **Santa Fe Public Library** at 145 Washington Ave. (© 505/955-6780), or retrieve your e-mail at **FedEx Kinko's,** 301 N. Guadalupe (© 505/982-6311).

Libraries **The Santa Fe Public Library** is half a block from the plaza, at 145 Washington Ave. (© 505/955-6780). There are branch libraries at Villa Linda Mall and at 1730 Llano St., just off St. Michaels Drive. **The New Mexico State Library** is at 1209 Camino Carlos Rey (© 505/476-9700). A new south-side branch at the intersection of Jaguar and Country Club was completed in 2006. Specialty libraries include the **Archives of New Mexico,** 1205 Camino Carlos Rey, and the **New Mexico History Library,** 120 Washington Ave.

Liquor Laws The legal drinking age is 21 throughout New Mexico. Bars may remain open until 2am Monday to Saturday and until midnight on Sunday. Wine, beer, and spirits are sold at licensed supermarkets and liquor stores, but there are no package sales on election days until after 7pm, and on Sundays before noon. It is illegal to transport liquor through most Native American reservations.

Lost Property Contact the **city police** at © 505/955-5030.

Newspapers & Magazines The *New Mexican*—Santa Fe's daily paper—is the oldest newspaper in the West. Its offices are at 202 E. Marcy St. (© 505/983-3303; www.santafenewmexican.com). The weekly *Santa Fe Reporter,* 132 E. Marcy St. (© 505/988-5541; www.sfreporter.com), published on Wednesday and available free at stands all over town, is often more willing to be controversial, and its entertainment listings are excellent. Regional magazines published locally are *New Mexico* magazine (monthly, statewide interest; www.nmmagazine.com) and the *Santa Fean* magazine (10 times a year, Southwestern lifestyles; www.santafean.com).

Pharmacies **Del Norte Pharmacy,** at 1691 Galisteo St. (© 505/988-9797), is open Monday to Friday, 8:30am to 6pm, and Saturday, 9am to noon. Delivery service is available.

Police In case of emergency, dial © **911.** For all other inquiries, call the **Santa Fe Police Department,** 2515 Camino Entrada (© 505/428-3710). The **Santa Fe County Sheriff,** with jurisdiction outside the city limits, is at 35 Camino Justicia (© 505/986-2400).

Post Offices The **main post office** is at 120 S. Federal Place (© 505/988-2239), 2 blocks north and 1 block west of the plaza. It's open from 8am to 5:30pm. The **Coronado Station branch** is at 2071 S. Pacheco St. (© 800/275-8777), and is open Monday to Friday 8am to 6pm, and Saturday 9am to 4pm. Some of the major hotels have stamp machines and mailboxes with twice-daily pickup. The zip code for central Santa Fe is 87501.

Radio Local radio stations are **BLU** (102.9), which plays contemporary jazz, and **KBAC** (98.1), which plays alternative rock and folk music.

Safety Although the tourist district appears very safe, Santa Fe is not on the whole a safe city; theft and the number of reported rapes have risen. The good news is that Santa Fe's overall crime statistics do appear to be falling. Still, when walking the city streets, guard your purse carefully because there are many bag-grab thefts, particularly during the summer tourist months. Also, be as aware of your surroundings as you would in any other major city.

Taxes A tax of 7.625% is added to all purchases, with an additional 5% added to lodging bills.

Taxis See "Getting Around," above.

Television There are five Albuquerque network affiliates: **KOB-TV** (Channel 4, NBC), **KOAT-TV** (Channel 7, ABC), **KQRE-TV** (Channel 13, CBS), **KASA-TV** (Channel 2, FOX), and **KNME-TV** (Channel 5, PBS).

Time Zone New Mexico is on **Mountain Standard Time**, 1 hour ahead of the West Coast and 2 hours behind the East Coast. When it's 10am in Santa Fe, it's noon in New York, 11am in Chicago, and 9am in San Francisco. Starting in 2007, daylight saving time will be observed from the second Sunday in March to the first Sunday in November.

Useful Telephone Numbers Information on **road conditions** in the Santa Fe area can be obtained by calling the State Highway and Transportation Department (© **800/432-4269**). For **time and temperature,** call © **505/473-2211.**

Weather For **weather forecasts,** call © **505/988-5151.**

5

Where to Stay in Santa Fe

It's difficult to find a bad place to stay in Santa Fe. From downtown hotels to Cerrillos Road motels, ranch-style resorts to quaint bed-and-breakfasts, the standard of accommodations is almost universally high.

You should be aware of the seasonal nature of the tourist industry in Santa Fe. Accommodations are often booked solid through the summer months, and most places raise their prices accordingly. Rates increase even more during Indian Market, the third weekend of August. During these periods, it's essential to make reservations well in advance.

Still, there seems to be little agreement on what constitutes the tourist season; one hotel may raise its rates July 1 and lower them again in mid-September, while another may raise its rates from May to November. Some hotels recognize a shoulder season, so it pays to shop around during the in-between seasons of May through June and September through October.

No matter the season, discounts are often available to seniors, affiliated groups, corporate employees, and others. If you have any questions about your eligibility for these lower rates, be sure to ask.

A combined city-state tax of about 14.6% is added to every hotel bill in Santa Fe. And unless otherwise indicated, all recommended accommodations come with a private bathroom.

RESERVATIONS SERVICES Year-round reservation assistance is available from **Santa Fe Hotels.com** (© 800/745-9910), the **Accommodation Hot Line** (© 800/338-6877), **All Santa Fe Reservations** (© 877/737-7366), and **Santa Fe Stay,** which specializes in casitas (© 800/995-2272). **Emergency Lodging Assistance** is available free after 4pm daily (© **505/986-0038**). All of the above are private companies and may have biases toward certain properties. Do your own research before calling.

1 Downtown

Everything within the horseshoe-shaped Paseo de Peralta and east a few blocks along either side of the Santa Fe River is considered downtown Santa Fe. All these accommodations are within walking distance of the plaza.

VERY EXPENSIVE

Eldorado Hotel & Spa ★★ Since its opening in 1986, the Eldorado has been a model hotel for the city. In a large structure, the architects managed to meld pueblo revival style with an interesting cathedral feel, inside and out. The lobby has a high ceiling that continues into the court area and the cafe, all adorned with well over a million dollars' worth of Southwestern art. The spacious, quiet rooms received a makeover in 2006, maintaining an artistic motif, with a warm feel created by custom-made furniture in all and kiva fireplaces in many. You'll find families, businesspeople, and conference-goers staying here. Most of the rooms have views of downtown Santa

Downtown Santa Fe Accommodations

Santa Fe

Downtown

OLD FORT MARCY PARK

SANTA FE RIVER PARK

Plaza

State Capitol Complex

DE VARGAS PARK

Church ✝
Post Office ⊠
Information ⓘ

Adobe Abode **2**	Hotel Plaza Real **12**	The Lodge at Santa Fe **1**
AdobeStar Inn **3**	Hotel St. Francis **7**	The Madeleine **17**
Don Gaspar Inn **23**	Hotel Santa Fe **29**	Old Santa Fe Inn **27**
Eldorado Hotel & Spa **4**	Inn & Spa at Loretto **9**	Pueblo Bonito **24**
El Farolito **26**	Inn of the Anasazi **11**	Santa Fe Motel and Inn **28**
El Paradero **25**	Inn of the Five Graces **21**	Santa Fe Plaza
Fort Marcy Hotel Suites **14**	Inn of the Governors **8**	Travelodge **30**
Four Kachinas Inn **22**	Inn on the Alameda **19**	Santa Fe Sage Inn **31**
Garrett's Desert Inn **20**	La Fonda **10**	Ten Thousand Waves **15**
Hacienda Nicholas **16**	La Posada de Santa Fe	Territorial Inn **13**
Hilton of Santa Fe **6**	Resort & Spa **18**	Water Street Inn **5**

Fe, many from balconies. If you're really indulging, join the ranks of Mick Jagger, Geena Davis, and King Juan Carlos of Spain and try the penthouse five-room presidential suite for $1,500 per night. The recently opened Nidah Spa offers a full range of treatments, including a turquoise gemstone therapy, worth sampling. The Eldorado also manages the nearby Zona Rosa condominiums, which are two-, three-, and four-bedroom suites with full kitchens. The hotel's innovative and elegant restaurant, The Old House (p. 91), serves creative American cuisine.

309 W. San Francisco St., Santa Fe, NM 87501. © 800/286-6755 or 505/988-4455. Fax 505/995-4544. www.eldoradohotel.com. 219 units. High season $169–$319 double; low season $119–$199 double. Ski and other package rates are available. AE, DC, DISC, MC, V. Valet parking $16 per night. Pets accepted. **Amenities:** 2 restaurants; bar; heated rooftop pool; medium-size health club (with a view); Jacuzzi; his-and-hers saunas and steam baths; spa; concierge; business center; salon; room service; massage; laundry service; dry cleaning. *In room:* A/C, TV, high-speed Internet, minibar, coffeemaker, hair dryer, iron, safe.

Hilton of Santa Fe ℛ   With its landmark bell tower, the Hilton encompasses a full city block (1 block from the plaza) and incorporates most of the historic landholdings of the 350-year-old Ortiz family estate. It's built around a lovely courtyard pool and patio area, and it's a fine blend of ancient and modern styles. A renovation late in 2004 has brought more style to the rooms and common areas, with handcrafted furnishings and hip Southwestern decor. Rooms vary slightly in size; my favorites are a little smaller than some but have balconies opening onto the courtyard. The Hilton also has the Casa Ortiz de Santa Fe, luxury casitas with kitchens situated in a 1625 coach house adjacent to the hotel.

100 Sandoval St. (P.O. Box 25104), Santa Fe, NM 87501-2131. © 800/336-3676, 800/HILTONS, or 505/988-2811. Fax 505/986-6439. www.santafe.hilton.com. 157 units. $159–$299 double; $239–$549 suite; $419–$559 casita, depending on time of year. Additional person $20. AE, DC, DISC, MC, V. Parking $10 per night. **Amenities:** 2 restaurants; bar; outdoor pool; exercise room; Jacuzzi; concierge; car-rental desk; business center; room service; laundry service; dry cleaning. *In room:* A/C, TV, dataport, wireless Internet, coffeemaker, hair dryer, iron, safe.

Inn of the Anasazi ℛℛℛ   The designers of this fine luxury hotel have crafted a feeling of grandness in a very limited space, and in 2006 a remodel added even finer touches, including new bedding and decor in the rooms, with bold splashes of color from indigenous rugs and handwoven fabrics. Flagstone floors and vigas create a warm and welcoming ambience that evokes the feeling of an Anasazi cliff dwelling. Oversize cacti complete the look. Accents are appropriately Navajo, in a nod to the fact that the Navajo live in the area the Anasazi once inhabited. A half block off the plaza, this hotel was built in 1991 to cater to travelers who know their hotels. On the ground floor are a living room and library with oversize furniture and replicas of Anasazi pottery and Navajo rugs. A library expansion and a new exercise room were completed in 2004. Even the smallest rooms are spacious, with pearl-finished walls and decor in cream tones accented by novelties such as iron candle sconces, original art, four-poster beds, gaslit kiva fireplaces, and humidifiers. All the rooms are quiet and comfortable, though none have dramatic views. The Anasazi Restaurant (p. 86) serves creative Southwestern cuisine.

113 Washington Ave., Santa Fe, NM 87501. © 800/688-8100 or 505/988-3030. Fax 505/988-3277. www.innoftheanasazi.com. 56 units. Jan 5–Feb 26 $269–$469; Feb 27–Apr 28 $325–$525; Apr 29–June 23 $325–$525; June 24–Jan 4 $325–$525 double. AE, DC, DISC, MC, V. Valet parking $15 per day. **Amenities:** Restaurant; concierge; room service; in-room massage; laundry service; library/boardroom. *In room:* A/C, TV/DVD, wireless Internet, coffeemaker, hair dryer, iron, safe.

Inn of the Five Graces ℛℛ *Finds*   In the historic Barrio de Analco, just a few blocks from the Plaza, this inn holds true to its stated theme: "Here the Orient and the Old West meet, surprisingly at home in each other's arms." With floral-decked courtyards, elaborately decorated suites with kilim rugs, ornately carved beds, and often beautiful mosaic tile work in the bathrooms, this is truly a "sheik" place. All but a few suites are medium size, most with small bathrooms, and some with fireplaces. The lower-priced rooms are smaller. Request one of the suites in the buildings on the north side of East de Vargas Street; they're more spacious and substantially built. Travelers seeking an exotic stay will like this place; it's of the same caliber as Inn of the Anasazi, but with more flair. And although the inn doesn't have a full-service restaurant, a new kitchen now serves a variety of hot breakfasts and tapas (small plates) as options for lunch and dinner. All rooms have robes, stocked fridges, patios, and CD players; some have kitchenettes. Wireless Internet access is available in the lobby.

150 E. de Vargas St., Santa Fe, NM 87501. ℰ 505/992-0957. www.fivegraces.com. 23 units. $295–$750 double, depending on the season and type of room. Price includes extended breakfast and afternoon treats. AE, MC, V. Free parking. Pets welcome with fee and deposit. **Amenities:** Concierge. *In room:* A/C, TV, fridge, coffeemaker, hair dryer, iron, CD player, microwave.

Inn & Spa at Loretto ℱ This much-photographed hotel, just 2 blocks from the plaza, was built in 1975 to resemble Taos Pueblo. Light and shadow dance upon the five-level structure as the sun crosses the sky. With ongoing refinements, this hotel has become a comfortable and chic place to stay. Decor is a Southwest/Montana ranch style, with faux-painted walls and a moodily lit lobby lounge. The hotel's rooms and bathrooms are standard size, with the same decor as the rest of the hotel. Be aware that the Loretto likes convention traffic, so sometimes service lags for travelers. Overall, it is fairly quiet and has nice views—especially on the northeast side, where you'll see both the historic St. Francis Cathedral and the Loretto Chapel (with its "miraculous" spiral staircase; see "More Attractions," in chapter 7). The newly added Spa Terre offers a range of treatments, from facials to massages, in intimate, Southwest-meets-Asia rooms.

211 Old Santa Fe Trail (P.O. Box 1417), Santa Fe, NM 87501. ℰ 800/727-5531 or 505/988-5531. Fax 505/984-7968. www.innatloretto.com. 134 units. Jan–Mar $159–$275 double; Apr–June $185–$300 double; July–Oct $215–$499 double; Nov–Dec $185–$299 double. Additional person $25. Children 17 and under stay free in parent's room. AE, DC, DISC, MC, V. Valet parking $15 per night. **Amenities:** Restaurant; lounge; outdoor pool (heated year-round); spa; concierge; business center with audiovisual conferencing equipment; room service; valet laundry. *In room:* A/C, TV, wireless Internet, fridge, coffeemaker, hair dryer, iron.

La Fonda ℱ Whether you stay in this hotel or not, it's worth strolling through just to get a sense of how Santa Fe once was—and in some ways still is. This was the inn at the end of the Santa Fe Trail; it saw trappers, traders, and merchants, as well as notables such as President Rutherford B. Hayes and General Ulysses S. Grant. The original inn was dying of old age in 1920 when it was razed and replaced by the current La Fonda. Its architecture is pueblo revival: imitation adobe with wooden balconies and beam ends protruding over the tops of windows. Inside, the lobby is rich and slightly dark, with people bustling about, sitting in the cafe, and buying jewelry from Native Americans.

The hotel has seen some renovation through the years, as well as a whole new wing recently completed to the east, where you'll find deluxe suites and new meeting spaces. If you want a feel of the real Santa Fe, this is the place to stay. Overall, however, this hotel isn't the model of refinement. For that, you'd best go to the Hotel Santa Fe or other newer places. No two rooms are the same here, and while each has its own funky touch, some are more kitsch than quaint. Some have refrigerators, fireplaces, and private balconies. A recently added spa offers a variety of treatments from massages to salt glows, as well as a sauna and Jacuzzi. The French Pastry Shop is the place to get cappuccino and crepes, La Fiesta Lounge draws many locals to its economical New Mexican food lunch buffet, and La Plazuela offers some of the best new Southwestern cuisine in town, in a skylit garden patio. The Bell Tower Bar is the highest point in downtown Santa Fe—a great place for a cocktail and a view of the city.

100 E. San Francisco St. (P.O. Box 1209), Santa Fe, NM 87501. © **800/523-5002** or 505/982-5511. Fax 505/988-2952. www.lafondasantafe.com. 167 units. $219–$299 standard double; $239–$319 deluxe double; $349–$549 suite. Additional person $15. Children under 12 stay free in parent's room. AE, DC, DISC, MC, V. Parking $10 per day in a covered garage. **Amenities:** Restaurant; 2 bars; outdoor pool; spa; exercise room; 2 indoor Jacuzzis; concierge; tour desk; business center; room service; massage room and in-room massage; babysitting; laundry service; dry cleaning. *In room:* A/C, TV, dataport, wireless Internet, coffeemaker, hair dryer, iron, safe.

La Posada de Santa Fe Resort and Spa ★★ If you're in the mood to stay in a

little New Mexico adobe village, you'll enjoy this luxury hotel just 3 blocks from the plaza. The main building is an odd mix of architecture. The original part was a Victorian mansion built in 1882 by Abraham Staab, a German immigrant, for his bride, Julia. Later it was adobeized—an adobe structure was literally built around it—so that now the Victorian presence is only within the charming bar (which was refurbished in 2006) and four rooms, which still maintain the original brick and high ceilings. It is said that Julia Staab, who died in 1896, continues to haunt the place. Mischievous but good-natured, she is Santa Fe's best-known and most frequently witnessed ghost. If you like Victorian interiors more than Santa Fe style, these rooms are a good bet.

The rest of the hotel follows in the pueblo-style construction and is quaint; it's especially nice in the summer, when surrounded by acres of green grass. Here, you get to experience squeaky maple floors, vigas and *latillas,* and, in many rooms, kiva fireplaces. Be aware that unless you've secured a suite, most rooms tend to be fairly small. Fortunately, the hotel benefited from a $23-million face-lift completed in 1999, and all the bathrooms in historic rooms were renovated in 2004. Last summer, the hotel invested $1.5 million to improve its soft goods. Most notable are the Zen-Southwestern-style Avanyu spa and pool and spacious spa rooms, as well as a few "gallery suites," appointed with original artwork from some of the region's most prestigious artists. Travelers who are reluctant to trust the whims of older adobe construction should reserve one of the spa rooms or any of the other 40 new rooms. The hotel attracts travelers and a fair number of families, though it is pushing for more convention business. Most rooms don't have views but have outdoor patios, and most are tucked back into the quiet compound. The top-notch onsite restaurant, Fuego (p. 89), serves artfully prepared international cuisine in a romantic, Spanish-colonial dining room.

330 E. Palace Ave., Santa Fe, NM 87501. © **800/727-5276** or 505/986-0000. Fax 505/982-6850. www.rockresorts.com. 157 units. $199–$359 double; suites $289 and way up, depending on the season. Various spa packages available. AE, DC, DISC, MC, V. Valet parking $15 per day. **Amenities:** 2 restaurants; bar; outdoor pool; exercise room; spa with full treatments; Jacuzzi; conference center; bike rental; concierge; salon; room service; in-room massage; babysitting; dry cleaning. *In room:* A/C, TV, DVD, CD player, wireless Internet, minibar, coffeemaker, hair dryer, iron, safe.

EXPENSIVE

Don Gaspar Inn ★★ *(Finds)* If you'd like to pretend that you live in Santa Fe during

your vacation, that you're blessed with your very own Southwestern-style home, in a historic neighborhood, full of artful touches such as Native American tapestries and a kiva fireplace, this is your inn. A 10-minute walk from the plaza, the Don Gaspar occupies three homes, connected by brilliant gardens and brick walkways. Rooms vary in size, though all are plenty spacious, most with patios, some with kitchenettes, and there's even a full house for rent. Travelers looking for an adventure beyond a hotel stay, but without the close interaction of a B&B, enjoy this place. Though the rooms don't have views, all are quiet. The Courtyard Casita, with a kitchenette and a sleeper couch in its own room, is nice for a small family. The Territorial Suite, with carpet throughout and Italian marble in the bath, is perfect for a romantic getaway. All rooms have bathrobes and fireplaces. The friendly and dedicated staff serves a full breakfast such as green-chile stew with fresh baked items on the patio under a peach tree (the fruit from which they make cobbler) in the warm months and in the atrium in winter.

623 Don Gaspar, Santa Fe, NM 87505. ☏ **888/986-8664** or 505/986-8664. Fax 505/986-0696. www.dongaspar.com. 12 units. $115–$165 double; $165–$205 suite; $185–$245 casita; $295–$355 house. Rates include full breakfast. AE, MC, V. Free parking. **Amenities:** Babysitting; same-day laundry service. *In room:* A/C, TV/VCR, high-speed Internet, hair dryer, iron.

Hotel Plaza Real 🌣 *Value*

This New Orleans–meets–Santa Fe Territorial–style hotel built in 1990 provides comfortable rooms near the plaza. The construction and decor of the lobby are rustically elegant, built around a fireplace with balconies perched above. Clean and attractively decorated rooms have Southwestern-style furniture, many with French doors opening onto balconies or terraces that surround a quiet courtyard decorated with *ristras* (strung chiles). Beds are comfortably soft and baths small but with an outer sink vanity. The junior suites have an especially nice layout, with a sitting area near a fireplace and good light from the north and south. The place could use some sprucing up, but such a low price this close to the plaza makes it a value.

125 Washington Ave., Santa Fe, NM 87501. ☏ **877/901-7666** or 505/988-4900. Fax 505/983-9322. www. buynewmexico.com. 56 units. $119–$149 double, $149–$289 suite, depending on time of year and type of room. Additional person $20. Children under 12 stay free in parent's room. AE, DC, DISC, MC, V. Parking $12 per day. Pets $50 per stay. **Amenities:** Lounge; laundry service; dry cleaning. *In room:* A/C, TV, dataport, wireless Internet, coffeemaker, hair dryer, iron.

Hotel St. Francis 🌣

If you long for the rich fabrics, fine antiques, and slow pace of a European hotel, this is your place. The building was first constructed in the 1880s; it became fairly dilapidated but was renovated in 1986. Now elegantly redecorated, the lobby is crowned by a Victorian fireplace with hovering cherubs, a theme repeated throughout the hotel. The rooms continue the European decor, each with its own unique bent. You'll find a fishing room, a golf room, a garden room, and a music room, with each motif evoked by the furnishings: a vintage set of golf clubs here, a sheet of music in a dry-flower arrangement there. The hotel, which attracts individual travelers as well as families and many Europeans, is well cared for by a concierge who speaks six languages. Enjoy high tea in the lobby 3 to 5:30pm daily. Request a room facing east, and you'll wake each day to a view of the mountains, seen through lovely lace. Larger rooms have coffeemakers and hair dryers.

210 Don Gaspar Ave., Santa Fe, NM 87501. ☏ **800/529-5700** or 505/983-5700. Fax 505/989-7690. www.hotelst francis.com. 82 units. $99–$349 all rooms, depending on the season. Children under 12 stay free in parent's room. AE, DC, DISC, MC, V. Parking $5 per day. **Amenities:** Restaurant; bar; exercise room, access to nearby spa; concierge; room service; laundry service; dry cleaning; library and gaming tables. *In room:* A/C, TV, wireless Internet, fridge, iron, safe.

Hotel Santa Fe 🌣 *Finds*

About a 10-minute walk south of the plaza you'll find this newer three-story establishment, the only Native American–owned hotel in Santa Fe. It is a good choice for consistent, well-planned lodgings. Picuris Pueblo is the majority stockholder here, and part of the pleasure of staying here is the culture the Picuris bring to your visit. This is not to say that you'll get any sense of the rusticity of a pueblo in your accommodations—this sophisticated 16-year-old hotel is decorated in Southwestern style, with a few novel aspects such as an Allan Houser bronze buffalo dancer watching over the front desk and a fireplace surrounded by comfortable furniture in the lobby. The rooms are medium size, with clean lines and comfortable beds, the decor accented with pine Taos-style furniture. Rooms on the north side get less street noise from Cerrillos Road and have better views of the mountains, but they don't have the sun shining onto their balconies. You will get a strong sense of the Native American presence on the patio during the summer, when Picuris dancers come to perform and bread bakers uncover the *horno* (oven) and prepare loaves for sale.

Opened in October 2001, The Hacienda at Hotel Santa Fe is a unique addition and features 35 luxurious rooms and suites, all with cozy fireplaces, 10-foot ceilings, handcrafted Southwestern furnishings, and plush duvets to snuggle into on chilly nights. The Amaya restaurant serves a standard breakfast, but for lunch and dinner you can dine on what they call "native" cuisine from all over the Americas. Expect elk and game hen instead of beef and chicken. Wireless Internet access is available in the lobby.

1501 Paseo de Peralta, Santa Fe, NM 87501. ⒸⒸ **800/825-9876** or 505/982-1200. Fax 505/984-2211. www.hotel santafe.com. 163 units. $99–$199 double; $129–$269 junior suite, depending on the season. Hacienda rooms and suites $199–$459. Additional person $20. Children 17 and under stay free in parent's room. AE, DC, DISC, MC, V. Free parking. Pets accepted with $20 fee. **Amenities:** Restaurant; outdoor pool; Jacuzzi; concierge; car-rental desk; room service; in-room massage; babysitting; dry cleaning. *In room:* A/C, TV, high-speed Internet, minibar, iron, safe.

Inn of the Governors ⒻⒻ   Rooms in this inn tucked 2 blocks from the plaza have the feel of a Southwestern home but come with the service and amenities of a fine hotel. The building (situated where the governor's mansion once was) is Territorial style, with a brick-trimmed roofline and distinctive portals. Built in 1965, it received a lovely remodel in 2004; the rooms received new bedding, including white down comforters, set against the bold reds and blacks of Native American weavings hanging on the walls. The medium-size rooms have Native American accents and delightful touches such as Mexican tile in the bathrooms, robes, and comfortable beds; many have fireplaces. Rooms on the north side look toward downtown and the mountains, and many have balconies. Unlike any other downtown hotel, this one serves a complimentary full breakfast buffet in the morning and sherry and cookies in the afternoon. The Del Charro Saloon serves food until midnight, a rarity in Santa Fe. Wireless Internet access is available in the lobby.

101 W. Alameda., Santa Fe, NM 87501. ⒸⒸ **800/234-4534** or 505/982-4333. Fax 505/989-9149. www.innofthe governors.com. 100 units. $99-$359 depending on season. Additional person $15. Rates include full breakfast buffet and sherry and cookies in the afternoon. Children 16 and under stay free in parent's room. AE, DC, DISC, MC, V. Free parking. **Amenities:** Restaurant; bar; outdoor pool (heated year-round); concierge; limited room service; laundry service. *In room:* A/C, TV, fridge, hair dryer, iron.

Inn on the Alameda ⒻⒻ   Just across the street from the bosque-shaded Santa Fe River sits the Inn on the Alameda, a cozy stop for those who like the services of a hotel with the intimacy of an inn. Built in 1986, with additions over the years, it now rambles across four buildings. There are casita suites to the west, two three-story buildings at the center, and another one-story building that contains suites. All are pueblo-style adobe, ranging in age, but most were built in the late 1980s. The owner, Joe Schepps, appreciates traditional Southwestern style; he's used red brick in the dining area and Mexican *equipae* (wicker) furniture in the lobby, as well as thick vigas and shiny *latillas* in a sitting area set around a grand fireplace. The rooms follow a similar good taste, some with refrigerators, CD players, safes, Jacuzzi tubs, and kiva fireplaces. The newer deluxe rooms and suites in the easternmost building are in the best shape. The traditional rooms are quaint, some with interesting angled bed configurations. The trees surrounding the inn—cottonwoods and aspens—make you feel as though you're in a tree house when you step out on some of the balconies. If you're an art shopper, this is an ideal spot because it's a quick walk to Canyon Road. A full-service bar is open nightly. Wireless Internet access is available in the lobby.

303 E. Alameda, Santa Fe, NM 87501. ☎ **800/289-2122** or 505/984-2121. Fax 505/986-8325. www.innonthe alameda.com. 71 units. $120–$220 queen; $135–$235 king; $255–$375 suites; reduced off-season rates are available. Rates include breakfast and afternoon wine and cheese reception. AE, DC, DISC, MC, V. Free parking. Small pets under 30 pounds welcome. **Amenities:** Bar; medium-size fitness facility; 2 open-air Jacuzzis; concierge; massage; child care by arrangement; coin-op laundry; same-day dry cleaning; pet amenities and a pet-walking map. *In room:* A/C, TV, hair dryer, iron.

Ten Thousand Waves ★ *(Moments)*   Longing for a little Zen in your life? This inn provides minimalist Japanese-adobe accommodations nestled within piñon trees below Ten Thousand Waves Japanese Health Spa (p. 133), a truly unique place renowned for its hot tubs and spa treatments. Inn guests receive complimentary use of communal baths. About a 10-minute drive from the plaza, the place is en route to Santa Fe Ski area. Travelers seeking to enjoy the silence of their own being seek out this place. They need to be fit because the paths connecting the rooms with the spa have enough steps to make you gasp during your mantra. Rooms are aesthetically bare, medium-size with clean lines and with paper lamps, kimonos, and such hanging about. All have wood-burning fireplaces, robes, CD players, and balconies; four have full kitchens; and most have TV/VCRs. Fresh fruit, rice milk, granola, coffee, and tea are provided in each room. The High Moon is the most elaborate room, with a full kitchen, two balconies, and lots of space. More spartan and small is the Zen room, decorated in minimalist decor, and with no TV. Wireless Internet access is available in the lobby, and wireless and high-speed Internet connections are in some of the rooms.

3451 Hyde Park Rd., Santa Fe, NM 87501. ☎ **505/982-9304** or 505/992-5025. Fax 505/989-5077. www.ten thousandwaves.com. 13 units. $99–$279 double. Additional person $20. Rates include use of communal baths. AE, DISC, MC, V. Free parking. One or more pets welcome, with advance notice, for $20 per night. **Amenities:** Spa with full treatments; coin-op laundry. *In room:* Fridge, coffeemaker, hair dryer, iron, CD player, microwave.

MODERATE

Garrett's Desert Inn *(Value)*   Completion of this hotel in 1957 prompted the Historic Design Review Board to implement zoning restrictions throughout downtown. Apparently, residents were appalled by the huge air conditioners adorning the roof. Though they're still unsightly, the hotel offers decent accommodations just 3 blocks from the plaza. It's a clean, two-story, concrete-block building around a broad parking lot. The hotel underwent a complete remodel in 1994, with touch-ups through the years, though new carpet and updated furnishings are now needed. It has managed to maintain some '50s touches, such as Art Deco tile in the bathrooms and plenty of space in the rooms. If you're traveling in winter, ask for a south-facing room and you might be able to sunbathe under the portal. Minisuites have refrigerators and microwaves. The outdoor pool here is one of the nicest in town. Wireless Internet access is available in the restaurant.

311 Old Santa Fe Trail, Santa Fe, NM 87501. ☎ **800/888-2145** or 505/982-1851. Fax 505/989-1647. www.garretts desertinn.com. 83 units. $89–$165, depending on season and type of room. AE, DISC, MC, V. **Amenities:** Restaurant; outdoor pool heated year-round. *In room:* A/C, TV, dataport, coffeemaker, hair dryer.

Old Santa Fe Inn ★ *(Finds)* Want to stay downtown and savor Santa Fe–style ambience without wearing out your plastic? This is your hotel. A multi-million-dollar renovation to this 1930s court motel has created a comfortable, quiet inn just a few blocks from the plaza. Rooms verge on small but are decorated with such lovely handcrafted colonial-style furniture that you probably won't mind. All have small Mexican-tiled bathrooms, each with an outer vanity; most have gas fireplaces. You have a choice of king, queen, or twin bedrooms as well as suites. Breakfast is served in an atmospheric dining room next to a comfortable library. This inn jacks prices *way* up during special event times such as the Indian Market.

320 Galisteo St., Santa Fe, NM 87501. © **800/745-9910** or 505/995-0800. Fax 505/995-0400. www.oldsantafeinn. com. 43 units. $80–$400 depending on season. Rates include continental breakfast. AE, DC, DISC, MC, V. *In room:* A/C, TV/VCR, high-speed Internet, fridge, coffeemaker, CD player.

Santa Fe Motel and Inn ★ If you like walking to the plaza and restaurants but don't want to pay big bucks, this little compound is a good choice. Rooms here are larger than at the Old Santa Fe Inn and have more personality than those at Garrett's Desert Inn. Ask for one of the casitas in back—you'll pay more but get a little turn-of-the-20th-century charm, plus more quiet and privacy. Some have vigas; others have skylights, fireplaces, and patios. The main part of the motel, built in 1955, is two-story Territorial style, with upstairs rooms that open onto a portal with a bit of a view. All guest rooms are decorated with a Southwest motif and some have antique furnishings. All have medium-size baths and comfortable beds. Some rooms have kitchenettes, with refrigerators, microwaves, stoves, coffeemakers, and toasters. A full breakfast, including Sage Bakehouse bread, is served each morning in the Southwest-style dining room or on a quaint patio.

510 Cerrillos Rd., Santa Fe, NM 87501. © **800/930-5002** or 505/982-1039. Fax 505/986-1275. www.santafemotel. com. 23 units. $69–$149, depending on the season and type of room. Additional person $10. Rates include full breakfast. AE, DC, MC, V. Free parking. *In room:* A/C, TV, high-speed Internet, hair dryer, iron.

Territorial Inn *(Value)* This inn, just 2 blocks from the plaza, offers sweetly appointed rooms at a good price. It was formerly located in a lovely Territorial-style building next door, but—who knows why—they moved into a 1960s building that fronts Marcy Street. The hallways are a bit dark and the rooms themselves don't offer much outdoor light, but they do offer plenty of space with some antique furnishings, all decorated in calming earth tones. All rooms are equipped with ceiling fans, and some are suites with two full bedrooms, great for travelers who like their own space. Guests enjoy an extended continental breakfast in a common area at the inn's center. The spa upstairs has a down-home style, with hardwood floors, a low ceiling, and a hot tub under a skylight. Wireless Internet access is available in the lobby.

215 Washington Ave., Santa Fe, NM 87501. © **866/230-7737** or 505/989-7737. Fax 505/986-9212. www.territorial inn.com. 15 units. $69–$159 double; $169–$329 suite. Additional person $20. Rates include extended continental breakfast. AE, DC, DISC, MC, V. Free parking. Children under 10 not accepted. **Amenities:** 2 Jacuzzis; massage; concierge; laundry service; dry cleaning. *In room:* A/C, TV, hair dryer.

INEXPENSIVE

Santa Fe Sage Inn *(Value) (Kids)* If you're looking for a convenient, almost-downtown location at a reasonable price, this is one of your best bets. This two-story stucco adobe motel with portals is spread through three buildings and is about a 10-minute walk from the plaza. Built in 1985, it was remodeled in 2005. The smallish rooms have Southwestern furnishings, with comfortable beds and small baths. It's near McDonald's, and there's

---

(Kids) Family-Friendly Hotels

Bishop's Lodge Ranch Resort & Spa (below)   Riding lessons, tennis courts with instruction, a pool with a lifeguard, a stocked trout pond just for kids, a summer daytime program, horseback trail trips, and more make this a veritable day camp for all ages.

El Rey Inn (p. 77)   A picnic area and playground in a courtyard set back away from the street make this a nice place for families to commune in summer.

Fort Marcy Hotel Suites (p. 76)   An indoor pool and condo amenities, such as kitchens and patios, make these a good option for families that don't like to eat out every meal.

The Lodge at Santa Fe (p. 76)   Built above the city, with a bit of a country-club feel, this place offers a nice outdoor pool and condo units that serve family needs well.

Residence Inn (p. 77)   Spacious suites house families comfortably. An outdoor pool, fully equipped kitchens, patio grills, and a grocery-shopping service add to the appeal.

Santa Fe Sage Inn (p. 74)   With its fenced-in pool and reasonable prices, this is a good spot for families.

---

a park in the back and an outdoor pool set in a secluded fenced area, a good place for kids. To avoid street noise, ask for a room at the back of the property.

725 Cerrillos Rd., Santa Fe, NM 87501. © **866/433-0335** or 505/982-5952. Fax 505/984-8879. www.santa fesageinn.com. 160 units. $58–$72 double; includes continental breakfast. Additional person $10. AE, DC, DISC, MC, V. Free parking. **Amenities:** Outdoor pool. *In room:* A/C, TV, dataport, wireless Internet, coffeemaker, hairdryer, iron.

Santa Fe Plaza Travelodge   You can count on this motel near Hotel Santa Fe (6 blocks to the plaza) on busy Cerrillos Road for comfort and convenience. The rooms, completely remodeled in 2003, have furnishings with clean lines, some with a rustic, pine, Santa Fe style. All rooms are clean, nicely lit, and, despite the busy location, relatively quiet. They offer a little more space than those at Santa Fe Sage, but Sage offers some rooms farther back from the road; choose according to your needs.

646 Cerrillos Rd., Santa Fe, NM 87501. © **800/578-7878** or 505/982-3551. Fax 505/983-8624. www. travelodge.com. 48 units. May–Oct $67–$89 double; Nov–Apr $40–$70 double. AE, DC, DISC, MC, V. Free parking. **Amenities:** Outdoor pool. *In room:* A/C, TV, wireless Internet, fridge, coffeemaker.

2 The North Side

Within easy reach of the plaza, the north side encompasses the area that lies north of the loop of Paseo de Peralta.

VERY EXPENSIVE

Bishop's Lodge Ranch Resort & Spa ✦✦ (Kids)   This resort holds special significance for me because my parents met in the lodge and were later married in the chapel. It's a place rich with history. More than a century ago, when Bishop Jean-Baptiste Lamy was the spiritual leader of northern New Mexico's Roman Catholic population, he often escaped clerical politics by hiking into this valley called Little Tesuque. He built a retreat and a humble chapel (now on the National Register of Historic Places) with high-vaulted ceilings and a hand-built altar. Today, Lamy's 1,000-acre getaway has become Bishop's Lodge.

In recent years, a $17-million renovation spruced up the place and added a spa and 10,000 square feet of meeting space. The guest rooms, spread through many buildings, feature handcrafted furniture and regional artwork. Standard rooms are spacious, and many have balconies, while deluxe rooms feature traditional kiva fireplaces, a combination bedroom/sitting room, and private decks or patios. The newest rooms are luxurious, and some have spectacular views of the Jemez Mountains. The Bishop's Lodge is an active resort three seasons of the year, with activities such as horseback riding, nature walks, and cookouts; in the winter, it takes on the character of a romantic country retreat. A children's program keeps kids busy for much of the day.

Bishop's Lodge Rd. (P.O. Box 2367), Santa Fe, NM 87504. © **505/983-6377.** Fax 505/989-8939. www. bishopslodge.com. 111 units. Summer $399–$459 double; fall and spring $299–$399 double; midwinter $189–$269 double. Resort fee $15 per person per day. Additional person $15. Children 3 and under stay free in parent's room. Ask about packages that include meals. AE, DC, DISC, MC, V. Free parking. **Amenities:** Restaurant; outdoor pool; tennis courts; spa; Jacuzzi; concierge; courtesy shuttle; room service; in-room massage; babysitting; laundry service. *In room:* A/C, TV, high-speed Ethernet, coffeemaker.

EXPENSIVE

Fort Marcy Hotel Suites *(Kids)*   About an 8-minute walk from the plaza, these condominiums climb up a hill north of town and are a decent choice for those who like the amenities a condo offers. They are privately owned, so decor and upkeep vary. All have fireplaces and full kitchens, with microwave ovens, ranges, and refrigerators, and most have dishwashers. The units have plenty of space, and the grounds are well kept, with some nature trails winding about. Some of the units, however, are showing their age (built in 1975). Wireless Internet access is available in the lobby.

320 Artist Rd., Santa Fe, NM 87501. © **800/561-0898** or 505/982-6636. Fax 505/992-1804. www.santafehotels. com. 100 units. $59–$239 1-bedroom (up to 3 adults); $79–$299 2-bedroom (up to 5 adults); $109–$339 2-bedroom town house (up to 5 adults); $139–$399 3-bedroom town house (up to 7 adults). Special events $319–$599. Children 18 and under stay free in parent's room. Rates include continental breakfast. AE, DC, DISC, MC, V. Free on- and off-street parking. **Amenities:** Indoor pool; business center; coin-op laundry. *In room:* A/C, TV/DVD, dataport, kitchen, hair dryer, iron.

The Lodge at Santa Fe *(✶ Kids)*   Once the Radisson Hotel, this property has received a new name and complete multi-million-dollar face-lift. Set on a hill as you head north toward the Santa Fe Opera, this three-story hotel is a convenient and relaxing place to stay. The new theme here is Native American, with Anasazi-style stacked sandstone throughout the lobby and dining room, a theme that carries into the guest rooms. They are medium size, decorated in earth tones with bold prints, some with views of the mountains, others overlooking the pool. Premium rooms are more spacious, some with large living rooms and private balconies. Each parlor suite has a Murphy bed and kiva fireplace in the living room, a big dining area, a wet bar and refrigerator, and a jetted bathtub. The condo units nearby come with fully equipped kitchens, fireplaces, and private decks.

750 N. St. Francis Dr., Santa Fe, NM 87501. © **800/333-3333** or 505/992-5800. Fax 505/992-5856. www.the lodgeatsantafe.com. 135 units. $89–$179 double; $129–$199 suite; $200–$300 condo. AE, DC, DISC, MC, V. Free parking. **Amenities:** Outdoor pool; free shuttle service to downtown. *In room:* A/C, TV, high-speed and wireless Internet, hair dryer, iron.

3 The South Side

Santa Fe's major strip, Cerrillos Road, is US 85, the main route to and from Albuquerque and the I-25 freeway. It's about 5¼ miles from the plaza to the Santa Fe Place, which marks the southern boundary of the city. Most motels are on this strip, although several of them are to the east, closer to St. Francis Drive (US 84) or the Las Vegas Highway.

EXPENSIVE

Residence Inn by Marriott   *Kids*   Designed to look like a neighborhood, this inn provides the efficient stay you'd expect from a Marriott, and a renovation in 2006 brought freshness to the rooms and some common areas. It's a 10-minute drive away from the plaza, through a few quiet neighborhoods. The lobby and breakfast area are warmly decorated in tile, with a fireplace and Southwestern accents such as *bancos* and drums. There are three sizes of suites, each roomy, each with a fully equipped kitchen. All rooms have fireplaces and balconies and are decorated with Southwestern furnishings. Outside, there are plenty of amenities to keep family members happy, including barbecue grills on the patio. Most who stay here are leisure travelers, but you'll also encounter some government workers and business travelers, all of whom benefit from free high-speed Internet access. Guests gather for complimentary hors d'oeuvres Monday through Thursday from 5 to 6:30pm.

1698 Galisteo St., Santa Fe, NM 87505. ✆ **800/331-3131** or 505/988-7300. Fax 505/988-3243. www.residenceinn. com. 120 suites. $109–$199 studio suite; $119–$199 studio double suite; $129–$239 penthouse suite. Rates vary according to season and include continental breakfast and Mon–Thurs evening hors d'oeuvres. AE, DC, DISC, MC, V. Free parking. **Amenities:** Outdoor pool; sports court; exercise room; 3 Jacuzzis; coin-op laundry; laundry service; dry cleaning; jogging trail. *In room:* A/C, TV, high-speed Internet, kitchen.

MODERATE

El Rey Inn   *Finds*   *Kids*   Staying at "The King" makes you feel like you're traveling the old Route 66 through the Southwest. The white stucco buildings of this court motel are decorated with bright trim around the doors and hand-painted Mexican tiles on the walls. Opened in the 1930s, it received additions in the 1950s, and remodeling is ongoing. The lobby has vigas and tile floors, and it is decorated with Oriental rugs and dark Spanish furniture. No two rooms are alike. The oldest section, nearest the lobby, feels a bit cramped, though the rooms have style, with Art Deco tile in the bathrooms and vigas on the ceilings. Some have little patios. Be sure to request a room as far back as possible from Cerrillos Road. The two stories of suites around the Spanish colonial courtyard are the sweetest deal I've seen in all of Santa Fe. These rooms make you feel like you're at a Spanish inn, with carved furniture and cozy couches. Some rooms have kitchenettes. To the north sit 10 deluxe units around the courtyard. These rooms offer more upscale amenities and gas log fireplaces, as well as distinctive furnishings and artwork. A complimentary continental breakfast is served in a sunny room or on a terrace in the warmer months. There's also a sitting room with a library and games tables, as well as a picnic area, a playground, and an exercise room. Wireless Internet access is available in the lobby.

1862 Cerrillos Rd. (P.O. Box 4759), Santa Fe, NM 87502. ✆ **800/521-1349** or 505/982-1931. Fax 505/989-9249. www.elreyinnsantafe.com. 85 units. $95–$165 double; $120–$225 suite. Rates include continental breakfast. AE, DC, DISC, MC, V. Free parking. **Amenities:** Outdoor pool; exercise room; 2 Jacuzzis; sauna; coin-op laundry. *In room:* A/C, TV, dataport, fridge, coffeemaker, hair dryer, iron, safe.

Accommodations & Dining on Cerrillos Road

ACCOMMODATIONS ■

El Rey Inn **7**
La Quinta Inn **1**
Los Campos RV Resort **4**
Residence Inn by Marriott **8**
Santa Fe Courtyard
by Marriott **5**
Super 8 Motel **3**

DINING ◆

Blue Corn Café
and Brewery **2**
Marisco's La Playa **6**

INEXPENSIVE

La Quinta Inn *Value*   Though it's a good 15-minute drive from the plaza, this is my top choice of economical Cerrillos Road chain hotels. Built in 1986, it has been fully remodeled in a very comfortable and tasteful way. The rooms within the three-story white-brick buildings have an unexpectedly elegant feel, with lots of deep colors and Art Deco tile in the bathrooms. There's plenty of space in these rooms, and they're lit for mood as well as for reading. A complimentary continental breakfast is served in the intimate lobby. The outdoor kidney-shaped pool has a nice lounging area and is open and heated May to October. The hotel is just across a parking lot from the Santa Fe Place mall, which shoppers and moviegoers will appreciate. The Flying Tortilla coffee shop is adjacent.

4298 Cerrillos Rd., Santa Fe, NM 87507. *(C)* **800/531-5900** or 505/471-1142. Fax 505/438-7219. www.lq.com. 130 units. June to mid-Oct $89–$110 double; late Oct to May $60–$66 double. Children 18 and under stay free in parent's room. Discount for AAA members. Rates include continental breakfast. AE, DC, DISC, MC, V. Free parking. Maximum 2 pets stay free. **Amenities:** Outdoor heated pool; coin-op laundry; executive-level rooms. *In room:* A/C, TV, wireless Internet, coffeemaker, hair dryer, iron.

Santa Fe Courtyard by Marriott   This is a good choice if you don't mind mixing business with pleasure. Since it caters to a lot of conference traffic, there's a definite business feel to this hotel. Built in 1986, it received a $3.5-million renovation after being acquired by Marriott. The decor is tasteful Southwestern, with rooms opening onto cavelike balconies or walkways bordered by grass. Though it's situated on busy Cerrillos Road, the rooms are placed so that they are quiet. The newly remodeled cafe serves breakfast and dinner. Wireless Internet access is available in the lobby.

3347 Cerrillos Rd., Santa Fe, NM 87505. *(C)* **800/777-3347** or 505/473-2800. Fax 505/473-4905. www.santafe courtyard.com. 213 units. $59–$89 double; $90–$249 suite. AE, DC, DISC, MC, V. Free parking. **Amenities:** Restaurant; indoor pool; exercise room; 2 Jacuzzis; room service; laundry service; dry cleaning; executive-level rooms; ballroom. *In room:* A/C, TV, dataport, fridge, coffeemaker, hair dryer, iron.

Super 8 Motel *Value*   It's nothing flashy, but this pink-stucco, boxy motel, which has received the Pride of Super 8 award, attracts regulars who know precisely what to expect. You'll get a clean room with a comfortable bed or beds and a few other amenities at a great price.

3358 Cerrillos Rd., Santa Fe, NM 87507. *(C)* **800/800-8000** or 505/471-8811. Fax 505/471-3239. www.super8.com. 96 units. $45–$80 double, depending on the season. Rates include continental breakfast. AE, DC, DISC, MC, V. Free parking. **Amenities:** Coin-op laundry. *In room:* A/C, TV, wireless Internet, coffeemaker, safe.

4 Bed & Breakfasts

If you prefer a homey, intimate setting to the sometimes-impersonal ambience of a large hotel, one of Santa Fe's bed-and-breakfast inns may be right for you. All those listed here are in or close to the downtown area and offer comfortable accommodations at expensive to moderate prices.

Adobe Abode   A short walk from the plaza, in the same quiet residential neighborhood as the Georgia O'Keeffe Museum, Adobe Abode is one of Santa Fe's most imaginative B&Bs. The living room is cozy, decorated with folk art. The creativity shines in each of the guest rooms as well, some in the main house, which was built in 1907. Others, in back, are newer. The Galisteo Suite is decorated with Spanish colonial furniture and artwork, while the Bronco Room is filled with cowboy paraphernalia: hats, Pendleton blankets, pioneer chests, and an entire shelf lined with children's cowboy boots. Two rooms have fireplaces, and several have private patios. Complimentary sherry, fruit, and cookies are served daily in the living room. Every morning, a full breakfast of fresh fruit and a hot dish such as green-chile corn soufflé is served in the country-style kitchen.

202 Chapelle St., Santa Fe, NM 87501. ℭ **505/983-3133**. Fax 505/983-3132. www.adobeabode.com. 6 units. $139–$179 double. Rates include breakfast and afternoon snacks. DISC, MC, V. Limited free parking. *In room:* A/C, TV, wireless Internet, coffeemaker, hair dryer, iron.

AdobeStar Inn 🏵 This inn, formerly the Spencer House B&B, is near the O'Keeffe Museum, and offers a cozy, homelike feel with a bit of Southwest elegance. New ownership has brought refinement to the small- to medium-size rooms here, each with a different Southwestern theme. The O'Keeffe room has bold primary colors along with O'Keeffe prints on the walls, while the Chimayo room—my favorite—is set in a quiet spot in back of the house and has wood floors, a kiva fireplace and warm earth tones. Also in back, an 800-square-foot casita has been split into two separate rooms, each with a full bath and whirlpool tub, one with a full kitchen, fireplace, and private patio. It's a great space but could use an update. All bathrooms are modern and very clean. In summer, a full breakfast—delights such as a chile relleno casserole or blueberry bread pudding—is served on the outdoor patio. In winter, guests dine in an atrium. Some rooms have coffeemakers, TVs, and telephones. All have wireless Internet access.

222 McKenzie St., Santa Fe, NM 87501. ℭ **800/647-0530** or 505/988-3024. Fax 505/983-3132. www.adobestarinn. com. 6 units. $135–$185 double. Rates include full breakfast. MC, V. **Amenities:** Concierge; laundry service. *In room:* A/C, wireless Internet, hair dryer, iron.

El Farolito 🏵🏵 The owners of this inn, which is within walking distance of the plaza, have created an authentic theme experience for guests in each room. The themes include the Native American Room, decorated with rugs and pottery; the South-of-the-Border Room, with Mexican folk art with a full-size sleeper sofa; and the elegant Santa Fe–style Opera Room, with hand-carved, lavishly upholstered furniture. A two-room suite has been added in the main building, with a queen-size iron bed and Southwestern decor. The walls of most of the rooms are rubbed with beeswax during plastering to give them a smooth, golden finish. All rooms have kiva fireplaces and private patios. The common area displays works by notable New Mexico artists. Part of the inn was built before 1912, and the rest is new, but the old-world elegance carries through. For breakfast, the focus is on healthy food with a little decadence thrown in. You'll enjoy fresh fruit and home-baked breads and pastries. Under the same stellar ownership (but a little less expensive) is the nearby **Four Kachinas Inn** 🏵 (ℭ **888/ 634-8782;** www.fourkachinas.com), where Southwestern-style rooms sit around a sunny courtyard. A little less lavish than those at El Farolito, these rooms are sparkly clean, all with patios.

514 Galisteo St., Santa Fe, NM 87501. ℭ **888/634-8782** or 505/988-1631. Fax 505/988-4589. www.farolito.com. 8 units. $150–$280 casita. Rates include expanded continental breakfast. AE, DISC, MC, V. Free parking. **Amenities:** Babysitting by appointment; valet laundry. *In room:* A/C, TV, coffeemaker, hair dryer, iron.

El Paradero 🏵 About a 10-minute walk from the plaza, El Paradero ("the stopping place") provides reliable, unpretentious accommodations and good service. It began in 1810 as a Spanish adobe farmhouse, and it doubled in size in 1878 when Territorial-style details were added. In 1912, Victorian touches were incorporated in the styling of its doors and windows. Innkeepers Ouida MacGregor and Thom Allen opened it as one of Santa Fe's first bed-and-breakfasts over 20 years ago. They're great resources; they can direct visitors to unexpected sights and activities. Nine ground-level rooms surround a central courtyard and offer a clean, white decor, hardwood or brick floors, folk art, and hand-woven textiles on the walls. Three more luxurious upstairs rooms feature tile floors and bathrooms as well as private balconies. Five rooms have fireplaces. Two suites occupying a brick 1912 coachman's house, a railroad-era Victorian building, are elegantly decorated with period antiques and provide living rooms with fireplaces, kitchen nooks, TVs, and phones. The ground floor of the main building has a parlor, a living room with a piano and fireplace, and a Mexican-style breakfast room where a full gourmet breakfast and afternoon tea are served daily.

220 W. Manhattan Ave., Santa Fe, NM 87501. ℂ 505/988-1177. Fax 505/988-3577. www.elparadero.com. 14 units. May–Oct $95–$170 double; Nov–Dec and Mar–Apr $95–$155 double; Jan–Feb $80–$135 double. Rates include full breakfast and afternoon tea. AE, MC, V. Free parking. Pets accepted, $15 per night. **Amenities:** Concierge. *In room:* A/C.

Hacienda Nicholas 𝕰𝕰   This inn, a few blocks from the plaza, has a delightful Southwest hacienda feel. Rooms surround a sunny patio; my favorites are the bright Cottonwood, with a serene feel created by the sunshine-colored walls, wood floors, and a kiva fireplace. Even more luxurious, the Sunflower has French doors, plenty of space, and also a fireplace. The rooms off the sitting room in the house are more modest but also have a warm "Southwest meets Provence" feel. All beds are comfortable and baths range from small with showers only to larger with tub/showers. A full breakfast—including such delicacies as homemade granola and red-and-green breakfast burritos—and afternoon wine and cheese are served in the lovely Great Room or on the patio, both with fireplaces. Service in this inn is excellent. Under the same ownership, **Alexander's Inn** (ℂ **888/321-5123** or 505/986-1431; www.alexanders-inn. com), has long been one of the city's finest B&Bs. In recent years, the inn itself has closed, but the same managers rent four casitas in the older district of Santa Fe. Each is a fully equipped home, with a kitchen, including fridge, range, and microwave. All have unique Southwestern furnishings and plenty of charm.

320 E. Marcy St., Santa Fe, NM 87501.. **888/284-3170** or 505/992-8385; www.haciendanicholas.com. Fax 505/982-8572. 7 units. $110–$210 double. Additional person $25. Rates include breakfast and afternoon wine and cheese. AE, DISC, MC, V. Free parking. Pets accepted with $20 deposit. **Amenities:** Concierge; activities desk. *In room:* A/C, TV, dataport, hair dryer.

The Madeleine 𝕰𝕰   Lace, flowery upholstery, and stained glass surround you at this 1886 Queen Anne–style inn just 5 blocks east of the plaza. All rooms have terry robes and some offer fireplaces. One of my favorites is the Morning Glory, with a king-size bed, a corner fireplace, and lots of sun. All rooms have comfortable beds and those in the main house have small baths. An adjacent cottage built in 1987 received an award for compatible architecture from the Santa Fe Historical Association. The two rooms in the cottage are larger than the other rooms, with king-size beds and bay windows, some of the nicest rooms in the city. In winter, a full breakfast is served family style at the adjacent Hacienda Nicholas, which is under the same excellent management. In the Victorian-cum-Asian lobby and out on a flagstone patio surrounded by flowers and fruit trees, visitors enjoy chai from the **Absolute Nirvana Spa, Tea Room & Gardens** (ℂ **505/983-7942;** www.absolutenirvana.com). This creation, voted one of the three best spas in town by the *Santa Fe Reporter,* offers luscious chai and imaginative Indo-Asian spa treatments and facials. For more details about Nirvana, see p. 133.

106 Faithway St., Santa Fe, NM 87501. ℂ **888/877-7622** or 505/982-3465. Fax 505/982-8572. www.madeleineinn. com. 7 units. $110–$210 double. Additional person $25. Rates include full breakfast and afternoon wine and cheese. AE, DISC, MC, V. Free parking. **Amenities:** Spa with steam showers and soaking tubs; concierge. *In room:* A/C, TV/VCR, wireless Internet, hair dryer.

Pueblo Bonito   Private courtyards and narrow flagstone paths give a look of elegance to this 19th-century adobe hacienda and stables, a few blocks south of the Santa Fe River. This is a good choice if you like more of an inn feel rather than a home feel in a B&B. Each guest room is named for a Pueblo tribe of the surrounding countryside. Every room—decorated with Native American rugs on wood or brick floors— has a queen-size bed and a fireplace. Bathrooms are small but attractively tiled. Six rooms are suites, each with a fully stocked kitchen, a living/dining room with fireside seating, and a bedroom. The remainder are standard units with locally made headboards and couches, dining alcoves, and old Spanish-style lace curtains. Afternoon margaritas and wine are served daily.

138 W. Manhattan Ave., Santa Fe, NM 87501. ℂ **800/461-4599** or 505/984-8001. Fax 505/984-3155. www. pueblobonitoinn.com. 18 units. $90–$165 double. Rates include continental breakfast and afternoon refreshments. AE, DISC, MC, V. Free parking. **Amenities:** Concierge; laundry. *In room:* A/C, TV, high-speed Internet.

Water Street Inn ★★   An award-winning adobe restoration 4 blocks from the plaza, this friendly inn features beautiful Mexican-tile bathrooms, several kiva fireplaces and wood stoves, and antique furnishings. Each room is decked out with Southwestern art and books. All rooms are decorated in a Moroccan/Southwestern style. Room no. 3 provides a queen-size hideaway sofa to accommodate families. Room no. 4 features special regional touches in its decor and boasts a chaise longue, a fur rug, built-in seating, and a corner fireplace. Four new suites have elegant contemporary Southwestern furnishings and outdoor private patios with fountains. Most rooms have balconies or terraces. In the afternoon, a happy hour, with quesadillas and margaritas, is offered in the living room or on the upstairs portal, where an extended continental breakfast is also served.

427 W. Water St., Santa Fe, NM 87501. ℂ **800/646-6752** or 505/984-1193. Fax 505/984-6235. www.water streetinn.com. 12 units. $100–$250 double. Rates include continental breakfast and afternoon hors d'oeuvres and refreshments. AE, DISC, MC, V. Free parking. Children and pets welcome with prior approval. **Amenities:** Jacuzzi; concierge; room service. *In room:* A/C, TV/VCR, wireless Internet, hair dryer.

5 RV Parks & Campgrounds

RV PARKS

At least four private camping areas, mainly for recreational vehicles, are located within a few minutes' drive of downtown Santa Fe. Typical rates are $28 for full RV hookups, $18 for tents. Be sure to book ahead at busy times.

Los Campos RV Resort   The resort has 95 spaces with full hookups, picnic tables, and a covered pavilion for use with reservation at no charge. It's just 5 miles south of the plaza, so it's plenty convenient, but keep in mind that it is surrounded by the city. The campground honors a variety of discounts. Wireless Internet access is available in half the park.

3574 Cerrillos Rd., Santa Fe, NM 87507. ℂ **800/852-8160**. Fax 505/471-9220. http://hometown.aol.com/loscampossf. $28–$33 daily; $172–$212 weekly; $450 monthly/winter; $500 monthly/summer. MC, V. Pets welcome. **Amenities:** Outdoor pool; concierge; coin-op laundry; restrooms; showers; grills; vending machines; free cable TV.

Rancheros de Santa Fe Campground ⚑ Tents, motor homes, and trailers requiring full hookups are welcome here. The park's 127 sites are situated on 22 acres of piñon and juniper forest. Cabins are also available. It's about 6 miles southeast of Santa Fe and is open March 15 to October 31. Free wireless Internet access too. Wireless Internet access is available throughout the park and high-speed Internet access is available in the lobby.

736 Old Las Vegas Hwy. (exit 290 off I-25), Santa Fe, NM 87505. ℭ **800/426-9259** or 505/466-3482. www. rancheros.com. Tent site $18–$20; RV hookup $24–$36. AE, DISC, MC, V. **Amenities:** Outdoor pool; coin-op laundry; restrooms; showers; grills; cable TV hookups; grocery store; recreation room; tables; fireplaces; nature trails; playground; free nightly movies May–Sept; public telephones; propane.

Santa Fe KOA This campground, about 11 miles northeast of Santa Fe, sits among the foothills of the Sangre de Cristo Mountains, an excellent place to enjoy Northern New Mexico's pine-filled high desert. It offers full hookups, pull-through sites, and tent sites. Wireless Internet access is available throughout the park.

934 Old Las Vegas Hwy. (exit 290 or 294 off I-25), Santa Fe, NM 87505. ℭ **800/KOA-1514** or 505/466-1419 for reservations. www.koa.com. Tent site $22–$25; RV hookup $26–$31. MC, V. **Amenities:** Coin-op laundry; restrooms; showers; store/gift shop; recreation room; playground; picnic tables; propane; dumping station.

CAMPGROUNDS

There are three forested sites along NM 475 on the way to Ski Santa Fe. All are open from May to October. Overnight rates start at about $12.

Hyde Memorial State Park About 8 miles from the city, this pine-surrounded park offers a quiet retreat. Seven RV pads with electrical pedestals and an RV dumping station are available. There are nature and hiking trails and a playground as well as a small winter skating pond.

740 Hyde Park Rd., Santa Fe, NM 87501. ℭ **505/983-7175**. www.nmparks.com. **Amenities:** Shelters; water; tables; vault toilets.

Santa Fe National Forest ⚑⚑ You'll reach Black Canyon campground, with 44 sites, before you arrive at Hyde State Park. It's one of the only campgrounds in the state for which you can make a reservation (ℭ **877/444-6777**; www.reserveusa.com). The sites sit within thick forest, with hiking trails nearby. Big Tesuque, a first-come, first-served campground with 10 newly rehabilitated sites, is about 12 miles from town. The sites here are closer to the road and sit at the edge of aspen forests. Both Black Canyon and Big Tesuque campgrounds, along the Santa Fe Scenic Byway, NM 475, are equipped with vault toilets.

P.O. Box 1689, Santa Fe, NM 87504. ℭ **505/438-7840** or 505/753-7331. www.fs.fed.us/r3/sfe. **Amenities:** Water; vault toilets.

6

Where to Dine in Santa Fe

Santa Fe abounds in dining options, with hundreds of restaurants in all categories. Competition among them is steep, and spots are continually opening and closing. Locals watch closely to see which ones will survive. Some chefs create dishes that incorporate traditional Southwestern foods with ingredients not indigenous to the region; their restaurants are referred to in the listings as "creative Southwestern." There is also standard regional New Mexican cuisine, and beyond that, diners can opt for excellent steak and seafood, as well as Continental, European, Asian, and, of course, Mexican menus. On the south end of town, Santa Fe has the requisite chain establishments such as **Outback Steakhouse,** 2574 Camino Entrada (© **505/424-6800**), **Olive Garden,** 3781 Cerrillos Rd. (© **505/438-7109**), and **Red Lobster,** 4450 Rodeo Rd. (© **505/473-1610**).

Especially during peak tourist seasons, dinner reservations may be essential. Reservations are always recommended at better restaurants.

1 Restaurants by Cuisine

AMERICAN
Cafe Dominic ✿ (Downtown, $, p. 99)
Cowgirl Hall of Fame ✿ (Downtown, $$, p. 95)
Plaza Cafe ✿ (Downtown, $, p. 100)
Second Street Brewery (South Side, $, p. 104)
Tesuque Village Market (North Side, $$, p. 102)
Zia Diner ✿ (Downtown, $, p. 101)

ASIAN
Chow's ✿ (South Side, $$, p. 103)
mu du noodles ✿✿ (South Side, $$, p. 103)
Shohko Cafe ✿✿ (Downtown, $$, p. 97)

BARBECUE/CAJUN
Cowgirl Hall of Fame ✿ (Downtown, $$, p. 95)

BISTRO
315 ✿✿ (Downtown, $$$, p. 93)

CONTINENTAL
Aquasanta ✿✿ (Downtown, $$, p. 86)
Fuego ✿✿✿ (Downtown, $$$, p. 89)
Geronimo ✿✿✿ (Downtown, $$$, p. 90)
Old House ✿✿✿ (Downtown, $$$, p. 91)
The Pink Adobe ✿ (Downtown, $$$, p. 92)
Señor Lucky's at the Palace ✿✿ (Downtown, $$$, p. 93)

CREATIVE SOUTHWESTERN
Anasazi Restaurant ✿✿✿ (Downtown, $$$, p. 86)
Atomic Grill (Downtown, $, p. 98)

Key to Abbreviations: $$$$ = Very Expensive $$$ = Expensive $$ = Moderate $ = Inexpensive

Cafe Pasqual's ✺✺ (Downtown, $$$, p. 88)

Coyote Café ✺✺ (Downtown, $$$, p. 88)

La Casa Sena ✺✺ (Downtown, $$$, p. 90)

Santacafé ✺✺✺ (Downtown, $$$, p. 93)

DELI/CAFE

Cafe Dominic ✺ (Downtown, $, p. 99)

Plaza Cafe ✺ (Downtown, $, p. 100)

Sage Bakehouse ✺ (Downtown, $, p. 100)

FRENCH

Ristra ✺✺ (Downtown, $$$, p. 92)

315 ✺✺ (Downtown, $$$, p. 93)

GREEK

Plaza Cafe ✺ (Downtown, $, p. 100)

INDIAN

India Palace ✺ (Downtown, $$, p. 96)

ITALIAN

Andiamo! ✺ (Downtown, $$, p. 94)

Il Piatto Cucina Italiano ✺✺ (Downtown, $$, p. 96)

Osteria d'Assisi ✺ (Downtown, $$, p. 96)

Pranzo Italian Grill ✺✺ (Downtown, $$, p. 97)

Trattoria Nostrani ✺✺ (Downtown, $$$, p. 94)

Upper Crust Pizza ✺ (Downtown, $, p. 101)

LATIN

Coyote Café ✺✺ (Downtown, $$$, p. 88)

MEXICAN

Bumble Bee's Baja Grill ✺ (Downtown, $, p. 98)

Felipe's Tacos (South Side, $, p. 103)

Los Mayas ✺ (Downtown, $$, p. 96)

Marisco's La Playa (South Side, $, p. 104)

MICROBREWERY

Blue Corn Café (Downtown, $, p. 98)

Second Street Brewery (South Side, $, p. 104)

NATIVE AMERICAN

Anasazi Restaurant ✺✺✺ (Downtown, $$$, p. 86)

Cafe San Estevan ✺ (Downtown, $$, p. 94)

NEW AMERICAN

Celebrations Restaurant ✺ (Downtown, $$, p. 95)

The Compound ✺✺✺ (Downtown, $$$, p. 88)

O'Keeffe Café ✺ (Downtown, $$$, p. 91)

Old House ✺✺✺ (Downtown, $$$, p. 91)

Santacafé ✺✺✺ (Downtown, $$$, p. 93)

Railyard Restaurant & Saloon ✺✺ (Downtown, $$, p. 97)

NEW MEXICAN

Blue Corn Café (Downtown, $, p. 98)

Cafe San Estevan ✺ (Downtown, $$, p. 94)

Guadalupe Cafe ✺✺ (Downtown, $, p. 99)

La Choza ✺✺ (Downtown, $, p. 99)

Ore House on the Plaza ✺ (Downtown, $$$, p. 91)

Plaza Cafe ✺ (Downtown, $, p. 100)

The Shed ✺✺ (Downtown, $, p. 100)

Tía Sophia's ✺ (Downtown, $, p. 101)

Tomasita's Cafe ✺ (Downtown, $, p. 101)

PIZZA

Upper Crust Pizza ✺ (Downtown, $, p. 101)

SOUTHWESTERN

The Pink Adobe ✶ (Downtown, $$$, p. 92)

Tesuque Village Market (North Side, $$, p. 102)

SPANISH

El Farol ✶ (Downtown, $$$, p. 89)

El Meson ✶✶ (Downtown, $$$, p. 89)

STEAK/SEAFOOD

El Nido ✶ (North Side, $$$, p. 102)

Marisco's La Playa (South Side, $, p. 104)

Ore House on the Plaza ✶ (Downtown, $$$, p. 91)

Railyard Restaurant & Saloon ✶✶ (Downtown, $$, p. 97)

Rio Chama Steakhouse ✶✶ (Downtown, $$$, p. 92)

Steaksmith at El Gancho ✶ (South Side, $$, p. 103)

Vanessie of Santa Fe ✶ (Downtown, $$$, p. 94)

2 Downtown

This area includes the circle defined by the Paseo de Peralta and St. Francis Drive, as well as Canyon Road.

EXPENSIVE

Anasazi Restaurant ✶✶✶ CREATIVE SOUTHWESTERN/NATIVE AMERICAN   This ranks as one of Santa Fe's more interesting dining experiences. It's part of the Inn of the Anasazi (p. 68), but it's a fine restaurant in its own right. You'll dine surrounded by diamond-finished walls and stacked flagstone, which create an Anasazi feel to this restaurant, named for the ancient people who once inhabited the area. There's no pretension here; the waitstaff is friendly but not overbearing, and tables are spaced nicely, making it a good place for a romantic dinner. All the food is inventive, especially now that Chef Martin Rios has come over from the Old House. He made his mark there and now brings his bold and elegant palate to mostly organic meats and vegetables here. For breakfast, try the breakfast burrito with homemade chorizo, green-chile potatoes, and refried Anasazi beans. For lunch, I've enjoyed the crispy ahi tuna tacos with mango salsa. Lunch portions are moderate size, so if you're hungry, order an appetizer as well. For dinner, try cinnamon-chili-rubbed beef tenderloin with potato bone-marrow purée, oyster mushrooms, and asparagus. A favorite dessert is the almond milk panna cotta parfait. There are daily specials, as well as a nice list of wines by the glass and special wines of the day.

At the Inn of the Anasazi, 113 Washington Ave. © **505/988-3236.** Reservations recommended. Main courses $7.50–$12 breakfast, $9.50–$15 lunch, $25–$36 dinner. AE, DISC, MC, V. Daily 7–10:30am, 11:30am–2:30pm, and 5:30–10pm.

Aquasanta ✶✶ *Finds* NEW AMERICAN   This is one of my favorite newer Santa Fe restaurants. Tucked into a little nook along the Santa Fe River, it could easily go unnoticed, but it already has a strong following of locals who enjoy the serene environment and delectable offerings. The food itself is the star here. The atmosphere is like a quaint country hacienda with a touch of elegance created by hardwood floors, a kiva fireplace, cream-colored walls, and fine art. Service is excellent, though cooking times run a little long. The chef employs organic meats and vegetables when possible. At lunch, I've enjoyed the lamb burger on a homemade roll, served with fingerling

Santa Fe

Downtown

Church ✝
Post Office ✉
Information ⓘ

Anasazi Restaurant **19**
Andiamo! **31**
Aquasanta **15**
Atomic Grill **22**
Blue Corn Café **13**
Bumble Bee's Baja Grill **8**
Cafe Dominic **36**
Cafe Pasqual's **23**
Cafe San Estevan **38**
Cowgirl Hall of Fame **37**
Coyote Café **14**
El Meson **4**
El Nido **1**
Guadalupe Cafe **29**
Il Piatto Cucina Italiano **5**

India Palace **22**
La Casa Sena **21**
Los Mayas **10**
O'Keeffe Café **6**
The Old House **12**
Ore House
  on the Plaza **17**
Osteria d' Assisi **2**
The Pink Adobe **27**
Plaza Cafe **18**
Pranzo Italian Grill **34**
Railyard Restaurant &
  Saloon **32**
Rio Chama Steakhouse **28**
Ristra **39**

Sage Bakehouse **30**
Santacafé **3**
Señor Lucky's at
  the Palace **16**
The Shed **20**
Tía Sophia's **13**
Shohko Cafe **7**
Trattoria Nostrani **11**
Tesuque Village
  Market **1**
Tomasita's Cafe **33**
315 **25**
Upper Crust Pizza **26**
Vanessie of Santa Fe **9**
Zia Diner **35**

potatoes. At dinner, the northern halibut with Manila clams is exquisite. For dessert, try the panna cotta or Meyer lemon tart. A carefully chosen beer and wine list compliments the menu. In warmer months, you might want to request a table on the patio where you can sit under a cherry tree. If you want a peaceful and delectable meal out, this is the spot to have it.

451 W. Alameda. © **505/982-6297.** Reservations recommended. Main courses $10–$15 lunch, $10–$25 dinner. AE, MC, V. Wed–Fri noon–2pm; Tues–Sat 5:30–9pm.

Cafe Pasqual's ★★ CREATIVE SOUTHWESTERN/MEXICAN "You have to become the food, erase the line between it as an object and you," says Pasqual's owner Katharine Kagel, who uses mostly organic ingredients in her dishes. Her attitude is apparent in this restaurant, where the walls are lined with murals depicting voluptuous villagers playing guitars, drinking, and even flying. Needless to say, it's a festive place, though it's also excellent for a romantic dinner. Service is jovial and professional. My favorite dish for breakfast or lunch is the *huevos motuleños* (two eggs over easy on blue-corn tortillas and black beans topped with sautéed bananas, feta cheese, salsa, and green chile). Soups and salads are also served for lunch, and there's a delectable grilled-salmon burrito with herbed goat cheese and cucumber salsa. The frequently changing dinner menu offers grilled meats and seafood, plus vegetarian specials. Start with the Iroquois corn tamale with roasted poblano, zucchini, and asadero cheese, and move on to the spinach, jack cheese, and red-onion enchiladas. There's a communal table for those who would like to meet new people over a meal. Pasqual's offers imported beers and wine by the bottle or glass. Try to go at an odd hour—late morning or afternoon—or make a reservation for dinner; otherwise, you'll have to wait.

121 Don Gaspar Ave. © **505/983-9340.** Reservations recommended for dinner. Main courses $8–$15 breakfast, $9–$15 lunch, $19–$37 dinner. AE, MC, V. Mon–Sat 7am–3pm; Sun–Thurs 5:30–9:30pm; Fri–Sat 5:30–10pm; summer daily 5:30–10:30pm. Brunch Sun 8am–2pm.

The Compound ★★★ NEW AMERICAN This reincarnation of one of Santa Fe's classic restaurants serves some of the most flavorful and daring food in town. Inside, it's an elegant old adobe with white walls often offset by bold splashes of flowers. Outside, during warm months, a broad patio shelters diners from the city bustle. With friendly, efficient service, this is an excellent place for a romantic dinner or a relaxing lunch. Chef and owner Mark Kiffin, after nearly eight years as chef at Coyote Café (see below), lets his creativity soar. For lunch, monkfish chorizo with watercress is outrageously tasty. At dinner, you might start off with tuna tartare topped with Osetra caviar. For an entree, a signature dish is the grilled beef tenderloin with Italian potatoes and foie gras hollandaise. Finish with a bittersweet chocolate torte. A carefully selected beer and wine list accompanies the menu.

653 Canyon Rd. © **505/982-4353.** Reservations recommended. Main courses $12–$20 lunch, $22–$44 dinner. AE, DC, DISC, MC, V. Mon–Fri noon–2pm; daily 6–9pm; bar opens nightly at 5pm.

Coyote Café ★★ CREATIVE SOUTHWESTERN/LATIN World-renowned chef and cookbook author Mark Miller has been "charged with single-handedly elevating the chile to haute status." That statement from the *New York Times Magazine* sums up the experience of eating at this trendy nouveau Southwestern restaurant about a block from the plaza. The atmosphere is contemporary with an imaginative blend of warm colors and creative lighting. The waitstaff is efficient and friendly. It's the place to go for a fun night out, or you can sample the great food for lunch at a fraction of the price.

The menu changes seasonally, so the specific dishes I mention may not be available. Start your meal with Coyote cocktails that might include a Brazilian daiquiri or margarita del Maguey. Then look for delights such as chipotle tiger prawns with griddled corn cakes or a duck tamale for appetizers. Move on to a braised-ancho lamb shank or horseradish-crusted Maine haddock. You can order drinks from the full bar or wine by the glass. Smoking is not allowed.

Coyote Café has an adjunct establishment. In summer, the place to be seen is the **Rooftop Cantina,** where light Latino/Cuban fare and cocktails are served on a festively painted terrace. (Try the chicken skewers on sugar cane.)

132 Water St. ⓒ **505/983-1615.** Reservations highly recommended. Main courses $6–$16 (Rooftop Cantina), $19–$36 (Coyote Café). AE, DC, DISC, MC, V. Rooftop Cantina: daily 11:30am–9pm. Dining room: daily 5:30–9pm.

El Farol ☆ SPANISH   This is the place to head for local ambience and old-fashioned flavor. El Farol (The Lantern) is the Canyon Road artists' quarter's original neighborhood bar. The restaurant has cozy low ceilings and hand-smoothed adobe walls. Thirty-five varieties of tapas are offered, including such delicacies as *gambas al ajillo* (shrimp with chile, garlic, Madeira, and lime) and *conejo y vino* (stewed rabbit). You can make a meal out of two or three tapas shared with your friends or order a full dinner such as the paella or the grilled lamb chops with cranberry salsa. There is live entertainment 7 nights a week—including jazz/swing, folk, and Latin guitar music—starting at 9:30pm. In summer, two outdoor patios are open to diners.

808 Canyon Rd. ⓒ **505/983-9912.** Reservations recommended. Tapas $4.50–$12; main courses $8–$15 lunch, $26–$32 dinner. AE, DC, DISC, MC, V. Daily 11:30am–3pm and 5:30–10pm (bar is open until 2am Mon–Sat., until midnight Sun).

El Meson ☆☆ SPANISH   In an elegantly rustic setting reminiscent of an old Spanish hacienda, this restaurant serves up enticing tapas and dynamic entertainment. The service is efficient and knowledgeable. My favorite tapas are the steamed mussels in herbs and the blue-crab cakes with a garlic-caper aioli. But most of all I can't pass up the paella here, made the way the Spaniards do in Valencia with prawns, calamari, shrimp, mussels, chicken, and chorizo all cooked slowly with saffron rice. For dessert, try the tres leches, one of the creamiest concoctions imaginable. **Chispa!** (p. 147), the neighboring tapas bar, offers live entertainment—jazz combos, guitar duos—Tuesday through Saturday night. Most notable are the tango Tuesdays, in which the city's tango adepts turn out to burn up the floor.

213 Washington Ave. ⓒ **505/983-6756.** Reservations recommended. AE, MC, V. Tapas $3–$12. Main courses $18–$28. Tues–Sat 5–10pm. Chispa! 5–11pm.

Fuego ☆☆☆ *Moments* INTERNATIONAL   A revamp of this restaurant has made it one of Santa Fe's most stylish and sophisticated dining experiences, though the change comes at a price. The restaurant offers the ambience of a traditional Southwestern hacienda, accented with colorful paintings from local galleries, grand iron chandeliers hanging from high ceilings, and comfortable couches, along with a broad dining patio that's one of Santa Fe's best. Service is excellent.

Some locals consider the "Rancher's Brunch" one of the town's finest. Fusing traditional New Mexican ingredients with sophisticated elements, it includes some of Chef Rahm Fama's favorites from growing up in New Mexico. Try the Southwestern omelet, which melds creamy goat cheese with toasted chilies, sun-dried tomatoes, ham, and avocado. As for lunch or dinner, either should start with the pear-and-ginger consommé, a light broth with a wonton-like "purse" on top filled with duck and mascarpone cheese that breaks open to create a real flavor burst. The pan-seared fillet of black cod served over layered potato, fennel, and sunchoke with an anchovy-and-parsley sauce is a good choice, as is the Sika deer-loin medallions, served with buttermilk biscuits with caramelized onion-and-mole relish. The chef recommends a dinner tasting menu with three, five, or seven courses of petite portions. An example is a lobster menu that includes a lobster bake and foie gras and lobster tail "surf 'n' turf." For dessert, try selections from a world-class artisanal farmhouse cheese cart or the macaroon with pistachio and hazelnut ice cream. Bring your heaviest plastic; this is one of the most expensive spots in Santa Fe, but a well-worth-it, memorable choice for special occasions.

330 E. Palace Ave. (at La Posada de Santa Fe Resort and Spa). ℂ 800/727-5276 or 505/954-9670. Reservations recommended. Main courses $45 adult, $25 children under 12 brunch; $15–$28 lunch; $25–$45 dinner. Prix fixe tasting menus at dinner $75–$125. AE, DC, DISC, MC, V. Breakfast daily 7–11am; Lunch Mon–Sat 11:30am–2:30pm; Brunch Sun 11:30am–2pm; Dinner daily 6–9pm and summer 5:30–9pm.

Geronimo ✿✿✿ CONTINENTAL   This elegant restaurant offers delectable dining. Occupying an old adobe structure known as the Borrego House—which was built by Geronimo Lopez in 1756 but has since been completely restored—it retains the feel of an old Santa Fe home. I especially recommend lunch here, when you can get a taste of this complex food for a fraction of the dinner price. Reserve a spot on the porch and watch the action on Canyon Road. For lunch, try the grilled mahimahi pineapple salad. For a dinner appetizer, the warm tomato tart with fresh goat cheese is delicious. If you want to try one of Santa Fe's most renowned entrees, order the peppery elk tenderloin, or as a seafood alternative the mesquite-grilled lobster tails. For dessert, you won't be disappointed by the trio of brûlées—espresso chocolate, Chambord, and orange—or the Belgian chocolate Grand Marnier cake. The menu changes seasonally, and there's an excellent wine list.

724 Canyon Rd. ℂ 505/982-1500. Reservations recommended. Main courses $20–$29 lunch, $30–$50 dinner. AE, MC, V. Tues–Sun 11:30am–2pm; Sun–Thurs 5:45–9pm; Fri–Sat 5:45–9:30pm.

La Casa Sena ✿✿ CREATIVE SOUTHWESTERN   Combining alluring ambience and tasty food, this is a favorite restaurant among Santa Feans, though the food here isn't as precise and flavorful as at Santacafé or Geronimo. It sits within the Sena compound, a prime example of a Spanish hacienda, in a Territorial-style adobe house built in 1867 by Civil War–hero Major José Sena. The house, which surrounds a garden courtyard, is today a veritable art gallery, with museum-quality landscapes on the walls and Taos-style handcrafted furniture. The cuisine in the main dining room might be described as northern New Mexican with a continental flair. One of my favorite lunches is the flash-fried Baja sea bass fish tacos with mango salsa. In the evening, diners might start with a salad of garden greens and grilled mushrooms, then move to a grilled lamb rack marinated with Dijon and mint and accompanied by roasted root vegetables and green peppercorn sauce.

In the adjacent **La Cantina,** waiters and waitresses sing Broadway show tunes as they carry platters from the kitchen to the table. The more moderately priced Cantina menu offers the likes of cornmeal-breaded trout and grilled stuffed pork loin with peach-onion sauce. Both restaurants have exquisite desserts; try the black-and-white bittersweet chocolate terrine with raspberry sauce. The award-winning wine list features more than 850 selections. There's patio dining in summer, and the setting is wonderful.

125 E. Palace Ave. ℂ **505/988-9232.** Reservations recommended. La Casa Sena main courses $11–$19 lunch, $24–$42 dinner; 5-course chef's tasting menu $42, with wine $58; La Cantina main courses $13–$28. AE, DC, DISC, MC, V. Mon–Sat 11:30am–3pm; Sun brunch 11am–3pm; daily 5:30–10pm.

O'Keeffe Café ☞ NEW AMERICAN   Following Georgia O'Keeffe's appreciation for sparse interiors, this restaurant has refined minimalist decor, with much more elaborate food. It's a place of clean lines and innovative color use. Large black-and-white photographs of O'Keeffe stirring stew and serving tea adorn the walls. This is a good place to stop in between museums or, in the warm months, to sit on the open patio and watch the summer scene pass by. The food is excellent, but for a nice dinner (in winter), the atmosphere lags behind that of places in a similar price range, such as Santacafé and Geronimo. The menu is eclectic, with a good balance of chicken, lamb, fish, and vegetarian dishes, some in fancy salad and sandwich form (at lunch), along with more elaborate entree offerings. Most recently, I had the crab cakes with chipotle aioli, and my friend tried duck confit on a sun-dried tomato and roasted garlic cake topped with crispy carrots and finished with a saffron-and-basil-infused tomato jus. There's also a children's menu. The restaurant has a notable wine list and offers periodic wine tasting menus.

217 Johnson St. ℂ **505/946-1065.** Lunch $8–$21; dinner $9–$35. AE, MC, V. Mon–Sat 11am–3pm and 5:30–9:30pm (wine bar 3–5:30pm); Sun brunch 11am–3pm.

Old House ☞☞☞ NEW AMERICAN/CONTINENTAL   Located within the Eldorado Hotel (p. 66), this restaurant consistently rates as Santa Fe's best eatery in local publications' polls. In a Southwestern atmosphere, rich with excellent Native American art, the Old House serves quality meats, poultry, and seafood in refined sauces. The menu changes seasonally, with some signature dishes that remain year-round. A must here, as either an appetizer or entree, is the pan-seared Dungeness crab cakes with an organic watercress salad. For entrees, you might try the hand-harvested sea scallops with creamed corn or the wood-roasted tenderloin of beef with ancho chile grits and buttermilk onion rings. The marscarpone cheesecake here is excellent, but my favorite dessert is the warm Tanzanian chocolate cake. The wine list is a *Wine Spectator* award-winner.

309 W. San Francisco St. (in the Eldorado Hotel). ℂ **505/988-4455,** ext. 130. Reservations recommended. Main courses $12–$20 lunch, $24–$40 dinner. AE, DC, DISC, MC, V. Mon–Fri 11:30am–2pm; daily 5:30–9:30pm. Lounge 11:30am–closing.

Ore House on the Plaza ☞ STEAK/SEAFOOD/NEW MEXICAN   The Ore House's second-story balcony, at the southwest corner of the plaza, is an ideal spot from which to watch the passing scene while you enjoy cocktails and hors d'oeuvres. In fact, it is the place to be between 4 and 6pm every afternoon. Inside, the decor is Southwestern, with plants and lanterns hanging amid white walls and booths. The menu offers fresh seafood and steaks, as well as some Nueva Latina dishes that incorporate some interesting sauces. Daily fresh-fish specials include salmon and swordfish (poached, blackened, teriyaki, or lemon), rainbow trout, lobster, and shellfish. The salmon with spinach-pecan pesto has become a new favorite, and you can't go wrong with the Steak Ore House (wrapped in bacon and topped with crabmeat and béarnaise sauce). The Ore House offers vegetable platters for noncarnivores.

The bar, offering live music nightly Thursday to Sunday, serves more than 65 different custom margaritas. It offers a selection of domestic and imported beers and an excellent wine list. An appetizer menu is served from 2:30 to 10pm daily, and the bar stays open until midnight or later (on Sun it closes at midnight).

50 Lincoln Ave. ⓒ **505/983-8687.** Reservations recommended. Main courses $5–$13 lunch, $16–$30 dinner. AE, MC, V. 11:30am–10pm daily (bar until midnight or later).

The Pink Adobe ✿ CONTINENTAL/SOUTHWESTERN   More show than flavor? Probably. This restaurant, a few blocks off the plaza, offers a swirl of local old-timer gaiety and food that is more imaginative than flavorful, but The Pink Adobe has remained popular since it opened in 1944. I remember eating my first lamb curry here, and my mother ate her first blue-corn enchilada, back in the '50s, and was taken aback by the odd colors. The restaurant occupies an adobe home believed to be at least 350 years old. Guests enter through a narrow side door into a series of quaint, informal dining rooms with tile or hardwood floors. Stuccoed walls display original modern art and Priscilla Hoback pottery on built-in shelves. For lunch, I always have a chicken enchilada topped with an egg. The gypsy stew (chicken, green chile, tomatoes, and onions in sherry broth) sounds great but is on the bland side. At the dinner hour, The Pink Adobe offers the likes of escargot and shrimp rémoulade as appetizers. The local word here is that the steak Dunigan, with sautéed mushrooms and green chile, is "the thing" to order. You can't leave without trying the hot French apple pie.

Under the same ownership, the charming bar (a real local scene) has its own menu, offering traditional New Mexican food. Locals come to eat hearty green-chile stew.

406 Old Santa Fe Trail. ⓒ **505/983-7712.** Reservations recommended. Main courses $5–$9 lunch, $15–$28 dinner. AE, DC, DISC, MC, V. Mon–Fri 11:30am–2pm; daily 5:30pm–closing. Bar: Mon–Fri 11:30am–midnight; Sat–Sun 5pm–midnight.

Rio Chama Steakhouse ✿✿ STEAK/SEAFOOD   Serving up tasty steaks in a refined ranch atmosphere, this is one of Santa Fe's most popular restaurants. It's a good spot for a business lunch or a fun-filled evening, and the patio is a bright spot during warm months. Service is efficient, and there's a full bar. I suggest sticking to the steaks here, as the fish isn't always as fresh as it ought to be. My favorite for lunch is the buffalo patty. Lunch also brings a good selection of salads and sandwiches, as well as steaks at more reasonable prices than dinner. Evenings, the prime rib is a big seller, as is the filet mignon. For dessert, try chocolate cake. The bar here romps during happy hour, when the booths fill up and martinis nearly overflow.

414 Old Santa Fe Trail. ⓒ **505/955-0765.** Reservations recommended on weekend nights. Main courses $8–$24 lunch, $18–$39 dinner. AE, DC, DISC, MC, V. Daily 11am–3pm and 5–10pm; patio bar 5pm–closing.

Ristra ✿✿ NEW AMERICAN   Restaurateur Eric Lamalle describes the food at his restaurant as "spirited," and anything you order here will likely be unique, with flavors that may startle but will certainly please you. Hearing the specials alone is like poetry: a blend of American favorites prepared with French and Southwestern accents. It's a quiet, comfortable restaurant within a century-old Victorian house decorated with contemporary art. The food is in a similar vein as Santacafé's (without the Asian influence; p. 93), but the atmosphere here is quieter. Best of all is the patio during warm months, when you can watch the sun set. The service is completely professional but without pretense. You may want to start with squash beignets or tiger prawn flautas. For a main course, try the achiote elk tenderloin served with morel barley or the seared coriander Alaskan halibut with sweet potato puree. For dessert, try the almond butter cake, with warm spiced apples and mascarpone caramel sauce. A long wine list covers the best wine regions of California and France; beer is also served. During warm months, request a table on the lovely patio.

548 Agua Fria St. ℂ 505/982-8608. www.ristrarestaurant.com. Reservations recommended. Main courses $22–$38. AE, MC, V. Daily 5:30–9:30pm.

Santacafé ✿✿✿ (Moments) NEW AMERICAN/CREATIVE SOUTHWESTERN When you eat at this fine restaurant, be prepared for spectacular bursts of flavor. The food combines the best of many cuisines, from Asian to Southwestern, served in an elegant setting with minimalist decor that accentuates the graceful architecture of the 18th-century Padre Gallegos House, 2 blocks from the plaza. The white walls are decorated only with deer antlers, and each room contains a fireplace. In warm months you can sit under elm trees in the charming courtyard. Beware that on busy nights the rooms are noisy. The dishes change to take advantage of seasonal specialties, each served with precision. For a starter, try the shiitake and cactus spring rolls with Southwestern ponzu. One of my favorite main courses is the Alaskan halibut with English peas and saffron couscous. A heartier eater might try the bacon-wrapped black angus filet mignon with roasted-garlic mashed potatoes. There's an extensive wine list, with wine by the glass, as well. Desserts, as elegant as the rest of the food, are made in-house; try the warm chocolate upside-down cake with vanilla ice cream.

231 Washington Ave. ℂ 505/984-1788. Reservations recommended. Main courses $9–$15 lunch, $19–$40 dinner. AE, DISC, MC, V. Mon–Sat 11:30am–2pm; daily 5:30–10pm. Sunday brunch served in summer, Easter Sunday, and Mother's Day.

Señor Lucky's at the Palace ✿✿ AMERICAN/MEXICAN Great food and a relaxing atmosphere at an affordable price—that's what this reincarnation of The Palace promises, and it delivers. Clif Skoglund and Eric DiStefano—the folks who have cast Geronimo into the top restaurants in the region list for the past decade—have brought their eye for quality and their imaginative palate to this fun spot decorated in earthy colors, with sepia photograph murals of horses and cowboys. The service is good, though, during busy hours, overworked. The restaurant has a historic setting: Santa Fe's 19th-century matriarch, Doña Tules, operated a thriving gambling hall and bordello here. From the place's remains came a brass door knocker, half shaped like a horseshoe, and the other half like a saloon girl's stockinged leg, now the restaurant's logo. Hearkening back to those old days, Señor Lucky's serves excellent drinks including big bowl-style margaritas (best savored out on the patio in warmer months) and Cactus Hearts made with silver tequila and prickly pear fruit juice. The food ranges broadly, from spaghetti with meat balls to enchiladas. My favorite for lunch or dinner is the chicken or pork tacos—perfectly seasoned and served on hand-patted tortillas, with a choice of salsas. The baby back pork ribs with coleslaw and tempura chili fries are also excellent. For lighter appetites, there are smaller "plates"—a fish of the day cooked in banana leaves, for instance. The wine list is long and well considered. A lovely patio and a lively bar are locals' favorites.

142 W. Palace Ave. ℂ 505/982-9891. Reservations recommended. Lunch $7–$16; dinner $12–$34. AE, DC, DISC, MC, V. Daily 11:30am–2:30pm and 5:30–10pm. Bar menu served 2:30–5:30pm.

315 ✿✿ FRENCH This classy French bistro enjoyed instant success when it opened in 1995 because the food is simply excellent. The elegant atmosphere provides a perfect setting for a romantic meal, and during warm months the patio is a popular place to people-watch. The menu changes seasonally; on my last visit there, I started with a smooth and flavorful lobster bisque and moved on to lamb chops served with a tart mustard sauce and mashed potatoes. My favorite dessert here is the flourless chocolate cake: not too sweet, and luscious. Because the restaurant is so popular, reservations are an absolute must.

315 Old Santa Fe Trail. ℂ 505/986-9190. www.315santafe.com. Reservations highly recommended. Main courses $9–$15 lunch, $20–$29 dinner. AE, DISC, MC, V. Summer Mon–Sat 11:30am–2pm, Sun–Thurs 5:30–9:00pm, Fri–Sat 5:30–9:30pm; winter 5:30–9pm daily.

Trattoria Nostrani ✶✶ NORTHERN ITALIAN   What was previously Rociada has transformed into this award-winning Italian treasure. It was the only restaurant in the state to receive the International Wine and Food Society Award of Excellence and the Wine Enthusiast Ultimate Award of Distinction. *Mountain Living Magazine* named it one of the top 10 restaurants in the western United States. Classically trained chefs Nelli Maltezos and Eric Stapelman spend time in Italy to keep expanding their talents. In a cozy romantic-chic setting accented by the wood floors and smooth walls of a historic building they serve such delicacies as roasted quail with sweet Italian sausage and soft polenta, or a grilled rack of lamb with potatoes and artichokes and a black truffle reduction. They also serve a range of pastas, all homemade. Try the pumpkin ravioli with brown butter and pesto. Over 500 wine selections are available to accompany your meal.

304 Johnson St. ℂ 505/983-3800. www.trattorianostrani.com. Reservations recommended. Main courses including pasta dishes $16–$40. MC, V. Jan–Feb Tues–Sat 5:30–10pm. Mar–Dec Mon–Sat 5:30–10pm.

Vanessie of Santa Fe ✶ STEAK/SEAFOOD   Vanessie is as much a piano bar as it is a restaurant. The talented musicians Doug Montgomery and Charles Tichenor hold forth at the keyboard, caressing the ivories with a repertoire that ranges from Bach to Barry Manilow. A 10-item menu, served at large, round, wooden tables beneath hanging plants in the main dining room or on a covered patio, never varies: rotisserie chicken, fresh fish, New York sirloin, filet mignon, Australian rock lobster, grilled shrimp, and rack of lamb. I especially like the rotisserie chicken. Portions are large; however, they're served a la carte, which bumps this restaurant up into the expensive category. For sides, you can order fresh vegetables, sautéed mushrooms, a baked potato, or an onion loaf (my mom raves about this). For dessert, the slice of cheesecake served is large enough for three diners. There's a short wine list.

434 W. San Francisco St. (parking entrance is on Water St.). ℂ 505/982-9966. Reservations recommended. Dinner $15–$27. AE, DC, DISC, MC, V. Daily 5:30–10:30pm (earlier in off season).

MODERATE

Andiamo! ✶ CONTEMPORARY ITALIAN   A local favorite, this neighborhood trattoria features an excellent daily-changing menu with antipasto, pasta, and excellent desserts. Though it doesn't quite have the spaciousness or fine service of Pranzo (p. 97), the prices are a little lower and the atmosphere is fun. In the summer, you can dine on a patio. I enjoyed the Caesar salad and the penne with merguez, which has a bit of musky flavor from the lamb sausage. For dessert, I'd recommend the polenta pound cake with lemon crème anglaise. Beer and wine are served.

322 Garfield St. ℂ 505/995-9595. Reservations recommended. Main courses $9.50–$20. AE, DISC, MC, V. Sun–Thurs 5:30–9pm; Fri–Sat 5:30–9:30pm.

Cafe San Estevan ✶ NEW MEXICAN/NATIVE AMERICAN WITH FRENCH ACCENTSA   Franciscan monk with a passion for saints, Estevan Garcia says he grew to love his art while cooking for friars and was inspired by angels to further his cooking skills. Thus was born this interesting twist on local cuisine. Though you can

(Kids) Family-Friendly Restaurants

Blue Corn Café (p. 98)   A relaxed atmosphere and their own menu pleases kids, while excellent brewpub beer pleases parents.

Bumble Bee's Baja Grill (p. 98)   A casual atmosphere allows parents to relax while their kids chow down on quesadillas and burritos.

Upper Crust Pizza (p. 101)   Many people feel it has the best pizza in town, and it'll deliver it to tired tots and their families at downtown hotels.

order a classic enchilada just as you can at so many Santa Fe restaurants, here you'll find closer attention to sauce flavors and some innovation in food combinations. For instance, Garcia has on the menu one of my favorites, a veggie enchilada, which has calabacitas (squash cooked with corn and chile) inside. He also serves a rib-eye steak with potatoes, calabacitas, and chile caribe (red chile). If your party has varying needs, his menu can accommodate, with dishes such as *burguesa* (hamburger) or salmon served with calabacitas and salsa tropical (a salsa made with mango, jalapeno, and cilantro). The service is friendly and efficient, and the decor is casual Southwestern, a sort of hacienda feel, with vigas on the ceiling and woven tapestries on the walls. Best of all is the street-side dining, for which, during the warmer months, you might have to make a reservation. Wine (from an extensive list) and beer are served.

428 Agua Fria St. ℂ 505/995-1996. Reservations recommended in evenings. Main courses $6–$12 lunch, $10–$24 dinner. AE, MC, V. Tues–Fri 11am–2pm; Sat–Sun 10am–2pm; daily 5:30–9pm.

Celebrations Restaurant ☞ NEW AMERICAN   Housed in a former art gallery with artful stained-glass windows and a kiva fireplace, Celebrations boasts the ambience of a bistro and the simple charm of another era. In summer, guests can dine on a brick patio facing Canyon Road. The meals here are a delicious melding of flavors, particularly those that cook awhile, such as the étouffée and stew. Three meals are served daily, starting with breakfast—an omelet with black beans or French toast with orange syrup, for example. Lunch choices include soups, salads, pasta specials, and sandwiches. Casseroles and potpies are always available in winter. The dinner menu changes with the chef's whims, but recent specialties have included sautéed pecan trout and my favorite, crawfish étouffée. All desserts (including the red-chile piñon ice cream) are homemade. There is a choice of beers and fine wines by the bottle or glass.

613 Canyon Rd. ℂ 505/989-8904. Reservations recommended. Main courses $5–$9 breakfast and lunch, $11–$20 dinner. AE, DISC, MC, V. Daily 8am–2:30pm; Wed–Sat 5–9pm.

Cowgirl Hall of Fame ☞ REGIONAL AMERICAN/BARBECUE/CAJUN   This raucous bar/restaurant serves decent food in a festive atmosphere. The main room is a bar—a hip hangout spot, and a good place to eat as well. The back room is quieter, with wood floors and tables and plenty of cowgirl memorabilia. Best of all is sitting out on a brick patio lit with strings of white lights during the warm season. The service is at times brusque, and the food varies. In winter, my favorite is a big bowl of gumbo or crawfish étouffée, and the rest of the time, I order Jamaican jerk chicken or pork tenderloin when it's a special. Careful, both can be hot. The daily blue-plate special is a real buy, especially on Tuesday nights, when it's chile rellenos. There's even a special "kid's corral" that has horseshoes, a rocking horse, a horse-shaped rubber tire swing, hay bales, and a beanbag toss. Happy hour is from 3 to 6pm. There is also live music almost every night, a pool hall, and a deli.

319 S. Guadalupe St. ℂ 505/982-2565. Reservations recommended. Main courses $6–$12 lunch, $7–$22 dinner. AE, DISC, MC, V. Mon–Fri 11am–midnight; Sat 8:30am–midnight; Sun 8:30am–11pm. Bar: Mon–Sat until 2am; Sun until midnight.

Il Piatto Cucina Italiano 🌟🌟 *Value* NORTHERN ITALIAN   This simple Italian cafe brings innovative flavors to thinner wallets. It's simple and elegant, with contemporary art on the walls—nice for a romantic evening. Service is efficient, though on a busy night, overworked. The menu changes seasonally, complemented by a few perennial standards. For a starter, try the grilled calamari with shaved fennel and aioli. Among entrees, my favorite is the pancetta-wrapped trout with grilled polenta and wild mushrooms, though you can't go wrong with the jumbo scampi risotto with sweet peppers. The Gorgonzola-walnut ravioli is a favorite of many, though not quite enough food to fill me up. A full wine and beer menu is available.

95 W. Marcy St. ℂ 505/984-1091. Reservations recommended. Main courses $13–$19. AE, DISC, MC, V. Mon–Fri 11:30am–2pm; daily 5:30–9pm. Closed July 4th.

India Palace 🌟 *Value* INDIAN   Once every few weeks, I get a craving for the lamb vindaloo served at this restaurant in the center of downtown. A festive ambience, with pink walls painted with mosque shadows, makes this a nice place for a romantic meal. The service is efficient, and most of the waiters are from India, as is chef Amarjit Behal. The tandoori chicken, fish, lamb, and shrimp are rich and flavorful, as is the *baingan bhartha* (eggplant in a rich sauce). A lunch buffet provides an excellent selection of vegetarian and nonvegetarian dishes at a reasonable price. Beer and wine are available, or you might want some chai tea.

227 Don Gaspar Ave. (inside the Water St. parking compound). ℂ 505/986-5859. Reservations recommended. Main courses $11–$26; luncheon buffet $9. AE, DC, DISC, MC, V. Daily 11:30am–2:30pm and 5–10pm. Closed Super Bowl Sunday.

Los Mayas 🌟 *Moments* MEXICAN   If you're looking to be transported to a Mexican village cafe—with excellent service—come here. Within easy walking distance of most downtown hotels, this little gem has three cozy, brightly painted rooms where a fire crackles in winter. In summer, there's lovely patio dining. Every night live music plays, often flamenco or Latin, to enhance the intimate ambience. The food is a refreshing alternative to New Mexican. Dishes such as enchilada banana (corn tortillas stuffed with plantains, topped with mole sauce) and *nopal asado* (grilled cactus, topped with squash and corn) are innovative openers reflecting the Oaxacan and Puebloan influences here. Main courses include meat, fish, poultry, and vegetarian offerings in good sauces. My favorites are the *camarones á la diabla* (shrimp in chipotle cream sauce) and the tenderloin with raspberry chipotle sauce. Most entrees come with beans and rice, but they can be exchanged for alternatives. Round out your meal with an agave margarita or a selection from a decent and affordable wine and beer list.

409 W. Water St. (1 block south of W. San Francisco St., just west of Guadalupe). ℂ 505/986-9930. Main courses $9–$15 lunch, $14–$20 dinner. AE, DISC, MC, V. Daily 11am–10pm.

Osteria d'Assisi 🌟 NORTHERN ITALIAN   A couple blocks from the plaza, this restaurant offers authentic Italian food in a fun atmosphere. The place has a quaint country Italian decor with simple wooden furniture and the sound of Italian from chef

Fabrezio Ventricini, of Rome, Italy, punctuating the air. In summer, the patio offers a country villa feel. For antipasto, I enjoyed the *caprese* (fresh mozzarella with tomatoes and basil, garnished with baby greens in a vinaigrette dressing). For pasta, I recommend the lasagna, and for fish, try the delightful Italian seafood stew. All meals are served with homemade Italian bread, and there are a number of special desserts, as well as a full bar.

58 S. Federal Place. ✆ **505/986-5858**. Main courses $6.50–$13 lunch, $12–$25 dinner. AE, MC, V. Mon–Sat 11am–3pm and 5–10pm; Sun 5–10pm.

Pranzo Italian Grill ✮✮ REGIONAL ITALIAN   Housed in a renovated warehouse and freshly decorated in warm Tuscan colors, this Santa Fe staple came under new ownership in 2005, bringing a few menu changes and slightly higher prices. The restaurant still has a contemporary atmosphere of modern abstract art and very fresh food prepared on an open grill. Homemade pastas, soups, salads, and creative thin-crust pizzas are among the less expensive menu items. *Linguine alla capasante* (linguine with bay scallops, artichoke hearts, and diced tomatoes in a white-wine butter sauce) and *pizza alla funghi* (pizza with marinara, mushrooms, sun-dried tomatoes, artichokes, mozzarella, and truffle oil) are consistent favorites. Steak, chicken, veal, and fresh seafood grills dominate the dinner menu. The bar offers the Southwest's largest collection of grappas, as well as a wide selection of wines and champagnes by the bottle or glass. The upstairs rooftop terrace is lovely for seasonal moon-watching over a glass of wine.

540 Montezuma St. (Sanbusco Center). ✆ **505/984-2645**. Reservations recommended. Main courses $6–$10 lunch, $6–$24 dinner. AE, DC, DISC, MC, V. Mon–Sat 11:30am–3pm and 5pm–midnight; Sun 1–10pm.

Railyard Restaurant & Saloon ✮✮ *Finds* NEW AMERICAN   Santa Fe locals' most talked-about new spot, the Railyard, is a fun and thoughtful addition to the restaurant scene. Set in one of the city's old railroad buildings, the place offers a comfortable ambience and imaginative food at not-too-steep prices. The space has clean lines, with maroon walls and spacious booths and tables set under an industrial ceiling with visible ductwork. Service is friendly and knowledgeable. This is the creation of Louis Moskow, who put 315 on the map. Here, he's offering a slice of Americana, with dishes such as an outstanding rib-eye and tasty pan-fried pork chop, but also some less American fare such as, my favorite, sesame-and-panko-crusted tuna. All menu items are a la carte, but the side portions you'll order separately are large enough to share. Select from a carefully considered wine list or from the full bar. An excellent but more limited selection of food is available all day at the bar.

530 S. Guadalupe (¼ block north of Paseo de Peralta). ✆ **505/989-3300**. Reservations recommended on weekend nights. Main courses $7.50–$23 lunch, $8–$23 dinner. Mon–Sat 11:30am–2:30pm; Sun–Thur 5:30–9:30pm; Fri–Sat 5:30–10pm. Bar is open Mon–Thur 11:30am–10pm; Fri–Sat 11:30am–11pm.

Shohko Cafe ✮✮ JAPANESE/SUSHI   Santa Fe's favorite sushi restaurant serves fresh fish in a 150-year-old adobe building that was once a bordello. The atmosphere is sparse and comfortable, a blending of New Mexican decor (such as ceiling vigas and Mexican tile floors) with traditional Japanese decorative touches (rice-paper screens, for instance). Up to 30 fresh varieties of raw seafood, including sushi and sashimi, are served at plain pine tables in various rooms or at the sushi bar. Request the sushi bar, where the atmosphere is coziest, and you can watch the chefs at work. My mother likes the tempura combination with veggies, shrimp, and scallops. On an odd night, I'll order the salmon teriyaki, but most nights I have sushi, particularly the *anago* and spicy tuna roll—though if you're daring, you might try the Santa Fe Roll (with green chile, shrimp tempura, and *masago*). My new favorite is a caterpillar, with eel and lots of avocado, shaped like its crawling namesake. Wine, imported beers, and hot sake are available.

321 Johnson St. ℭ 505/982-9708. Reservations recommended. Main courses $5–$17 lunch, $8.50–$25 dinner. AE, DISC, MC, V. Mon–Fri 11:30am–2pm; Sun–Thurs 5:30–9pm; Fri–Sat 5:30–9:30pm.

INEXPENSIVE

Atomic Grill CREATIVE SOUTHWESTERN A block south of the plaza, this cafe offers decent patio dining at reasonable prices. Of course, there's indoor dining as well. The whole place has a hip and comfortable feel, and the food is prepared imaginatively. This isn't my first choice for downtown restaurants, but it's great if you're dining at an odd hour, particularly late at night. For breakfast try the raspberry French toast made with home-baked challah bread, served with apricot butter and maple syrup. For lunch, the green-chile stew is tasty, although it could use more chicken habañero sausage. The fish tacos are also nice, if a little bland (ask for extra salsa), and the burgers are good. They also have wood-fired pizzas; try the grilled chicken pesto one. For dessert, the carrot cake is big enough to share and is quite tasty. Wine by the glass and 100 different beers are available. The restaurant also delivers to the downtown area from 11am to midnight.

103 E. Water St. ℭ 505/820-2866. Most items under $10. AE, DC, DISC, MC, V. Mon–Thur 11am–3am; Fri 10am–3 am; Sat 9am–3am; Sun 9am–1am.

Blue Corn Café (Kids) NEW MEXICAN/MICROBREWERY If you're ready for a fun and inexpensive night out to eat decent New Mexican food, this is your place. Within a clean and breezy decor—wooden tables and abstract art—you'll find a raucous and buoyant atmosphere; it's a good place to bring kids. The overworked waitstaff may be slow, but they're friendly. I recommend sampling dishes from the combination menu. You can get two to five items served with your choice of rice, beans, or one of the best *posoles* (hominy and chile) that I've tasted. I had the chicken enchilada, which I recommend, and the chalupa, which I don't because it was soggy. You can have tacos, tamales, and rellenos, too. Kids have their own menu and crayons to keep them occupied. There are nightly specials—the shrimp fajitas are tasty, served with a nice guacamole and the usual toppings. Since this is also a brewery, you might want to sample the High Altitude Pale Ale or the Plaza Porter. My beverage choice is the prickly-pear iced tea (black tea with enough cactus juice to give it a zing). The Spanish flan is tasty and large enough to share. **The Blue Corn Cafe & Brewery** (4056 Cerrillos Rd., Suite G; ℭ 505/438-1800), on the south side at the corner of Cerrillos and Rodeo roads, has similar fare and atmosphere.

133 W. Water St. ℭ 505/984-1800. Reservations accepted for parties of 6 or more. Main courses $9.50–$18. AE, DC, DISC, MC, V. Daily 11am–10pm.

Bumble Bee's Baja Grill (⋆) (Finds) (Kids) MEXICAN This new "beestro" offers a refreshing twist on fast food: It's actually healthy! The secret? Tacos are made Mexican style, with a tortilla folded around quality meat, fish, and poultry grilled with veggies. You pick from an array of salsas. Waist watchers can sample from a selection of salads, including one with grilled chicken and avocado. Rotisserie chicken and various burritos round out the main menu, while kids have their own options, such as the quesadillas. Diners order at a counter, and a waiter brings the food. The decor is a bit Formica-esque for my tastes, though the primary colors are fun. During warm months, I try to nab a patio table. Evenings often offer live jazz music, when folks sit back and sip beer and wine. There's also a drive-through window. There's another **Bumble Bee's Baja Grill** (3777 Cerrillos Rd., ℂ **505/988-3278**), with similar decor and offerings, on the south side of town.

301 Jefferson (from W. San Francisco St., take Guadalupe 2 blocks north). ℂ **505/820-2862**. Main courses $6–$12. AE, MC, V. Mon–Sat 11am–9pm.

Cafe Dominic ℛ AMERICAN/DELI   This cafe offers sophisticated flavors with casual ease in a comfortable urban environment. Diners order at a counter, and a waiter brings the food. The restaurant serves a variety of breakfasts as well as soups, salads, sandwiches, New Mexican food, grilled fish and meat, and pasta. My favorite is the cobb salad, which comes with crisp bacon, grilled chicken, Gorgonzola cheese, avocado, and egg wedges. For a real City Different bargain, try the grilled salmon, served with beans, rice, salad, and grilled foccacia. When dessert rolls around, you can feast on a caramel turtle cheesecake or four-layer chocolate cake.

320 S. Guadalupe. ℂ **505/982-4743**. Main courses $5–$13. AE, MC, V. Mon 7am–3pm; Tues–Sat 7am–9pm; Sun 7am–3pm.

Guadalupe Cafe ℛℛ NEW MEXICAN   When I want New Mexican food, I go to this restaurant, and like many Santa Feans, I go there often. This casually elegant cafe is in a white stucco building that's warm and friendly and has a nice-size patio for dining in warmer months. Service is generally friendly and conscientious. For breakfast, try the spinach-mushroom burritos or huevos rancheros, and for lunch, the chalupas or stuffed *sopaipillas*. Any other time, I'd start with fresh roasted ancho chiles (filled with a combination of Montrachet and Monterey Jack cheeses and piñon nuts, and topped with your choice of chile) and move on to the sour-cream chicken enchilada or any of the other Southwestern dishes. Order both red and green chile ("Christmas") so that you can sample some of the best sauces in town. Beware, though: The chile here can be hot, and the chef won't put it on the side. Diners can order from a choice of delicious salads, such as a Caesar with chicken. Daily specials are available, and don't miss the famous chocolate-amaretto adobe pie for dessert. Beer and wine are served.

422 Old Santa Fe Trail. ℂ **505/982-9762**. Breakfast $4.50–$8.75; lunch $6–$12; dinner $7–$15. DISC, MC, V. Tues–Fri 7am–2pm; Sat–Sun 8am–2pm; Tues–Sat 5:30–9pm.

La Choza ℛℛ NEW MEXICAN   This sister restaurant of The Shed (p. 100) offers some of the best New Mexican food in town at a convenient location near the intersection of Cerrillos Road and St. Francis Drive. When other restaurants are packed, you'll only wait a little while here. It's a warm, casual eatery with vividly painted walls; it's especially popular on cold days, when diners gather around the wood-burning stove and fireplace. The patio is delightful in summer. Service is friendly and efficient. The menu offers enchiladas, tacos, and burritos on blue-corn tortillas, as well as green-chile stew, chile con carne, and carne adovada. The portions are medium size, so if you're hungry, start with guacamole or nachos. For years, I've ordered the cheese or chicken enchilada, two dishes I will always recommend. My new favorite, though, is the blue-corn burritos (tortillas stuffed with beans and cheese) served with *posole;* the dish can be made vegetarian if you'd like. For dessert, you can't leave without trying the mocha cake (chocolate cake with a mocha pudding filling, served with whipped cream). Vegetarians and children have their own menus. Beer and wine are available.

905 Alarid St. ℭ **505/982-0909.** Lunch or dinner $7.95–$10. AE, DISC, MC, V. Summer Mon–Sat 11am–9pm; winter Mon–Thurs 11am–8pm, Fri–Sat 11am–9pm.

Plaza Cafe ⭑ AMERICAN/DELI/NEW MEXICAN/GREEK   Santa Fe's best example of diner-style eating, this cafe has excellent food in a bright and friendly atmosphere right on the plaza. I like to meet friends here, sit in a booth, eat, and laugh about life. A restaurant since the turn of the 20th century, it's been owned by the Razatos family since 1947. The decor has changed only enough to stay comfortable and clean, with red upholstered banquettes, Art Deco tile, and a soda fountain–style service counter. Service is always quick and conscientious, and only during the heavy tourist seasons will you have to wait long for a table. Breakfasts are excellent and large, and the hamburgers and sandwiches are good. I also like the soups and New Mexican dishes, such as the bowl of green-chile stew, or, if you're more adventurous, the pumpkin *posole.* Check out the Greek dishes, such as vegetable moussaka or beef and lamb gyros. Wash it down with an Italian soda, in flavors from vanilla to Amaretto. Alternatively, you can have a shake, a piece of coconut cream pie, or Plaza Cafe's signature dessert, *cajeta* (apple and pecan pie with Mexican caramel). Beer and wine are available.

54 Lincoln Ave. (on the plaza). ℭ **505/982-1664.** No reservations. Main courses $8–$15. AE, DISC, MC, V. Daily 7am–9pm.

Sage Bakehouse ⭑ GOURMET CAFE   Restaurants all over Santa Fe use elegantly sharp sourdough bread from this bakery on Cerrillos Road across from the Hotel Santa Fe. And whenever I'm going visiting, I'll stop and pick up a peasant loaf or some rich olive bread. If you're a bread lover, you might want to stop in for breakfast or lunch. The atmosphere is quiet and hip, with lots of marble and metal, a rounded counter, and a few small tables, as well as sidewalk seating during the warm months. Breakfasts include good espressos and mochas, and a bread basket that allows you to sample some of the splendid treats. There are also large blueberry muffins. Lunches are simple, with only a few sandwiches from which to choose, but you can bet they're good. Try the Black Forest ham and gruyere on rye or the roasted red bell pepper and goat cheese on olive. People all over town are talking about the chocolate chip cookies—rumor has it there's more chocolate than cookie in them.

535-C Cerrillos Rd. ℭ **505/820-SAGE.** All menu items under $8. MC, V. Mon–Fri 7am–5pm; Sat 7am–2pm.

The Shed ⭑⭑ NEW MEXICAN   This longtime locals' favorite is so popular that during lunch lines often form outside. Half a block east of the plaza, a luncheon institution since 1953, it occupies several rooms and the patio of a rambling hacienda that was built in 1692. Festive folk art adorns the doorways and walls. The food is delicious, some of the best in the state, and a compliment to traditional Hispanic and Pueblo cooking. The cheese enchilada is renowned in Santa Fe. Tacos and burritos are good, too, all served on blue-corn tortillas, with pinto beans on the side. The green-chile soup is a local favorite. The Shed's Joshua Carswell has added vegetarian and low-fat Mexican foods to the menu, as well as a variety of soups and salads and grilled chicken and steak. Don't leave without trying the mocha cake, possibly the best dessert you'll ever eat. In addition to wine and a number of beers, there's full bar service.

113½ E. Palace Ave. ℭ **505/982-9030.** Reservations accepted at dinner. Lunch $5.75–$9.50; dinner $8–$17. AE, DC, DISC, MC, V. Mon–Sat 11am–2:30pm and 5:30–9pm.

Sol Café ⭑ *Moments* NEW AMERICAN   So you're on Canyon Road but you already wore out your plastic buying art? Here's your spot. Sol is a casual dining spot at the top of Santa Fe's art haven, offering gourmet burgers and comfort fare. Inside, wooden chairs and tables and a painted rug on the floor lend a whimsical European bistro feel. In summer, it's an excellent spot to sit out on the patio and watch the world. For breakfast, try the Beligan waffles or a number of egg dishes. These are served all day. Lunch and dinner bring a broad range of food, ranging from an Asian chicken salad, with blueberries and fried wontons, to barbecue, and five-cheese mac and cheese. Many lunch items are available for dinner, with some more high-brow specials such as a wild mahimahi with macadamia crust. Wash it all down with your choice of 18 kinds of beer and selections from a seasonally changing wine list. If you go for dinner, make it an early one; the restaurant closes early.

802 Canyon Rd. *C* 505/989-1949. Reservations recommended on summer weekends. Breakfast $5–$10; lunch $8–$11; dinner $8–$19. AE, DISC, MC, V. Summer: Mon–Thur 11:30am–8pm; Fri–Sat 11:30am–9pm; Sun 9am–3pm; winter: Wed–Thur 11:30am–8pm; Fri–Sat 11:30am–9pm.

Tía Sophia's *Finds* NEW MEXICAN   If you want to see how real Santa Fe locals look and eat, go to this friendly downtown restaurant, now in its 33rd year. You'll sit at big wooden booths and sip diner coffee. Daily breakfast specials include eggs with blue-corn enchiladas (Tues) and burritos with chorizo, potatoes, chile, and cheese (Sat). My favorites are the breakfast burrito and huevos rancheros (eggs over corn tortillas, smothered with chile). Beware of what you order because, as the menu states, Tía Sophia's is "not responsible for too hot chile." Because this is a popular place, be prepared to wait for a table.

210 W. San Francisco St. *C* **505/983-9880**. Breakfast $2–$9.50; lunch $4–$9.50. MC, V. Mon–Sat 7am–2pm.

Tomasita's Cafe NEW MEXICAN   When I was in high school, I used to eat at Tomasita's, a little dive on a back street. I always ordered a burrito, and I think people used to bring liquor in bags. It's now in a modern building near the train station, and its food has become renowned. The atmosphere is simple—hanging plants and wood accents—with lots of families sitting at booths or tables and a festive spillover from the bar, where many come to drink margaritas. Service is quick, even a little rushed, which is my biggest gripe about Tomasita's. Sure, the food is still tasty, but unless you go at some totally odd hour, you'll wait for a table, and once you're seated, you may eat and be out again in less than an hour. The burritos are still excellent, though you may want to try the chile rellenos, a house specialty. Vegetarian dishes, burgers, steaks, and daily specials are also offered. There's full bar service.

500 S. Guadalupe St. *C* 505/983-5721. No reservations; large parties call ahead. Lunch $5.25–$14; dinner $5.75–$14. AE, DISC, MC, V. Mon–Sat 11am–10pm.

Upper Crust Pizza *Kids* PIZZA/ITALIAN   Upper Crust serves Santa Fe's best pizzas, in an adobe house near the old San Miguel Mission. The atmosphere is plain, with wooden tables; in summer, the outdoor patio overlooking Old Santa Fe Trail is more inviting. Meals-in-a-dish include the Grecian gourmet pizza (feta and olives) and the whole-wheat vegetarian pizza (topped with sesame seeds). You can either eat here or request free delivery (it takes about 30 min.) to your downtown hotel. Beer and wine are available, as are salads, calzones, sandwiches, and stromboli.

329 Old Santa Fe Trail. *C* 505/982-0000. Pizzas $7.95–$16. DISC, MC, V. Summer daily 11am–midnight; winter Sun–Thurs 11am–10pm, Fri–Sat 11am–11pm.

Zia Diner INTERNATIONAL/AMERICAN   Santa Fe's alternative weekly, *The Reporter,* awarded this local favorite the prize for the "Best Comfort Food" in town, and that phrase describes the place well. In a renovated 1880 coal warehouse, it's an Art Deco diner with a turquoise-and-mauve color scheme. It boasts a stainless-steel soda fountain and a shaded patio. Extended hours make it a convenient stopover after a movie or late outing; however, during key meals on weekends, it can get crowded and the wait can be long. The varied menu features homemade soups, salads, fish and chips, scrumptious piñon meatloaf, and, of course, enchiladas. Specials range from turkey potpie to Yankee pot roast to three-cheese calzone. I like the corn, green-chile, and asiago pie, as well as the soup specials. There are fine wines, a full bar, great desserts (for example, tapioca pudding, apple pie, and strawberry-rhubarb pie), and an espresso bar. You can get malts, floats, and shakes anytime.

326 S. Guadalupe St. ✆ **505/988-7008**. Reservations accepted only for parties of 6 or more. Main courses $5.95–$9.95 breakfast, $5.95–$11 lunch, $5.95–$17 dinner. AE, DISC, MC, V. Daily 7am–10pm.

3 The North Side
EXPENSIVE
El Nido ✿ STEAK/SEAFOOD   This has long been a celebration spot for my family and for many Santa Fe old-timers. In the warm atmosphere, decorated with bird-cages and smooth adobe partitions and *bancos,* you're likely to encounter interesting characters. In the 1950s and '60s, locals packed this place to party and dance into the wee hours of the morning. Indeed, El Nido (the Nest) has been a landmark for many years. Built as a residence in the 1920s, it was a dance hall and Ma Nelson's brothel before it became a restaurant in 1939.

The food here is fresh and well prepared, with just a touch of fusion (European and Cajun influences) added to the specials. I'd suggest coming here if you like fairly traditional steak-house fare. The place is roomy, and the service is friendly and informal. You might start with ceviche. For entrees, I enjoy the salmon, which is broiled, with a light dill sauce on the side. Friends order the broiled lamb chops, served with a light and tasty spinach mint sauce. All meals come with salad and baked potato, rice, or french fries. For dessert, try the crème brûlée, or, if you're a chocolate lover, try the chocolate piñon torte. There's a full bar, including a good selection of wines and local microbrewed beers.

Bishop's Lodge Rd., at the center of Tesuque Village. ✆ **505/988-4340**. Reservations recommended. Main courses $15–$26. AE, DC, MC, V. Tues–Sun 5:30–9:30pm.

MODERATE
Tesuque Village Market AMERICAN/SOUTHWESTERN   You'll see sparkly Range Rovers parked alongside beat-up ranch trucks in front of this charming market and restaurant, an indication that the food here has broad appeal. Located under a canopy of cottonwoods at the center of this quaint village, the restaurant doesn't have the greatest food but makes for a nice adventure 15 minutes north of town. During warmer months, you can sit on the porch; in other seasons, the interior is comfortable, with plain wooden tables next to a deli counter and upscale market. For me, this is a breakfast place, where blue-corn pancakes rule. Friends of mine like the breakfast burritos and huevos rancheros. Lunch and dinner are also popular, and there's always a crowd (though, if you have to wait for a table, the wait is usually brief). For lunch, I recommend the burgers, and for dinner, one of the hearty specials, such as lasagna. For dessert, there's a variety of house-made pastries and cakes at the deli counter, as well as fancy granola bars and oversize cookies in the market. A kids' menu is available.

At the junction of Bishop's Lodge Rd. and NM 591, in Tesuque Village. ✆ **505/988-8848**. Reservations recommended for holidays. Main courses $5–$8 breakfast, $6–$12 lunch, $8–$20 dinner. MC, V. Daily 7am–9pm.

4 The South Side

Santa Fe's motel strip and other streets south of Paseo de Peralta have their share of good, reasonably priced restaurants.

MODERATE

Chow's ♠ CREATIVE CHINESE   This refined but casual restaurant, near the intersection of St. Francis and St. Michael's, is Chinese with a touch of health-conscious Santa Fe. The tasteful decor has lots of wood and earth tones, while the food is unconventional as well, and cooked without MSG. You can get standard pot stickers and fried rice, but you may want to investigate imaginatively named dishes such as Firecracker Dumplings (carrots, onions, ground turkey, and chile in a Chinese pesto-spinach sauce), Nuts and Birds (chicken, water chestnuts, and zucchini in a Szechuan sauce), or my favorite, Pearl River Splash (whole steamed boneless trout in a ginger-onion sauce). For dessert, try the chocolate-dipped fortune cookies. Wine by the bottle or glass as well as beer is available. Chow's also has Chow's Chinese Bistro in Albuquerque, also with tasty food.

720 St. Michaels Dr. ℂ **505/471-7120.** Main courses $8–$17. AE, MC, V. Mon–Sat 11:30am–2pm and 5–9pm.

mu du noodles ♠♠ PACIFIC RIM   If you're ready for a light, healthy meal with lots of flavor, head to this small restaurant about an 8-minute drive from downtown. There are two rooms, with plain pine tables and chairs and sparse Asian prints on the walls. The carpeted back room is cozier, and a woodsy-feeling patio is definitely worth requesting during the warmer months. The waitstaff is friendly and unimposing. I almost always order the Malaysian *laksa,* thick rice noodles in a blend of coconut milk, hazelnuts, onions, and red curry, stir-fried with chicken or tofu and julienned vegetables and sprouts. If you're eating with others, you may each want to order a different dish and share. The pad Thai is lighter and spicier than most, served with a chile-vinegar sauce. A list of beers, wines, and sakes is available, tailored to the menu. I'm especially fond of the ginseng ginger ale. Menu items change seasonally.

1494 Cerrillos Rd. ℂ **505/983-1411.** Reservations for parties of 3 or larger only. Main courses $9–$18. AE, DC, DISC, MC, V. Mon–Sat 5:30–9pm (sometimes 10pm in summer).

Steaksmith at El Gancho ♠ STEAK/SEAFOOD   Surrounded by piñon and juniper about 15 minutes southeast of town on Old Pecos Trail, with a decor accented by raw wood, this steakhouse is a favorite for many Santa Fe locals. In fact, my mother and her best friend eat here regularly. They like the fairly traditional food and the festive atmosphere (there's often a crowd). I find the service quite uneven, especially for large parties. A creative appetizer menu of tapas ranges from ceviche to deep-fried avocado. My mother orders the grilled shrimp, and her friend orders the baby back ribs. Steak and Alaskan King crab are other friends' favorites. There is also a choice of salads and homemade desserts, plus a full bar and lounge (serving a tapas menu from 4pm) that even caters to cappuccino lovers.

At the intersection of Old Las Vegas Hwy. and El Gancho Way. ℂ **505/988-3333.** Reservations recommended. Main courses $9–$27. AE, DC, DISC, MC, V. Daily 4–9:30pm.

INEXPENSIVE

Felipe's Tacos MEXICAN   Locals buzz around this small rapid-food restaurant like *moscas en miel* (flies on honey), and it's no wonder—the food is *muy sabrosa* (very flavorful) and prepared with lean meats and fresh ingredients—no lard is used. You order at a counter, and the food generally comes quickly, ready for you to apply your own choice of a variety of salsas. As far as I'm concerned, there's only one thing to order here—it's so good, why bother with anything else? That's the original chicken burrito, charbroiled chicken with cheese, beans, avocado, and salsa. You can also get it with steak. I see plenty of quesadillas served as well, and during the morning hours, *la Mexicana burrito* (eggs, pico de gallo, potatoes, and beans) is popular. Avoid the tacos, which are bland. No alcoholic beverages are served.

1711 A Llano St., in St. Michael's Village. © 505/473-9397. All menu items under $7. No credit cards. Mon–Sat 9am–3:30pm.

Marisco's La Playa MEXICAN/SEAFOOD   What this Mexican seafood restaurant lacks in ambience, it makes up for in *comida sabrosa* (tasty food). Set in a small shopping mall not far from St. Francis Drive, it has a beach scene mural on one wall and stark luminescent lighting from above. It was opened by two cousins who wanted to bring good Mexican *playa* (beach) food to the drylands, and judging from the crowds here (you may have to wait 15–20 min., but it's worth it), they've succeeded. It features such dishes as shrimp or fish tacos and *pescado a la plancha* (trout seasoned with butter, garlic, and paprika). Some locals complain that the place is too pricey, but I say for good fish, it's a bargain. My Chinese doctor friend, Michael, says my favorite dish is excellent for my chi: The *caldo vuelve a la vida* (come-back-to-life soup) is a huge bowl, even if you order the small, of shrimp, octopus, scallops, clams, crab legs, and calamari in a tasty broth. Wash it down with a domestic or imported beer. There is a now a second location as well, at 2875 Cerrillos Rd. (© **505/473-4594**).

537 Cordova Rd. © 505/982-2790. Main courses $8.95–$14. AE, DISC, MC, V. Fri–Wed 11am–9pm.

Second Street Brewery MICROBREWERY/AMERICAN PUB FARE   In a metal building, tucked back off 2nd Street, this brewery has managed to create a lively pub scene and fairly warm atmosphere, and inside it's smoke-free. The walls, painted in gold hues, enclose a room containing interesting contemporary art and wooden tables. It's a party type of place, especially during the warm months, when diners and beer savorers sit out on the patio. The beers are quite tasty—I like the amber ale, and my friend enjoys the cream stout. You can even get a 4-ounce sampler size for $1 and try a few different brews. The food isn't extremely memorable, but in winter, it can warm a hearty appetite with such home-style dishes as chicken potpie (as a special) and shepherd's pie. The fish and chips is a big seller as are the burgers, topped with green chile and cheese. The menu also offers lighter fare, such as quiches, soups, and salads. There's a kids' menu, and wines are available. Look for their "Hoppy" Hour, when beer prices are reduced. There are also darts all the time and live entertainment several nights a week.

1814 2nd St. (at the railroad tracks). © 505/982-3030. Main courses $4–$10. AE, DISC, MC, V. Sun noon–10pm; Mon–Sat 11am–11pm (bar open later; call).

Celebrations Restaurant
  and Bar **3**
Chow's **10**
The Compound **2**
El Farol **1**
Felipe's Tacos **9**
Geronimo **4**

La Choza **5**
Marisco's La Playa **6**
mu du noodles **7**
Second Street Brewery **8**
Sol Café **1**
Steaksmith at
  El Gancho **11**

7

What to See & Do in Santa Fe

One of the oldest cities in the United States, Santa Fe has long been a center for the creative and performing arts, so it's not surprising that most of the city's major sights are related to local history and the arts. The city's Museum of New Mexico, art galleries and studios, historic churches, and cultural sights associated with local Native American and Hispanic communities all merit a visit. It would be easy to spend a full week sightseeing in the city, without ever heading out to any nearby attractions. Of special note is the **Georgia O'Keeffe Museum.**

1 The Top Attractions

Museum of Fine Arts � Opposite the Palace of the Governors, this was one of the first pueblo revival–style buildings constructed in Santa Fe (in 1917). The museum's permanent collection of more than 20,000 works emphasizes regional art and includes landscapes and portraits by all the Taos masters, *los Cincos Pintores* (a 1920s organization of Santa Fe artists), and contemporary artists. The museum also has a collection of photographic works by such masters as Ansel Adams, Edward Weston, and Elliot Porter. Modern artists are featured in temporary exhibits throughout the year. Two sculpture gardens present a range of three-dimensional art, from the traditional to the abstract.

Graceful **St. Francis Auditorium,** patterned after the interiors of traditional Hispanic mission churches, adjoins the art museum (see "The Performing Arts," in chapter 9). A museum shop sells gifts, art books, prints, and postcards of the collection.

107 W. Palace (at Lincoln Ave.). © 505/476-5072. www.museumofnewmexico.org. Admission $7 adults, free for seniors Wed, free for children 16 and under, free for all Fri 5–8pm. 4-day passes (good at all 4 branches of the Museum of New Mexico and the Museum of Spanish Colonial Art) $15 for adults. Tues–Sun 10am–5pm (Fri until 8pm). Closed New Year's Day, Easter, Thanksgiving, Christmas.

Palace of the Governors ⋆⋆ In order to fully appreciate this structure, it's important to know that this is where the only successful Native American uprising took place in 1680. Prior to the uprising, this was the local seat of power, and after de Vargas reconquered the natives, it resumed that position. Built in 1610 as the original capitol of New Mexico, the palace has been in continuous public use longer than any other structure in the United States. A watchful eye can find remnants of the conflicts this building has seen through the years. Begin out front, where Native Americans sell jewelry, pottery, and some weavings under the protection of the portal. This is a good place to buy, and it's a fun place to shop, especially if you take the time to visit with the artisans about their work. When you buy a piece, you may learn its history, a treasure as valuable as the piece itself.

Inside, a map illustrates 400 years of New Mexico history, from the 16th-century Spanish explorations through the frontier era and modern times. A rickety stagecoach

Downtown Santa Fe Attractions

Catholic Museum &
  Lamy Garden **7**
Georgia O'Keeffe Museum **2**
Institute of American
  Indian Arts Museum **5**
Loretto Chapel Museum **8**
Mission of San Miguel **10**

Museum of Fine Arts **3**
New Mexico State Capitol
  (Roundhouse) **9**
Palace of the Governors **4**
Santuario de Nuestra Señora
  de Guadalupe **1**
St. Francis Cathedral **6**

Value **Museum Binging**

If you're a museum buff, pick up one of Museum of New Mexico's 4-day passes. It's good at all 4 branches of the Museum of New Mexico: the Palace of the Governors, the Museum of Fine Arts, the Museum of International Folk Art, and the Museum of Indian Arts & Culture, with the Museum of Spanish Colonial Art thrown in for good measure. The cost is $15 for adults.

contains tools, such as farm implements and kitchen utensils, used by early Hispanic residents. There's a replica of a mid-19th-century chapel, with a simple, bright-colored altarpiece made in 1830 for a Taos church by folk artist José Rafael Aragón. What I find most interesting are the period photos scattered throughout. The building's exterior seems elaborate now, but it was once a simple flat-topped adobe with thin posts. You can see a fireplace and chimney chiseled into the adobe wall, and, in the west section of the museum, a cutaway of the adobe floor. Farther in that direction, unearthed in a recent excavation, are storage pits where the Pueblo Indians kept corn, wheat, barley, and other goods.

The museum focuses little on regional Native American culture. (Most Native American artifacts previously housed here have been moved to the Museum of Indian Arts & Culture.) However, a world-class collection of pre-Columbian art objects has been added. You'll see South and Central American ceramics, gold, and stonework dating from 1500 B.C. to A.D. 1500. There's also an impressive 18th-century Segesser Hide painting collection and an exhibit called "Jewish Pioneers of America."

Governors' offices from the Mexican and 19th-century U.S. eras have been restored and preserved. My favorite display is a set of spurs ranging from the 16th to the late 19th centuries, including a spur with 5-inch rowels. There are two shops of particular interest. One is the bookstore, which has one of the finest selections of art, history, and anthropology books in the Southwest. The other is the print shop and bindery, where limited-edition works are produced on hand-operated presses.

The palace is the flagship of the Museum of New Mexico system; the main office is at 113 Lincoln Ave. (© **505/476-5060**). The system comprises five state monuments and four Santa Fe museums: the Palace of the Governors, the Museum of Fine Arts, the Museum of International Folk Art, and the Museum of Indian Arts & Culture.

North plaza. © 505/476-5100. www.palaceofthegovernors.org. Admission $7 adults, free for children 16 and under, free for all 5–8pm Fri. 4-day passes (good at all 4 branches of the Museum of New Mexico and the Museum of Spanish Colonial Art) $15 for adults. Tues–Sun 10am–5pm. Closed New Year's Day, Thanksgiving, Christmas.

St. Francis Cathedral ⋒   Santa Fe's grandest religious structure is an architectural anomaly in Santa Fe because its design is French. Just a block east of the plaza, it was built between 1869 and 1886 by Archbishop Jean-Baptiste Lamy in the style of the great cathedrals of Europe. French architects designed the Romanesque building—named after Santa Fe's patron saint—and Italian masons assisted with its construction. The small adobe Our Lady of the Rosary chapel on the northeast side of the cathedral has a Spanish look. Built in 1807, it's the only portion that remains from Our Lady of the Assumption Church, founded along with Santa Fe in 1610. The new cathedral was built over and around the old church.

A wooden icon set in a niche in the wall of the north chapel, Our Lady of Peace, is the oldest representation of the Madonna in the United States. Rescued from the old church during the 1680 Pueblo Rebellion, it was brought back by Don Diego de Vargas on his (mostly peaceful) reconquest 12 years later—thus, the name. Today, Our Lady of Peace plays an important part in the annual Feast of Corpus Christi in June and July.

The cathedral's front doors feature 16 carved panels of historic note and a plaque memorializing the 38 Franciscan friars who were martyred during New Mexico's early years. There's also a large bronze statue of Archbishop Lamy himself; his grave is under the main altar of the cathedral.

Cathedral Place at San Francisco St. ℭ 505/982-5619. Donations appreciated. Open daily. Visitors may attend Mass Mon–Sat 7am and 5:15pm; Sun 8am, 10am, noon, and 5:15pm. Free parking in city lot next to the cathedral to attend church services.

Santa Fe Plaza 𝄪𝄪 *Moments*   This square has been the heart and soul of Santa Fe, as well as its literal center, since its concurrent establishment with the city in 1610. Originally designed as a meeting place, it has been the site of innumerable festivals and other historical, cultural, and social events. Long ago the plaza was a dusty hive of activity as the staging ground and terminus of the Santa Fe Trail. Today, those who congregate around the central monument enjoy the best people-watching in New Mexico. Live music and dancing are often staged on the gazebo/bandstand in summer. At Christmas time the plaza is decked out with lights. Santa Feans understandably feel nostalgic for the days when the plaza, now the hub of the tourist trade, still belonged to locals rather than outside commercial interests.

At the corner of San Francisco St. and Lincoln Ave. Open daily 24 hours.

2 More Attractions
MUSEUMS
Catholic Museum and the Archbishop Lamy Commemorative Garden   This museum will be especially interesting if you've read Willa Cather's *Death Comes for the Archbishop,* a fictional account of Archbishop Lamy's experience in northern New Mexico. If you haven't read it, as you visit the St. Francis Cathedral, The Bishop's Lodge, and other areas around Santa Fe, pay attention to tales of the Archbishop because he's central to the area's history. The exhibition changes every few years, but you're likely to see a portrait of the determined, thin-lipped Frenchman—who resolutely battled what he felt was apostasy on the part of the Spanish clergy in New Mexico—and some of Lamy's personal items. All of the museum's changing exhibits feature objects and information about the 400-year-old history of the Catholic Church in New Mexico. The adjacent Lamy garden isn't much to see, but the gift shop has a nice collection of locally made religious articles.

223 Cathedral Place. ℭ 505/983-3811. Donations appreciated. Mon–Fri 9am–noon and 1–4pm.

Georgia O'Keeffe Museum 𝄪𝄪   The Georgia O'Keeffe museum, inaugurated in July 1997, contains the largest collection of O'Keeffes in the world: currently 117 oil paintings, drawings, watercolors, and pastels, and more than 50 works by other artists of note. It's the largest museum in the United States dedicated solely to one woman's work. You can see such remarkable O'Keeffes as *Jimson Weed,* painted in 1932, and *Evening Star No. VII,* from 1917. The rich and varied collection adorns the walls of a

Greater Santa Fe

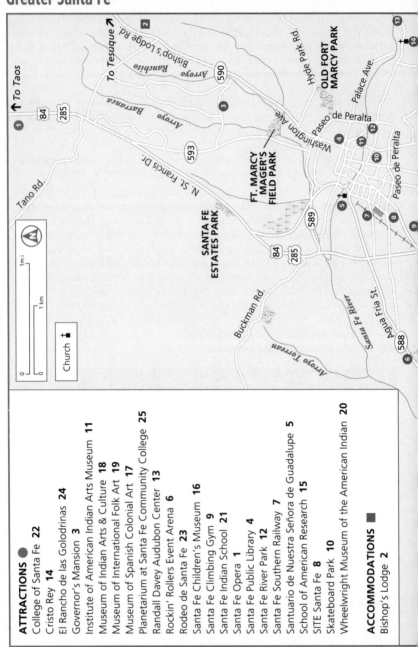

cathedral-like, 13,000-square-foot space—a former Baptist church with adobe walls. O'Keeffe's images are tied inextricably to local desert landscapes. She first visited New Mexico in 1917 and returned for extended periods from the '20s through the '40s.

217 Johnson St. ℂ 505/946-1000. www.okeeffemuseum.org. Admission $8, free for students, free for all Fri 5–8pm. July–Oct daily 10am–5pm (Fri until 8pm); Nov–June Thurs–Tues 10am–5pm (Fri until 8pm).

Indian Arts Research Center ⭐   Having grown up in New Mexico, surrounded by Native American arts, I had a hodgepodge knowledge of whose work looked like what. The center put my knowledge into an understandable framework. The School of American Research, of which the Indian Arts Research Center is a division, was established in 1907 as a center for advanced studies in anthropology and related fields. It sponsors scholarship, academic research, and educational programs, all in the name of keeping traditional arts alive.

The school has collected more than 10,000 objects, in the process compiling one of the world's finest collections of Southwest Indian pottery, jewelry, weavings, kachinas, paintings, baskets, and other arts that span from the prehistoric era (around 300–500 A.D.) to the present. You'll be led through temperature- and humidity-controlled rooms filled with work separated by tribe. Admission, however, is by tour only; see below for details.

School of American Research, 660 Garcia St. (off Canyon Rd.). ℂ 505/954-7205. www.sarweb.org/iarc/iarc.htm. Free admission for Native Americans and SAR members; $15 fee for others. Public tours given most Fri 2pm (call for reservations). Group tours can also be arranged. Limited parking.

Institute of American Indian Arts Museum ⭐   A visit to this museum (the most comprehensive collection of contemporary Native American art in the world) offers a profound look into the lives of a people negotiating two worlds: traditional and contemporary. Here, you'll see cutting-edge art that pushes the limits of many media, from creative writing to textile manufacturing to painting. Much of the work originates from artists from The Institute of American Indian Arts (IAIA), the nation's only congressionally chartered institute of higher education devoted solely to the study and practice of the artistic and cultural traditions of all American Indian and Alaskan native peoples.

Exhibits change periodically, while a more permanent collection of Allan Houser's monumental sculpture is on display in the museum's Art Park. The museum store offers a broad collection of contemporary jewelry, pottery, and other crafts, as well as books and music.

108 Cathedral Place. ℂ 505/983-8900. www.iaiancad.org. Admission $4 adults, $2 seniors and students, free for children 16 and under. Oct–May Mon–Sat 10am–5pm, Sun noon–5pm; June–Sept daily 9am–5pm.

Cultural Chow

If you get hungry while visiting the Museum of Indian Arts & Culture, the Museum of International Folk Art, the Wheelwright Museum of the American Indian, and the Museum of Spanish Colonial Art (all located together, southeast of the plaza), you can now feast on more than your fingernails. The **Museum Hill Café** ⭐ (ℂ 505/820-1776) opens Tuesday through Saturday for beverages and snacks at 10am, and a tasty lunch from 11am to 3pm; it serves brunch on Sunday from 11am to 3pm.

Museum of Indian Arts & Culture ✦✦   An interactive permanent exhibit here has made this one of the most exciting Native American museum experiences in the Southwest. "Here, Now and Always" takes visitors through thousands of years of Native American history. More than 70,000 pieces of basketry, pottery, clothing, carpets, and jewelry—much of it quite old—are on continual rotating display. You begin by entering through a tunnel that symbolizes the *sipapu,* the ancestral Puebloan (Anasazi) entrance into the upper worlds; you're greeted by the sounds of trickling water, drums, and Native American music. Videos show Native Americans telling creation stories. Visitors can reflect on the lives of modern-day Native Americans by juxtaposing a traditional Pueblo kitchen with a modern kitchen. You can step into a Navajo hogan and stroll through a trading post. The rest of the museum houses a lovely pottery collection as well as changing exhibits. There's always a contemporary show.

Look for demonstrations of traditional skills by tribal artisans and regular programs in a 70-seat multimedia theater. Call for information on year-round lectures and classes on native traditions and arts, as well as performances of Native American music and dancing by tribal groups. In February, look for an annual fiber show, and in June, a presentation on oral traditions.

The laboratory, founded in 1931 by John D. Rockefeller, Jr., is itself a point of interest. Designed by the well-known Santa Fe architect John Gaw Meem, it is an exquisite example of pueblo revival architecture.

710 Camino Lejo. ✆ 505/476-1250. www.miaclab.org. Admission $7 adults, free for kids 16 and under. 4-day passes (good at all 4 branches of the Museum of New Mexico and the Museum of Spanish Colonial Art) $15 for adults. Tues–Sun 10am–5pm. Drive southeast on Old Santa Fe Trail (beware: Old Santa Fe Trail takes a left turn; if you find yourself on Old Pecos Trail, you missed the turn). Look for signs pointing right onto Camino Lejo.

Museum of International Folk Art ✦✦ (Kids)   This branch of the Museum of New Mexico may not seem quite as typically Southwestern as other Santa Fe museums, but it's the largest of its kind in the world. With a collection of some 130,000 objects from more than 100 countries, it's my favorite city museum, well worth an hour or two of perusing. It was founded in 1953 by the Chicago collector Florence Dibell Bartlett, who said, "If peoples of different countries could have the opportunity to study each other's cultures, it would be one avenue for a closer understanding between men." That's the basis on which the museum operates today.

The special collections include Spanish colonial silver, traditional and contemporary New Mexican religious art, Mexican tribal costumes and majolica ceramics, Brazilian folk art, European glass, African sculptures, East Indian textiles, and the marvelous Morris Miniature Circus. Particularly delightful are numerous dioramas of people around the world at work and play in typical town, village, and home settings. Recent acquisitions include American weather vanes and quilts, Palestinian costume jewelry and amulets, and Bhutanese and Indonesian textiles.

Children love to look at the hundreds of toys on display throughout the museum, many of which are from a collection donated in 1982 by Alexander Girard, a notable architect and interior designer, and his wife, Susan. The couple spent their lives traveling the world collecting dolls, animals, fabrics, masks, and dioramas. They had a home in Santa Fe, where they spent many years before they died. Their donation included more than 100,000 pieces, 10,000 of which are exhibited at the museum.

The Hispanic Heritage Wing houses the country's finest collection of Spanish colonial and Hispanic folk art. Folk-art demonstrations, performances, and workshops are often presented here. The 80,000-square-foot museum also has a lecture room, a research library, and a gift shop, where a variety of folk art is available for purchase.

706 Camino Lejo. (©) 505/476-1200. www.moifa.org. Admission $8 adults, free for kids 11 and under. 4-day passes (good at all 4 branches of the Museum of New Mexico) $15 for adults. Tues–Sun 10am–5pm. The museum is about 2 miles southeast of the plaza. Drive southeast on Old Santa Fe Trail (beware: Old Santa Fe Trail takes a left turn; if you find yourself on Old Pecos Trail, you missed the turn). Look for signs pointing right onto Camino Lejo.

Museum of Spanish Colonial Art ✮   Beauty often follows in the tragic wake of imperialism. A good example of this point is Spanish colonial art, which has flourished from Europe across the Americas and even in the Philippines. This newer museum, located in the same compound as the Museum of International Folk Art, the Museum of Indian Arts & Culture, and the Wheelwright Museum of the American Indian, celebrates this art with a collection of 3,000 devotional and decorative works and utilitarian artifacts. Housed in a home built by noted architect John Gaw Meem, the museum displays *retablos* (religious paintings on wood), *bultos* (free-standing religious sculptures), furniture, metalwork, and textiles and, outside, an 18th-century wooden colonial house from Mexico.

750 Camino Lejo. (©) 505/982-2226. www.spanishcolonial.org. Admission $6 adults, free for kids 16 and under. 4-day passes (good at all 4 branches of the Museum of New Mexico and the Museum of Spanish Colonial Art) $15 for adults. Tues–Sun 10am–5pm. The museum is located about 2 miles southeast of the plaza. Drive southeast on Old Santa Fe Trail (beware: Old Santa Fe Trail takes a left turn; if you find yourself on Old Pecos Trail, you missed the turn). Look for signs pointing right onto Camino Lejo.

SITE Santa Fe ✮   This not-for-profit, 18,000-square-foot contemporary art space without a permanent collection has made a place for itself in the City Different, as well as in the international art scene. It's no wonder, with shows by some of the world's most noted contemporary artists—in 2006, for example, Cai Guo-Qiang presented an installation of stunning sculptural tigers. As well as bringing cutting-edge visual art to Santa Fe, SITE sponsors an art and culture series of lectures, multidisciplinary programs, and artist dialogues. SITE sponsors other events; in 2008, look for their International Biennial starting in July and running through the end of the year.

1606 Paseo de Peralta. (©) 505/989-1199. www.sitesantafe.org. $10 adults, $5 students and seniors, free for SITE Santa Fe members, free for all Fri. Wed–Sun 10am–5pm (Fri until 7pm). Closed Thanksgiving, Christmas Eve, Christmas, New Year's Eve, New Year's Day. Call for information about docent tours and tours in Spanish.

Wheelwright Museum of the American Indian ✮ *Kids*   Next door to the folk art museum, this museum resembles a Navajo hogan, with its doorway facing east (toward the rising sun) and its ceiling formed in the interlocking "whirling log" style. It was founded in 1937 by Boston scholar Mary Cabot Wheelwright, in collaboration with a Navajo medicine man, Hastiin Klah, to preserve and document Navajo ritual beliefs and practices. Klah took the designs of sand paintings used in healing ceremonies and adapted them into the woven pictographs that are a major part of the museum's treasure. In 1976, the museum's focus was altered to include the living arts of all Native American cultures. The museum offers three or four exhibits per year. You may see a basketry exhibit, mixed-media Navajo toys, or amazing contemporary Navajo rugs. An added treat here is the Case Trading Post, an arts-and-crafts shop built to resemble the typical turn-of-the-20th-century trading post found on the Navajo reservation. Docent tours of the exhibition are Monday to Wednesday and Friday at 2pm and Saturday at 11am. Year-round each Saturday and Tuesday morning at 10:15am and Sunday at 2pm, the Trading Post presents a lively and informative introduction to Southwestern Indian art. The museum has excellent access for travelers with disabilities.

Fun Fact **Fetishes: Gifts of Power**

According to Zuni lore, in the early years of human existence, the Sun sent down his two children to assist humans, who were under siege from earthly predators. The Sun's sons shot lightning bolts from their shields and destroyed the predators. For generations, Zunis, traveling across their lands in western New Mexico, have found stones shaped like particular animals. The Zunis believe the stones to be the remains of those long-lost predators, still containing their souls or last breaths.

In many shops in Santa Fe, you too can pick up a carved animal figure called a *fetish*. According to belief, the owner of the fetish is able to absorb the power of that creature. Many fetishes were long ago used for protection and might in the hunt. Today, a person might carry a bear for health and strength or an eagle for keen perspective. A mole might be placed in a home's foundation for protection from elements underground, a frog buried with crops for fertility and rain, a ram carried in the purse for prosperity. For love, some locals recommend pairs of fetishes—often foxes or coyotes carved from a single piece of stone.

Many fetishes, arranged with bundles on top and attached with sinew, serve as an offering to the animal spirit that resides within the stone. Fetishes are still carved by many of the pueblos. A good fetish is not necessarily one that is meticulously carved. Some fetishes are barely carved at all, since the original shape of the stone already contains the form of the animal. When you have a sense of the quality and elegance available, decide which animal (and power) suits you best. Native Americans caution, however, that the fetish cannot be expected to impart an attribute you don't already possess. Instead, it will help elicit the power that already resides within you. Good sources for fetishes are **Price-Dewey Galleries Limited,** 53 Old Santa Fe Trail, second floor (on the plaza; © **505/982-8632**) and **Keshi,** 227 Don Gaspar (© **505/989-8728**). Expect to pay $25 to $50 for a good one.

704 Camino Lejo. © **800/607-4636** or 505/982-4636. Fax 505/989-7386. www.wheelwright.org. Donations appreciated. Mon–Sat 10am–5pm; Sun 1–5pm. Closed New Year's Day, Thanksgiving, Christmas. Drive southeast on Old Santa Fe Trail (beware: Old Santa Fe Trail takes a left turn; if you find yourself on Old Pecos Trail, you missed the turn). Look for signs pointing right onto Camino Lejo.

CHURCHES

Cristo Rey This Catholic church ("Christ the King," in Spanish), a huge adobe structure, was built in 1940 to commemorate the 400th anniversary of Coronado's exploration of the Southwest. Parishioners did most of the construction work, even making adobe bricks from the earth where the church stands. The local architect John Gaw Meem designed the building, in missionary style, as a place to keep some magnificent stone *reredos* (altar screens) created by the Spanish during the colonial era and recovered and restored in the 20th century.

Upper Canyon Rd. © **505/983-8528**. Free admission. Mon–Fri 8am–5pm.

Loretto Chapel Museum ☆   Though no longer consecrated for worship, the Loretto Chapel is an important site in Santa Fe. Patterned after the famous Sainte-Chapelle church in Paris, it was constructed in 1873—by the same French architects and Italian masons who were building Archbishop Lamy's cathedral—as a chapel for the Sisters of Loretto, who had established a school for young women in Santa Fe in 1852.

The chapel is especially notable for its remarkable spiral staircase: It makes two complete 360-degree turns, with no central or other visible support. The structure is steeped in legend. The building was nearly finished in 1878, when workers realized the stairs to the choir loft wouldn't fit. Hoping for a solution more attractive than a ladder, the sisters made a novena to St. Joseph—and were rewarded when a mysterious carpenter appeared astride a donkey and offered to build a staircase. Armed with only a saw, a hammer, and a T-square, the master constructed this work of genius by soaking slats of wood in tubs of water to curve them and holding them together with wooden pegs. Then he disappeared without bothering to collect his fee.

207 Old Santa Fe Trail (between Alameda and Water sts.). © 505/982-0092. www.lorettochapel.com. Admission $2.50 adults, $2 children 7–12 and seniors over 65, free for children 6 and under. Mon–Sat 9am–5pm; Sun 10:30am–5pm.

Mission of San Miguel   If you really want to get the feel of colonial Catholicism, visit this church. Better yet, attend Mass here. You won't be disappointed. Built in 1610, the church has massive adobe walls, high windows, an elegant altar screen (erected in 1798), and a 780-pound San José bell (now found inside), which was cast in Spain in 1356. If that doesn't impress you, perhaps the buffalo-hide and deerskin Bible paintings used in 1630 by Franciscan missionaries to teach the Native Americans will. Anthropologists have excavated near the altar, down to the original floor that some claim to be part of a 12th-century pueblo. A small store just off the sanctuary sells religious articles.

401 Old Santa Fe Trail (at E. de Vargas St.). © 505/983-3974. Admission $1 adults, free for children under 6. Mon–Sat 9am–5pm; Sun 10am–4pm. Summer hours start earlier. Mass Sun 5pm.

Santuario de Nuestra Señora de Guadalupe ☆   This church, built between 1776 and 1796 at the end of El Camino Real by Franciscan missionaries, is believed to be the oldest shrine in the United States honoring the Virgin of Guadalupe, the patron saint of Mexico. Better known as Santuario de Guadalupe, the shrine's adobe walls are almost 3-feet thick, and the deep-red plaster wall behind the altar was dyed with oxblood in traditional fashion when the church was restored early in the 20th century.

It is well worth a visit to see photographs of the transformation of the building over time; its styles have ranged from flat-topped pueblo to New England town meeting and today's northern New Mexico style. On one wall is a famous oil painting, *Our Lady of Guadalupe,* created in 1783 by the renowned Mexican artist José de Alzibar. Painted expressly for this church, it was brought from Mexico City by mule caravan.

100 S. Guadalupe St. © 505/988-2027. Donations appreciated. Mon–Sat 9am–4pm. Labor Day–Memorial Day 9am–6pm. Masses: Mon–Fri 6:30am, Sat 8am, Sun noon.

PARKS & REFUGES

Arroyo de los Chamisos Trail   This trail, which meanders through the southwestern part of town, is of special interest to those staying in hotels along Cerrillos Road. The 2.5-mile paved path follows a chamisa-lined arroyo (stream) and has mountain views. It's great for walking or bicycling; dogs must be leashed.

Begin at Santa Fe High School on Yucca St. or on Rodeo Rd. near Sam's Club. © 505/955-2103.

Old Fort Marcy Park   Marking the 1846 site of the first U.S. military reservation in the Southwest, this park overlooks the northeast corner of downtown. Only a few mounds remain from the fort, but the Cross of the Martyrs, at the top of a winding brick walkway from Paseo de Peralta near Otero Street, is a popular spot for bird's-eye photographs. The cross was erected in 1920 by the Knights of Columbus and the Historical Society of New Mexico to commemorate the Franciscans killed during the Pueblo Rebellion of 1680. It has since played a role in numerous religious processions. The park's open daily 24 hours, though it's dark and not likely safe at night.

617 Paseo de Peralta (or travel 3 blocks up Artist Rd. and turn right).

Randall Davey Audubon Center ⚡   Named for the late Santa Fe artist who willed his home to the National Audubon Society, this wildlife refuge occupies 135 acres at the mouth of Santa Fe Canyon. Just a few minutes' drive from the plaza, it's an excellent escape. More than 100 species of birds and 120 types of plants live here, and varied mammals have been spotted—including black bears, mule deer, mountain lions, bobcats, raccoons, and coyotes. Trails winding through more than 100 acres of the nature sanctuary are open to day hikers, but not to dogs. There's also a natural history bookstore on site.

1800 Upper Canyon Rd. ℭ **505/983-4609.** Trail admission $2 adults, $1 children. Daily 9am–5pm. House tours conducted 2pm Mon $5 per person. Gift shop daily 10am–4pm (call for winter hours). Free 1-hr. guided bird walk every Sat at 8:30am.

Santa Fe River Park   This is a lovely spot for an early morning jog, a midday walk beneath the trees, or perhaps a sack lunch at a picnic table. The green strip follows the midtown stream for about 4 miles as it meanders along Alameda from St. Francis Drive upstream beyond Camino Cabra, near its source. It's open daily 24 hours, but it's not a safe place to linger at night.

Alameda St. ℭ **505/955-2103.**

OTHER ATTRACTIONS

El Rancho de las Golondrinas ⚡ *Kids*   This 200-acre ranch, about 15 miles south of the plaza via I-25, was once the last stopping place on the 1,000-mile El Camino Real from Mexico City to Santa Fe. Today, it's a living 18th- and 19th-century Spanish village, comprising a hacienda, a village store, a schoolhouse, and several chapels and kitchens. There's also a working molasses mill, wheelwright and blacksmith shops, shearing and weaving rooms, a threshing ground, a winery and vineyard, and four water mills, as well as dozens of farm animals. A walk around the entire property is 1¾ miles in length, with amazing scenery and plenty of room for the kids to romp.

The Spring Festival (the first full weekend of June) and the Harvest Festival (the first full weekend of Oct) are the year's highlights at Las Golondrinas (The Swallows). On these festival Sundays, the museum opens with a procession and Mass dedicated to San Ysidro, patron saint of farmers. Volunteers in authentic costumes demonstrate shearing, spinning, weaving, embroidery, wood carving, grain milling, blacksmithing, tinsmithing, soap making, and other activities. There's an exciting atmosphere of Spanish folk dancing, music, theater, and food.

334 Los Pinos Rd. ℭ **505/471-2261.** www.golondrinas.org. Admission $5 adults, $4 seniors and teens, $2 children 5–12, free for children under 5. Festival weekends $7 adults, $5 seniors and teens, $3 children 5–12. June–Sept Wed–Sun 10am–4pm; Apr–May and Oct open by advance arrangement. Closed Nov–Mar. From Santa Fe, drive south on I-25, taking exit 276; this will lead to NM 599 going north; turn left on W. Frontage Rd.; drive ½ mile; turn right on Los Pinos Rd.; travel 3 miles to the museum.

New Mexico State Capitol (Roundhouse)   Some are surprised to learn that this is the only round capitol building in the U.S. Built in 1966, it's designed in the shape of a Zia Pueblo emblem (or sun sign, which is also the state symbol). It symbolizes the Circle of Life: four winds, four seasons, four directions, and four sacred obligations. Surrounding the capitol is a lush 6½-acre garden boasting more than 100 varieties of plants, including roses, plums, almonds, nectarines, Russian olive trees, and sequoias. Inside you'll find standard functional offices, with New Mexican art hanging on the walls. Check out the Governor's Gallery and the Capitol Art Collection. Self-guided tours are available 8am to 5pm Monday through Friday year-round; Memorial Day to Labor Day guided tours are available Monday through Saturday at 10am and 2pm. All tours and self-guided brochures are free to the public.

Paseo de Peralta and Old Santa Fe Trail. (℃ **505/986-4589.** www.legis.state.nm.us. Free admission. Mon–Sat 8am–5pm. Free parking.

Santa Fe Climbing Gym   The walls of this two-story, cavernous gym are covered with foot- and handholds, making it a perfect place to frolic, especially in winter. Rental gear is available.

825 Early St. (℃ **505/986-8944.** Daily passes $12 adults, $6 kids under 12. Weekdays 5–10pm; Sat 1–8pm.

Santa Fe Southern Railway ⟡   "Riding the old Santa Fe" always referred to riding the Atchison, Topeka & Santa Fe railroad. Ironically, the main route of the AT&SF bypassed Santa Fe, which probably forestalled some development for the capital city. A spur was run off the main line to Santa Fe in 1880, and today, an 18-mile ride along that spur offers views of some of New Mexico's most spectacular scenery.

The Santa Fe Depot is a well-preserved tribute to the Mission architecture that the railroad brought to the West in the early 1900s. Characterized by light-colored stuccoed walls, arched openings, and tile roofs, this style was part of an architectural revolution in Santa Fe at a time that builders snubbed the traditional pueblo style.

Inside the restored coach, passengers are surrounded by aged mahogany and faded velvet seats. The train snakes through Santa Fe and into the Galisteo Basin, broad landscapes spotted with piñon and chamisa, with views of the Sandia and Ortiz mountains. Arriving in the small track town of Lamy, you get another glimpse of a Mission-style station, this one surrounded by spacious lawns where passengers picnic. Check out the sunset rides on weekends and specialty trains throughout the year.

410 S. Guadalupe St. (℃ **888/989-8600** or 505/989-8600. Fax 505/983-7620. www.sfsr.com. Tickets range from $15 (children) to $25 (adults), $30–$80 Fri–Sat evening rides (Apr–Oct). Depending on the season, trains depart the Santa Fe Depot (call to check winter schedule) 9:30am–1pm Mon–Sat. Rides also available Fri–Sat evening and Sun afternoon.

COOKING, ART & PHOTOGRAPHY CLASSES

If you're looking for something to do that's a little off the beaten tourist path, you might consider taking a class.

You can master the flavors of Santa Fe with an entertaining 3-hour demonstration cooking class at the **Santa Fe School of Cooking and Market** ⟡, on the upper level of the Plaza Mercado, 116 W. San Francisco St. (℃ **505/983-4511;** fax 505/983-7540; www.santafeschoolofcooking.com). The class teaches about the flavors and history of traditional New Mexican and contemporary Southwestern cuisines. "Cooking Light" classes are available as well. Prices range from $40 to $88 and include a meal; call for a class schedule. The adjoining market offers a variety of regional foods and cookbooks, with gift baskets available.

THE TRAVELOCITY GUARANTEE

...THAT SAYS EVERYTHING YOU BOOK WILL BE RIGHT, OR WE'LL WORK WITH OUR TRAVEL PARTNERS TO MAKE IT RIGHT, RIGHT AWAY.

To drive home the point,
we're going to use the word "right" in every single sentence.

Let's get right to it. Right to the meat! Only Travelocity guarantees everything about your booking will be right, or we'll work with our travel partners to make it right, right away. Right on!

Here's a picture taken smack dab right in the middle of Antigua, where the Guarantee also covers you.

The Guarantee covers all but one of the items pictured to the right.

For example, what if the ocean view you booked actually looks out at a downright ugly parking lot? You'd be right to call – we're there for you. And no one in their right mind would be pleased to learn the rental car place has closed and left them stranded. Call Travelocity and we'll help get you back on the right track.

Now, you may be thinking, "Yeah, right, I'm so sure." That's OK; you have the right to remain skeptical. That is until we mention help is always right around the corner. Call us right off the bat, knowing our customer service reps are there for you 24/7. Righting wrongs. Left and right.

Now if you're guessing there are some things we can't control, like the weather, well you're right. But we can help you with most things – to get all the details in righting,* visit travelocity.com/guarantee.

*Sorry, spelling things right is one of the few things not covered under the Guarantee.

I'd give my right arm for a guarantee like this, although I'm glad I don't have to.

travelocity
You'll never roam alone.

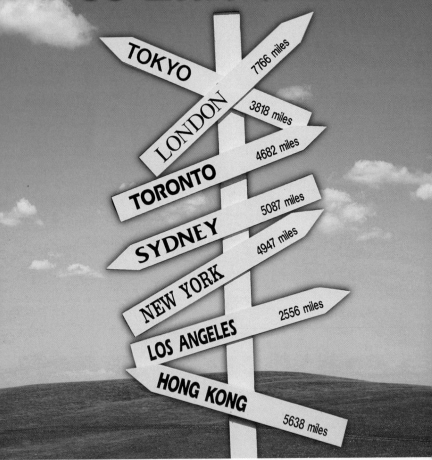

If Southwestern art has you hooked, you can take a drawing and painting class led by Santa Fe artist Jane Shoenfeld. Students sketch such outdoor subjects as the Santa Fe landscape and adobe architecture. In case of inclement weather, classes are held in the studio. Each class lasts for 3 hours, and art materials are included in the fee, which ranges from $85 to $90. Private lessons can also be arranged. All levels of experience are welcome. Children's classes can be arranged. You can create your own personal art adventure with one of Shoenfeld's 1-day classes at Ghost Ranch in Abiquiu, or a 5-day intensive class (also held at Ghost Ranch). Contact Jane at **Sketching Santa Fe,** P.O. Box 5912, Santa Fe, NM 87502 (© **505/986-1108;** fax 505/986-3845; www. skyfields.net).

Some of the world's most outstanding photographers convene in Santa Fe at various times during the year for the **Santa Fe Photography & Digital Workshops,** P.O. Box 9916, Santa Fe, NM 87504, at a delightful campus in the hills on the east side of town (© **505/983-1400;** www.santafeworkshops.com). Most courses are full-time, lasting a week. Food and lodging packages are available.

WINE TASTINGS

If you enjoy sampling regional wines, consider visiting the wineries within easy driving distance of Santa Fe: **Balagna Winery/Il Santo Cellars,** 223 Rio Bravo Dr., in Los Alamos (White Rock) (© **505/672-3678**), north on US 84/285 and then west on NM 502; **Santa Fe Vineyards,** with a retail outlet at 235 Don Gaspar Ave., in Santa Fe (© **505/982-3474**), or the vineyard itself about 20 miles north of Santa Fe on US 84/285 (© **505/753-8100**); **Madison Vineyards & Winery,** in Ribera (© **505/421-8028**), about 45 miles east of Santa Fe on I-25 North; and the **Black Mesa Winery,** 1502 Hwy. 68, in Velarde (© **800/852-6372**), north on US 84/285 to NM 68. Be sure to call in advance to find out when the wineries are open for tastings and to get specific directions.

3 Especially for Kids

Don't miss taking the kids to the **Museum of International Folk Art,** where they'll love the international dioramas and the toys (discussed earlier in this chapter). Also visit the tepee at the **Wheelwright Museum of the American Indian** (discussed earlier in this chapter), where storyteller Joe Hayes spins traditional Spanish *cuentos,* Native American folk tales, and Wild West tall tales on weekend evenings. **The Bishop's Lodge** has extensive children's programs during the summer. These include horseback riding, swimming, arts-and-crafts programs, and special activities, such as archery and tennis. Kids are sure to enjoy **El Rancho de las Golondrinas** (discussed above), a living 18th- and 19th-century Spanish village comprising a hacienda, a village store, a schoolhouse, and several chapels and kitchens.

The **Genoveva Chavez Community Center** is a full-service family recreation center on the south side of Santa Fe (3221 Rodeo Rd.). The complex includes a 50m pool, a leisure pool, a therapy pool, an ice-skating rink, three gyms, a workout room, racquetball courts, and an indoor running track, as well as a spa and sauna. For hours and more information, call © **505/955-4001.**

Planetarium at Santa Fe Community College   The planetarium offers imaginative programs, combining star shows with storytelling and other interactive techniques. Among the planetarium's inventive programs: Rusty Rocket's Last Blast, in which kids launch a model rocket; and the Solar System Stakeout, in which kids build a solar system. There's also a 10-minute segment on the current night sky. Programs vary, from those designed for preschoolers to ones for high school kids.

6401 Richards Ave. (south of Rodeo Rd.). ℂ 505/428-1677, or 505/428-1777, for the information line. www.sfccnm. edu. Admission $5 adults, $3 seniors and children 12 and under. Live lecture 1st Wed of month 7–8pm; Celestial Highlights (live program mapping the night sky for that particular month) 1st Thurs of month 7–8pm; prerecorded shows 2nd and 4th Thurs of month.

Rockin' Rollers Event Arena   This roller rink offers public-skating sessions—what the owners call family nights—on Fridays, as well as lessons and rentals. There's also a concession area to buy snacks. In-line skates are allowed.

2915 Agua Fria St. ℂ 505/473-7755. $5. Fri 7–9pm.

Rodeo de Santa Fe ⊛   The rodeo is usually held sometime around June 21. It's a colorful and fun Southwestern event for kids, teens, and adults. (See "Northern New Mexico Calendar of Events," in chapter 2, for details.)

3237 Rodeo Rd. ℂ 505/471-4300.

Santa Fe Children's Museum ⊛   This museum offers interactive exhibits and hands-on activities in the arts, humanities, and science. The most notable features include a 16-foot climbing wall that kids—outfitted with helmets and harnesses—can scale, and a 1-acre Southwestern horticulture garden, complete with animals, wetlands, and a greenhouse. This fascinating area serves as an outdoor classroom for ongoing environmental educational programs. Special performances and hands-on sessions with artists and scientists are regularly scheduled. *Family Life* magazine named this as 1 of the 10 hottest children's museums in the nation.

1050 Old Pecos Trail. ℂ 505/989-8359. www.santafechildrensmuseum.org. Admission $4; children under 12 must be accompanied by an adult. Wed–Sat 10am–5pm; Sun noon–5pm.

Santa Fe Public Library   Special programs, such as storytelling and magic shows, can be found here weekly throughout the summer. The library is in the center of town, 1 block from the plaza.

145 Washington Ave. ℂ 505/955-6780. www.santafelibrary.org. Mon–Thurs 10am–9pm; Fri–Sat 10am–6pm; Sun 1–5pm. Call for additional information.

Skateboard Park   Split-level ramps for daredevils, park benches for onlookers, and climbing structures for youngsters are located at this park near downtown.

At the intersection of de Vargas and Sandoval sts. ℂ 505/955-2100. Free admission. Open 24 hr.

4 Santa Fe Strolls

Santa Fe, with its intricate streets and resonant historical architecture, lends itself to walking. The city's downtown core extends only a few blocks in any direction from the plaza, and the ancient Barrio de Analco and the Canyon Road artists' colony are a mere stone's throw away.

WALKING TOUR 1   THE PLAZA AREA

Start: The plaza.
Finish: Loretto Chapel.

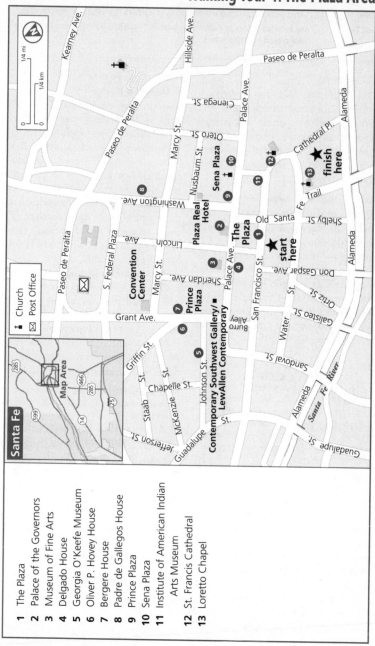

Santa Fe

Map Area

Church
Post Office

1 The Plaza
2 Palace of the Governors
3 Museum of Fine Arts
4 Delgado House
5 Georgia O'Keefe Museum
6 Oliver P. Hovey House
7 Bergere House
8 Padre de Gallegos House
9 Prince Plaza
10 Sena Plaza
11 Institute of American Indian
   Arts Museum
12 St. Francis Cathedral
13 Loretto Chapel

Time: 1 to 5 hours, depending on the length of visits to the museums and churches.

Best Times: Any morning before the afternoon heat, but after the Native American traders have spread out their wares.

---

❶ The Plaza

This square (see "The Top Attractions," earlier in this chapter) offers a look at Santa Fe's everyday life as well as many types of architecture, ranging from the Pueblo-style Palace of the Governors to the Territorial-style row of shops and restaurants on its west side.

Facing the plaza on its north side is the:

❷ Palace of the Governors

Today the flagship of the New Mexico State Museum system (see "The Top Attractions," earlier in this chapter), the Palace of the Governors has functioned continually as a public building since it was erected in 1610 as the capitol of Nuevo Mexico. Every day, Native American artisans spread out their crafts for sale beneath its portal.

 TAKE A BREAK
Even though you're only two stops into this walking tour, you might want to fortify your strength for the rest of the walk. I recommend the *carnitas* (fajitas—grilled meat and chile in a tortilla) or tamales from the street vendor on the plaza.

If you stopped at Lincoln and Palace avenues for a *carnita*, you're now in front of the:

❸ Museum of Fine Arts

Located at 107 W. Palace Ave., this museum holds works by Georgia O'Keeffe and other famed 20th-century Taos and Santa Fe artists. The building is a fine example of pueblo revival–style architecture, and it's home to the renowned St. Francis Auditorium (see "The Top Attractions," earlier in this chapter and "The Performing Arts," in chapter 9).

Virtually across the street is the:

❹ Delgado House

This Victorian mansion (at 124 W. Palace Ave.) is an excellent example of local adobe construction, modified by late-19th-century architectural detail. It was built in 1890 by Felipe B. Delgado, a merchant most known for his business of running mule and ox freight trains over the Santa Fe Trail to Independence and the Camino Real to Chihuahua. The home remained in the Delgado family until 1970. It now belongs to the Historic Santa Fe Foundation.

If you continue west on Palace Avenue, you'll come to **LewAllen Contemporary,** where you'll find an array of paintings, sculptures, ceramics, and work in other media that may make you stop and ponder.

Nearby, you'll see a narrow lane—Burro Alley—jutting south toward San Francisco Street, with an interesting burro sculpture.

Head back to Palace Avenue, make your way north on Grant Avenue, and turn left on Johnson Street to the:

❺ Georgia O'Keeffe Museum

Opened in 1997, this museum houses the largest collection of O'Keeffe works in the world. The 13,000-square-foot space is the largest museum in the United States dedicated solely to one woman's work. You might also want to stop at the museum's **O'Keeffe Café** (discussed in more detail in chapter 6) for one of its creative lunch or dinner entrees.

Head back to Grant Avenue, and continue north to 136 Griffin St., where you'll find the:

❻ Oliver P. Hovey House

Constructed between 1857 and 1859 in Territorial style, this adobe (located at 136 Griffin St.) is unique because it is actually painted brick. It's not surprising that a flamboyant man like Hovey would go to the trouble to dress up a home in such a fancy style (red brick was a rare commodity in this outpost town back then), but such stunts might be what made people call him the Great Lord Hovey, when he was no lord at all.

Across the street (135 Griffin St.) is the:

7 Bergere House

Built around 1870, this house (135 Grant Ave.) hosted U.S. President Ulysses S. Grant and his wife Julia during their 1880 visit to Santa Fe.

Proceed north on Grant, turning right on Marcy. On the north side of this corner was the **Sweeney Convention Center;** at this writing the center had been razed and construction begun on the city's new convention center.

Three blocks farther east, through an office and restaurant district, turn left on Washington Ave. Walk a short distance to 227–237 Washington Ave., where you'll see the:

8 Padre de Gallegos House

This house was built in 1857 in the Territorial style. Padre de Gallegos was a priest who, in the eyes of newly arrived Archbishop Jean-Baptiste Lamy, kept too high a social profile and was therefore defrocked in 1852. Gallegos later represented the territory in Congress and eventually became the federal superintendent of Native American affairs.

Reverse course and turn south again on Washington Avenue, passing en route the public library.

TAKE A BREAK
This is a good time to stop for refreshments at **Holy Spirit Espresso** near the Plaza Real; during the summer, you'll find a variety of drinks served on the veranda, and in the winter, the small bar inside can be quite cozy.

Leaving the coffee shop, you'll notice the entrance to the Palace of the Governors Museum Shop, a good place to purchase quality regional memorabilia. As you approach the plaza, turn left (east) on Palace Avenue. A short distance farther on your left, at 113 E. Palace Ave., is:

9 Prince Plaza

A former governor's home, this Territorial-style structure, which now houses **The Shed** restaurant, had huge wooden gates to keep out tribal attacks.

Next door is:

10 Sena Plaza

This city landmark offers a quiet respite from the busy streets, with its parklike patio. **La Casa Sena** restaurant (a great place to stop for lunch or dinner) is the primary occupant of what was once the 31-room Sena family adobe hacienda, built in 1831. The Territorial legislature met in the upper rooms of the hacienda in the 1890s.

Turn right (south) on Cathedral Place to no. 108, which is the:

11 Institute of American Indian Arts Museum

Here you'll find the most comprehensive collection of contemporary Native American art in the world (see "More Attractions," above).

Across the street, step through the doors of the:

12 St. Francis Cathedral

Built in Romanesque style between 1869 and 1886 by Archbishop Lamy, this is Santa Fe's grandest religious edifice. It has a famous 17th-century wooden Madonna known as *Our Lady of Peace* (see "The Top Attractions," above).

After leaving the cathedral, walk around the backside of the illustrious La Fonda Hotel—south on Cathedral Place and west on Water Street—to the intersection of the Old Santa Fe Trail. Here, in the northwest corner of the Hotel Loretto, you'll find the:

⓭ Loretto Chapel

This chapel is more formally known as the Chapel of Our Lady of Light. Lamy was also behind the construction of this chapel, built for the Sisters of Loretto. It is remarkable for its spiral staircase, which has no central or other visible support (see "More Attractions," above).

TAKE A BREAK
By now you may be tired and hungry. I recommend heading straight back to the plaza to a small store called **Five and Dime General Store**, where F. W. Woolworth's, the now-defunct, legendary five-and-dime store, once stood. Like Woolworth's, the store serves a cherished local delicacy called Frito pie: a bag of Fritos smothered in chile con carne, served in a plastic bag with a spoon and a napkin.

WALKING TOUR 2 | BARRIO DE ANALCO & CANYON ROAD

Start:	Don Gaspar Avenue and East de Vargas Street.
Finish:	Any of the quaint restaurants on Canyon Road.
Time:	1 to 3 hours, depending on how long you spend in the art galleries.
Best Times:	Anytime.

The Barrio de Analco, now called East de Vargas Street, is one of the oldest continuously inhabited avenues in the United States. Spanish colonists, with their Mexican and Native American servants, built homes here in the early 1600s, when Santa Fe was founded; some of the structures survive to this day.

Most of the houses you'll see as you walk east on de Vargas are private residences, not open for viewing. Even so, they are well worth looking at because of the feeling they evoke of a Santa Fe now relegated to bygone days. Most have interpretive historical plaques on their outer walls.

The first house you'll see is:

❶ Tudesqui House

Dating from the early 19th century, this house (135 E. de Vargas St.), once owned by a merchant, is now recognizable for the wisteria growing over its adobe walls. The L-shaped Territorial-style residence is noted for its brick coping, three-foot-thick adobe walls, and deeply inset windows.

Across the street is the:

❷ Gregoria Crespin House

The records of this house (132 E. de Vargas St.) date back at least to 1747, when it was sold for 50 pesos. Originally of pueblo design, it later had Territorial embellishments added in the trim of bricks along its roofline.

Just down the road is the:

❸ Santa Fe Playhouse

Home to the oldest existing thespian group in New Mexico, this original adobe theater (at 142 E. de Vargas St.) still holds performances. (See "The Performing Arts," in chapter 9.)

On the next block, at 401 Old Santa Fe Trail, is the:

❹ Mission of San Miguel

Built around 1612, this ranks as one of the oldest churches in the United States (see "More Attractions," above). Today, it's maintained and operated by the Christian Brothers.

Across de Vargas Street from the Mission of San Miguel is the so-called:

Walking Tour 2: Barrio de Analco & Canyon Road

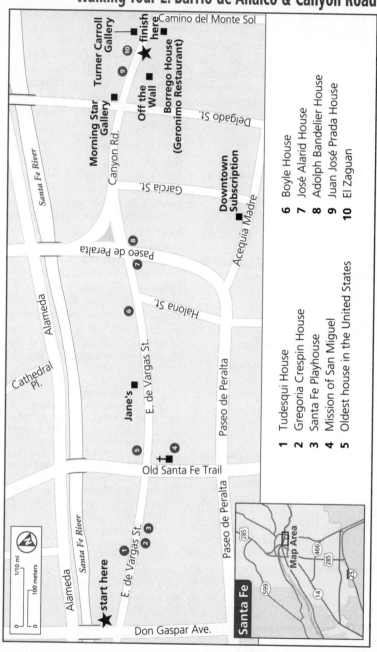

Camino del Monte Sol

Turner Carroll Gallery

finish here

Morning Star Gallery

Off the Wall

Borrego House (Geronimo Restaurant)

Delgado St.

Canyon Rd.

Garcia St.

Downtown Subscription

Acequia Madre

Santa Fe River

Paseo de Peralta

Alameda

Halona St.

E. de Vargas St.

Cathedral Pl.

Jane's

Paseo de Peralta

Old Santa Fe Trail

Santa Fe River

Paseo de Peralta

Alameda

start here

Don Gaspar Ave.

1/10 mi

100 meters

Santa Fe

285

466

285

25

599

14

Map Area

1 Tudesqui House
2 Gregoria Crespin House
3 Santa Fe Playhouse
4 Mission of San Miguel
5 Oldest house in the United States

6 Boyle House
7 José Alarid House
8 Adolph Bandelier House
9 Juan José Prada House
10 El Zaguan

5 Oldest House in the United States

Whether or not this is true is anybody's guess, but this is among the last of the poured-mud adobe houses and may have been built by Pueblo people. The new owners, who run a crafts shop here, date the place between 1200 and 1646.

>
> **TAKE A BREAK**
> This might be a good time to stop in at the **Mission Café and Sweet Shop,** 237 E. de Vargas, which serves excellent coffee and tea and tasty chocolates under shady elm trees.

There are more homes at the east end of de Vargas, before its junction with Canyon Road. Among them is the:

6 Arthur Boyle House

This house (at 327 E. de Vargas St.) on the left side of the street was built in the mid–18th century as a hacienda.

Up the block and across the street is the:

7 José Alarid House

Built in the 1830s, this house (at 338 E. de Vargas St.) is a one-story house with a pitched metal roof in the grand style of a hacienda.

East de Vargas crosses Paseo de Peralta, entering an alleyway. Immediately on the right is the:

8 Adolph Bandelier House

This house (at 352 E. de Vargas St.; also listed as 1005 Paseo de Peralta) was the home of the famous archaeologist who unearthed the prehistoric ruins at Bandelier National Monument. It has recently undergone a fine restoration, and houses Sherwoods, a gallery specializing in Native American artifacts.

Extending for a mile or so before you, Canyon Road was once a Native American trail used by the Pueblo tribes and traders. When the Pueblo tribes came to launch their 1680 insurrection against the Spanish colonists, they used this route. Today, it's lined with art galleries, shops, and restaurants. Its historic buildings include the:

9 Juan José Prada House

This house (at 519 Canyon Rd.) dates from about 1760. A few doors before you get to it, you'll come to **Morning Star Gallery,** a great place to glimpse and buy museum-quality Native American arts and artifacts.

Farther up the road is:

10 El Zaguan

This building (located at 545 Canyon Rd.) is a beautiful example of a Spanish hacienda. In warmer months, be sure to walk through the garden, subject of many Santa Fe paintings. El Zaguan is the headquarters of the **Historic Santa Fe Foundation** (© **505/983-2567;** www.historicsantafe.com). A publication of the foundation, *Old Santa Fe Today* ($10 for nonmembers), gives detailed descriptions, with a map and photos, of approximately 80 sites within walking distance of the plaza. The office is generally open weekdays 9am to 5pm; closed Sunday.

>
> **TAKE A BREAK**
> If you're ready for a break, look for **Cruz,** a gallery and coffee shop on your right. It serves drinks and pastries in a cozy, colorful atmosphere. Farther up Canyon Road, you may want to stop at the old Borrego House, which is now **Geronimo Restaurant,** for lunch or dinner. Across the street is **Turner Carroll Gallery,** where you'll find very eclectic art.

If you have the stamina to continue, turn right on Camino del Monte Sol, then right again on Camino del Poniente, and bear right onto Acequia Madre (Mother Ditch). This narrow lane winds through one of Santa Fe's oldest and most notable residential districts. It follows the mother ditch, used for centuries to irrigate gardens in the area. A 20- to 30-minute walk will bring you to **Downtown Subscription,** where you can have some excellent coffee and baked goods. From there, you can take Garcia Street north, back to the base of Canyon Road.

5 Organized Tours

BUS, CAR & TRAM TOURS

LorettoLine   For an open-air tour of the city covering history and sights, contact this company that has been running tours for 17 years. Tours last 1¼ hours and are offered daily from April to October. They depart at 10am, noon, and 2pm—and sometimes more frequently in high summer.

At the Hotel Loretto, 211 Old Santa Fe Trail. Tours depart from the Loretto Chapel. *C* **505/983-3701.** Tours $14 adults, $10 children under 12.

WALKING TOURS

As with the independent strolls described above, the following are the best way to get an appreciable feel for Santa Fe's history and culture.

Storytellers and the Southwest: A Literary Walking Tour ⊛   Barbara Harrelson, a former Smithsonian museum docent and local writer, takes you on a 2-hour literary walking tour of downtown, exploring the history, legends, characters, and authors of the region through its landmarks and historic sites. It's a great way to absorb the unique character of Santa Fe. Tours take place by appointment.

924 Old Taos Hwy. *C* **505/989-4561.** barabarah@newmexico.com. Apr–Oct. Tours $15 per person, 2-person minimum.

Walking Tour of Santa Fe ⊛   One of Santa Fe's best walking tours begins under the T-shirt tree at Tees & Skis, 107 Washington Ave., near the northeast corner of the plaza (at 9:30am and 1:30pm). It lasts about 2½ hours.

54½ E. San Francisco St. (tour meets at 107 Washington Ave.). *C* **800/338-6877** or 505/983-6565. Tours $10 adults, free for children under 12.

MISCELLANEOUS TOURS

Pathways Customized Tours ⊛   Don Dietz offers several planned tours, including a downtown Santa Fe walking tour, a full city tour, a trip to the cliff dwellings and native pueblos, a "Taos adventure," and a trip to Georgia O'Keeffe country (with a focus on the landscape that inspired the art now viewable in the O'Keeffe Museum). He will try to accommodate any special requests you might have. These tours last anywhere from 2 to 9 hours, depending on the one you choose. Don has extensive knowledge of the area's culture, history, geology, and flora and fauna, and will help you make the most of your precious vacation time.

161-F Calle Ojo Feliz. *C* **505/982-5382.** www.santafepathways.com. Tours $60–$200+ per day per couple. No credit cards.

Rain Parrish ⊛   A Navajo (or *Diné*) anthropologist, artist, and curator, Rain Parrish offers custom guide services focusing on cultural anthropology, Native American arts, and the history of the Native Americans of the Southwest. Some of these are true adventures to insider locations. Ms. Parrish includes visits to local Pueblo villages.

704 Kathryn St. *C* **505/984-8236.** Tours $130 per couple for 4½ hr., $230 per couple for 7 hr.

Recursos de Santa Fe/Royal Road Tours   This organization is a full-service destination management company, emphasizing custom-designed itineraries to meet the

Indoor/Outdoor Adventuring

If you're one of those people who wants it all, hook up with **Santa Fe Mountain Adventures** (© 800/965-4010 or 505/988-4000; www.santefemountain adventures.com). They lead programs that combine outdoor adventures with arts and cultural experiences, with spa treatments massaged in for good measure. You might start the day with fly fishing or white-water rafting, and then in the afternoon take a cooking or pottery-making class. Families especially enjoy the guided geo-caching adventure, a scavenger hunt using a global positioning device. Prices range from $99 to $120 per day depending on the length of participation and whether you stay at one of their "partner hotels."

interests of any group. They specialize in the archaeology, art, literature, spirituality, architecture, environment, food, and history of the Southwest. Call or visit the website for a calendar and information about their annual writers' conferences and the international bead expo that they sponsor in Santa Fe on even years in March.

826 Camino de Monte Rey. © 505/982-9301. www.recursos.org.

Rojo Tours & Services Customized and private tours are arranged to pueblos, cliff dwellings, ruins, hot air ballooning, backpacking, or white-water rafting. Rojo also provides planning services for groups.

P.O. Box 15744. © 505/474-8333. Fax 505/474-2992. www.rojotours.com.

Santa Fe Detours ⚘ Santa Fe's most extensive tour-booking agency accommodates almost all travelers' tastes, from bus and rail tours to river rafting, backpacking, and cross-country skiing. The agency can also facilitate hotel reservations, from budget to high end.

54½ E. San Francisco (summer tour desk, 107 Washington Ave.). © 800/338-6877 or 505/983-6565. www.sf detours.com.

Southwest Safaris ⚘⚘ This tour is one of the most interesting Southwestern experiences available. You'll fly in a small plane 1,000 feet off the ground to various destinations while pilot Bruce Adams explains millions of years of geologic history. En route to the Grand Canyon, for instance, you may pass by the ancient ruins of Chaco Canyon and over the vivid colors of the Painted Desert, and then, of course, over the spectacular Grand Canyon itself. Trips to many Southwestern destinations are available, including Monument Valley, Mesa Verde, Canyon de Chelly, and Arches/Canyonlands, as well as a trip to Capulin Volcano and the ruins at Aztec, New Mexico. Local 1- and 2-hour scenic flights are available as well, to places such as the Rio Grande Gorge, the back route in to Acoma Pueblo, and Abiquiu Valley—Georgia O'Keeffe country. Tours depart from the Santa Fe Airport.

P.O. Box 945. © 800/842-4246 or 505/988-4246. Tours $149–$699 per person.

6 Outdoor Activities

Set between the granite peaks of the Sangre de Cristo Mountains and the subtler volcanic Jemez Mountains, and with the Rio Grande flowing through, the Santa Fe area offers outdoor enthusiasts many opportunities to play. This is the land of high desert, where temperatures vary with the elevation, allowing for a full range of activities throughout the year.

BALLOONING

New Mexico is renowned for its spectacular Balloon Fiesta, which takes place annually in Albuquerque (p. 19). If you want to take a ride, you'll probably have to go to Albuquerque or Taos, but you can book your trip in Santa Fe through **Santa Fe Detours,** 54½ E. San Francisco St. (tour desk for summer, 107 Washington Ave.; © **800/338-6877** or 505/983-6565). Flights take place early in the day. Rates begin at around $175 a flight. If you have your heart set on a balloon flight, I suggest that you reserve a time early in your trip because flights are sometimes canceled due to bad weather. That way, if you have to reschedule, you'll have enough time to do so.

BIRD-WATCHING

Bird-watchers flock to the **Randall Davey Audubon Center** ⚘ (see "Parks & Refuges," earlier in this chapter), 1800 Upper Canyon Rd (© **505/983-4609),** to see more than 100 species of birds and many other animals. For guided bird-watching tours all over the region, contact **Wings West** at © **800/583-6928;** http://home. earthlink.net/wingswestnm. Bill West guides half-day tours to local spots such as the Santa Fe Mountains and Cochiti Lake ($95 for 1–2 people) and full-day ones farther afield ($175 for 1–2 people).

BIKING

You can cycle along main roadways and paved country roads year-round in Santa Fe, but be aware that traffic is particularly heavy around the plaza—and all over town, motorists are not particularly attentive to bicyclists, so you need to be especially alert. Mountain-biking interest has exploded here and is especially popular in the spring, summer, and fall; the high-desert terrain is rugged and challenging, but mountain bikers of all levels can find exhilarating rides. The Santa Fe Convention and Visitors Bureau can supply you with bike maps.

I recommend the following trails: West of Santa Fe, the **Caja del Rio** area has nice dirt roads and some light-to-moderate technical biking; the **railroad tracks south of Santa Fe** provide wide-open biking on beginner-to-intermediate technical trails; and the **Borrego Trail** up toward the Santa Fe Ski Area is a challenging technical ride that links in with the **Windsor Trail,** a nationally renowned technical romp with plenty of verticality.

In Santa Fe bookstores, or online at sites like Amazon.com, look for *Frommer's Great Outdoor Guide to Arizona and New Mexico* by Lesley King, *Mountain Biking in Northern New Mexico: Historical and Natural History Rides* by Craig Martin, and *The Mountain Biker's Guide to New Mexico* by Sarah Bennett. All of them are excellent guides to trails in Santa Fe, Taos, and Albuquerque, and outline tours for beginner, intermediate, and advanced riders. **Santa Fe Mountain Sports,** 606 Cerrillos Rd. (© **505/988-3337),** rents hard-tail mountain bikes for $20/half day and $25/full day, or full-suspension bikes for $35/full day. **Mellow Velo Bikes,** 102 E. Water St. (© **505/ 982-8986;** www.mellowbike.com), rents front-suspension mountain bikes for $23/half-day and $30/full day. Town cruisers run $23/half-day and $30/full day. Full-suspension bikes run $43 per day. Add $7, and Mellow Velo will deliver to and pick up from your hotel (in the Santa Fe area). Multiday rentals can be arranged. Both shops supply accessories such as helmets, rent locks, maps, and trail information, usually at an additional cost. **Mellow Velo** also runs a private guided tour service, which includes back-country guided adventures starting from $60 to $95 per person. On their guided train tour, clients cycle to Lamy and take a train back.

FISHING

In the lakes and waterways around Santa Fe, anglers typically catch trout (there are five varieties in the area). Other local fish include bass, perch, and kokanee salmon. The most popular fishing holes are Cochiti and Abiquiu lakes as well as the Rio Chama, Pecos River, and the Rio Grande. A world-renowned fly-fishing destination, the **San Juan River,** near Farmington, is worth a visit and can make for an exciting 2-day trip in combination with a tour around **Chaco Culture National Historic Park** (see chapter 10). Check with the **New Mexico Game and Fish Department** (© 505/ 476-8000) for information (including maps of area waters), licenses, and fishing proclamations. **High Desert Angler,** 435 S. Guadalupe St. (© 505/988-7688), specializes in fly-fishing gear and guide services.

GOLF

There are three courses in the Santa Fe area: the 18-hole **Santa Fe Country Club,** on Airport Road (© 505/471-2626); the often-praised 18-hole **Cochiti Lake Golf Course,** 5200 Cochiti Hwy., Cochiti Lake, about 35 miles southwest of Santa Fe via I-25 and NM 16 and 22 (© 505/465-2239); and Santa Fe's newest 18-hole course, **Marty Sanchez Links de Santa Fe,** 205 Caja del Rio (© 505/955-4400). Both the Santa Fe Country Club and the Marty Sanchez Links offer driving ranges as well. North of Santa Fe on Pojoaque Pueblo land, the **Towa Golf Resort** (Cities of Gold Casino Resort, U.S. 285/84, © 877/465-3489 or 505/455-9000; www.towagolf.com), offers 27 holes designed by Hale Irwin and William Phillips, set with views of the Jemez and Sangre de Cristo Mountains.

HIKING

It's hard to decide which of the 1,000 miles of nearby national forest trails to tackle. Four wilderness areas are nearby, most notably **Pecos Wilderness,** with 223,000 acres east of Santa Fe. Also visit the 58,000-acre **Jemez Mountain National Recreation Area.** Information on these and other wilderness areas is available from the **Santa Fe National Forest,** P.O. Box 1689 (1474 Rodeo Rd.), Santa Fe, NM 87504 (© 505/ 438-7840). If you're looking for company on your trek, contact the Santa Fe branch of the **Sierra Club,** 1472 S. St. Francis (© 505/983-2703). You can pick up a hiking schedule in the local newsletter outside the office. Some people enjoy taking a chairlift ride to the summit of the **Santa Fe Ski Area** (© 505/982-4429; www.skisantafe.com)

Moments Retro Cruising

If you want to see Santa Fe's downtown the old-fashioned way, check out Mellow Velo Bikes '50s retro cruisers. These reproduction bicycles come with a basket on the front, so shoppers can cruise the plaza and Canyon Road and have a place to stash their goods. If you rent one, take a spin through some of Santa Fe's old neighborhoods on Acequia Madre and Garcia Street. Town cruisers run $23 for a half-day and $30 for a full day. Contact **Mellow Velo Bikes,** 102 E. Water St. (© 505/982-8986; www.mellowbike.com).

Trail Closures

The drought that has spread across the Southwest in recent years has caused the U.S. Forest Service to close trails in many New Mexico mountains during the summer in order to reduce fire hazard. Before you head out in this area, contact the **Santa Fe National Forest** (*©* **505/438-7840**).

and hiking around up there during the summer. You might also consider purchasing *The Hiker's Guide to New Mexico* (Falcon Press Publishing Co., Inc.) by Laurence Parent; it outlines 70 hikes throughout the state. *Frommer's Great Outdoor Guide to Arizona and New Mexico* (Wiley Publishing, Inc.), written by yours truly, details many of my favorite hikes. A popular guide with Santa Feans is *Day Hikes in the Santa Fe Area,* put out by the local branch of the Sierra Club. The most popular hiking trails are the **Borrego Trail,** a moderate 4-mile jaunt through aspens and ponderosa pines, ending at a creek, and **Aspen Vista,** an easy 1- to 5-mile hike through aspen forest with views to the east. Both are easy to find; simply head up Hyde Park Road toward Ski Santa Fe. The Borrego Trail is 8¼ miles up, while Aspen Vista is 10 miles. In recent years an energetic crew has cut the **Dale Ball Trails** (*©* **505/955-2103**), miles of hiking/biking trails throughout the Santa Fe foothills. The easiest access is off Hyde Park Road toward Ski Santa Fe. Drive 2 miles from Bishop's Lodge Road and watch for the trail head on the left. If you're looking for "outspiration" (versus inspiration) on a guided day-hiking experience, call **Outspire** *©* **505/660-0394;** www.outspire.com). They'll set you up with a guide and design just the hike for your ability level and interest. A 3- to 4-hour hike runs at a flat rate of $150, with prices going up from there. Outspire also guides snowshoeing trips.

HORSEBACK RIDING

Trips ranging in length from a few hours to overnight can be arranged by **Santa Fe Detours,** 54½ E. San Francisco St. (summer tour desk, 107 Washington Ave.; *©* **800/ 338-6877** or 505/983-6565). You'll ride with "experienced wranglers" and they can even arrange a trip that includes a cookout or brunch. Rides are also major activities at **The Bishop's Lodge** (see "The North Side," in chapter 5). The **Broken Saddle Riding Company** (*©* **505/424-7774;** www.brokensaddle.com) offers rides through the stunning Galisteo Basin south of Santa Fe.

HUNTING

Elk and mule deer are taken by hunters in the Pecos Wilderness and Jemez Mountains, as are occasional black bears and bighorn sheep. Wild turkeys and grouse are frequently bagged in the uplands, geese and ducks at lower elevations. Check with the **New Mexico Game and Fish Department** (*©* **505/476-8000**) for information and licenses.

RIVER RAFTING & KAYAKING

Although Taos is the real rafting center of New Mexico, several companies serve Santa Fe during the April-to-October white-water season. They include **New Wave Rafting,** 70 County Rd. 84B, Santa Fe, NM 87506 (*©* **800/984-1444** or 505/984-1444), and **Santa Fe Rafting Co.,** 1000 Cerrillos Rd., Santa Fe, NM 87505 (*©* **888/988-4914** or 505/988-4914; www.santaferafting.com). You can expect the cost of a full-day trip to range from about $90 to $125 before tax and the 3% federal land use fee. The day of the week (weekdays are less expensive) and group size may also affect the price.

RUNNING

Despite its elevation, Santa Fe is popular with runners and hosts numerous competitions, including the annual **Old Santa Fe Trail Run** on Labor Day. Each Wednesday, Santa Fe runners gather at 6pm at the plaza and set out on foot for runs in the surrounding area. This is a great opportunity for travelers to find their way and to meet some locals. **Santa Fe Striders** (www.santafestriders.org) sponsors various runs during the year.

SKIING

There's something available for every ability level at **Ski Santa Fe,** about 16 miles northeast of Santa Fe via Hyde Park (Ski Basin) Road. Lots of locals ski here, particularly on weekends; if you can, go on weekdays. It's a good family area and fairly small, so it's easy to split off from and later reconnect with your party. Built on the upper reaches of 12,000-foot Tesuque Peak, the area has an average annual snowfall of 225 inches and a vertical drop of 1,703 feet. Seven lifts, including a 5,000-foot triple chair and a new quad chair, serve 67 runs and 660 acres of terrain, with a total capacity of 7,800 riders an hour. Base facilities, at 10,350 feet, center around **La Casa Mall,** with a cafeteria, lounge, ski shop, and boutique. A restaurant, **Totemoff's,** has a mid-mountain patio.

The ski area is open daily from 9am to 4pm; the season often runs from Thanksgiving to early April, depending on snow conditions. Rates for all lifts are $51 for adults, $41 for teens (13–20 years), $37 for children and seniors; half-day a.m. or p.m. tickets run $37. Tickets are free for kids less than 46 inches tall (in their ski boots), and for seniors 72 and older. For more information, contact **Ski Santa Fe,** 2209 Brothers Rd., Suite 220 (✆ 505/982-4429; www.skisantafe.com). For 24-hour reports on snow conditions, call ✆ **505/983-9155. Ski New Mexico** (✆ 505/982-5300) gives statewide reports. Ski packages are available through **Santa Fe Hotels.com** (✆ 800/745-9910).

Cross-country skiers find seemingly endless miles of snow to track in the **Santa Fe National Forest** (✆ 505/438-7840). A favorite place to start is at the Black Canyon campground, about 9 miles from downtown en route to the Santa Fe Ski Area. In the same area are the **Borrego Trail** (high intermediate), **Aspen Vista Trail,** and the **Norski Trail,** all en route to Santa Fe Ski Area as well. Other popular activities at the ski area in winter include snowshoeing, snowboarding, sledding, and inner tubing. Ski, snowboard, and snowshoe rentals are available at a number of downtown shops and the ski area.

SWIMMING

There's a public pool at the **Fort Marcy Complex** (✆ 505/955-2500) on Camino Santiago, off Bishop's Lodge Road. Admission is $1.85 for adults, $1.50 for ages 13 to 18, 75¢ for ages 8 to 12, 30¢ for children 7 and under, and 75¢ for seniors.

TENNIS

Santa Fe has 44 public tennis courts and 4 major private facilities. The **City Recreation Department** (✆ 505/955-2100) can help you locate indoor, outdoor, and lighted public courts.

Getting Pampered: The Spa Scene

If traveling, skiing, or other activities have left you weary, Santa Fe has a number of relaxation options. Newest to the city is the **Absolute Nirvana Spa, Tea Room & Gardens** ☆☆ (✆ 505/983-7942; www.absolutenirvana.com). This creation, voted one of the best three spas in town by the *Santa Fe Reporter,* offers imaginative Indo-Asian spa "experiences" as well as massages and facials. Their signature treatment, the Javanese Lulur, includes a full-body massage with jasmine oil, a sandlewood/rice powder exfoliation and yogurt/honey wrap, followed by a steam shower and decadent rose petal bath, all accompanied by tea, fruit, and a house-made truffle. The tea room is open daily 10am to 6pm, and the spa is open Sunday to Thursday 10am to 6pm and Friday and Saturday 10am to 8pm. Prices range from $95 to $220.

Another option with a more Japanese bent is **Ten Thousand Waves** ☆☆, a spa about 3 miles northeast of Santa Fe on Hyde Park Road (✆ **505/982-9304;** www.tenthousandwaves.com). This serene retreat, nestled in a grove of piñons, offers hot tubs, saunas, and cold plunges, plus a variety of massage and other bodywork techniques. Bathing suits are optional in both the communal hot tub (during the day) and the women's communal tub, where you can stay as long as you want for $15. Nine private hot tubs cost $20 to $27 an hour, with discounts for seniors and children. A premium bath is offered at $59 for 85 minutes. You can also arrange therapeutic massage, hot-oil massage, in-water *watsu* massage, herbal wraps, salt glows, facials, dry brush aromatherapy treatments, Ayurvedic treatments, and the much-praised Japanese Hot Stone Massage. If you call far enough in advance, you may be able to find lodging at Ten Thousand Waves as well (see chapter 5). The spa is open Sunday, Monday, Wednesday, and Thursday from 10am to 10pm; Tuesday from 4:30 to 10pm; and Friday and Saturday from 10am to 11pm (winter hours are shorter, so be sure to call). Reservations are recommended, especially on weekends.

Decorated in Southwestern-cum-Asian style, with clean lines and lots of elegant stone, Santa Fe's chicest option is **Avanyu Spa** ☆☆ at La Posada de Santa Fe Resort and Spa (✆ **505/986-0000**). A full-service spa offering a range of treatments from massage to salt glows, this spot may initially seem expensive (about $120 for 60 min.), but treatments come with full use of the steam room, hot tub, and grass-surrounded pool.

Another option is **Vista Clara Ranch Spa Resort.** Located 25 minutes south of Santa Fe, just outside Galisteo (✆ **888/663-9772** or 505/466-4772; www.vistaclara.com), this resort/spa has a stunning setting and some fine amenities and programs, including a cooking school in the summer.

Another south-of-town option, **Sunrise Springs Inn and Retreat,** 242 Los Pinos Rd. (✆ **505/471-3600**), offers spa stays in a lovely pond-side setting. Some accommodations here retain a group-meeting feel—the inn's bread and butter; to avoid these request their newest additions, which are lovely. Even if you don't stay here, plan a meal at the inn's **Blue Heron Restaurant** ☆☆, where you'll feast on delectable new American cuisine with a healthy flair.

8

Santa Fe Shopping

Santa Fe offers a broad range of art, from very traditional Native American crafts and Hispanic folk art to extremely innovative contemporary work. Some locals call Santa Fe one of the top art markets in the world. Galleries speckle the downtown area, and as an artists' thoroughfare, Canyon Road is preeminent. The greatest concentration of Native American crafts is displayed beneath the portal of the Palace of the Governors.

Any serious arts aficionado should try to attend one or more of the city's great arts festivals—the Spring Festival of the Arts in May, the Spanish Market in July, The Indian Market in August, and the Fall Festival of the Arts in October.

1 The Shopping Scene

Few visitors to Santa Fe leave the city without acquiring at least one item from the Native American artisans at the Palace of the Governors. When you are thinking of making such a purchase, keep the following pointers in mind.

Silver jewelry should have a harmony of design, clean lines, and neatly executed soldering. Navajo jewelry typically features large stones, with designs shaped around the stone. Zuni jewelry usually has patterns of small or inlaid stones. Hopi jewelry rarely uses stones; it's usually a silver-on-silver overlay, darkly oxidized so the image stands out.

Turquoise of a deeper color is usually higher quality, so long as it hasn't been color treated (undesirable because the process adds false color to the stone). Often, turquoise is "stabilized," which means it has resin baked into the stone. This makes the stone less fragile but also prevents it from changing color with age and contact with body oils. Many people find the aging effect desirable. Beware of "reconstituted turquoise." In this process, the stone is disassembled and reassembled; it usually has a uniformly blue color that looks very unnatural.

Pottery is traditionally hand-coiled and made of natural clay, not thrown on a potter's wheel using commercial clay. It is hand-polished with a stone, hand-painted, and fired in an outdoor oven (usually an open fire pit) rather than an electric kiln. Look for an even shape; clean, accurate painting; a high polish (if it's a polished piece); and an artist's signature.

Navajo rugs are appraised according to tightness and evenness of weave, symmetry of design, and whether natural (preferred) or commercial dyes have been used.

The value of **kachina dolls** depends on the detail of their carving: fingers, toes, muscles, rib cages, feathers, and so on. Elaborate costumes are also desirable. Oil staining is preferred to the use of bright acrylic paints.

Sand paintings should display clean, narrow lines, even colors, balance, an intricacy of design, and smooth craftsmanship.

Local museums, particularly the Wheelwright Museum and the Institute of American Indian Arts Museum, can give you a good orientation to contemporary craftsmanship.

Contemporary artists are mainly painters, sculptors, ceramists, and fiber artists, including weavers. Peruse one of the outstanding **gallery catalogs** for an introduction to local dealers. They're available for free in many galleries and hotels. They include *The Collector's Guide to Art in Santa Fe and Taos* by Wingspread Incorporated (www.collectorsguide.com), *The Essential Guide* by Essential Guides, LLC (www.essentialguide.com), and others. For a current listing of gallery openings, with recommendations on which ones to attend, purchase a copy of the monthly magazine the *Santa Fean* by Santa Fean, LLC (466 W. San Francisco St., Santa Fe, NM 87501; www.santafean.com). Also check in the "Pasatiempo" section of the local newspaper, the *New Mexican* (www.santafenewmexican.com), every Friday.

Business hours vary quite a bit among establishments, but most are open at least Monday through Friday from 10am to 5pm, with mall stores open until 8 or 9pm. Most shops are open similar hours on Saturday, and many also open on Sunday afternoon during the summer. Winter hours tend to be more limited.

After the high-rolling 1980s, during which art markets around the country prospered, came the penny-pinching 1990s and the fearful 2000s. Many galleries in Santa Fe have been forced to shut their doors. Those that remain tend to specialize in particular types of art, a refinement process that has improved the gallery scene here. Some locals worry that the lack of serious art buyers in the area leads to fewer good galleries and more T-shirt and trinket stores. The plaza has its share of those but still has a good number of serious galleries, appealing to those buyers whose interests run to accessible art—Southwestern landscapes and the like. On Canyon Road, the art is often more experimental and diverse.

2 The Top Galleries

CONTEMPORARY ART

Adieb Khadoure Fine Art   Featuring contemporary artists Steven Boone, Hal Larsen, Robert Anderson, and Barry Lee Darling, the works here are shown in the gallery daily from 10am to 6pm. Adieb Khadoure also sells elegant rugs, furniture, and pottery from around the world. 610 Canyon Rd. ✆ **505/820-2666.**

Bellas Artes   Though a bit on the stuffy side, this lovely gallery down a side street near the Compound Restaurant sells art that stretches the imagination. You'll find works in many mediums by nationally known artists. Look for "architectural tapestries" by Olga de Amaral and inventive sculpture by Ruth Duckworth. 653 Canyon Rd. ✆ **505/984-2745.**

Canyon Road Contemporary Art   This gallery represents some of the finest emerging U.S. contemporary artists as well as internationally known artists. You'll find figurative, landscape, and abstract paintings, as well as raku pottery. 403 Canyon Rd. ✆ **505/983-0433.**

Hahn Ross Gallery   Owners Tom Ross and Elizabeth Hahn, a children's book illustrator and surrealist painter, respectively, specialize in representing artists who create colorful, fantasy-oriented works. Check out the sculpture garden here. 409 Canyon Rd. ✆ **505/984-8434.**

An Echo of Italy

If all the shopping has emptied more than your bank account, stop in at **Ecco** (105 E. Marcy St.; ✆ **505/986-9778**) for an organic espresso drink—the vanilla latte is legendary. Alongside your hot or cold drink, sample a cup or cone of gelato, Santa Fe's finest. The mango salsa and the chocolate banana could make Michelangelo's *David* smile. Ecco also serves sandwiches on farmhouse bread.

La Mesa of Santa Fe ✪ *(Finds)*   Step into this gallery and let your senses dance. Dramatically colored ceramic plates, bowls, and other kitchen items fill one room. Contemporary kachinas by Gregory Lomayesva—a real buy—line the walls, accented by steel lamps and rag rugs. An adventure. 225 Canyon Rd. ✆ **505/984-1688.**

LewAllen Contemporary ✪✪ *(Finds)*   This is one of Santa Fe's most prized galleries. You'll find bizarre and beautiful contemporary works in a range of media, from granite to clay to twigs. There are always exciting works on canvas. 129 W. Palace Ave. ✆ **505/988-8997.**

Linda Durham Contemporary Art ✪   The opening of this broad and bright art space in summer 2004 marks the return of one of Santa Fe's best galleries. Longtime gallery owner Linda Durham had moved her gallery 25 miles south of town, but has now returned, with a strong roster of talent including Greg Erf and Judy Tuwaletstiwa. 1101 Paseo de Peralta. ✆ **505/466-6600.**

Peyton Wright Gallery ✪   Housed within the Historic Spiegelberg House (a refurbished Victorian adobe), this excellent gallery offers contemporary, American Modernism, Spanish Colonial, Russian, and 18th-century New Mexico *bultos* and *santos*. In addition to representing such artists as Orlando Leyba, Roni Stretch, and Tim Murphy, the gallery features monthly exhibitions—including contemporary paintings, sculptures, and works on paper. 237 E. Palace Ave. ✆ **800/879-8898** or 505/989-9888.

Shidoni Foundry, Gallery, and Sculpture Gardens ✪✪ *(Moments)*   Shidoni Foundry is one of the area's most exciting spots for sculptors and sculpture enthusiasts. At the foundry, visitors may take a tour through the facilities to view casting processes. In addition, Shidoni Foundry includes a 5,000-square-foot contemporary gallery, a bronze gallery, and a wonderful sculpture garden—a great place for a picnic. Bishop's Lodge Rd., Tesuque. ✆ **505/988-8001.**

Waxlander Gallery   Primarily featuring the whimsical acrylics and occasional watercolors of Phyllis Kapp, this is the place to browse if you like bold color. 622 Canyon Rd. ✆ **800/342-2202** or 505/984-2202.

NATIVE AMERICAN & OTHER INDIGENOUS ART

Andrea Fisher Fine Pottery ✪   This expansive gallery is a wonderland of authentic Southwestern Indian pottery. You'll find real showpieces here, including the work of renowned San Ildefonso Pueblo potter Maria Martinez. 100 W. San Francisco St. ✆ **505/986-1234.**

Frank Howell Gallery   If you've never seen the wonderful illustrative hand of the late Frank Howell, you'll want to visit this gallery. You'll find a variety of works by contemporary American Indian artists. The gallery also features sculpture, jewelry, and graphics. 103 Washington Ave. ℂ 505/984-1074.

Michael Smith Gallery ⚝   This gallery's namesake has made his mark through the years by finding and displaying some of the region's most exciting rugs, baskets, jewelry, and paintings. It's a small shop with a big heart. 526 Canyon Rd. ℂ 505/995-1013.

Morning Star Gallery ⚝⚝ *Finds*   This is one of my favorite places to browse. Throughout the rambling gallery are American Indian art masterpieces, all elegantly displayed. You'll see a broad range of works, from late-19th-century Navajo blankets to 1920s Zuni needlepoint jewelry. 513 Canyon Rd. ℂ 505/982-8187.

Ortega's on the Plaza   A hearty shopper could spend hours here, perusing inventive turquoise and silver jewelry and especially fine strung beadwork, as well as rugs and pottery. An adjacent room showcases a wide array of clothing, all with a hip Southwestern flair. 101 W. San Francisco St. ℂ 505/988-1866.

Sherwoods ⚝   Set in the historic Bandelier House, this gallery features museum-quality Plains Indians antiquities such as an 1870 Nez Perce beaded dress and a Crow warshirt. Some paintings hang here as well, including works by Santa Fe masters such as J. H. Sharp and Gene Kloss. Firearm buffs will go ballistic over the gun room here. 1005 Paseo de Peralta. ℂ 505/988-1776.

PHOTOGRAPHY

Andrew Smith Gallery ⚝   I'm always amazed when I enter this gallery and notice works I've seen reprinted in major magazines for years. There they are, photographic prints, large and beautiful, hanging on the wall. Here, you'll see famous works by Edward Curtis, Henri Cartier-Bresson, Ansel Adams, Annie Leibovitz, and others. 203 W. San Francisco St. ℂ 505/984-1234.

Photo-Eye Gallery   You're bound to be surprised each time you step into this gallery a few blocks off Canyon Road. Dealing in contemporary photography, the gallery represents both internationally renowned and emerging artists. 370 Garcia St. ℂ 505/988-5152.

SPANISH & HISPANIC ART

Montez Gallery   This shop is rich with New Mexican (and Mexican) art, decorations, and furnishings such as *santos* (saints), *retablos* (paintings), *bultos* (sculptures), and *trasteros* (armoires). Sena Plaza Courtyard, 125 E. Palace Ave., Suite 33. ℂ 505/982-1828.

TRADITIONAL ART

Altermann Galleries   This is a well of interesting traditional art, mostly 19th-, 20th-, and 21st-century American paintings and sculpture. The gallery represents Remington and Russell, in addition to Taos founders, Santa Fe artists, and members of the Cowboy Artists of America and the National Academy of Western Art. Stroll through the sculpture garden among whimsical bronzes of children and dogs. 225 Canyon Rd. ℂ 505/983-1590.

Gerald Peters Gallery ⚝⚝   Displayed throughout a graceful pueblo-style building, the works here are so fine you'll feel as though you're in a museum. You'll find 19th-, 20th-, and 21st-century American painting and sculpture, featuring the art of Georgia O'Keeffe, William Wegman, and the founders of the Santa Fe and Taos artist colonies, as well as more contemporary works. 1011 Paseo de Peralta. ℂ 505/954-5700.

The Mayans Gallery Ltd.   Established in 1977, this is one of the oldest galleries in Santa Fe. You'll find 20th-century American and Latin American paintings, photography, prints, and sculpture. 601 Canyon Rd. (C) **505/983-8068.**

Nedra Matteucci Galleries (✭)   As you approach this gallery, note the elaborately crafted stone and adobe wall that surrounds it, merely a taste of what's to come. The gallery specializes in 19th-, 20th-, and 21st-century American art. Inside, you'll find a lot of high-ticket works such as those of early Taos and Santa Fe painters, as well as classic American Impressionism, historical Western modernism, and contemporary Southwestern landscapes and sculpture. 1075 Paseo de Peralta. (C) **505/982-4631.**

Owings-Dewey Fine Art (✭)   These are treasure-filled rooms. You'll find 19th-, 20th-, and 21st-century American painting and sculpture, including works by Georgia O'Keeffe, Robert Henri, Maynard Dixon, Fremont Ellis, and Andrew Dasburg, as well as antique works such as Spanish colonial *retablos, bultos,* and tin works. 76 E. San Francisco St., upstairs. (C) **505/982-6244.**

Zaplin Lampert Gallery (✭✭)   Art aficionados as well as those who just like a nice landscape will enjoy this gallery, one of Santa Fe's classics. Hanging on old adobe walls are works by some of the region's early masters, including Bert Phillips, Gene Kloss, and Gustauve Baumann. 651 Canyon Rd. (C) **505/982-6100.**

3 More Shopping A to Z

ANTIQUES

El Paso Import Company (✭)   Whenever I'm in the vicinity of this shop, I always stop in. It's packed—and I mean packed—with colorful, weathered colonial and ranchero furniture. The home furnishings and folk art here are imported from Mexico. 418 Sandoval St. (C) **505/982-5698.**

Arcade Shopping on the Plaza

Opened in 2004, the **Santa Fe Arcade,** 60 E. San Francisco St. ((C) **505/988-5792**), on the south side of the plaza, offers three stories of shops in a sleek, glassy European-style space. It's a far cry from the Woolworth's that once lived there. Showy Western wear, fine Indian jewelry, and hip clothing fill the display windows of some 60 spaces in the mall. If you like to pamper yourself with natural products, many made in northern New Mexico, step into **Sombria** (suite 222; (C) **888/480-5554** or 505/982-7383). Look for their margarita salt glow, made with salt from Utah's Great Salt Lake. Prima Fine Jewelry's **Oro Fino** (suite 218; (C) **505/983-9699**) sells contemporary and Southwestern inlaid jewelry in silver, gold, and platinum. After all the shopping, if you find yourself hungry, head to the **Rooftop Pizzeria** (✭) (top floor; (C) **505/984-0008**) for some of the city's best pizza. Two types of crust, an "artisan" or a blue corn, are topped with imaginative concoctions such as smoked duck and roasted garlic or wild mushroom and Alfredo sauce. Salads and pasta dishes, and beer and wine are also available. It's open Sunday through Thursday 11am to 10pm and Friday and Saturday 11am to 11pm.

Finds Gypsy Time

Even if you don't shop, you'll want to wander down Gypsy Alley, one of Canyon Road's older artist enclaves. Though the once-crooked shops and studios have been replaced by sleek galleries, it still retains a row of whimsically painted mail boxes—a great photo op. **Gypsy Baby,** 708 Canyon Rd. no. 4. (© 505/992-0865), sells bright clothes, beaded slippers, and mustang rocking horses, all mindful of the slogan "Born to be spoiled." There is another outpost of this store on Guadalupe Street (© 505/820-1898). **Chiaroscuro Gallery,** 708 Canyon Rd. (© 505/986-9197), presents contemporary fine art and photography. Especially look for Willy Heeks's lovely textured paintings. **Emilia Poochie,** 708 Canyon Rd. no. 3, (© 505/438-9663) likes to "pamper your pooch," and they're not kidding. If you take your doggie in with you, he or she will get treats and water, and can choose from an array of designer beds, dog houses, and games. Monopoly fans should check out the Dog-opoly.

Jackalope ★ *Kids* *Value*   Spread over 7 acres of land, this is a wild place to spend a morning or an afternoon browsing through exotic furnishings from India and Mexico, as well as imported textiles, pottery, jewelry, and clothing. It's a great place to find gifts. Kids will love the prairie-dog village. 2820 Cerrillos Rd. © 505/471-8539.

BELTS

Desert Son of Santa Fe ★ *Moments*   From belts to mules, everything in this narrow little shop is hand-tooled, hand-carved, and/or hand-stamped. As well as leather items, look for cowboy hats and exotic turquoise jewelry. It's a slip of a shop with lots of character, presided over by the artist herself, Mindy Adler. 725 Canyon Rd. © 505/982-9499.

BOOKS

Borders   With close to 200 stores nationwide, this chain provides a broad range of books, music, and videos, and it hosts in-store appearances by authors, musicians, and artists. 500 Montezuma Ave. © 505/954-4707.

Collected Works Bookstore   This is a good downtown book source, with carefully recommended books up front, in case you're not sure what you want, and shelves of Southwest, travel, nature, and other books. 208–B W. San Francisco St. © 505/988-4226.

Horizons—The Discovery Store *Kids*   Here, you'll find adult and children's books, science-oriented games and toys, telescopes, binoculars, and a variety of unusual educational items. I always find interesting gifts for my little nieces in this store. 328 S. Guadalupe St. © 505/983-1554.

Nicholas Potter, Bookseller   This bookstore handles rare and used hardcover books, as well as tickets to many local events. 211 E. Palace Ave. © 505/983-5434.

CRAFTS

Davis Mather Folk Art Gallery   This small shop is a wild animal adventure. You'll find New Mexican animal woodcarvings in shapes of lions, tigers, and bears—even chickens—as well as other folk and Hispanic arts. 141 Lincoln Ave. © 505/983-1660.

Nambe ⚝ *Finds*   The cooking, serving, and decorating pieces here are fashioned from an exquisite sand-cast and handcrafted alloy. These items are also available at the Nambe stores at 104 W. San Francisco St. (© **505/988-3574**) and in Taos at 113A Paseo del Pueblo Norte (© **505/758-8221**). 924 Paseo de Peralta. © **505/988-5528**.

FASHIONS

Back at the Ranch ⚝   This shop has chic western wear and what it calls the "largest selection of handmade cowboy boots in the country." 209 E. Marcy St. © **888/962-6687** or 505/989-8110; www.backattheranch.com.

Judy's Unique Apparel   Judy's has eclectic separates made locally and imported from around the globe. You'll find a wide variety of items here, many at surprisingly reasonable prices. 714 Canyon Rd. © **505/988-5746**.

Origins ⚝ *Moments*   A little like a Guatemalan or Turkish marketplace, this store is packed with wearable art, folk art, and the work of local designers. Look for good buys on ethnic jewelry. Throughout the summer there are trunk shows, which offer opportunities to meet the artists. 135 W. San Francisco St. © **505/988-2323**.

Overland Sheepskin Company   The rich smell of leather will draw you in the door, and possibly hold onto you until you purchase a coat, blazer, hat, or other finely made leather item. 74 E. San Francisco St. © **505/983-4727**.

FOOD

The Chile Shop   This store has too many cheap trinket-like items for me, but many people find some novelty items to take back home. You'll find everything from salsas to cornmeal and tortilla chips. The shop also stocks cookbooks and pottery items. 109 E. Water St. © **505/983-6080**.

Señor Murphy Candy Maker   Unlike any candy store you'll find in other parts of the country—everything here is made with local ingredients. The chile piñon-nut brittle is a taste sensation! Señor Murphy has another shop in the Santa Fe Place mall (© **505/471-8899**). 100 E. San Francisco St. (La Fonda Hotel). © **505/982-0461**.

FURNITURE

Asian Adobe   One of the Santa Fe Railyard district's treats, this shop marries the warmth of Southwestern decor with the austere grace of Asian. You'll find weathered wood tables and trasteros, colorful wall hangings, and moody rugs. 530 S. Guadalupe (in the Gross Kelly Warehouse). © **505/992-6846**.

Casa Nova   Also in the Santa Fe Railyard district, this colorful shop offers everything from dishware to furniture, all in bold and inventive colors. Those with whimsical

---

Kids **More than Dinosaurs**

A timeless adventure tucked into a small space, **Dinosaurs & More,** 102 W. San Francisco St., upstairs in Suite 5 (© **505/988-3299**), caters to children of all ages, even those simply young at heart. Rockhound Charlie Snell has been hunting and collecting fossils, minerals, and meteorites for 25 years. He displays and sells them here, with special attention to children's curiosity. At the back of the shop, kids can participate in the archaeology by brushing and scraping away rock and dust from real dinosaur bones.

---

natures will get happily lost here. 530 S. Guadalupe St. (in the Gross Kelly Warehouse). © 505/983-8558.

Southwest Spanish Craftsmen   The Spanish colonial and Spanish provincial furniture, doors, and home accessories in this store are a bit too elaborate for my tastes, but if you find yourself dreaming of carved wood, this is your place. 314 S. Guadalupe St. © 505/982-1767.

Taos Furniture   Here you'll find classic Southwestern furnishings handcrafted in solid ponderosa pine—both contemporary and traditional. Prices are a little better here than in downtown shops. 217 Galisteo St. © 800/443-3448 or 505/988-1229.

GIFTS & SOUVENIRS
El Nicho _Value_   If you want to take a little piece of Santa Fe home with you, you'll likely find it at this shop. You'll find handcrafted Navajo folk art as well as jewelry and other items by local artisans, including woodcarvings (watch for the *santos!*) by the renowned Ortega family. 227 Don Gaspar Ave. © 505/984-2830.

HATS
Montecristi Custom Hat Works ✦   This fun shop hand-makes fine Panama and felt hats in a range of styles, from Australian outback to Mexican bolero. 322 McKenzie St. © 505/983-9598. www.montecristihats.com.

JEWELRY
Packards ✦   Opened by a notable trader, Al Packard, and later sold to new owners, this store on the plaza is worth checking out to see some of the best jewelry available. You'll also find exquisite rugs and pottery. 61 Old Santa Fe Trail. © 505/983-9241.

Tresa Vorenberg Goldsmiths   You'll find some wildly imaginative designs in this jewelry store, where more than 40 artisans are represented. All items are handcrafted, and custom commissions are welcomed. 656 Canyon Rd. © 505/988-7215.

MALLS & SHOPPING CENTERS
de Vargas Center   There are approximately 50 merchants and restaurants in this mall just northwest of downtown. This is Santa Fe's small, struggling mall. Though there are fewer shops than at Villa Linda, this is where I shop because I don't tend to get the mall phobia I get in the more massive places. Open Monday to Friday 10am to 7pm, Saturday 10am to 6pm, and Sunday noon to 5pm. N. Guadalupe St. and Paseo de Peralta. © 505/982-2655.

Sanbusco Market Center ✦   Unique shops and restaurants occupy this remodeled warehouse near the old Santa Fe Railyard. Many of the shops are overpriced, but it's a fun place to window-shop. Open Monday to Saturday 10am to 6pm, Sunday noon to 5pm. 500 Montezuma St. © 505/989-9390.

Santa Fe Outlets   Outlet shopping fans will enjoy this open-air mall on the south end of town. Anchors include Brooks Brothers, Jones New York, and Coach. 8380 Cerrillos Rd. © 505/474-4000.

Santa Fe Place   Santa Fe's largest mall is near the southwestern city limits, not far from the I-25 on-ramp. If you're from a major city, you'll probably find shopping here very provincial. Anchors include JCPenney, Sears, Dillard's, and Mervyn's. Open Monday to Saturday 10am to 9pm, Sunday noon to 6pm. 4250 Cerrillos Rd. (at Rodeo Rd.). © 505/473-4253.

MARKETS

Santa Fe Farmers' Market *★★* *(Finds)* This farmers' market has everything from fruits, vegetables, and flowers to cheeses, cider, and salsas. Great local treats! If you're an early riser, stroll through and enjoy good coffee, excellent breakfast burritos, and music ranging from violin to fiddle. Open April to mid-November, Saturday and Tuesday 7am to noon. In winter, an abbreviated version takes place indoors. Look for the *Santa Fe Farmers' Market Cookbook,* a compilation of vendor and chef recipes from the region, with vivid photography, to be released in spring 2007. In the Santa Fe Railyard, off Paseo de Peralta, Lot H. *(C)* 505/983-4098.

Tesuque Flea Market *★* *(Moments)* If you're a flea-market hound, you'll be happy to discover this one. More than 500 vendors here sell everything from used cowboy boots (you might find some real beauties) to clothing, jewelry, books, and furniture, all against a big northern New Mexico view. Open March to late November, Friday to Sunday. Vendors start selling at about 7:30am and stay open until about 6:30pm, weather permitting. US 84/285 (about 8 miles north of Santa Fe). No phone.

NATURAL ART

Mineral & Fossil Gallery of Santa Fe You'll find ancient artwork here, from fossils to geodes in all sizes and shapes. There are also natural mineral jewelry and decorative items for the home, including lamps, wall clocks, furniture, art glass, and carvings. Mineral & Fossil also has galleries in Taos, and in Scottsdale and Sedona, Arizona. 127 W. San Francisco St. *(C)* 800/762-9777 or 505/984-1682.

Stone Forest *★* *(Finds)* Proprietor Michael Zimber travels to China and other Asian countries every year to collaborate with the stone carvers who create the fountains, sculptures, and bath fixtures that fill this inventive shop and garden not far from the plaza. 213 St Francis Dr. *(C)* 505/986-8883.

POTTERY & TILES

Artesanos Imports Company *★* *(Moments)* Coming here is like taking a trip south of the border, with all the scents and colors you'd expect on such a journey. You'll find a wide selection of Talavera tile and pottery, as well as light fixtures and many other accessories for the home. There's even an outdoor market where you can buy fountains, sculpture items, and outdoor furniture. A second store is located at 1414 Maclovia St. (*(C)* 505/471-8020). 222 Galisteo St. *(C)* 505/983-1743.

Santa Fe Pottery at Double Take The work of more than 120 master potters from New Mexico and the Southwest is on display here; you'll find everything from mugs and lamps to home furnishings. 323 S. Guadalupe St. *(C)* 505/989-3363.

RUGS

Seret & Sons Rugs, Furnishings, and Architectural Pieces *★* If you're like me and find Middle Eastern decor irresistible, you'll want to wander through this shop. You'll find kilims and Persian and Turkish rugs, as well as some of the Moorish-style ancient doors and furnishings that you see around Santa Fe. 224 Galisteo St. *(C)* 505/988-9151 or 505/983-5008.

9

Santa Fe After Dark

Santa Fe is a city committed to the arts, so it's no surprise that the Santa Fe night scene is dominated by highbrow cultural events, beginning with the world-famous Santa Fe Opera. The club and popular music scene runs a distant second.

Information on all major cultural events can be obtained from the **Santa Fe Convention and Visitors Bureau** (© 800/ 777-CITY or 505/955-6200) or from the **City of Santa Fe Arts Commission** (© 505/955-6707). Current listings are published each Friday in the "Pasatiempo" section of *The New Mexican* (www.santa fenewmexican.com), the city's daily newspaper, and in the *Santa Fe Reporter* (www. sfreporter.com), published every Wednesday.

Nicholas Potter, Bookseller, 211 E. Palace Ave. (© **505/983-5434**); **Candyman,** 851 St. Michaels Dr. (© **505/983-5906**), and **CD Café,** 301 N. Guadalupe (© **505/986-0735**), sell tickets for many events. You can also order by phone from **Ticketmaster** (© **505/883-7800**). Discount tickets may be available on the night of a performance; for example, the opera offers standing-room tickets on the day of the performance. Sales start at 10am.

A variety of free concerts, lectures, and other events are presented in the summer, cosponsored by the City of Santa Fe and the Chamber of Commerce. Many of these musical and cultural events take place on the plaza; check in the "Pasatiempo" section for current listings and information.

1 The Performing Arts

Many performing-arts groups flourish in this city of 65,000. Many of them perform year-round, but others are seasonal. The acclaimed Santa Fe Opera, for instance, has just a 2-month summer season: late June to August.

Note: Many companies noted here perform at locations other than their listed addresses, so check the site of the performance you plan to attend.

MAJOR PERFORMING ARTS COMPANIES
CHORAL GROUPS

Desert Chorale   This 28-member vocal ensemble recruits members from all over the United States. It's nationally recognized for its eclectic blend of Renaissance melodies and modern avant-garde compositions. During summer months, the chorale performs classical concerts at various locations, including the Cathedral Basilica of St. Francis and Loretto Chapel, as well as settings throughout Santa Fe and Albuquerque. The chorale also performs a popular series of Christmas concerts during December. Most concerts begin at 8pm. 811 St. Michael's Dr., Suite 208. © 800/244-4011 or 505/988-2282. www.desertchorale.org. Tickets $10–$50 adults, half price for students under 18.

Sangre de Cristo Chorale   This 34-member ensemble has a repertoire ranging from classical, baroque, and Renaissance works to more-recent folk music and spirituals,

A Home for the Arts

The Santa Fe arts scene's best venue, the **Lensic Performing Arts Center,** 211 W. San Francisco St. ((C) **505/988-7050**), hosts many of the city's major performances, including the Santa Fe Chamber Music Festival and the Santa Fe Symphony Orchestra and Chorus, among others. The setting is wonderfully atmospheric; a multimillion-dollar face-lift brought out the 1931 movie palace's Arabian Nights charm.

much of it presented a cappella. The group gives concerts in Santa Fe, Los Alamos, and Albuquerque. The Christmas dinner concert is extremely popular. P.O. Box 4462. (C) **505/662-5445**. www.sdc-chorale.org. Tickets $15–$60, depending on the season.

Santa Fe Women's Ensemble   This choral group of 13 semiprofessional singers offers classical works sung a cappella as well as with varied instrumental accompaniment during February, March, and December. The "Spring Offering" concert (in Feb and Mar) is held at the Santuario de Guadalupe (100 S. Guadalupe St.), and the "Christmas Offering" concert (in mid-Dec) is held in the Loretto Chapel (Old Santa Fe Trail at Water St.). Call for tickets. 424 Kathryn Place. (C) **505/954-4922**. www.sfwe.org. Tickets $20, $16 students.

OPERA & CLASSICAL MUSIC

Santa Fe Opera ✦✦✦   Many rank the Santa Fe Opera second only to the Metropolitan Opera of New York in the United States. Established in 1957, it consistently attracts famed conductors, directors, and singers. At the height of the season, the company is 500 strong. It's noted for its performances of the classics, little-known works by classical European composers, and American premieres of 21st-century works. The theater, completed for the 1998 season, sits on a wooded hilltop 7 miles north of the city, off US 84/285. It's partially open-air, with open sides. A controversial structure, this new theater replaced the original, built in 1968, but preserved the sweeping curves attuned to the contour of the surrounding terrain. At night, the lights of Los Alamos can still be seen in the distance under clear skies.

The 8-week, 40-performance opera season runs from late June through late August. Highlights for 2007 include a Santa Fe Opera–commissioned world premiere by Chinese-American composer Tan Dun—who won an Oscar for scoring *Crouching Tiger, Hidden Dragon*—titled *Tea: A Mirror of Soul.* Also slated are Puccini's passionate *La Bohème,* Mozart's *Così fan tutte,* Strauss's *Daphne,* and Jean-Philippe Rameau's French baroque masterwork *Platée.* All performances begin at 9pm, until the end of July when performances start at 8:30pm and the last week of the season when performances begin at 8pm. A small screen in front of each seat shows the libretto during the performance. A gift shop has been added, as has additional parking. The entire theater is wheelchair accessible. P.O. Box 2408. (C) **800/280-4654** or 505/986-5900. www.santafe opera.org. Tickets $25–$160; standing room $10; Opening Night Gala $1,700–$3,000. Backstage tours July–Aug Mon–Sat at noon; $5 adults, free for children ages 5–17.

ORCHESTRAL & CHAMBER MUSIC

Santa Fe Pro Musica Chamber Orchestra & Ensemble   This chamber ensemble performs everything from Bach to Vivaldi to contemporary masters. During Holy Week, the Santa Fe Pro Musica presents its annual Mozart and Hayden Concert at the St. Francis Cathedral. Christmas brings candlelight chamber ensemble concerts. Pro Musica's season runs September to May. 430 Manhattan, Suite 10. ☎ **505/988-4640.** www.santafepromusica.com. Tickets $15–$50.

Santa Fe Symphony Orchestra and Chorus   This 60-piece professional symphony orchestra has grown rapidly in stature since its founding in 1984. Matinee and evening performances of classical and popular works are presented in a subscription series at the Lensic Performing Arts Center from October to May. There's a preconcert lecture before each performance. During the spring, the orchestra presents music festivals (call for details). P.O. Box 9692. ☎ **800/480-1319** or 505/983-1414. www.sf-symphony.org. Tickets $15–$55 (5 seating categories).

Serenata of Santa Fe   This professional chamber-music group specializes in bringing lesser-known works of the masters to the concert stage. Concerts are presented September to May. Call for location, dates, and details. P.O. Box 8410. ☎ **505/989-7988.** Tickets $12 general admission, $15–$20 reserved seats.

MUSIC FESTIVALS & CONCERT SERIES

Santa Fe Chamber Music Festival ☆☆   An extraordinary group of international artists comes to Santa Fe every summer for this festival. Its 6-week season runs mid-July to mid-August and is held in the St. Francis Auditorium and the Lensic Performing Arts Center. Each festival features chamber-music masterpieces, new music by a composer in residence, jazz, free youth concerts, preconcert lectures, and open rehearsals. Performances are Monday, Tuesday, Thursday, and Friday at 8pm; Saturday at various evening times; and Sunday at 6pm. Open rehearsals, youth concerts, and preconcert lectures are free to the public. 239 Johnson St., Suite B (P.O. Box 2227). ☎ **505/983-2075** or 505/982-1890 for box office (after June 22). www.sfcmf.org. Tickets $16–$125.

Santa Fe Concert Association   Founded in 1937, this oldest musical organization in northern New Mexico has a September-to-May season that includes approximately 17 annual events. Among them are a "Great Performances" series and an "Adventures" series, both featuring renowned instrumental and vocal soloists and chamber ensembles. The association also hosts special holiday concerts around Christmas. Performances are held at the Lensic Performing Arts Center and the St. Francis Auditorium; tickets are available at the Lensic box office (☎ **505/988-1234**) and at ☎ **800/905-3315** (www.tickets.com) or 505/984-8759. 210 E. Marcy St. (P.O. Box 4626, 87502). Tickets $16–$75.

THEATER COMPANIES

Greer Garson Theater Center   In this graceful, intimate theater, the College of Santa Fe's Performing Arts Department produces four plays annually, with six presentations of each, given between October and May. Usually, the season consists of a comedy, a drama, a musical, and a classic. The college also sponsors studio productions and various contemporary music concerts. College of Santa Fe, 1600 St. Michael's Dr. ☎ **505/473-6511.** www.csf.edu. Tickets $10–$20 adults, $5 students.

Santa Fe Playhouse   Founded in the 1920s, this is the oldest extant theater group in New Mexico. Still performing in a historic adobe theater in the Barrio de Analco, it attracts thousands for its dramas, avant-garde theater, and musical comedy. Its popular one-act melodramas call on the public to boo the sneering villain and swoon for the damsel in distress. 142 E. de Vargas St.. © **505/988-4262**. www.santafeplayhouse.org. Tickets "Pay What You Wish"–$20, depending on the show.

Theater Grottesco ⟨★⟩ ⟨*Finds*⟩   This troupe combines the best of comedy, drama, and dance in its original productions performed each spring and summer in a renovated space at the Center for Contemporary Arts. Expect to be romanced, shocked, intellectually stimulated, and, above all, struck silly with laughter. Look for upcoming winter shows as well. 551 W. Cordova Rd. #8400. © **505/474-8400**. www.theatergrottesco.org. Tickets $10–$25.

Theaterwork Studio ⟨★⟩   A critic for the *Santa Fe New Mexican* called Theaterwork's performance of Chekhov's *Uncle Vanya* "the most rewarding experience I have yet had at a Santa Fe theater." That high praise is well deserved by this community theater that goes out of its way to present refreshing, at times risky, plays. In an intimate theater on the south end of town, Theaterwork offers seven main-stage productions a year, a broad variety including new plays and classics by regional and national playwrights. Expect to see works by such names as Brecht, Shakespeare, and Victor Hugo. 1336 Rufina Circle (mail: P.O. Box 842). © **505/471-1799**. www.theaterwork.org. Tickets $10–$18. Call for performance times.

DANCE COMPANIES

Aspen Santa Fe Ballet ⟨★⟩   In its 11th season, the Aspen Santa Fe Ballet brings classically trained dancers to Santa Fe and Aspen. Performances are an eclectic repertoire by some of the world's foremost choreographers. The season is year-round, with performances at the Lensic Performing Arts Center. 550-B St. Michael's Dr. © 505/983-5591; www.aspensantafeballet.com. Purchase tickets at the Lensic © **505/988-1234**. Tickets $15–$52.

María Benitez Teatro Flamenco ⟨★★⟩ ⟨*Finds*⟩   You won't want to miss this cultural treat. True flamenco is one of the most thrilling of dance forms, displaying the inner spirit and verve of the gypsies of Spanish Andalusia, and María Benitez, trained in Spain, is a fabulous performer. The Benitez Company's "Estampa Flamenca" summer series is performed nightly except Tuesday from late June to early September. The María Benitez Theater at The Lodge at Santa Fe is modern and showy, and yet it's intimate enough so you're immersed in the art. Institute for Spanish Arts, P.O. Box 8418. For tickets call © **888/435-2636**, or the box office (June 16–Sept 3, © **505/982-1237**). www.mariabenitez.com. Tickets $18–$50.

MAJOR CONCERT HALLS & ALL-PURPOSE AUDITORIUMS

Center for Contemporary Arts and Cinematheque   CCA presents the work of internationally, nationally, and regionally known contemporary artists in art exhibitions, dance, new music concerts, poetry readings, performance-art events, theater, and video screenings. The Cinematheque screens films from around the world nightly, with special series presented regularly. CCA's galleries are open daily noon to 7pm. 1050 Old Pecos Trail. © **505/982-1338**. www.ccasantafe.org. Film tickets $8. Art exhibitions are free; performances range broadly in price.

St. Francis Auditorium   This atmospheric music hall, patterned after the interiors of traditional Hispanic mission churches, is noted for its excellent acoustics. The hall hosts a wide variety of musical events, including the Santa Fe Chamber Music Festival in July and August. Museum of Fine Arts, Lincoln and Palace aves. © **505/476-5072**. Ticket prices vary; see above for specific performing-arts companies.

2 The Club & Music Scene

In addition to the clubs and bars listed below, there are a number of hotels whose bars and lounges feature some type of entertainment (see chapter 5.)

COUNTRY, JAZZ & LATIN

Chispa! ☆ A tapas bar with the *chispa* or "spark" of fun entertainment and dancing, this hot spot next to the dining room at El Meson (p. 89) draws locals of all types. Music ranges from guitar duos to jazz combos and Brazilian music, with flamenco dancers performing on some Saturday nights. On tango Tuesdays, locals turn out in their tightest dance clothes to party. The tapas are excellent. Open Tuesday to Saturday. 213 Washington Ave. ℂ 505/983-6756. Cover charge for select performances.

Cowgirl Hall of Fame It's difficult to categorize what goes on in this bar and restaurant, but there's live entertainment nightly. Some nights there's blues guitar, others folk music; you might also find "progressive rock," comedy, or cowboy poetry. In the summer, this is a great place to sit under the stars and listen to music. 319 S. Guadalupe St. ℂ 505/982-2565. No cover for music Sun, Mon, and Wed. Tue and Thurs–Sat $3 cover. Special performances $10.

Eldorado Hotel In a grand lobby-lounge full of fine art, classical guitarists and pianists perform nightly. 309 W. San Francisco St. ℂ **505/988-4455.**

El Farol ☆ This original neighborhood bar of the Canyon Road artists' quarter (its name means "the lantern") is the place to head for local ambience. Its low ceilings and dark-brown walls are home to Santa Fe's largest and most unusual selection of tapas (bar snacks and appetizers). Jazz, swing, folk, and most notably, salsa and flamenco musicians (and dancers)—some of national note—perform most nights. 808 Canyon Rd. ℂ **505/983-9912.** Cover $7.

La Fiesta Lounge ☆ Set in the notable La Fonda hotel on the plaza, this nightclub offers excellent country bands on weekends, with old- and new-timers two-stepping across the floor. This lively lobby bar offers cocktails, an appetizer menu, and live entertainment nightly. It's a great authentic Santa Fe spot. La Fonda Hotel, 110 E. San Francisco St. ℂ **505/982-5511.**

ROCK & DISCO

Catamount Bar and Grille The postcollege crowd hangs out at this bar, where there's live rock and blues music on weekends. Food is served until midnight, and there is also a billiards room. 125 E. Water St. ℂ **505/988-7222.**

3 The Bar Scene

The Dragon Room ☆ A number of years ago, *International Newsweek* named the Dragon Room at The Pink Adobe (p. 92) one of the top 20 bars in the world. The

Snub Out the Smokes

In 2006, smoking in Santa Fe bars and restaurants, including outdoor-dining areas, became illegal. The law was instituted mainly to protect entertainment and hospitality workers from secondhand smoke, but it will likely protect many others as well.

reason is its spirited but comfortable ambience, which draws students, artists, politi-cians, and even an occasional celebrity. The decor theme is dragons, which you'll find carved on the front doors as well as hanging from the ceiling, all within low-lit, aged elegance akin to the Pink Adobe's interior. Live trees also grow through the roof. In addition to the tempting lunch and bar menu, there's always a complimentary bowl of popcorn close at hand. 406 Old Santa Fe Trail. © 505/983-7712.

El Paseo Bar and Grill   You can almost always catch live music at this casual, unpretentious place (yet it's not a "sports bar"). The crowd here is somewhat younger than at most other downtown establishments, and on certain nights, the bar is com-pletely packed. In addition to the open mic night on Tuesdays, a variety of local bands play here regularly—cranking out many types of music, from blues to rock to jazz to bluegrass. 208 Galisteo St. © 505/992-2848. Cover $3–$5 weekends.

Evangelo's   A popular downtown hangout, with tropical decor and a mahogany bar, this place can get raucous at times. It's a bit seedy, but more than 60 varieties of imported beer are available, and pool tables are an added attraction. On Friday and Saturday nights starting at 9pm and Wednesdays at 7:30pm, live bands play (jazz, rock, or reggae). Evangelo's is extremely popular with the local crowd. You'll find your share of business people, artists, and even bikers here. Open Monday to Saturday noon to 1:30am and Sundays until midnight. 200 W. San Francisco St. © 505/982-9014. Cover for special performances only.

Swig ⊛ (Finds   Santa Fe's most happening bar stirs a splash of '60s retro in with a good shot of contemporary chic. The result? A smooth sip of fun. Catering to a broad variety of clientele, this martini bar serves classic and cutting-edge drinks along with delectable small plates of Asian food. The lounge serves until 11pm on weekdays and midnight on weekends, making it one of the few Santa Fe spots for late-night food. A new sushi bar added in 2006 is a great bonus. Open Tuesday through Saturday from 5pm to 2am. 135 W. Palace Ave., level 3. © 505/955-0400.

Vanessie of Santa Fe ⊛   This is unquestionably Santa Fe's most popular piano bar. The talented Doug Montgomery and Charles Tichenor have a loyal local follow-ing. Their repertoire ranges from Bach to Billy Joel, Gershwin to Barry Manilow. They play nightly from 8pm until closing, which could be anywhere from midnight to 2am. There's an extra microphone, so if you're daring (or drunk), you can stand up and accompany the piano and vocals (though this is *not* a karaoke scene). National celebri-ties have even joined in—including Harry Connick, Jr. (and he wasn't even drunk). Vanessie's offers a great bar menu. 434 W. San Francisco St. © 505/982-9966.

10

Excursions from Santa Fe

Native American pueblos and ruins, a national monument and national park, Los Alamos (the A-bomb capital of the United States), and the scenic and fascinating High Road to Taos are all easy day trips from Santa Fe. A longer drive will take you to Chaco Culture National Historic Park (well worth the time) and to Chama, home of the Cumbres & Toltec Scenic Railroad.

1 Exploring the Northern Pueblos

Of the eight northern pueblos, Tesuque, Pojoaque, Nambe, San Ildefonso, San Juan, and Santa Clara are within about 30 miles of Santa Fe. Picuris (San Lorenzo) is on the High Road to Taos (see section 3, below), and Taos Pueblo (p. 208) is just outside the town of Taos.

The six pueblos described in this section can easily be visited in a single day's round-trip from Santa Fe, though I suggest visiting just the two that really give a feel of the ancient lifestyle: San Ildefonso, with its broad plaza, and San Juan, including its arts cooperative. In an easy day trip from Santa Fe you can take in both, with some delicious New Mexican food in Española en route. If you're in the area at a time when you can catch certain rituals, that's when to see some of the other pueblos.

TESUQUE PUEBLO

Tesuque (te-*soo*-keh) Pueblo is about 9 miles north of Santa Fe on US 84/285. You'll know that you're approaching the pueblo when you see a large store near the highway. If you're driving north and you get to the unusual Camel Rock and a large roadside casino, you've missed the pueblo entrance.

The 400 pueblo dwellers at Tesuque are faithful to their traditional religion, rituals, and ceremonies. Excavations confirm that a pueblo has existed here at least since the year A.D. 1200; accordingly, this pueblo is now on the National Register of Historic Places. When you come to the welcome sign at the pueblo, turn right, go a block, and park on the right. You'll see the plaza off to the left. There's not a lot to see; in recent

Pueblo Etiquette

There are personal dwellings and/or important historic sites at pueblos that must be respected as such. Don't climb on the buildings or peek into doors or windows. Don't enter sacred grounds, such as cemeteries and kivas. If you attend a dance or ceremony, remain silent while it is taking place and refrain from applause when it's over. Many pueblos prohibit photography or sketches; others require you to pay a fee for a permit. If you don't respect the privacy of the Native Americans who live at the pueblo, you'll be asked to leave.

years renovation has brought a new look to some of the homes around it. There's a big open area where dances are held and the **San Diego Church,** completed in 2004 on the site of an 1888 structure that burned down recently. It's the fifth church on the pueblo's plaza since 1641. Visitors are asked to remain in this area.

Some Tesuque women are skilled potters; Ignacia Duran's black-and-white and red micaceous pottery and Teresa Tapia's miniatures and pots with animal figures are especially noteworthy. You'll find many crafts at a gallery on the plaza's southeast corner. The **San Diego Feast Day,** which may feature harvest, buffalo, deer, flag, or Comanche dances, is November 12.

The Tesuque Pueblo's address is Route 5, Box 360-T, Santa Fe, NM 87501 (© **505/ 983-2667**). Admission to the pueblo is free; however, there is a $20 charge for use of still cameras; special permission is required for filming, sketching, and painting. The pueblo is open daily from 9am to 5pm. **Camel Rock Casino** (© **505/984-8414**) is open Sunday to Wednesday from 8am to 4am, and Thursday to Saturday for 24 hours; it has a snack bar on the premises.

POJOAQUE PUEBLO

About 6 miles farther north of Tesuque Pueblo on US 84/285, at the junction of NM 502, Pojoaque (Po-*hwa*-keh) Pueblo provides a roadside peek into Pueblo arts. Though small (pop. 200) and without a definable village (more modern dwellings exist now), Pojoaque is important as a center for traveler services; in fact, Pojoaque, in its Tewa form, means "water-drinking place." The historical accounts of the Pojoaque people are sketchy, but we do know that in 1890 smallpox took its toll on the Pojoaque population, forcing most of the pueblo residents to abandon their village. Since the 1930s, the population has gradually increased, and in 1990, a war chief and two war captains were appointed. Today, visitors won't find much to look at, but the **Poeh Cultural Center and Museum,** on US 84/285, operated by the pueblo, features a museum, a cultural center, and artists' studios. It's situated within a complex of adobe buildings, including the three-story Sun Tower. There are frequent artist demonstrations, exhibitions, and, in the warmer months, traditional ceremonial dances. Indigenous pottery, embroidery, silverwork, and beadwork are available for sale at the Pojoaque Pueblo Visitor Center nearby.

If you leave US 84/285 and travel on the frontage road back to where the pueblo actually was, you'll encounter lovely orchards and alfalfa fields backed by desert and mountains. There's a modern community center near the site of the old pueblo and church. On December 12, the annual feast day of **Our Lady of Guadalupe** features a buffalo dance.

The pueblo's address is Route 11, Box 71, Santa Fe, NM 87506 (© **505/455-2278**). The pueblo is open every day during daylight hours. The Poeh Center is at 78 Cities of Gold Rd. (© **505/455-3334**). Admission is free. Open daily 8am to 5pm. Sketching, photography, and filming are prohibited.

NAMBE PUEBLO

If you're still on US 84/285, continue north from Pojoaque about 3 miles until you come to NM 503; turn right, and travel until you see the Bureau of Reclamation sign for Nambe Falls; turn right on NP 101. Approximately 2 miles farther is Nambe ("mound of earth in the corner"), a 700-year-old Tewa-speaking pueblo (pop. 450), with a solar-powered tribal headquarters, at the foot of the Sangre de Cristo range.

Only a few original pueblo buildings remain, including a large round kiva, used today in ceremonies. Pueblo artisans make woven belts, beadwork, and brown micaceous pottery. One of my favorite reasons for visiting this pueblo is to see the small herd of bison that roam on 179 acres set aside for them.

Nambe Falls make a stunning three-tier drop through a cleft in a rock face about 4 miles beyond the pueblo. You can reach the falls via a 15-minute hike on a rocky, clearly marked path that leaves from the picnic area. A recreational site at the reservoir offers fishing, boating (non-motor boats only), hiking, camping, and picnicking. The **Waterfall Dances** on July 4 and the **Saint Francis of Assisi Feast Day** on October 4, which has buffalo and deer dances, are observed at the pueblo. Recent dry weather has caused cancellations; before setting out, call the pueblo.

The address is Route 1, Box 117-BB, Santa Fe, NM 87506 (© **505/455-2036,** or 505/455-2304 for the Ranger Station). Admission to the pueblo is free, but there is a $10 charge for taking photographs. Filming and sketching are prohibited. The pueblo is open daily 8am to 5pm. The recreational site is open 8am to 8pm April 1 through October 1.

SAN ILDEFONSO PUEBLO ★★

Pox Oge, as San Ildefonso Pueblo is called in its own Tewa language, means "place where the water cuts down through," possibly named such because of the way the Rio

Grande cuts through the mountains nearby. Turn left on NM 502 at Pojoaque, and drive about 6 miles to the turnoff. This pueblo has a broad, dusty plaza, with a kiva on one side, ancient dwellings on the other, and a church at the far end. It's nationally famous for its matte-finish, black-on-black pottery, developed by tribeswoman María Martinez in the 1920s. One of the most visited pueblos in northern New Mexico, San Ildefonso attracts more than 20,000 visitors a year.

The San Ildefonsos could best be described as rebellious because this was one of the last pueblos to succumb to the reconquest spearheaded by Don Diego de Vargas in 1692. Within view of the pueblo is the volcanic Black Mesa, a symbol of the San Ildefonso people's strength. Through the years, each time San Ildefonso felt itself threatened by enemy forces, the residents, along with members of other pueblos, would hide out up on the butte, returning to the valley only when starvation set in. Today, a visit to the pueblo is valuable mainly in order to see or buy rich black pottery. A few shops surround the plaza, and there's the **San Ildefonso Pueblo Museum** tucked away in the governor's office beyond the plaza. I especially recommend visiting during ceremonial days. **San Ildefonso Feast Day,** on January 23, features the buffalo and Comanche dances in alternate years. **Corn dances,** held in late August or early September, commemorate a basic element in pueblo life, the importance of fertility in all creatures—humans as well as animals—and plants.

The pueblo has a 4½-acre fishing lake that is surrounded by *bosque* (Spanish for "forest"), open April to October. Picnicking is encouraged, though you may want to look at the sites before you decide to stay; some are nicer than others. Camping is not allowed.

The pueblo's address is Route 5, Box 315A, Santa Fe, NM 87506 (**(℃) 505/455-3549**). The admission charge is $5 per car. The charge for taking photographs is $10; you'll pay $20 to film and $25 to sketch. If you plan to fish, the charge is $10 for adults and $5 for seniors and children under 12 years, but you'll want to call to be sure the lake is open. The pueblo is open in the summer, daily, from 8am to 5pm; call for weekend hours. In the winter, it's open Monday to Friday from 8am to 4:30pm. It's closed for major holidays and tribal events.

OHKAY OWINGE (SAN JUAN PUEBLO) ✍

If you continue north on US 84/285, you will reach San Juan Pueblo, now renamed in Tewa language Ohkay Owinge, via NM 74, a mile off NM 68, about 4 miles north of Española.

The largest (pop. 1,950) and northernmost of the Tewa-speaking pueblos and headquarters of the Eight Northern Indian Pueblos Council, San Juan is on the east side of the Rio Grande—opposite the 1598 site of San Gabriel, the first Spanish settlement west of the Mississippi River and the first capital of New Spain. In 1598, the Spanish, impressed with the openness and helpfulness of the people of San Juan, decided to establish a capital there (it was moved to Santa Fe 10 years later), making San Juan Pueblo the first to be subjected to Spanish colonization. The Indians were generous, providing food, clothing, shelter, and fuel—they even helped sustain the settlement when its leader Conquistador Juan de Oñate became preoccupied with his search for gold and neglected the needs of his people.

The past and present cohabit here. Though many of the tribe members are Catholics, most of the San Juan tribe still practice traditional religious rituals. Thus, two rectangular kivas flank the church in the main plaza, and *caciques* (pueblo priests) share power with civil authorities. The annual **San Juan Fiesta** is held June 23 and 24;

The Great Pueblo Revolt

By the 17th century, the Spanish subjugation of the Native Americans in the region had left them virtual slaves, forced to provide corn, venison, cloth, and labor. They were forced to participate in Spanish religious ceremonies and to abandon their own religious practices. Under no circumstances were their ceremonies allowed; those caught participating in them were punished. In 1676, several Puebloans were accused of sorcery and jailed in Santa Fe. Later they were led to the plaza, where they were flogged or hanged. This incident became a turning point in Indian–Spanish relations, generating an overwhelming feeling of rage in the community. One of the accused, a San Juan Pueblo Indian named Po'Pay, became a leader in the Great Pueblo Revolt of 1680, which led to freedom from Spanish rule for 12 years.

it features buffalo and Comanche dances. Another annual ceremony is the **turtle dance** on December 26. The **Matachine dance,** performed here Christmas Day, vividly depicts the subjugation of the Native Americans by the Catholic Spaniards (p. 294).

The address of the pueblo is P.O. Box 1099, San Juan Pueblo, NM 87566 (© **505/ 852-4400** or 505/852-4210). Admission is free. Photography or sketching may be allowed with prior permission from the governor's office. For information, call the number above. The charge for fishing is $8 for adults and $5 for children and seniors. The pueblo is open every day during daylight hours.

The **Eight Northern Indian Pueblos Council** (© **505/747-1593**) is a sort of chamber of commerce and social-service agency.

A crafts shop, **Ohkay Owinge Arts and Crafts Cooperative** (© **505/852-2372**), specializes in local wares. This is a fine place to seek out San Juan's distinctive red pottery, a lustrous ceramic incised with traditional geometric symbols. Also displayed for sale are seed, turquoise, and silver jewelry; wood and stone carvings; indigenous clothing and weavings; embroidery; and paintings. Artisans often work on the premises, allowing visitors to watch. The co-op is open Monday through Saturday 9am to 4:30pm in winter, until 5pm in summer (but is closed San Juan Feast Day, June 24). **Sunrise Crafts,** another crafts shop, is to the right of the co-op. There, you'll find one-of-a-kind hand-crafted pipes, beadwork, and burned and painted gourds.

Fishing and picnicking are encouraged at the **San Juan Tribal Lakes,** open year-round. **Ohkay Casino** (© **505/747-1668**) offers table games and slot machines, as well as live music nightly Tuesday through Saturday. It's open 24 hours on weekends.

SANTA CLARA PUEBLO

Close to Española (on NM 5), Santa Clara, with a population of about 1,800, is one of the largest pueblos. You'll see the village sprawling across the river basin near the beautiful Black Mesa, rows of tract homes surrounding an adobe central area. Although it's in an incredible setting, the pueblo itself is not much to see; however, a trip through it will give a real feel for the contemporary lives of these people. Though stories vary, the Santa Clarans teach their children that their ancestors once lived in cliffside dwellings named Puye and migrated down to the river bottom in the 13th century. This pueblo is noted for its language program. Artisan elders work with children to teach them their native Tewa language, on the brink of extinction because so many now speak English. This pueblo is also the home of noted potter Nancy Youngblood, who comes from a long line of famous potters and now does alluring contemporary work.

Follow the main route to the old village, where you come to the visitor center, also known as the neighborhood center. There you can get directions to small shops that sell distinctive black incised Santa Clara pottery, red burnished pottery, baskets, and other crafts. One stunning sight here is the cemetery. Stop on the west side of the church and look over the 4-foot wall. It's a primitive site, with plain wooden crosses and some graves adorned with plastic flowers.

There are corn and harvest dances on **Santa Clara Feast Day** (Aug 12); information on other special days (including the corn or harvest dances, as well as children's dances) can be obtained from the pueblo office.

The famed **Puye Cliff Dwellings** (see below) are on the Santa Clara reservation.

The pueblo's address is P.O. Box 580, Española, NM 87532 (© **505/753-7326**). Admission is free. The charge for taking photographs is $5; filming and sketching are not allowed. The pueblo is open every day from 9am to 4pm; the visitor center is open Monday to Friday from 8am to 4:30pm.

PUYE CLIFF DWELLINGS

Well worth visiting, the Puye Cliff Dwellings offer a view of centuries of culture so well preserved you can almost hear ancient life clamoring around you. Unfortunately, recent fires devastated the area, so Santa Clara has closed the ruins and recreation area indefinitely. Call before setting out.

If you do get to see them, you'll first encounter dwellings believed to have been built around 1450. Above, on a 200-foot cliff face, are dwellings dating from 1200. By 1540, this community's population was at its height, and Puye was the center for a number of villages of the Pajarito Plateau. Today, this settlement, which typifies Pajaritan culture in the placement of its houses and its symbolic decorations, is a series of rooms and caves reached by sturdy ladders and steps that visitors can climb up and down, clambering in and out of the homes.

If you would like to visit the cliff dwellings, call © **505/753-7326** for opening times and admissions information (before the area was closed, admission was $6 for adults, $5 for children and seniors). To reach Puye: At the intersection of NM 502 and NM 30, head north for 4 miles to Indian Road 601. Travel this paved road for 7 miles.

2 Los Alamos & the Ancient Cliff Dwellings of Bandelier National Monument

Pueblo tribes lived in the rugged Los Alamos area for well over 1,000 years, and an exclusive boys' school operated atop the 7,300-foot plateau from 1918 to 1943. Then, the **Los Alamos National Laboratory** was established here in secrecy, code-named Site Y of the Manhattan Project, the hush-hush wartime program that developed the world's first atomic bombs.

Project director J. Robert Oppenheimer, later succeeded by Norris E. Bradbury, worked along with thousands of scientists, engineers, and technicians in research, development, and production of those early weapons. Today, more than 13,000 people work at the Los Alamos National Laboratory, making it one of the largest employers in northern New Mexico. Operated from the beginning by the University of California, currently under a contract through the U.S. Department of Energy, its 2,800 individual facilities and 42 separate technical areas occupy 36 square miles of mesa-top land.

The laboratory is known today as one of the world's foremost scientific institutions. While primarily focused on nuclear weapons research—the Trident and Minuteman strategic warheads were designed here, for example—it has many other interdisciplinary research programs, including international nuclear safeguards and nonproliferation, space, and atmospheric studies; supercomputing; theoretical physics; biomedical and materials science; and environmental restoration.

Current plans call on Los Alamos National Laboratory, in 2007, to begin building a limited number of replacement plutonium pits for use in the enduring U.S. nuclear weapons stockpile. The lab has the only plutonium-processing facility in the United States that is capable of producing those components.

ORIENTATION/USEFUL INFORMATION

Los Alamos is about 35 miles west of Santa Fe and about 65 miles southwest of Taos. From Santa Fe, take US 84/285 north approximately 16 miles to the Pojoaque junction, then turn west on NM 502. Driving time is only about 50 minutes.

Los Alamos is a town of 18,000, spread over the colorful, finger-like mesas of the Pajarito Plateau, between the Jemez Mountains and the Rio Grande Valley. As NM 502 enters Los Alamos from Santa Fe, it follows Trinity Drive, where accommodations, restaurants, and other services are located. Central Avenue parallels Trinity Drive and has restaurants, galleries, and shops, as well as the **Los Alamos Historical Museum** (1921 Juniper St.; © **505/662-4493;** free) and the **Bradbury Science Museum** (15th St. and Central Ave.; © **505/667-4444;** free). In the spring of 2000, the town was evacuated due to a forest fire that destroyed 400 families' homes. Though no lives were lost, the appearance of Los Alamos and particularly the forest surrounding it—47,000 acres of which burned—were forever changed.

The **Los Alamos Chamber of Commerce,** P.O. Box 460, Los Alamos, NM 87544 (© **505/662-8105;** fax 505/662-8399), runs a visitor center that is open Monday to Saturday 9am to 5pm and Sunday 10am to 3pm. It's at 109 Central Park Sq. (across from the Bradbury Science Museum).

EVENTS

The Los Alamos events schedule includes a **Sports Skiesta** in mid-March; **arts-and-crafts fairs** in May, August, and November; a **county fair, rodeo,** and **arts festival** in August; and a **triathlon** in August/September.

WHAT TO SEE & DO

Aside from the sights described below, Los Alamos offers the **Pajarito Mountain ski area,** Camp May Road (P.O. Box 155), Los Alamos, NM 87544 (© **505/662-5725**), with five chairlifts—it's only open on Friday through Sunday and federal holidays. It's an outstanding ski area that rarely gets crowded; many trails are steep and have moguls. Los Alamos also offers the **Los Alamos Golf Course,** 4250 Diamond Dr. (© **505/662-8139**), at the edge of town, where greens fees are around $25, and the **Larry R. Walkup Aquatic Center,** 2760 Canyon Rd. (© **505/662-8170**), the highest-altitude indoor Olympic-size swimming pool in the United States. Not far from downtown is an outdoor ice-skating rink, with a snack bar and skate rentals, open Thanksgiving to late February (© **505/662-4500**). It's at 4475 West Rd. (take Trinity

Dr. to Diamond St., turn left, and watch for the sign on your right). There are no outstanding restaurants in Los Alamos, but if you get hungry, you can stop at the **Blue Window,** 800 Trinity Dr. (✆ **505/662-6305**), a country-style restaurant serving pasta, sandwiches, and salads, with a view of the Sangre de Cristo Mountains. The Chamber of Commerce has maps for self-guided historical walking tours, and you can find self-guided driving-tour tapes at stores and hotels around town.

The Art Center at Fuller Lodge   This is a public showcase for work by visual artists from northern New Mexico and the surrounding region. Two annual arts-and-crafts fairs are also held here—in August and October. The gallery shop sells local crafts at good prices.

In the same building is the **Los Alamos Arts Council** (✆ **505/663-0477**), a multidisciplinary organization that sponsors an art fair in May, as well as evening and noontime cultural programs.

2132 Central Ave., Los Alamos. ✆ 505/662-9331. www.artfulnm.org. Free admission. Mon–Sat 10am–4pm.

Black Hole (Finds)   This store/museum is an engineer's dream world, a creative photographer's heaven, and a Felix Unger nightmare. Owned and run by Edward Grothus, it's an old grocery store packed to the ceiling with the remains of the nuclear age, from Geiger counters to giant Waring blenders. If you go, be sure to visit with Grothus. He'll point out an A-frame building next door that he's christened the "First Church of High Technology," where he says a "critical mass" each Sunday. In this business for over 50 years, Grothus has been written about in *Wired* magazine and has supplied props for the movies *Silkwood, Earth II,* and *The Manhattan Project.*

4015 Arkansas, Los Alamos. ✆ 505/662-5053. Free admission. Mon–Sat 10am–5pm.

Bradbury Science Museum 🔆   This is a great place to get acquainted with what goes on at a weapons production facility after nuclear proliferation. Although the museum is run by Los Alamos National Laboratory, which definitely puts a positive spin on the business of producing weapons, it's a fascinating place to explore and it includes more than 35 hands-on exhibits.

Begin in the History Gallery, where you'll learn about the evolution of the site from the Los Alamos Ranch School days through the Manhattan Project to the present, including a 1939 letter from Albert Einstein to President Franklin D. Roosevelt, suggesting research into uranium as a new and important source of energy. Next, move into the Research and Technology Gallery, where you can see work that's been done on the Human Genome Project, including a computer map of human DNA. You can try out a laser and learn about the workings of a particle accelerator. Meanwhile, listen for announcement of the film *The Town That Never Was,* an 18-minute presentation on this community that grew up shrouded in secrecy (shown in the auditorium). Further exploration will take you to the Defense Gallery, where you can test the heaviness of plutonium against that of other substances, see an actual 5-ton Little Boy nuclear bomb (like the one dropped on Hiroshima), and see firsthand how Los Alamos conducts worldwide surveillance of nuclear explosions. The museum also has an exhibit on national defense. It presents issues related to nuclear weapons: why we have them, how they work, how scientists ensure that aging weapons will still work, what treaties govern them, and what environmental problem sites resulted from their production. It includes a 16-minute film, computer-based activities for visitors, and displays of bombs, a cruise missile, and warhead casings.

15th St. and Central Ave., Los Alamos. Ⓒ 505/667-4444. Free admission. Tues–Sat 10am–5pm; Sun–Mon 1–5pm. Closed Thanksgiving, Christmas, New Year's Day.

Los Alamos Historical Museum ⭐ Fuller Lodge, a massive vertical-log building built by John Gaw Meem in 1928, is well worth the visit. The log work is intricate and artistic, and the feel of the old place is warm and majestic. It once housed the dining and recreation hall for the Los Alamos Ranch School for boys and is now a National Historic Landmark. Its current occupants include the museum office and research archives and The Art Center at Fuller Lodge (see above). The museum, located in the small log-and-stone building to the north of Fuller Lodge, depicts area history from prehistoric cliff dwellers to the present. Exhibits range from Native American artifacts to school memorabilia and an excellent Manhattan Project exhibit that offers a more realistic view of the devastation resulting from use of atomic bombs than is offered at the Bradbury Science Museum.

1921 Juniper St., Los Alamos. Ⓒ 505/662-4493. Free admission. Summer Mon–Sat 9:30am–4:30pm, Sun 11am–5pm; winter Mon–Sat 10am–4pm, Sun 1–4pm. Closed Thanksgiving, Dec 25, Easter.

NEARBY
Bandelier National Monument ⭐⭐⭐ Less than 15 miles south of Los Alamos along NM 4, this National Park Service area contains stunningly preserved ruins of the ancient cliff-dwelling ancestral Puebloan (Anasazi) culture within 46 square miles of canyon-and-mesa wilderness. The national monument is named after the Swiss-American archaeologist Adolph Bandelier, who explored here in the 1880s. During busy summer months, head out early; there can be a waiting line for cars to park.

After an orientation stop at the visitor center and museum to learn about the culture that flourished here between 1100 and 1550, most visitors follow a trail along Frijoles Creek to the principal ruins. The pueblo site, including an underground kiva, has been stabilized. The biggest thrill for most folks is climbing hardy ponderosa pine ladders to visit an alcove—140 feet above the canyon floor—that was once home to prehistoric people. Tours are self-guided or led by a National Park Service ranger. Be aware that dogs are not allowed on trails.

On summer nights, rangers offer campfire talks about the history, culture, and geology of the area. The guided night walks offered some summer evenings reveal a different, spooky aspect of the ruins and cave houses, outlined in the two-dimensional chiaroscuro of the thin light from the starry sky. During the day, nature programs are sometimes offered for adults and children. The small museum at the visitor center displays artifacts found in the area.

Elsewhere in the monument area, 70 miles of maintained trails lead to more tribal ruins, waterfalls, and wildlife habitats. However, a recent fire has decimated parts of this area, so periodic closings will take place in order to allow the land to reforest.

The separate **Tsankawi** section, reached by an ancient 2-mile trail close to **White Rock,** has a large unexcavated ruin on a high mesa overlooking the Rio Grande Valley. The town of White Rock, about 10 miles southeast of Los Alamos on NM 4, offers spectacular panoramas of the river valley in the direction of Santa Fe; the **White Rock Overlook** is a great picnic spot. Within Bandelier, areas have been set aside for picnicking and camping.

NM 4 (HCR 1, Box 1, Suite 15, Los Alamos). Ⓒ 505/672-3861, ext 517. www.nps.gov/band. Admission $12 per vehicle. Open daily during daylight hours. No pets allowed on trails. Closed Christmas, New Year's Day.

Inside a Volcano

While you're in the area, check out the **Valles Caldera National Preserve,** past Bandelier National Monument on NM 4, beginning about 15 miles from Los Alamos. The reserve is all that remains of a volcanic caldera created by a collapse after eruptions nearly a million years ago. When the mountain spewed ashes and dust as far away as Kansas and Nebraska, its underground magma chambers collapsed, forming this great valley—one of the largest volcanic calderas in the world. Lava domes that pushed up after the collapse obstruct a full view across the expanse, but the beauty of the place is still within grasp. Visitors have many guided options for exploring the preserve, from sleigh rides in winter to fly-fishing in summer. For more information, check out www.vallescaldera.gov.

3 Along the High Road to Taos ★★

Unless you're in a hurry to get from Santa Fe to Taos, the High Road—also called the Mountain Road or the King's Road—is by far the most fascinating route between the two cities. It begins in lowlands of mystically formed pink and yellow stone, passing by apple and peach orchards and chile farms in the weaving village of **Chimayo.** Then it climbs toward the highlands to the village of **Cordova,** known for its woodcarvers, and higher still to **Truchas,** a renegade arts town where Hispanic traditions and ways of life continue much as they did a century ago. Though I've described this tour from south to north, the most scenic way to see it is from north to south, when you travel down off the mountains rather than up into them. This way, you see more expansive views.

CHIMAYO

About 28 miles north of Santa Fe on NM 76/285 is the historic weaving center of Chimayo. It's approximately 16 miles past the Pojoaque junction, at the junction of NM 520 and NM 76 via NM 503. In this small village, families still maintain the tradition of crafting hand-woven textiles initiated by their ancestors seven generations ago, in the early 1800s. One such family is the Ortegas, and **Ortega's Weaving Shop** (© 505/351-4215) and **Galeria Ortega** ★ (© 505/351-2288), both at the corner of NM 520 and NM 76, are fine places to take a close look at this ancient craft. A more humble spot is **Trujillo Weavings** (© 505/351-4457) on NM 76. If you're lucky enough to find the proprietors in, you might get a weaving history lesson. You can see an 80-year-old loom and a 100-year-old shuttle carved from apricot wood. The weavings you'll find are some of the best of the Rio Grande style, with rich patterns, many made from naturally dyed wool. Also on display are some fine Cordova woodcarvings. Near the Santuario de Chimayo, just off the plaza, look for the **High Road Marketplace** ★ (© 866/343-5381 or 505/351-1078), an artists' co-op gallery with a variety of offerings ranging from jewelry to landscape paintings to a broad range of crosses made from tin, rusted metal, and nails. Also check out **Centinela Traditional Arts,** 946 NM 76 (© 877/351-2180 or 505/351-2180), for a good selection of rugs made by weavers from up and down the Rio Grande Valley. Watch for the chenille shawls by Scarlet Rose.

One of the best places to shop in Chimayo, **Chimayo Trading and Mercantile** *GF* (*(C)* **505/351-4566**), on Highway 76, is a richly cluttered store carrying local arts and crafts as well as select imports. It has a good selection of kachinas and Hopi corn maidens, as well as specialty items such as elaborately beaded cow skulls. Look for George Zarolinski's "smoked porcelain."

Many people come to Chimayo to visit **El Santuario de Nuestro Señor de Esquipulas (the Shrine of Our Lord of Esquipulas)** *GFGF*, better known simply as "El Santuario de Chimayo." Ascribed with miraculous powers of healing, this church has attracted thousands of pilgrims since its construction in 1814 to 1816. Up to 30,000 people participate in the annual Good Friday pilgrimage, many of them walking from as far away as Albuquerque.

Although only the earth in the anteroom beside the altar is presumed to have the gift of healing powers, the entire shrine radiates true serenity. A National Historic Landmark, the church has five beautiful *reredos* (panels of sacred paintings)—one behind the main altar and two on each side of the nave. Each year during the fourth weekend in July, the military exploits of the 9th-century Spanish saint Santiago are celebrated in a weekend fiesta, including the historic play *Los Moros y Los Cristianos (The Moors and the Christians).*

A good place to stop for a quick bite, **Leona's Restaurante de Chimayo** (*(C)* **505/351-4569**) is right next door to the Santuario de Chimayo. Leona herself presides over this little taco and burrito stand with plastic tables inside and, during warm months, out. Leona has gained national fame for her flavored tortilla—such delicacies as raspberry and chocolate really are tasty. Burritos and soft tacos made with chicken, beef, or veggie-style with beans will definitely tide you over en route to Taos or Santa Fe. Open 11am to 5pm, closed Tuesday and Wednesday.

Nearby **Santa Cruz Lake** provides water for Chimayo Valley farms and also offers a recreation site for trout fishing and camping at the edge of the Pecos Wilderness. During busy summer months, trash might litter its shores. To reach the lake from Chimayo, drive 2 miles south on NM 520, then turn east on NM 503 and travel 4 miles.

WHERE TO STAY

Casa Escondida *GF*   On the outskirts of Chimayo, this inn offers a lovely retreat and a good home base for exploring the Sangre de Cristo Mountains and their many soulful farming villages. This hacienda-feeling place has a cozy living room with a large kiva fireplace. Decor is simple and classic, with Mission-style furniture lending a colonial feel. The breakfast room is a sunny atrium with French doors that open out in summer to a grassy yard spotted with apricot trees. The rooms are varied; all of my favorites are within the main house. The Sun Room catches all that passionate northern New Mexico sun upon its red brick floors and on its private flagstone patio as well. It has an elegant feel and connects with a smaller room, so it's a good choice for families. The Vista is on the second story. Its dormer windows give it an oddly shaped roofline. It has a wrought-iron queen-size bed as well a twin, and it opens out onto a large deck offering spectacular sunset views. The casita adjacent to the main house has a kiva fireplace, a stove, and a minirefrigerator, as well as nice meadow views.

P.O. Box 142, Chimayo, NM 87522. *(C)* **800/643-7201** or 505/351-4805. Fax 505/351-2575. www.casaescondida.com. 8 units. $95–$155 double. Rates include full breakfast. MC, V. Pets welcome for a small fee; prearrangement required. **Amenities:** Jacuzzi; in-room massage.

Fun Fact **High on Art**

If you really like art and want to meet artists, check out one of the **Art Studio Tours** held in the fall in the region. Artists spend months preparing their best work, and then open their doors to visitors. Wares range from pottery and paintings to furniture and woodcarvings to ristras and dried-flower arrangements. The most notable tour is the **High Road Studio Art Tour** (www.high roadnewmexico.com) in mid- to late September. If you're not in the region during that time, watch the newspapers (such as the *Santa Fe New Mexican's* Friday edition "Pasatiempo") for notices of other art-studio tours. Good ones are held in **Galisteo** (in mid-Oct; www.galisteostudiotour.com); **Abiquiu** (early Sept; www.abiquiustudiotour.org); **El Rito** (mid-Oct; www.elritolibrary.org); and **Dixon** (early Nov; www.dixonarts.org). If you're not here during those times, you can still visit many of the galleries listed on the websites.

WHERE TO DINE

Restaurante Rancho de Chimayo ☆ NEW MEXICAN   For as long as I can remember, my family and many of my friends' families have scheduled trips into northern New Mexico to coincide with lunch or dinner at this fun restaurant. In an adobe home built by Hermenegildo Jaramillo in the 1880s, it's now run as a restaurant by his descendants. Unfortunately, over the years the restaurant has become so famous that tour buses now stop here. However, the food has suffered only a little. In the warmer months, request to dine on the terraced patio. During winter, you'll be seated in one of a number of cozy rooms with thick viga ceilings. The food is native New Mexican, prepared from generations-old Jaramillo family recipes. You can't go wrong with the enchiladas, served layered, northern New Mexico style, rather than rolled. For variety you might want to try the *combinación picante* (carne adovada, tamale, enchilada, beans, and posole). Each plate comes with two *sopaipillas*. With a little honey, who needs dessert? The full bar serves delicious margaritas.

300 County Rd. 98 (¼ mile west of the Santuario), Chimayo, NM 87522 (CTR 98). (℃ **505/351-4444.** Reservations recommended. Lunch $7.50–$13; dinner $10–$18. AE, DC, DISC, MC, V. Daily May–Oct 11:30am–9pm; Sat–Sun breakfast 8:30–10:30am. Closed Mon Nov 1–Apr 30.

CORDOVA

Just as Chimayo is famous for its weaving, the village of Cordova, about 7 miles east on NM 76, is noted for its woodcarving. It's easy to whiz by this village, nestled below the High Road, but don't. Just a short way through this truly traditional northern New Mexico town is a gem: **The Castillo Gallery** ☆ (℃ **505/351-4067**), a mile into the village of Cordova, carries moody and colorful acrylic paintings by Paula Castillo, as well as her metal welded sculptures. It also carries the work of Terry Enseñat Mulert, whose contemporary woodcarvings are treasures of the high country. En route to the Castillo, you may want to stop in at two other local carvers' galleries. The first you'll come to is that of **Sabinita Lopez Ortiz;** the second belongs to her cousin, **Gloria Ortiz.** Both are descendants of the well-noted José Dolores Lopez. Carved from cedar wood and aspen, the works range from simple statues of saints *(santos)* to elaborate scenes of birds.

TRUCHAS

Robert Redford's 1988 movie *The Milagro Beanfield War* featured the town of Truchas (which means "trout"). A former Spanish colonial outpost built on top of an 8,000-foot mesa, 4 miles east of Cordova, it was chosen as the site for the film in part because traditional Hispanic culture is still very much in evidence. Subsistence farming is prevalent here. The scenery is spectacular: 13,101-foot Truchas Peak dominates one side of the mesa, and the broad Rio Grande Valley dominates the other.

Be sure to find your way into **The Cordovas' Handweaving Workshop** (© **505/ 689-2437**). In the center of town, this tiny shop is run by Harry Cordova, a fourth-generation weaver with a unique style. His works tend to be simpler than many Rio Grande weavings, utilizing mainly stripes in the designs.

Just down the road from Cordovas' is **Hand Artes Gallery** (© **800/689-2441** or 505/689-2443), a definite surprise in this remote region. Here you'll find an array of contemporary as well as representational art from noted regional artists. Look for Sheila Keeffe's worldly painted panels, and Norbert Voelkel's colorful paintings and monoprints.

About 6 miles east of Truchas on NM 76 is the small town of **Las Trampas,** noted for its 1780 **San José de Gracia Church,** which, with its thick walls and elegant lines, might possibly be the most beautiful of all New Mexico churches built during the Spanish colonial period.

PICURIS (SAN LORENZO) PUEBLO

Near the regional education center of Peñasco, about 24 miles from Chimayo, near the intersection of NM 75 and NM 76, is the Picuris (San Lorenzo) Pueblo (© **505/ 587-2519**). The 375 citizens of this 15,000-acre mountain pueblo, native Tewa speakers, consider themselves a sovereign nation: Their forebears never made a treaty with any foreign country, including the United States. Thus, they observe a traditional form of tribal council government. A few of the original mud-and-stone houses still stand, as does a lovely church. A striking aboveground ceremonial kiva called "the Roundhouse," built at least 700 years ago, and some historic excavated kivas and storerooms are on a hill above the pueblo and are open to visitors. The **annual feast days** at San Lorenzo Church are August 9 and 10.

The people here are modern enough to have fully computerized their public showcase operations as Picuris Tribal Enterprises. Besides running the Hotel Santa Fe in the state capital, they own the **Picuris Pueblo Museum and Visitor's Center,** where weaving, beadwork, and distinctive reddish-brown clay cooking pottery are exhibited daily 9am to 6pm. Self-guided tours through the old village ruins begin at the museum and cost $5; the camera fee is $6; sketching and video camera fees are $25. There's also an information center, crafts shop, and restaurant. Fishing permits ($11 for adults, $8 for seniors, and $7 for children) are available, as are permits to camp ($8) at Tu-Tah Lake, which is regularly stocked with trout.

You might want to plan your High Road trip to include a visit to **Sugar Nymphs Bistro** ★★, 15046 NM 75 (© **505/587-0311**) for some inventive food. Inside a vintage theater in the little farming village of Peñasco, Kai Harper, former executive chef at Greens in San Francisco, prepares contemporary cuisine. Lunch brings imaginative pizza, salads, and burgers, while dinner includes a full range of entrees. Pork tenderloin with chipotle cream sauce is one favorite. In summer, the cafe is open Thursday to Saturday 11:30am to 3pm and 5:30 to 7:30 or 8pm, with Sunday brunch 11am to

2pm (from July to September, this schedule extends to include lunch Monday through Wednesday). Since it's a country place, this schedule isn't reliable. Call ahead to be sure it's open. In winter, the schedule will be abbreviated.

About a mile east of Peñasco on NM 75 is **Vadito,** the former center for a conservative Catholic brotherhood, the Penitentes, early in the 20th century. You'll see a small adobe chapel on the left. Also watch for Penitente crosses scattered about the area, often on hilltops.

DIXON & EMBUDO

Taos is about 24 miles north of Peñasco via NM 518, but day-trippers from Santa Fe can loop back to the capital by taking NM 75 west from Picuris Pueblo. Dixon, approximately 12 miles west of Picuris, and its twin village Embudo, a mile farther on NM 68 at the Rio Grande, are home to many artists and craftspeople who exhibit their works during the annual **autumn show** sponsored by the Dixon Arts Association. If you get to Embudo at mealtime, stop in at **Embudo Station** (© 800/852-4707 or 505/852-4707), a restaurant right on the banks of the Rio Grande. From mid-April to October—the only time it's open—you can sit on the patio under giant cottonwoods and sip the restaurant's own microbrewed beer (try the green-chile ale, its most celebrated) and signature wines while watching the peaceful Rio flow by. The specialty here is Southwestern food, but you'll find other tantalizing tastes as well. Try the rainbow trout roasted on a cedar plank. The restaurant is generally open Tuesday to Sunday noon to 9pm, but call before making plans. It's especially known for its Jazz on Sunday, an affair that PBS once featured.

To taste more of the local grape, follow signs to **La Chiripada Winery** (© 505/579-4437), whose product is surprisingly good, especially to those who don't know that New Mexico has a long winemaking history. Local pottery is also sold in the tasting room. The winery is open Monday to Saturday 10am to 5pm, Sunday noon to 5pm.

Two more small villages lie in the Rio Grande Valley at 6-mile intervals south of Embudo on NM 68. **Velarde** is a fruit-growing center; in season, the road here is lined with stands selling fresh fruit or crimson chile ristras and wreaths of native plants. **Alcalde** is the site of Los Luceros, an early-17th-century home that has been refurbished as an arts and history center. Also in the area and worth checking out is **Los Luceros Winery** (© 505-852-1085), which makes wine in a straw-bale winery. The unique **Dance of the Matachines,** a Moorish-style ritual brought from Spain, is performed here on holidays and feast days (p. 294).

ESPAÑOLA

The commercial center of Española (pop. 7,000) no longer has the railroad that led to its establishment in the 1880s, but it may have New Mexico's greatest concentration of **low riders.** These are late-model customized cars, so called because their suspension leaves them sitting quite close to the ground. For details, see the box below.

Sights of interest in Española include the **Bond House Museum** (© 505/747-8535), a Victorian-era adobe home that exhibits local history and art, and the **Santa Cruz Church,** built in 1733 and renovated in 1979, which houses many fine examples of Spanish colonial religious art. The **Convento,** built to resemble a colonial cathedral, on the Española Plaza (at the junction of NM 30 and US 84), houses a variety of shops, including a trading post and an antiques gallery, as well as a display room for the Historical Society. Major events include the July **Fiesta de Oñate,** commemorating the valley's founding in 1596; the October **Tri-Cultural Art Festival** on the

> (*Fun Fact* **Lowriders: Car Art**
>
> While cruising Española's main drag, don't drop your jaw if you see the front of a car raise up off the ground and then sink down again, or if you witness another that appears to be scraping its underbelly on the pavement. These novelties are part of a car culture that thrives in northern New Mexico. Traditionally, the owners use late-model cars, which they soup up with such novelties as elaborate chrome, metal chain steering wheels, even portraits of Our Lady of Guadalupe painted on the hood. If you're interested in seeing the "Custom Car and Truck Show" put on by local car clubs (and often cosponsored by local casinos), call the Española Valley Chamber of Commerce for information (© **505/753-2831**).

Northern New Mexico Community College campus; the weeklong **Summer Solstice** celebration staged in June by the nearby Ram Dass Puri ashram of the Sikhs (© **888/ 346-2420** or 505/367-1310); and **Peace Prayer Day,** an outdoor festival in mid-June—featuring art, music, food, guest speakers, and more—in the Jemez Mountains (© **877/707-3223**).

Complete information on Española and the vicinity can be obtained from the **Española Valley Chamber of Commerce,** 710 Paseo de Onate, Española, NM 87532 (© **505/753-2831**).

If you admire the work of Georgia O'Keeffe, try to plan a short trip to **Abiquiu,** a tiny town at a bend of the Rio Chama, 14 miles south of Ghost Ranch and 22 miles north of Española on US 84. When you see the surrounding terrain, it will be clear that this was the inspiration for many of her startling landscapes. **O'Keeffe's adobe home** ⊛ (where she lived and painted) is open for public tours. However, a reservation must be made in advance; the fee for adults is $25 for a 1-hour tour. A number of tours are given each week—on Tuesday, Thursday, and Friday (Mar–Nov only)—and a limited number of people are accepted per tour. Visitors are not permitted to take pictures. Fortunately, O'Keeffe's home remains as it was when she lived there (until 1986). Call several months in advance for reservations (© **505/685-4539**).

If you're in the area and need gas for your car or a snack for yourself (or goodies for a picnic), stop in at **Bode's** (on U.S. 84 in Abiquiu; © **505/685-4422**). The general store for the area, this place has shovels and irrigation boots, and better yet, cold drinks, gourmet sandwiches, and other deli items—even a hearty green chile stew.

WHERE TO STAY & DINE
El Paragua ⊛ NORTHERN NEW MEXICAN   This Española restaurant is a great place to stop en route to Taos, though some Santa Feans make a special trip here. Every time I enter El Paragua (which means "the umbrella"), with its red-tile floors and colorful Saltillo-tile trimmings, I feel as though I've stepped into Mexico. The restaurant opened in 1958 as a small taco stand owned by two brothers, and through the years it has flourished. It has received praise from many sources, including *Gourmet Magazine* and N. Scott Momaday, writing for the *New York Times.* You can't go wrong ordering the enchilada suprema, a chicken and cheese enchilada with onions and sour cream. Also on the menu are fajitas and a variety of seafood dishes and steaks,

including the *churrasco Argentino.* Served at your table in a hot brazier, it's cooked in a green herb *salsa chimichurri.* There's a full bar from which you may want to try Don Luis's Italian coffee, made with a coffee-flavored liquor called Tuaca. For equally excellent but faster food, skip next door to the kin restaurant **El Parasol** ☞ and order a chicken taco—the best ever.

Georgia O'Keeffe & New Mexico: A Desert Romance

In June 1917, during a short visit to the Southwest, the painter Georgia O'Keeffe (born 1887) visited New Mexico for the first time. She was immediately enchanted by the stark scenery; even after her return to the energy and chaos of New York City, her mind wandered frequently to New Mexico's arid land and undulating mesas. However, not until coaxed by the arts patron and "collector of people" Mabel Dodge Luhan 12 years later did O'Keeffe return to the multihued desert of her daydreams.

O'Keeffe was reportedly ill, both physically and emotionally, when she arrived in Santa Fe in April 1929. New Mexico seemed to soothe her spirit and heal her physical ailments almost magically. Two days after her arrival, Mabel Dodge Luhan persuaded O'Keeffe to move into her home in Taos. There, she would be free to paint and socialize as she liked.

In Taos, O'Keeffe began painting what would become some of her best-known canvases—close-ups of desert flowers and objects such as cow and horse skulls. "The color up there is different . . . the blue-green of the sage and the mountains, the wildflowers in bloom," O'Keeffe once said of Taos. "It's a different kind of color from any I've ever seen—there's nothing like that in north Texas or even in Colorado." Taos transformed not only her art, but her personality as well. She bought a car and learned to drive. Sometimes, on warm days, she ran naked through the sage fields. That August, a new, rejuvenated O'Keeffe rejoined her husband, photographer Alfred Stieglitz, in New York.

The artist returned to New Mexico year after year, spending time with Mabel Dodge Luhan as well as staying at the isolated Ghost Ranch. She drove through the countryside in her snappy Ford, stopping to paint in her favorite spots along the way. Until 1949, O'Keeffe always returned to New York in the fall. Three years after Stieglitz's death, though, she relocated permanently to New Mexico, spending each winter and spring in Abiquiu and each summer and fall at Ghost Ranch. Georgia O'Keeffe died in Santa Fe in 1986.

A great way to see Ghost Ranch is on a hike that climbs above the mystical area. Take US 84 north from Española about 36 miles to Ghost Ranch and follow the road to the Ghost Ranch office. The ranch is owned by the Presbyterian Church, and the staff will supply you with a primitive map for the **Kitchen Mesa** and **Chimney Rock** hikes. If you hike there, be sure to check in at the front desk, which is open Monday to Saturday from 8am to 5pm. For more information, contact **Ghost Ranch,** 401 Old Taos Hwy., Santa Fe (© **505/685-4333;** www.ghostranch.org).

603 Santa Cruz Rd., Española (off the main drag; turn east at Long John Silver's). (℃ **505/753-3211.** Reservations recommended. Main courses $11–$20. AE, DISC, MC, V. Daily 11am–9pm.

Rancho de San Juan ★★ (Moments   Just 38 miles from Santa Fe, set between Española and Ojo Caliente, this inn provides an authentic northern New Mexico desert experience with the comforts of a luxury hotel and the ease of staying with friends. In 2006, this place received some serious recognition; it was listed on the *Conde Nast Traveler* Gold List and named as one of the top six inns in the United States by *Executive Traveler.* It's the passion of architect and chef John Johnson, responsible for the design and cuisine, and interior designer David Heath, responsible for the elegant interiors. The original part of the inn comprises four recently renovated and enlarged rooms around a central courtyard. Additional casitas with kitchens are in the outlying hills. Rooms here are open, bright, and very elegant—stylishly decorated with a creative mix from the owners' personal art collections including contemporary paintings, tribal masks, and European antiques. From private patios, you'll have spectacular views of desert landscapes and distant, snow-capped peaks. The Kiva suite is the most innovative, with a round bedroom and a skylight just above the bed, perfect for stargazing.

A few minutes' hike from the inn is **"Windows in the Earth,"** an impressive shrine that the innkeepers commissioned to be carved into a sandstone outcropping, where weddings and other festivities are held. With a key, you can unlock the structure and go inside for a don't-miss experience—the feeling that you're in a life-size sandcastle.

Meals here are some of the best in the state. The weekly seasonal menus are original, flavorful, and beautifully presented. The selection of appetizers, entrees ($35), and desserts often take a French-inspired twist on local Southwest ingredients. Highlights last time we ate here included a fire-roasted poblano chile stuffed with pine nuts, sultanas, and goat cheese with tomato saffron coulis, followed by grilled swordfish steak with lemon-caper butter, wild rice and peach pilaf, and sautéed spinach. The restaurant also has an impressive wine list that includes more than 250 selections; it won *Wine Spectator's* "Award of Excellence" for the past five years.

US 285 (en route to Ojo Caliente), P.O. Box 4140, Fairview Station, Española, NM 87533. (℃ **505/753-6818.** www. ranchodesanjuan.com. 12 units. $275–$550 double. AE, MC, V. **Amenities:** Restaurant; concierge; in-room massage and other spa treatments; laundry service. *In room:* A/C, CD player, fridge with stocked beverages, fireplace, coffeemaker, hair dryer, dial-up Internet access.

OJO CALIENTE

Many locals from the area like to rejuvenate at **Ojo Caliente Mineral Springs,** Ojo Caliente, NM 87549 (℃ **800/222-9162** or 505/583-2233); it's on US 285, 50 miles (a 1-hr. drive) northwest of Santa Fe and 50 miles southwest of Taos. This National Historic Site was considered sacred by prehistoric tribes. When Spanish explorer Cabeza de Vaca discovered and named the springs in the 16th century, he called them "the greatest treasure that I found these strange people to possess." No other hot spring in the world has Ojo Caliente's combination of iron, soda, lithium, sodium, and arsenic. If the weather is warm enough, the outdoor mud bath is a treat. The dressing rooms are in fairly good shape; however, the whole place has an earthy feel. If you're a fastidious type, you won't be comfortable here. The resort offers herbal wraps and massages, lodging, and meals. It's open daily 8am to 8pm (to 9pm Fri–Sat). If you get hungry on your way there, you can get a burrito across from a general store at **El Rito** (1212 Main St., El Rito, NM 87530; (℃ 505/581-9509).

4 Pecos National Historic Park

About 15 miles east of Santa Fe, I-25 meanders through **Glorieta Pass,** site of an important Civil War skirmish. In March 1862, volunteers from Colorado and New Mexico, along with Fort Union regulars, defeated a Confederate force marching on Santa Fe, thereby turning the tide of Southern encroachment in the West.

Follow NM 50 east to **Pecos** for about 7 miles. This quaint town, well off the beaten track since the interstate was constructed, is the site of a noted **Benedictine monastery.** About 26 miles north of here on NM 63 is the village of **Cowles,** gateway to the natural wonderland of the **Pecos Wilderness.** There are many camping, picnicking, and fishing locales en route.

Pecos National Historical Park ✸✸ (✆ **505/757-6414;** www.nps.gov/peco), about 2 miles south of the town of Pecos off NM 63, contains the ruins of a 15th-century pueblo and 17th- and 18th-century missions that jut up spectacularly from a high meadow. Coronado mentioned Pecos Pueblo in 1540: "It is feared through the land," he wrote. The approximately 2,000 Native Americans here farmed in irrigated fields and hunted wild game. Their pueblo had 660 rooms and many kivas. By 1620, Franciscan monks had established a church and convent. Military and natural disasters took their toll on the pueblo, and in 1838, the 20 surviving Pecos went to live with relatives at the Jemez Pueblo.

The **E. E. Fogelson Visitor Center** tells the history of the Pecos people in a well-done, chronologically organized exhibit, complete with dioramas. A 1.5-mile loop trail begins at the center and continues through Pecos Pueblo and the **Misión de Nuestra Señora de Los Angeles de Porciuncula** (as the church was formerly called). This excavated structure—170 feet long and 90 feet wide at the transept—was once the most magnificent church north of Mexico City.

Pecos National Historical Park is open Memorial Day to Labor Day, daily 8am to 6pm; the rest of the year, daily 8am to 5pm. It's closed January 1 and December 25. Admission is $3 per person over age 16.

5 Chaco Culture National Historic Park ✸✸✸

A combination of a stunning setting and well-preserved ruins makes the long drive to **Chaco Culture National Historic Park,** often referred to as Chaco Canyon, worth the trip. Whether you come from the north or south, you drive in on a dusty (and sometimes muddy) road that seems to add to the authenticity and adventure of this remote New Mexico experience.

When you finally arrive, you walk through stark desert country that seems perhaps ill suited as a center of culture. However, the ancient Anasazi people successfully farmed the lowlands and built great masonry towns, which connected with other towns over a wide-ranging network of roads crossing this desolate place.

What's most interesting here is how changes in architecture—beginning in the mid-800s, when the Anasazi started building on a larger scale than they had previously—chart the area's cultural progress. The Anasazi used the same masonry techniques that tribes had used in smaller villages in the region (walls one stone thick, with generous use of mud mortar), but they built stone villages of multiple stories with rooms several times larger than in the previous stage of their culture. Within a century, six large pueblos were underway. This pattern of a single large pueblo with oversize rooms, surrounded by conventional villages, caught on throughout the region. New communities built along these lines sprang up. Old villages built similarly large pueblos. Eventually there were more than 75 such towns, most of them closely tied to Chaco by an extensive system of roads. Aerial photos show hundreds of miles of roads connecting these towns with the Chaco pueblos, one of the longest running 42 miles straight north to Salmon Ruins and the Aztec Ruins. It is this road network that leads some scholars to believe that Chaco was the center of a unified Anasazi society.

This progress led to Chaco becoming the economic center of the San Juan Basin by A.D. 1000. As many as 5,000 people may have lived in some 400 settlements in and around Chaco. As masonry techniques advanced through the years, walls rose more than four stories in height. Some of these are still visible today.

Chaco's decline after 1½ centuries of success coincided with a drought in the San Juan Basin between A.D. 1130 and 1180. Scientists still argue vehemently over why the site was abandoned and where the Chacoans went. Many believe that an influx of outsiders may have brought new rituals to the region, causing a schism among tribal members. Most agree, however, that the people drifted away to more hospitable places in the region and that their descendants are today's Pueblo people.

This is an isolated area, and there are **no services** available within or close to the park—no food, gas, auto repairs, firewood, lodging (besides the campground), and drinking water (other than at the visitor center) are available. Overnight camping is permitted year-round. If you're headed toward Santa Fe after a day at the park and looking for a place to spend the night, one nice option is the **Cañon del Rio–A Riverside Inn,** 16445 Scenic Hwy. 4, Jemez Springs, NM 87025 (✆ **505/829-4377;** www.canondelrio.com).

ESSENTIALS

GETTING THERE   To get to Chaco from Santa Fe, take I-25 south to Bernalillo, then US 550 northwest. Turn off US 550 at CR 7900 (3 miles southeast of Nageezi and about 50 miles west of Cuba at mile 112.5). Follow the signs from US 550 to the park boundary (21 miles). This route includes 5 miles of paved road (CR 7900) and 16 miles of rough dirt road (CR 7950). This is the recommended route. NM 57 from Blanco Trading Post is closed. The trip takes about 3½ to 4 hours. Farmington is the nearest population center, a 1½-hour drive away. The park can also be reached from Grants via I-40 west to NM 371, then north on NM 57 (with the final 19 miles ungraded dirt). This route is rough to impassable and is not recommended for RVs.

Whichever way you come, call ahead to inquire about **road conditions** (✆ **505/786-7014**) before leaving the paved highways. The dirt roads can get extremely muddy and dangerous after rain or snow, and afternoon thunderstorms are common in late summer. Roads often flood when it rains.

VISITOR INFORMATION   Ranger-guided walks and campfire talks are available in the summer at the visitor center where you can get self-guiding trail brochures and permits for the overnight campground (see "Camping," below). If you want information before you leave home, write to the Superintendent, Chaco Culture National Historical Park, 1808 County Rd. 7950, Nageezi, NM 87037 (✆ **505/786-7014;** www.nps.gov/chcu).

ADMISSION FEES & HOURS   Admission is $8 per car; a campsite is $10 extra. The visitor center is open daily from 8am to 5pm. Trails are open from sunrise to sunset.

SEEING THE HIGHLIGHTS

Exploring the ruins and hiking are the most popular activities here. A series of pueblo ruins stand within 5 or 6 miles of each other on the broad, flat, treeless canyon floor. Plan to spend at least 3 to 4 hours here driving to and exploring the different pueblos. A one-way road from the visitor center loops up one side of the canyon and down the other. Parking lots are scattered along the road near the various pueblos; from most, it's only a short walk to the ruins.

You may want to focus your energy on seeing **Pueblo Bonito,** the largest prehistoric Southwest Native American dwelling ever excavated. It contains giant kivas and 800 rooms covering more than 3 acres. Also, the **Pueblo Alto Trail** is a nice hike that takes you up on the canyon rim so that you can see the ruins from above—in the afternoon, with thunderheads building, the views are spectacular. If you're a cyclist, stop at the visitor center to pick up a map outlining ridable trails.

CAMPING

Gallo Campground, within the park, is quite popular with hikers. It's about 1 mile east of the visitor center; fees are $10 per night. The campground has 48 sites (group sites are also available), with fire grates (bring your own wood or charcoal), central toilets, and nonpotable water. Drinking water is available only at the visitor center. The campground cannot accommodate trailers over 30 feet.

As I said above, there's no place to stock up on supplies once you start the arduous drive to the canyon, so if you're camping, make sure to be well supplied, especially with water, before you leave home base.

6 Chama: Home of the Cumbres & Toltec Scenic Railroad

Some of my best outdoor adventuring has taken place in the area surrounding this pioneer village of 1,250 people at the base of the 10,000-foot Cumbres Pass. With a backpack on, I cross-country skied high into the mountains and stayed the night in a *yurt* (Russian hut), the next day waking to hundreds of acres of snowy fields to explore. Another time, we headed down **Rio Chama,** an official wild and scenic river, on rafts and in kayaks following the course that Navajos, Utes, and Comanches once traveled to raid the Pueblo Indians down river. The campsites along the way were pristine, with mule deer threading through the trees beyond our tents. In my most recent visit to the village, it was summertime, and I'd just come from Durango, which was packed with tourists, to hike, raft, and ride the train. Chama was still quiet, and I realized Chama is New Mexico's undiscovered Durango, without the masses. And now, with some new additions, the town is really looking up. A park, clock-tower, and, drum-roll please . . . sidewalks! give it a more friendly tone.

Bordered by three wilderness areas, the Carson, Rio Grande, and Santa Fe national forests, the area is indeed prime for hunting, fishing, cross-country skiing, snowmobiling, snowshoeing, and hiking.

Another highlight here is America's longest and highest narrow-gauge coal-fired steam line, the **Cumbres & Toltec Scenic Railroad,** which winds through valleys and mountain meadows 64 miles between Chama and Antonito, Colorado. The village of Chama boomed when the railroad arrived in 1881. A rough-and-ready frontier town, the place still maintains that flavor, with lumber and ranching making up a big part of the economy.

Landmarks to watch for are the **Brazos Cliffs** and waterfall and **Heron and El Vado lakes.** Tierra Amarilla, the Rio Arriba County seat, is 14 miles south, and is at the center—along with Los Ojos and Los Brazos—of a wool-raising and weaving tradition where local craftspeople still weave masterpieces. Dulce, governmental seat of the Jicarilla Apache Indian Reservation, is 27 miles west.

ESSENTIALS

GETTING THERE   From Santa Fe, take US 84 north (2 hr.). From Taos, take US 64 west (2½ hr.). From Farmington, take US 64 east (2¼ hr.).

VISITOR INFORMATION   The **New Mexico Visitor Information Center,** P.O. Box 697, Chama, NM 87520 (© **505/756-2235**), is at 2372 NM 17. It's open daily from 8am to 6pm in the summer, from 8am to 5pm in the winter. At the same address is the **Chama Valley Chamber of Commerce** (© **800/477-0149** or 505/756-2306).

ALL ABOARD THE HISTORIC C&T RAILROAD

Cumbres & Toltec Scenic Railroad ☆☆ *(Moments*   If you have a passion for the past and for incredible scenery, climb aboard America's longest and highest narrow-gauge steam railroad, the historic C&T. It operates on a 64-mile track between Chama and Antonito, Colorado. Built in 1880 as an extension of the Denver and Rio Grande line to serve the mining camps of the San Juan Mountains, it is perhaps the finest surviving example of what once was a vast network of remote Rocky Mountain railways.

The C&T passes through forests of pine and aspen, past striking rock formations, and over the magnificent Toltec Gorge of the Rio de los Pinos. It crests at the 10,015-foot Cumbres Pass, the highest in the United States used by scheduled passenger trains.

Halfway through the route, at Osier, Colorado, the *New Mexico Express* from Chama meets the *Colorado Limited* from Antonito. They stop to exchange greetings, engines, and through passengers. Round-trip day passengers return to their starting point after enjoying a picnic or catered lunch beside the old water tank and stock pens in Osier. Through passengers continue on to Antonito and return by van. Be aware that both trips are nearly full-day events. Those who find it uncomfortable to sit for long periods may instead want to opt for hiking or skiing in the area. Ask about their Parlor Car, a more luxurious alternative to coach seating.

A walking-tour brochure, describing 23 points of interest in the Chama railroad yards, can be picked up at the 1899 depot in Chama. A registered National Historic Site, the C&T is owned by the states of Colorado and New Mexico. Special cars with lifts for people with disabilities are available with a 7-day advance reservation.

500 Terrace Ave., Chama, NM 87520. © **888/CUMBRES** or 505/756-2151. Fax 505/756-2694. www.cumbresand toltec.com. Lunch is included with all fares. Round-trip to Osier: adults $70, children age 11 and under $37. Through

---

Steam Power Shopping

After sitting on the steam train, you may want to stroll for a while, hitting a few of the shops in Chama. One of note is the **Local Color Gallery,** 567 Terrace Ave. (© **888/756-2604** or 505/756-2604) in the center of town. Here you'll find all kinds of locally made arts and crafts, from pottery to moody candles painted with petroglyph symbols to picturesque watercolors of the Chama area. Nearby, the **Trackside Emporium,** 611 Terrace Ave. (© **505/ 756-1848**), offers train books and videos and model cars.

trip to Antonito, return by van (or to Antonito by van, return by train): adults $65, children $35. Reservations highly recommended. Memorial Day to mid-Oct trains leave Chama daily at 10am; vans depart for Antonito at 8am.

WHERE TO STAY IN CHAMA

Most accommodations in this area are found on NM 17 or south of the US 64/84 junction, known as the "Y."

HOTELS/LODGES

Chama Trails Inn　This stucco building adorned with chile *ristras* (decorative strung chiles) houses homey motel-style rooms at a reasonable price. The place is impeccably kept, and the medium-size rooms feature custom-made pine furnishings and minirefrigerators. Be aware that the rooms are a bit dark because of stucco-colored walls. A few rooms have ceiling fans, gas fireplaces, and/or Mexican-tile bathroom floors. A new gazebo in the front grassy area provides a great place for a picnic lunch or dinner. Most noteworthy, the owners take great care of this place and are on hand to make your stay pleasant.

2362 Hwy. 17 (P.O. Box 975), Chama, NM 87520. ✆ **800/289-1421** or 505/756-2156. Fax 505/756-2855. www.chama trailsinn.com. 15 units. $50–$85 double, depending on the season. AE, DC, DISC, MC, V. Pets accepted with $10 fee. **Amenities:** Exercise room; Jacuzzi; sauna. *In room:* TV, dataport, fridge, coffeemaker, iron.

River Bend Lodge　Set on a bend of the Chama River, this lodging offers the best cabins in town and clean motel rooms. Though they're prefab cabins, they're better than some of the more authentic and overly rustic ones at nearby lodgings. If you can reserve cabin no. 40, 50, or 60 at the back of the property, you'll have a sweet riverside stay. Some of these are split level, with a queen-size sleeping loft and a bedroom—not great for privacy, but good for a family that doesn't mind sharing space. Others are similar, but without the loft. Every cabin has a fold-out futon in the living room, an efficient little kitchen, and a small bathroom. The motel rooms are medium-size, with basic furnishing and a long portal to relax on in the afternoons.

2625 US 84/64, Chama, NM 87520. ✆ **800/288-1371** or 505/756-2264. Fax 505/756-2664. www.chamariverbend lodge.com. 20 units. Motel rooms $65–$78 double; cabins $89–$129 double. Additional person $10. Children under 13 stay free in parent's room. AE, DC, DISC, MC, V. Pets accepted with $10 fee. **Amenities:** Jacuzzi; river for fishing and wading. *In-room:* A/C, TV, fridge, coffeemaker (upon request), microwave (upon request).

The Timbers at Chama 🔍　This luxury lodge, set on 400 acres of meadow, with only streams, birds, and elk to disturb your sleep, is one of the region's real gems. Designed as a hunting and fishing lodge, the place has an elegant great room on the first floor, with vaulted ceilings, a giant stone fireplace, and a big-screen TV. One wall is devoted to a vast display of game heads, a detail that nonhunters may find disturbing. Outside is a broad deck with a hot tub and outdoor fireplace overlooking a little pond. The rooms, all decorated in an elegant Montana ranch style, are medium size (the suite is large) with heavy pine furniture, views, and medium-size bathrooms. The beds are comfortably firm and have fine linens. All rooms have VCRs, jet tubs, and robes, and are decorated with original art. An adjacent guest house has a kitchen—a great place for families. Hunting and fishing guides are available, as are horses for guests to ride, all for an additional charge.

Off NM 512 to the Brazos (HC 75, Box 136), Chama, NM 87520. ✆ **505/588-7950**. Fax 505/588-7051. www.the timbersatchama.com. 5 units. $100–$175 double. Guest house $200 double. Rates include full breakfast, except for guest house. DISC, MC, V. **Amenities:** Jacuzzi. *In room:* TV/VCR, coffeemaker, hair dryer, safe.

BED & BREAKFASTS

Gandy Dancer Bed & Breakfast Inn 🍴   In a 1912 two-story Victorian from the early railroad era, this B&B offers an old-world feel with up-to-date amenities. New owners have added color and a more cowboy–railroad atmosphere to the place. Rooms range in size, all with medium-size bathrooms and comfortable beds. Attractive antiques make each room—all named with railroad lingo—unique. The upstairs Caboose, with a king-size bed, sky-blue walls, and lots of light from all directions, is one pick of the place, but my favorite is the downstairs Main Line, a large room with a king-size bed and a purple iris theme. The full breakfast is well worth waking up for. The spinach quiche served with Canadian bacon and an almond French pancake from my last stay is still memorable.

299 Maple Ave. (P.O. Box 810), Chama, NM 87520. ✆ **800/424-6702** or 505/756-2191. Fax 505/756-2649. www.gandydancerbb.com. 7 units. $109–$139 double. Additional person $15. Rates include full breakfast. AE, MC, V. **Amenities:** Jacuzzi. *In room:* A/C, TV, VCR.

CAMPING

At **Rio Chama RV Campground** (✆ **505/756-2303**), you're within easy walking distance of the Cumbres & Toltec Scenic Railroad depot. This shady campground with 94 sites along the Rio Chama is ideal for RVers and tenters who plan to take train rides. The campground also offers great photo opportunities of the old steam trains leaving the depot. Hot showers, a dump station, and complete hookups are available. It's open from May to mid-October only. The campground is 2¼ miles north of the US 84/64 junction on NM 17.

   Twin Rivers Trailer Park (✆ **505/756-2218;** www.twinriversonline.net) has 50 sites and 40 full hookups; phone hookups are offered. Tenting is available, as are laundry facilities and ice and picnic tables. River swimming and fishing are popular activities; other sports facilities include basketball, volleyball, badminton, and horseshoes. Twin Rivers is open from April 15 to November 15 and is 100 yards west of the junction of NM 17 and US 84/64.

WHERE TO DINE IN CHAMA

Cookin' Books 🍴 *Finds* DELI/AMERICAN   This is Chama's new gem, a fun community-style cafe serving creative, delectable food. The main room has a vaulted ceiling with bookshelves on one side and lots of windows. Diners order at a counter and serve themselves water and coffee, while the food is made fresh and brought to them. The menu ranges broadly. You might start with shrimp ceviche or a chicken quesadilla. For an entree, the tastiest sandwich is the roast turkey, goat cheese, and pesto served on a fresh ciabatta roll. The Reuben on rye is also delicious. Lighter appetites may select from a few salad options such as a grilled salmon steak on organic greens. During my most recent visit, I had the daily special: a stellar chicken putanesca (chicken cooked with olives, tomatoes, and onions), served with a salad. While you wait for your food, be sure to peruse the community room/gallery in back, displaying local art including "found" pieces by Bruce McIntosh. Beer and wine accompany the menu.

2449 US 84/64, at the Y, Chama. ✆ **505/756-1717.** All menu items under $9. MC, V. Thurs–Mon 10am–8pm.

High Country Restaurant and Saloon 🍴 STEAKS/SEAFOOD/NEW MEXICAN This is definitely a country place, with functional furniture, orange vinyl chairs, brown carpet, and a big stone fireplace. But it's *the* place innkeepers recommend, and one traveling couple I spoke to had eaten lunch and dinner here every day of their weeklong stay. The steaks are a big draw here. More sophisticated appetites may like the *trucha con piñon,* trout dusted in flour and cooked with pine nuts, garlic, and shallots. Meals are served with a salad and choice of potato. The New Mexican food is also good. The attached saloon has a full bar and bustles with people eating peanuts and throwing the shells on the floor. Breakfast on Sunday is country-style, with offerings such as steak and eggs and biscuits and gravy topping the menu, as well as omelets, pancakes, and huevos rancheros (eggs atop tortillas smothered in chile sauce).

Main St. (¹/₁₀ mile north of the Y), Chama. ℂ 505/756-2384. Breakfast $4–$10; lunch $6–$12; dinner $4–$20; Sun breakfast buffet $8.95. AE, DISC, MC, V. Mon–Sat 11am–10pm; Sun 8am–10pm. Closed Easter, Thanksgiving, Christmas.

CHAMA AFTER DARK

Summer evenings in Chama now include entertainment beyond watching the river flow in its banks or the beer flow in the local tavern. The Elkhorn Lodge, 2663 S. US 84 (ℂ 800/532-8874 or 505/756-2105; www.elkhornlodge.net), sponsors a **Chuck-wagon Cowboy Dinner** Saturday and Sunday evenings. Guests chow down on beef brisket, beans, and corn bread while watching a historical western narrative told through guitar music and singing. Kids like the food and the fun story. Reservations required; contact Elkhorn Lodge. Performances start at 6:30pm, and prices run $16 for adults and $9 for children under 14; children under 2 eat free.

ON THE ROAD: WHAT TO SEE & DO ON US 84 SOUTH

Distinctive yellow earth provided a name for the town of **Tierra Amarilla,** 14 miles south of Chama at the junction of US 84 and US 64. Throughout New Mexico, this name is synonymous with a continuing controversy over the land-grant rights of the descendants of the original Hispanic settlers. But the economy of this community of 1,000 is dyed in the wool—literally.

The organization *Ganados del Valle* (Livestock Growers of the Valley) is at work to save the longhaired Spanish churro sheep from extinction, to introduce other unusual wool breeds to the valley, and to perpetuate a 200-year-old tradition of shepherding, spinning, weaving, and dyeing. Many of the craftspeople work in conjunction with **Tierra Wools** ✸, P.O. Box 229, Los Ojos, NM 87551 (ℂ 505/588-7231; www. handweavers.com), which has a showroom and workshop in a century-old mercantile building just north of Tierra Amarilla. One-of-a-kind blankets and men's and women's apparel are among the products displayed and sold.

Just down the street, across from the Los Ojos General Store, is an interesting little art studio worth checking out. **Yellow Earth Studio** (ℂ 505/588-7807), the passion of Paul Trachtman, the resident artist, is a great place to see and purchase enchanting scenes of the Los Ojos area in the form of paintings and monotype, woodcut, and metal engraving prints. His work is part of the permanent collection of the New Mexico State Capitol. Paul will likely be working away in his studio in back, and if you're fortunate, he'll guide you through some of his techniques.

Two state parks are a short drive west from Tierra Amarilla. **El Vado Lake State Park,** 14 miles southwest on NM 112 (ℂ 505/588-7247), offers boating and water-skiing, fishing, and camping in summer; cross-country skiing and ice fishing in winter. **Heron Lake State Park,** 11 miles west on US 64 and NM 95 (ℂ 505/588-7470), has a no-wake speed limit for motor vessels, adding to its appeal for fishing, sailing, windsurfing, canoeing, and swimming. The park has an interpretive center, plus camping, picnic sites, hiking trails, and cross-country skiing in the winter. The 5½-mile Rio Chama trail connects the two lakes.

East of Tierra Amarilla, the Rio Brazos cuts a canyon through the Tusas Mountains and around 11,403-foot Brazos Peak. Just north of Los Ojos, NM 512 heads east 7½ miles up the **Brazos Box Canyon.** High cliffs that rise straight from the valley floor give it a Yosemite-like appearance—which is even more apparent from an overlook on US 64, 18 miles east of Tierra Amarilla en route to Taos. **El Chorro,** an impressive waterfall at the mouth of the canyon, usually flows only from early May to mid-June. Several resort lodges are in the area.

About 37 miles south of Tierra Amarilla on US 84, and 3 miles north of Ghost Ranch, is **Echo Canyon Amphitheater** (© **505/684-2486**), a U.S. Forest Service campground and picnic area. The natural "theater," hollowed out of sandstone by thousands of years of erosion, is a natural work of art with layers of stone ranging from pearl-color to blood red. The walls send back eerie echoes and even clips of conversations. It's just a 10-minute walk from the parking area. The fee is $2 per car. Some 13 miles west of here, via the dirt Forest Service road 151 into the Chama River Canyon Wilderness, is the isolated **Monastery of Christ in the Desert** (www.christdesert.org), built in 1964 by Benedictine monks. The brothers produce crafts, sold at a small gift shop, and operate a guest house.

Along the same road (FS 151) is access to the Chama River, a good place to hike, mountain bike, kayak, and camp. The **Rim Vista Trail** will take you to the top of the rim, with vast views out across Abiquiu Lake and Ghost Ranch. Primitive campsites can be found all along the river.

A 3-mile drive from there is **Ghost Ranch,** a collection of adobe buildings that make up an adult study center maintained by the United Presbyterian Church. A number of hauntingly memorable hikes originate from this place, which gets its name from the *brujas,* or witches, said to inhabit the canyons. Most popular among the hikes is spectacular **Chimney Rock,** but even more notable in our opinion is **Kitchen Mesa.** Directions for the hikes can be obtained at the visitor center. World-renowned painter Georgia O'Keeffe spent time at Ghost Ranch painting these canyons and other land formations. Eventually she bought a portion of the ranch and lived in a humble adobe house there. The ranch now offers seminars on a variety of topics, ranging from art to literature to religion, that are open to all. For information, contact **Ghost Ranch,** 401 Old Taos Hwy., Santa Fe (© **505/982-8539;** www.ghostranch.org).

The **Florence Hawley Ellis Museum of Anthropology** has interpretative exhibits of a Spanish ranch house and Native American anthropology, and the **Ruth Hall Paleontology Museum** (both museums © **505/685-4333;** www.ghostranch.org) displays fossils of the early dinosaur named coelophysis found on the ranch. A lightly built creature, it was very fast when chasing prey. It roamed the area 250 million years ago, making it the oldest dinosaur found in New Mexico.

Many dinosaur skeletons have been found in rocks along the base of cliffs near **Abiquiu Reservoir** (© **505/685-4371**), a popular boating and fishing spot formed by the Abiquiu Dam.

A good place to stay in the area is the **Abiquiu Inn,** a small country inn, restaurant, art gallery, and gift shop, ½ mile north of the village of Abiquiu (© **505/685-4378**). The casitas are especially nice. Rates are $139 to $199.

Heading south from Abiquiu, watch for **Dar al Islam** (© **505/685-4515**), a spiritual center with a circular Middle Eastern–style mosque made of adobe; the small community of **Mendanales,** where you'll find the shop of renowned weaver Cordelia Coronado; and **Hernandez,** the village immortalized in Ansel Adams's famous 1941 photograph *Moonrise, Hernandez, New Mexico.* **Rancho de San Juan** (p. 165) is a wonderful nearby place to stay and dine.

11

Getting to Know Taos

New Mexico's favorite arts town sits in a masterpiece setting. It's wedged between the towering peaks of the Rocky Mountains and the plunging chasm of the Rio Grande Gorge.

Located about 70 miles north of Santa Fe, this town of 5,000 residents combines 1960s hippiedom (thanks to communes set up in the hills back then) with the ancient culture of Taos Pueblo (some people still live without electricity and running water, as their ancestors did 1,000 years ago). It can be an odd place, where some completely eschew materialism and live "off the grid" in half-underground houses called earthships. But there are plenty of more mainstream attractions as well—Taos boasts some of the best restaurants in the state, a hot and funky arts scene, and incredible outdoors action, including world-class skiing.

Its history is rich. Throughout the Taos valley, ruins and artifacts attest to a Native American presence dating back 5,000 years. The Spanish first visited this area in 1540, colonizing it in 1598. In the last 2 decades of the 17th century, they put down three rebellions at Taos Pueblo. During the 18th and 19th centuries, Taos was an important trade center: New Mexico's annual caravan to Chihuahua, Mexico, couldn't leave until after the annual midsummer **Taos Fair.** French trappers began attending the fair in 1739. Even though the Plains tribes often attacked the pueblos at other times, they would attend the market festival under a temporary annual truce. By the early 1800s, Taos

had become a meeting place for American mountain men, the most famous of whom, Kit Carson, made his home in Taos from 1826 to 1868.

Taos remained loyal to Mexico during the U.S.–Mexican War of 1846. The town rebelled against its new U.S. landlord in 1847, even killing newly appointed Governor Charles Bent in his Taos home. Nevertheless, the town was eventually incorporated into the Territory of New Mexico in 1850. During the Civil War, Taos fell into Confederate hands for 6 weeks; afterward, Carson and two other men raised the Union flag over Taos Plaza and guarded it day and night. Since that time, Taos has had the honor of flying the flag 24 hours a day.

Taos's population declined when the railroad bypassed it in favor of Santa Fe. In 1898, two East Coast artists—Ernest Blumenschein and Bert Phillips—discovered the dramatic, varied effects of sunlight on the natural environment of the Taos valley and depicted them on canvas. By 1912, thanks to the growing influence of the **Taos Society of Artists,** the town had gained a worldwide reputation as a cultural center. Today, it is estimated that more than 15% of the population are painters, sculptors, writers, or musicians, or in some other way earn their income from artistic pursuits.

The town of Taos is merely the focal point of rugged 2,200-square-mile Taos County. Two features dominate this sparsely populated region: the high desert mesa, split in two by the 650-foot-deep

Downtown Taos & Environs

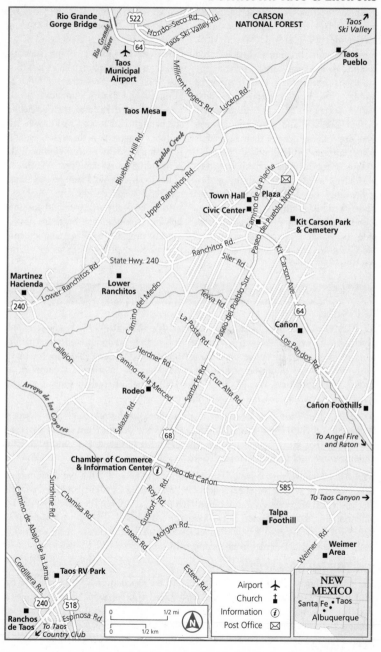

Rio Grande Gorge Bridge

522

Hondo–Seco Rd.

Taos Ski Valley Rd.

CARSON NATIONAL FOREST

Taos Ski Valley

64

Rio Grande River

Taos Municipal Airport

Millicent Rogers Rd.

Lucero Rd.

Taos Pueblo

Taos Mesa

Pueblo Creek

Blueberry Hill Rd.

Upper Ranchitos Rd.

Camino de la Placita

Town Hall
Plaza

Civic Center

Paseo del Pueblo Norte

Kit Carson Park & Cemetery

Ranchitos Rd.

Siler Rd.

Kit Carson Ave.

State Hwy. 240

Lower Ranchitos Rd.

Martinez Hacienda

240

Lower Ranchitos

Camino del Medio

Tewa Rd.

Paseo del Pueblo Sur

La Posta Rd.

64

Cañon

Los Pandos Rd.

Callejon

Herdner Rd.

Camino de la Merced

Santa Fe Rd.

Cruz Alta Rd.

Arroyo de los Coyotes

Rodeo

Salazar Rd.

Cañon Foothills

68

To Angel Fire and Raton

Chamber of Commerce & Information Center ⓘ

Paseo del Cañon

585

To Taos Canyon →

Sunshine Rd.

Chamisa Rd.

Roy Rd.

Gusdorf Rd.

Talpa Foothill

Camino de Abajo de la Lama

Morgan Rd.

Estees Rd.

Weimer Rd.

Weimer Area

Cordillera Rd.

Taos RV Park

Estees Rd.

240 518

Espinosa Rd.

To Taos Country Club

Ranchos de Taos

Airport	✈
Church	✝
Information	ⓘ
Post Office	✉

0 1/2 mi
0 1/2 km

N

NEW MEXICO

Santa Fe • • Taos

• Albuquerque

175

chasm of the **Rio Grande;** and the **Sangre de Cristo** range, which tops out at 13,161-foot Wheeler Peak, New Mexico's highest mountain. From the forested uplands to the sage-carpeted mesa, the county is home to a large variety of wildlife. The human element includes Native Americans who are still living in ancient pueblos and Hispanic farmers who continue to irrigate their farmlands using centuries-old methods.

Taos is also inhabited by many people who have chosen to retreat from, or altogether drop out of, mainstream society. There's a laid-back attitude here, even more pronounced than the general *mañana* attitude for which New Mexico is known. Most Taoseños live here to play here—and that means outdoors. Many work at the ski

area all winter (skiing whenever they can) and work for raft companies in the summer (to get on the river as much as they can). Others are into rock climbing, mountain biking, and backpacking. That's not to say that Taos is just a resort town. With the Hispanic and Native American populations' histories in the area, there's a richness and depth here that most resort towns lack.

Taos's biggest task these days is to try to stem the tide of overdevelopment that is flooding northern New Mexico. In "Life Today—From Flamenco to Craps" (p. 285), I address the city's success in battling back airport expansion and some housing developments. A grassroots community program has been implemented that gives neighborhoods a say in how their area is developed.

1 Orientation

ARRIVING

BY PLANE   The **Taos Municipal Airport** (© **505/758-4995**) is about 8 miles northwest of town on US 64. Most people opt to fly into Albuquerque International Sunport, rent a car, and drive up to Taos from there. The drive takes approximately 2½ hours. If you'd rather be picked up at Albuquerque International Sunport, call **Faust's Transportation, Inc.** (© **505/758-3410**), which offers daily service, as well as taxi service between Taos and Taos Ski Valley.

BY BUS   The **Taos Bus Center** is 5 miles south of the plaza at 1386 Paseo del Pueblo Sur (© **505/758-1144**). **TNM&O** arrives and departs from this depot several times a day. For more information on this and other bus services to and from Albuquerque and Santa Fe, see "Getting There," in chapter 2.

BY CAR   Most visitors arrive in Taos via either NM 68 or US 64. Northbound travelers should exit I-25 at Santa Fe, follow US 285 as far as Española, and then continue on the divided highway when it becomes NM 68. Taos is about 79 miles from the I-25 junction. Southbound travelers from Denver on I-25 should exit about 6 miles south of Raton at US 64 and then follow it about 95 miles to Taos. Another major route is US 64 from the west (214 miles from Farmington).

VISITOR INFORMATION

The **Taos County Chamber of Commerce,** at the junction of NM 68 and NM 585 (P.O. Drawer I), Taos, NM 87571 (© **800/732-TAOS** or 505/758-3873; www.taos chamber.com), is open in summer, daily 9am to 5pm. It's closed on major holidays. **Carson National Forest** also has an information center in the same building.

CITY LAYOUT

The **plaza** is a short block west of Taos's major intersection—where US 64 (Kit Carson Rd.) from the east joins NM 68, **Paseo del Pueblo Sur.** US 64 proceeds north from the intersection as **Paseo del Pueblo Norte. Camino de la Placita (Placita Rd.)** circles the west side of downtown, passing within a block of the other side of the plaza. Many of the streets that join these thoroughfares are winding lanes lined by traditional adobe homes, many of them over 100 years old.

Most of the art galleries are located on or near the plaza, which was paved over with bricks several years ago, and along neighboring streets. Others are in the **Ranchos de Taos** area, a few miles south of the plaza.

MAPS   To find your way around town, pick up a free Taos map from the **Chamber of Commerce at Taos Visitor Center,** 1139 Paseo del Pueblo Sur (✆ **505/758-3873**). Good, detailed city maps can be found at area bookstores as well (see "Shopping," in chapter 14).

2 Getting Around

BY CAR

With offices at the Taos airport, **Enterprise** (✆ **505/369-4226**) is reliable and efficient. Other car-rental agencies are available out of Albuquerque. See "Getting Around," in chapter 15, for details.

PARKING   Parking can be difficult during the summer rush, when the stream of tourists' cars moving north and south through town never ceases. If you can't find parking on the street or in the plaza, check out some of the nearby roads (Kit Carson Rd., for instance); there are plenty of metered and unmetered lots in Taos.

ROAD CONDITIONS   Information on highway conditions throughout the state can be obtained from the **State Highway Department** (✆ **800/432-4269**).

BY BUS & TAXI

If you're in Taos without a car, you're in luck because there's local bus service, provided by **Chile Line Town of Taos Transit** (✆ **505/751-4459**). It operates on the half-hour Monday to Saturday 7am to 7pm in summer, 7am to 6pm in winter, and on the hour Sunday 8am to 5pm. Two simultaneous routes run southbound from Taos Pueblo and northbound from the Ranchos de Taos Post Office. Each route makes stops at the casino and various hotels in town, as well as at Taos RV Park. Bus fares are 50¢ one-way, $1 round trip, $5 for a 7-day pass, and $20 for a 31-day pass.

In addition, **Faust's Transportation** (✆ **505/758-3410**) has a taxi service linking town hotels and Taos Ski Valley. Faust's Transportation also offers shuttle service and on-call taxi service daily from 7am to 8:30pm, with fares of about $10 anywhere within the city limits for up to two people ($2 per additional person).

Warning for Drivers

En route to many recreation sites, reliable paved roads often give way to poorer forest roads. When you get off the main roads, you don't find gas stations or cafes. Four-wheel-drive vehicles are recommended on snow and much of the unpaved terrain of the region. If you're doing some off-road adventuring, it's wise to go with a full gas tank, extra food and water, and warm clothing—just in case. At the higher-than-10,000-foot elevations of northern New Mexico, sudden summer snowstorms are not unheard of.

BY BICYCLE

Bicycle rentals are available from **Gearing Up Bicycle Shop,** 129 Paseo del Pueblo Sur (℗ **505/751-0365**); daily rentals run $35 for a full day and $25 for a half day for a mountain bike with front suspension. From April to October, **Native Sons Adventures,** 1033-A Paseo del Pueblo Sur (℗ **800/753-7559** or 505/758-9342), rents no-suspension bikes for $15/half day and $20/full day, front-suspension bikes for $25/half day and $35/full day, and full-suspension bikes for $35/half day and $45/full day. It also rents car racks for $5. Each shop supplies helmets and water bottles with rentals.

FAST FACTS: Taos

Airport See "Orientation," above.

Area Code The telephone area code for all of New Mexico is **505**; however, at press time, plans were in the works to add new codes.

ATMs You can find ATMs (also known as *cash pueblos*) all over town, at supermarkets, banks, and drive-throughs.

Business Hours Most **businesses** are open at least Monday to Friday 10am to 5pm, though some may open an hour earlier and close an hour later. Many **tourist-oriented shops** are also open on Saturday morning, and some **art galleries** are open all day Saturday and Sunday, especially during peak tourist seasons. **Banks** are generally open Monday to Thursday 9am to 5pm and often for longer hours on Friday. Some may be open Saturday morning. Most branches have cash machines available 24 hours. Call establishments for specific hours.

Car Rentals See "Getting Around Northern New Mexico," in chapter 2, or "Getting Around," above.

Climate Taos's climate is similar to that of Santa Fe. Summer days are dry and sunny, except for frequent afternoon thunderstorms. Winter days are often bracing, with snowfalls common but rarely lasting too long. Average **summer temperatures** range from 50°F to 87°F (10°C–31°C). **Winter temperatures** vary between 9°F and 40°F (–13°C–4°C). **Annual rainfall** is 12 inches; annual snowfall is 35 inches in town and 300 inches at Taos Ski Valley, where the elevation is 9,207 feet. (A foot of snow is equal to an inch of rain.)

Currency Exchange Foreign currency can be exchanged at the **Centinel Bank of Taos,** 512 Paseo del Pueblo Sur (℗ **505/758-6700**).

Dentists If you need dental work, try **Dr. Walter Jakiela,** 1392 Weimer Rd. (℗ **505/758-8654**); **Dr. Michael Rivera,** 107 Plaza Garcia, Suite E (℗ **505/758-0531**); or **Dr. Tom Simms,** 1392 Weimer Rd. (℗ **505/758-8303**).

Doctors Members of the **Taos Medical Group,** on Weimer Road (℗ **505/758-2224**), are highly respected. Also recommended are **Family Practice Associates of Taos,** 630 Paseo del Pueblo Sur, Suite 150 (℗ **505/758-3005**).

Embassies & Consulates See "Fast Facts: For the International Traveler," in chapter 2.

Emergencies Dial ℗ **911** for police, fire, and ambulance.

Hospital **Holy Cross Hospital,** 1397 Weimer Rd., off Paseo del Canyon (© **505/ 758-8883**), has 24-hour emergency service. Serious cases are transferred to Santa Fe or Albuquerque.

Hot Lines The **crisis hot line** (© **505/758-9888**) is available for emergency counseling.

Information See "Visitor Information," under "Orientation," above.

Internet Access You can retrieve your e-mail at **Magic Circle Bagels,** 710 Paseo del Pueblo Sur (© **505/758-0045**).

Library The **Taos Public Library,** 402 Camino de la Placita (© **505/758-3063** or 505/737-2590), has a general collection for Taos residents, a children's library, and special collections on the Southwest and Taos art.

Liquor Laws The legal drinking age is 21 in New Mexico, as it is throughout the United States. Bars may remain open until 2am Monday to Saturday and until midnight on Sunday. Wine, beer, and spirits are sold at licensed supermarkets and liquor stores, but there are no package sales on election days until after 7pm. It is illegal to transport liquor through most Native American reservations.

Lost Property Check with the **Taos police** at © **505/758-2216.**

Newspapers & Magazines *The Taos News* (© **505/758-2241**; www.taosnews. com) and the *Sangre de Cristo Chronicle* (© **505/377-2358**; www.sangre chronicle.com) are published every Thursday. *Taos Magazine* is also a good source of local information. The *Albuquerque Journal* (www.abqjournal.com) and the *New Mexican* (from Santa Fe; www.santafenewmexican.com) are easily obtained at book and convenience stores.

Pharmacies There are several full-service pharmacies in Taos. **Raley's Pharmacy** (© **505/758-1203**), **Smith's Pharmacy** (© **505/758-4824**), and **Wal-Mart Pharmacy** (© **505/758-2743**) are all on Pueblo Sur and are easily seen from the road.

Police In case of emergency, dial © **911.** All other inquiries should be directed to the **Taos police,** Civic Plaza Drive (© **505/758-2216**). The **Taos County Sheriff,** with jurisdiction outside the city limits, is in the county courthouse on Paseo del Pueblo Sur (© **505/758-3361**).

Post Offices The main **Taos post office** is at 318 Paseo del Pueblo Norte (© **505/ 758-2081**), a few blocks north of the plaza traffic light. There are smaller offices in **Ranchos de Taos** (© **505/758-3944**) and at **El Prado** (© **505/758-4810**). The zip code for Taos is 87571.

Radio A local station is **KTAO-FM** (101.9), which broadcasts an entertainment calendar daily (© **505/758-5826**); National Public Radio can be found on **KUNM-FM** (98.5) from Albuquerque.

Taxes Gross receipts tax for the city of Taos is 7%, and for Taos County it's 6.31%. There is an additional local bed tax of 4.5% in the city of Taos and 5% on hotel rooms in Taos County.

Taxis See "Getting Around," above.

Television **Channel 2,** the local access station, is available in most hotels. For a few hours a day it shows local programming. Cable networks carry Santa Fe and Albuquerque stations.

Time As is true throughout New Mexico, Taos is on **Mountain Standard Time.** It's 2 hours earlier than New York, 1 hour earlier than Chicago, and 1 hour later than Los Angeles. A new law will extend daylight savings time in 2007. Clocks will change the second Sunday in March and the first Sunday in November.

Useful Telephone Numbers For **emergency road service** in the Taos area, call the state police at *①* **505/758-8878;** for **road conditions** dial *①* **800/432-4269** (within New Mexico) for the state highway department. **Taos County offices are at** *①* **505/737-6300.**

Weather Taos has no number to call for weather forecasts, but if you're hooked up, log on to www.taoschamber.com.

12

Where to Stay in Taos

A tiny town with a big tourist market, Taos has thousands of rooms in hotels, motels, condominiums, and bed-and-breakfasts. Many new properties have recently opened, turning this into a buyer's market. In the slower seasons, in January through early February and April through early May, when competition for travelers is steep, you may even want to try bargaining your room rate down. Most of the hotels and motels are on Paseo del Pueblo Sur and Norte, with a few scattered just east of the town center, along Kit Carson Road. The condos and bed-and-breakfasts are generally scattered throughout Taos's back streets.

During peak seasons, visitors without reservations may have difficulty finding vacant rooms. **Taos Chamber of Commerce,** 1139 Paseo del Pueblo Sur (© **505/758-3873**), might be able to help. If you're looking to hook up to the Internet in this town, head for the plaza, which offers wireless access anywhere you sit.

Fifteen hundred or so of Taos County's beds are in condominiums and lodges at or near Taos Ski Valley. The **Taos Valley Resort Association,** P.O. Box 85, Taos Ski Valley, NM 87525 (© **800/776-1111** or 505/776-2233; fax 505/776-8842; www.visitnewmexico.com), can book these, as well as rooms in Taos and all the rest of northern New Mexico, and it can book private home rentals.

Reservations of Taos, 1033-A Paseo del Pueblo Sur, Taos, NM 87571 (© **505/751-1292**), will help you find accommodations from bed-and-breakfasts to home rentals, hotels, RV parks, and cabins throughout Taos and the rest of northern New Mexico. It'll also help you arrange package prices for outdoor activities such as white-water rafting, horseback riding, hot-air ballooning, snowmobiling, fishing, and skiing.

There are two high seasons in Taos: winter (the Christmas-to-Easter ski season, except for Jan, which is notoriously slow) and summer. Spring and fall are shoulder seasons, often with lower rates. The period between Easter and Memorial Day is also slow in the tourist industry here, and many proprietors of restaurants and other businesses take their annual vacations at this time. Book well ahead for ski holiday periods (especially Christmas) and for the annual arts festivals (late May to mid-June and late Sept to early Oct).

1 The Taos Area

HOTELS/MOTELS
EXPENSIVE
El Monte Sagrado ★★★ *(Moments)* New to Taos in 2003, this resort near the center of town offers a feast for the senses. Water running over falls, clear air, and delicious food and drink lull guests into a sweet *samadhi,* or state of relaxation, while the eyes luxuriate in the beauty of rooms impeccably decorated. These range in theme

from the Caribbean casita, a medium-size room with a medium-size bathroom, which evokes the feel of an African jungle, to the Argentina global suite, a huge two-bedroom decorated in cowboy-contemporary style with wood floors, leather furniture, iron and copper accents, and two large bathrooms featuring stone and glass mosaic-decorated showers, not to mention its own patio and outdoor hot tub, to the Kamasutra Suite, with suggestive carvings throughout, a room resort owner Tom Worrell describes as "the first honeymoon suite to come with instructions." All rooms are quiet and lovely, with patios or balconies and views. In line with Worrell's plan to preserve the earth's environment through responsible development and sustainable technologies, the resort recycles its water and makes much of its own electricity. All rooms rim a grassy, cottonwood-shaded "Sacred Circle," which also has trout and koi ponds. The intimate spa, with a waiting area that resembles a greenhouse filled with light and large plants, offers a full range of excellent treatments. The **Anaconda Bar** (see chapter 14) and **De La Tierra** restaurant (see chapter 13) combine a contemporary feel with elegant Asian touches. The only area where there's room to improve is the service; hopefully, the staff was just going through a rough patch the last time we visited.

317 Kit Carson Rd., Taos, NM 87571. ⓒ **800/828-TAOS** or 505/758-3502. www.elmontesagrado.com. 36 units. $245–$299 historic 1-bedroom casita; $349–$399 Native American suite; $549 Bali and Tibet premier suite; $699 2-bedroom global suite. AE, DC, DISC, MC, V. Valet parking $12. **Amenities:** Restaurant (p.196); bar (p. 224); indoor pool; well-equipped health club and spa; Jacuzzi; concierge; babysitting; laundry service. *In room:* A/C, TV, CD player, high-speed Ethernet and wireless, hair dryer, safe.

Fechin Inn 🐾🐾   This masterfully created luxury hotel provides comfort, quiet, and charm. Built next door to Russian artist Nicolai Fechin's 1927 home (see the discussion of the Taos Art Museum in chapter 14), the hotel features elegantly carved wood furniture and artwork by Jeremy Morelli of Santa Fe. The hotel is next to Kit Carson Park and a 10-minute walk from the plaza. The two-story lobby is airy, with a bank of windows and French doors looking south to a portal where diners can eat breakfast in the warmer months. The spacious rooms have Southwestern decor with thoughtful touches including guest robes, hickory furniture, and flagstone-topped tables; some have balconies or patios. Suites have kiva fireplaces. The bathrooms are delightful, with Italian tile and warm, adjustable lighting. There's a library where you can play chess or backgammon. For an additional cost, you can eat a continental breakfast here. In the evenings, drinks are available. Wireless Internet access is available in the lobby and the library.

227 Paseo del Pueblo Norte, Taos, NM 87571. ⓒ **800/811-2933** or 505/751-1000. Fax 505/751-7338. www.fechin inn.com. 84 units. $127–$177 double; $282–$512 suite. Rates vary according to season. Additional person $15. AE, DC, DISC, MC, V. Free parking. Pets accepted with some restrictions and extra fee. **Amenities:** Medium-size health club; Jacuzzi; massage; coin-op laundry; same-day dry-cleaning and laundry service. *In room:* A/C, TV, dataport, fridge, coffeemaker, hair dryer.

The Historic Taos Inn 🐾   It's rare to see a hotel that has withstood the years with grace, but the Historic Taos Inn has done just that. Here, you'll be surrounded by 20th-century luxury without ever forgetting that you're within the thick walls of a number of 19th-century Southwestern homes. Dr. Thomas Paul Martin, the town's first physician, purchased the complex in 1895. In 1936, a year after the doctor's death, his widow, Helen, enclosed the plaza—now the inn's darling two-story lobby— and turned it into a hotel. In 1981–82, the inn was restored; it's now listed on both the State and National Registers of Historic Places.

Taos Area Accommodations

Abominable Snowmansion
  Skiers' Hostel **3**
Adobe & Pines Inn **17**
Adobe and Stars Bed
  and Breakfast Inn **3**
Adobe Sun God Lodge **14**
Alma del Monte
  (Spirit of the Mountain) **1**
Best Western Kachina Lodge **4**
Carson National Forest **1**
Casa del las Chimeneas **13**
Comfort Suites **17**
Cottonwood Inn **1**
El Monte Sagrado **8**
Fechin Inn **5**
Hacienda del Sol **2**

The Historic Taos Inn **6**
Hotel La Fonda de Taos **9**
Inger Jirby's Guest Houses **10**
Inn on La Loma Plaza **12**
La Posada de Taos **11**
Little Tree Bed & Breakfast **3**
Mabel Dodge Luhan House **7**
Old Taos Guesthouse
  Bed & Breakfast **15**
Questa Lodge **3**
Sagebrush Inn **17**
Salsa del Salto **3**
San Geronimo Lodge **16**
Taos RV Park **17**
Taos Valley RV Park
  and Campground **17**

The lobby doubles as the **Adobe Bar,** a popular local gathering place, with adobe *bancos* (benches) and a sunken fireplace, all surrounding a wishing well that was once the old town well. A number of rooms open onto a balcony that overlooks this area. If you like community and don't mind the sound of jazz and flamenco drifting up toward your room, these rooms are for you. However, if you appreciate solitude and silence, request one of the courtyard rooms downstairs. All the rooms are unique and comfortable, decorated with Spanish colonial art, Taos-style furniture, and interesting touches, such as hand-woven Oaxacan bedspreads and little niches decorated with Mexican pottery; many rooms have fireplaces. A wireless Internet connection is available in the lobby.

I should note that in recent years I've had complaints from guests about the temperamental nature of these old buildings. You may encounter problems such as windows not staying open and some not having screens.

Doc Martin's, with nouveau Southwestern cuisine and a hint of Asia, is a good bet for dinner (see chapter 13).

125 Paseo del Pueblo Norte, Taos, NM 87571. ℰ **800/TAOS-INN** or 505/758-2233. Fax 505/758-5776. www.taos inn.com. 36 units. $70–$250, depending on the type of room and season. AE, DISC, MC, V. **Amenities:** Restaurant (p. 196); bar; seasonal outdoor pool; Jacuzzi; room service; coffee or refreshments in lobby. *In room:* A/C, TV, VCR on request, hair dryer, iron.

Hotel La Fonda de Taos ✿

Finally, Taos has a recommendable hotel on the plaza. A $3-million renovation to this historic property built in 1880 has turned it into a comfortable, fun spot with a stellar location. The charismatic Taos figure Saki Kavaras put this hotel on the society map in the 1930s, when, most notably, British author D. H. Lawrence frequented it. His legacy is preserved in a unique D. H. Lawrence Forbidden Art Museum, where some of his risqué paintings hang—a must-see even if you don't stay here (free for guests; $3 for nonguests). Rooms are set off broad hallways, each styled in earth tones, Southwestern furnishings, and tile bathrooms. Standards are small, each with a queen-size bed. Your better bet is to reserve a plaza or deluxe plaza room, or a suite. These are larger, with king beds. My favorite rooms are nos. 201 and 301, which overlook the plaza. Groups can rent the whole top floor (or the whole hotel), which includes a full kitchen suite. **Joseph's Table** (see p. 196), one of Taos' finest restaurants, is off the lobby.

108 South Plaza, Taos, NM 87571. ℰ **800/833-2211** or 505/758-2211. Fax 505/758-8508. www.lafondataos.com. 24 units. $99–$149 standard double; $139–$209 plaza and deluxe plaza double; $189–$239 suite. AE, DC, DISC, MC, V. Free parking. **Amenities:** Restaurant; coffee shop; bar. *In room:* A/C, TV, high-speed Internet, hair dryer, iron.

Inger Jirby's Guest Houses ✿✿

You can't have a better address in Taos than this artist has, 2 blocks from the plaza, between the R.C. Gorman Gallery and the Ernest L. Blumenschein Museum. Inger Jirby has chosen this for her gallery space as well as a home for travelers. From the remains of a 400-year-old adobe, she's carved and added these lively dwellings and adorned them with her unique style. Full of rich Mexican and Balinese art, and then accented by her own vivid landscapes of the Southwest and beyond, the casitas are artsy as well as comfortable. Each has a full kitchen, with range, dishwasher, microwave, and washer/dryer. The larger two have flagstone floors, large windows, and sleeping lofts. (Very big people might have trouble maneuvering the spiral staircases in these.) These also have foldout couches, so they're a great option for families. The third casita has a large kitchen, a smaller bedroom, and an atrium. All are equipped with stereos and robes. More than anywhere else in town, these casitas provide a real home away from home. The attached Inger Jirby Gallery provides Internet access for guests.

207 Ledoux St., Taos, NM 87571. © 505/758-7333. www.jirby.com. 3 units. $125–$175 double; $175–$250 double during holidays. Additional person $25. *In room:* TV/VCR, kitchen, hair dryer.

MODERATE

Best Western Kachina Lodge & Meeting Center ☆ *Value* *Kids*   Built in the early 1960s, this lodge on the north end of town, in walking distance of the plaza, has a lot of charm despite the fact that it's a motor hotel. Remodeling is ongoing in the solidly built Southwestern-style rooms—some have couches and most have Taos-style *trasteros* (armoires) that hold the TVs. Beds are comfortable and baths are small, but functional and very clean. Rooms sit around a grassy courtyard studded with huge blue spruce trees, allowing kids room to run. In the center is a stage where a family from Taos Pueblo builds a bonfire and dances nightly in the summer and explains the significance of the dances—a real treat for anyone baffled by the Pueblo rituals. A full, hot breakfast is served in a very retro kiva-shaped café.

413 Paseo del Pueblo Norte (P.O. Box NM), Taos, NM 87571. © 800/522-4462 or 505/758-2275. Fax 505/758-9207. www.kachinalodge.com. 118 units. $59–$139 double; includes full breakfast. Additional person $10. Children under 12 stay free in parent's room. AE, DC, DISC, MC, V. **Amenities:** 2 restaurants; lounge; outdoor pool; courtesy shuttle; salon; coin-op laundry. *In room:* A/C, TV, high-speed Internet, coffeemaker, hair dryer, iron.

Comfort Suites   New, clean, predictable: That's what you'll get in this chain hotel about 5 minutes (by car) from the plaza. Each room has a small living/dining area, with a sleeper sofa, microwave, minirefrigerator, and coffeemaker, and a bedroom with hand-crafted wood furniture and a comfortable king-size or queen-size bed. Bathrooms are medium size. If you have kids, you might want a ground-floor poolside room. Though the pool isn't landscaped, it's warm, roomy, and accompanied by a hot tub. This hotel shares ownership with the Sagebrush Inn, so guests have easy access to its nightlife, hot breakfast (at an extra charge), and spacious grounds. Wireless Internet access is available in the lobby.

1500 Paseo del Pueblo Sur (P.O. Box 1268), Taos, NM 87571. © 888/751-1555 or 505/751-1555. Fax 505/751-1991. www.comfortsuites.com. 60 units. $69–$149 double. Rates include continental breakfast. AE, DC, DISC, MC, V. **Amenities:** Outdoor pool; Jacuzzi; in-room massage; same-day dry cleaning. *In room:* A/C, TV, high-speed Internet, fridge, microwave, coffeemaker, hair dryer.

Sagebrush Inn   Three miles south of Taos, surrounded by acres of sage, this inn is housed in an adobe building that has been added on to decade after decade, creating an interesting mix of accommodations. The original structure was built in 1929, and the roof was held in place with hand-hewn vigas. Its three floors and 12 rooms, hand-sculpted from adobe, remain. The rooms are small and cozy and have the feel of old Taos—in fact, Georgia O'Keeffe lived and worked here for 10 months in the late 1930s. But for those more accustomed to refined style, it might feel dated.

The treasure of this place is the large grass courtyard dotted with elm trees, where visitors sit and read in the warm months. Be aware that some of the rooms added in the '50s through '70s have a tackiness not overcome by the vigas and tile work. The rooms are dark and need updating. More recent additions (to the west) are more skillful; these suites away from the hotel proper are spacious and full of amenities, but they, too, with their heavy Spanish colonial furnishings have a dark aspect to them.

The lobby-cum-cantina has an Old West feel that livens at night when it becomes a venue for country/western dancing and one of Taos's most active nightspots for live music (see "Taos After Dark," in chapter 14). Traditionally, this has been a family hotel, but with a new convention center and the addition of a Comfort Suites hotel on the property, management is working to appeal to convention guests as well. A high-speed Internet connection is available in the conference center.

1508 Paseo del Pueblo Sur (P.O. Box 557), Taos, NM 87571. ℂ 800/428-3626 or 505/758-2254. Fax 505/758-5077. www.sagebrushinn.com. 97 units. $70–$95 double; $95–$165 deluxe or small suite; $130–$185 executive suite. Additional person $10. Children under 17 stay free in parent's room. Rates include full breakfast. AE, DC, DISC, MC, V. Pets welcome, $7 per night fee. **Amenities:** 2 restaurants; bar; outdoor pool; tennis courts; Jacuzzi; courtesy shuttle; business center; in-room massage; same-day dry cleaning; executive-level rooms. *In room:* A/C, TV, dataport, coffeemaker, hair dryer, iron.

INEXPENSIVE

Abominable Snowmansion Skiers' Hostel ` Since I was a kid, I've traveled past this hostel and marveled at the name; it was a treat for me to finally experience the inside. Set in the quaint village of Arroyo Seco, about 8 miles north of Taos and 10 miles from Taos Ski Valley, it offers clean beds (in dorm rooms or private ones) for reasonable prices, and a nice community experience. The common room has a pool table, piano, and circular fireplace. Best of all are the tepees that sit out around a grassy yard. They each sleep two to four people; an outdoor kitchen, showers, and toilets are nearby. High-speed and wireless Internet access is available in the common area, as is a guest computer.

476 Taos Ski Valley Rd. (Hwy. 150), Arroyo Seco (P.O. Box GG), Taos, NM 87571. ℂ 505/776-8298. Fax 505/776-2107. http://taoswebb.com/hotel/snowmansion. 60 beds. $15–$22 bed; $40–$54 double, depending on size of accommodation and season; $34 cabins and tepees; $12 camping. Rates include continental breakfast in winter. MC, V.

Adobe Sun God Lodge For a comfortable, economical stay with a northern New Mexico ambience, this is a good choice. This hotel, a 5-minute drive from the plaza, has three distinct parts spread across 1½ acres of landscaped grounds. The oldest was solidly built in 1958 and has some court-motel charm, with a low ceiling and large windows. To update the rooms, the owners added tile sinks, Taos-style furniture, and new carpeting. To the south is a section built in 1988. The rooms are small but have little touches that make them feel cozy, such as little *nichos* (niches) and hand-carved furnishings. In back to the east are the newest buildings, built in 1994. These are two-story structures with portal-style porches and balconies. Some rooms have kitchenettes, which include microwaves, refrigerators, and stoves; others have kiva fireplaces. The two suites on the northeast corner of the property are the quietest and have the best views.

919 Paseo del Pueblo Sur, Taos, NM 87571. ℂ 800/821-2437 or 505/758-3162. Fax 505/758-1716. www.sungod lodge.com. 53 units. $49–$99 double; $69–$139 suite. AE, DISC, MC, V. Pets allowed for $10 per day. **Amenities:** Jacuzzi. *In room:* A/C, TV, wireless Internet, coffeemaker.

BED & BREAKFASTS
EXPENSIVE

Adobe & Pines Inn 𐦂𐦂 The Adobe & Pines Inn seeks to create a magical escape, and it succeeds. Much of it's in a 150-year-old adobe directly off NM 68, less than half a mile south of St. Francis Plaza (about a 10-min. drive from Taos Plaza). The inn is set around a courtyard marked by an 80-foot-long grand portal and surrounded by pine and fruit trees. Each room has a private entrance and fireplace (three even have fireplaces in their bathrooms), and each is uniquely decorated. The theme here is the use of colors, which are richly displayed on the walls and in the furnishings. There's Puerta Azul, a cozy blue room with thick adobe walls, and Puerta Turquese, a separate whimsically painted guest cottage with a full kitchen. The two newest rooms, completed in 1996, have bold maroon and copper-yellow themes. The walls have handprints and petroglyph motifs, and each room is furnished with rich and comfortable couches. Most of the inn's rooms also have Jacuzzi tubs. Since this inn is near the highway, at times cars can be heard, but the rooms themselves are quiet. Morning brings a delicious full gourmet breakfast in the glassed-in breakfast room. A courtesy computer with Internet is available for guest use.

NM 68, Ranchos de Taos, NM 87557. ℂ 800/723-8267 or 505/751-0947. Fax 505/758-8423. www.adobepines.com. 7 units, 4 casitas. $95–$195 double; $185–$245 suite for up to 6 people. Rates include full gourmet breakfast. MC, V. Pets accepted with prior arrangement. **Amenities:** In-room massage; complimentary laundry facility available evenings. *In room:* TV, no phone, wireless Internet.

Adobe and Stars Bed and Breakfast Inn ★

On first appearance, this modern inn looks stark, sitting on the mesa between Taos town and Taos Ski Valley. However, once you're inside, you can see that innkeeper Judy Salathiel has an eye for detail. The breakfast area and common room are sunny, with large windows facing the mountains. A few rooms are upstairs, such as La Luna, my favorite, with views in every direction and a heart-shaped Jacuzzi tub for two. All rooms have kiva fireplaces and private decks or patios. Most of the downstairs rooms open onto a portal. All are decorated with hand-crafted Southwestern-style furniture, and many have Jacuzzi tubs. The full breakfast may vary from New Mexican dishes (such as breakfast burritos served with green-chile stew) to baked goods (apple and strawberry turnovers). In the afternoons, New Mexico wines are served with the inn's special salsa and blue-corn chips, as are sweets such as chocolate cake and piñon lemon bars. A courtesy computer with Internet is available for guest use.

At the corner of State Hwy. 150 and Valdez Rim Rd. (P.O. Box 2285), Taos, NM 87571. ℂ 800/211-7076 or 505/776-2776. Fax 505/776-2872. www.taosadobe.com. 8 units. $95–$190 double. Rates include full breakfast and hors d'oeuvres. AE, MC, V. Pets accepted with $20 per-pet fee and $50 damage deposit. **Amenities:** Jacuzzi. *In room:* Wireless Internet, hair dryer.

Alma del Monte (Spirit of the Mountain) ★

If you like views and the quiet of the country, you'll enjoy this bed-and-breakfast. Halfway between the ski area and the plaza, this house is a hacienda-shaped, pueblo-style adobe. Each room opens onto the courtyard, which is outfitted with a fountain and, in warm weather, hammocks. Proprietors Jan and Phyllis Waye have decorated the place with a bit of a hodgepodge of lovely antiques and modern furnishings that works better in some cases than in others. Each room has a Jacuzzi tub and kiva-style fireplace. Many have picture-window views and skylights, and some have private gardens. Above all, the rooms are quiet because no roads border the property. The three-course breakfast includes a smoothie and a specialty such as baked French toast. In the library, guests enjoy high-speed Internet access, television, and a good CD library.

372 Hondo Seco Rd., Taos, NM 87571. ℂ 800/273-7203 or 505/776-2721. Fax 505/776-8888. www.almaspirit.com. 5 units. $170–$210 double; prices vary with seasons and holidays. Rates include full breakfast and afternoon refreshments. AE, MC, V. Pets welcome to stay in the straw-bale doghouse; can also accommodate horses. *In room:* Wireless Internet, hair dryer, iron, CD player.

Casa de las Chimeneas ★★★

This 82-year-old adobe home set on spacious grounds has, since its opening as a luxury inn in 1988, been a model of Southwestern elegance. Adding to its appeal is a spa with a small fitness room and sauna, as well as complete massage and facial treatments for an additional charge. I recommend the Rio Grande and Territorial rooms, which are spacious and air-conditioned. Both of these rooms have heated Saltillo-tile floors, gas kiva fireplaces, and Jacuzzi tubs. If you prefer a more antique-feeling room, try the delightful older section, especially the Library Suite. Each room in the inn is decorated with original works of art and has elegant bedding, a private entrance, robes, and a minirefrigerator stocked with complimentary soft drinks, juices, and mineral water. All rooms have kiva fireplaces, and most look out on flower and herb gardens. Breakfasts are delicious. Specialties include an artichoke-heart and mushroom omelet or ricotta cream-cheese blintz, plus innkeeper Susan Vernon's special fruit frappé. In the evenings she serves a full dinner, which may include corn-crusted tilapia or roasted chicken served with vegetables from a local organic farm. End the day at the large hot tub in the courtyard. Smoking is not permitted. Ask about the spa specials. A courtesy computer with Internet is available for guest use.

405 Cordoba Rd., at Los Pandos Rd. (5303 NDCBU), Taos, NM 87571. ℂ 877/758-4777 or 505/758-4777. Fax 505/758-3976. www.visittaos.com. 8 units. $180–$290 double; $325 suite. Rates include breakfast and evening supper. AE, DC, DISC, MC, V. **Amenities:** Small exercise room; spa; Jacuzzi; sauna; concierge; car-rental desk; in-room massage; coin-op laundry; laundry service. *In room:* TV/VCR, wireless Internet, free stocked minibar, coffeemaker, hair dryer, iron, free movies.

Cottonwood Inn ✦   This inn provides cozy comfort in a rural setting. Built in 1947 by a flamboyant artist, it has high ceilings with vigas, and almost every room has a kiva fireplace. Innkeepers Kit and Bill Owen have made the place luxurious, using thick carpeting in many of the rooms and Saltillo tile in the bathrooms, as well as adding Jacuzzi tubs and steam baths to some rooms. The rooms have down pillows and comforters on the beds and are decorated in a subtle Southwestern style. The inn's location, halfway between Taos and the ski area, lends a pastoral quality to your stay, with a herd of sheep wandering in a meadow to the west. My favorite rooms are the ones that open into the main part of the house, but if you prefer a private entrance, you have that option, too. Smoking is not allowed here. Guests have access to a courtesy computer with Internet.

2 State Rd. 230 (HCR 74, Box 24609), Taos, NM 87529. ℂ 800/324-7120 or 505/776-5826. Fax 505/776-1141. www.taos-cottonwood.com. 8 units. $95–$195 double. Rates include full breakfast and afternoon snack. AE, DISC, MC, V. **Amenities:** Jacuzzi; concierge; in-room massage. *In room:* Wireless Internet, hair dryer.

Hacienda del Sol ✦✦   What's unique about this bed-and-breakfast is its completely unobstructed view of Taos Mountain. Because the 1¼-acre property borders Taos Pueblo, the land is pristine. The inn also has a rich history. It was once owned by arts patron Mabel Dodge Luhan, and it was here that author Frank Waters wrote *The People of the Valley.* You'll find bold splashes of color from the gardens—where in summer tulips, pansies, and flax bloom—to the rooms themselves—where woven bedspreads and original art lend a Mexican feel. The main house is 202 years old, so it has the wonderful curves of adobe as well as thick vigas. Some guest rooms are in this section. Others range from 7 to 25 years in age. The newer rooms are finely constructed, and I almost recommend them over the others because they're a little more private and the bathrooms are more refined. All rooms have robes and CD players, most have fireplaces, three have private Jacuzzis, and four have private steam showers. Some have minirefrigerators. A full and delicious breakfast, with favorites such as banana pancakes or scrambled eggs and turkey sausage, is served in the Spanish-hacienda-style dining area. The outdoor hot tub has a mountain view and is available for private guest use in half-hour segments. A courtesy computer with Internet is available for guest use.

109 Mabel Dodge Lane (P.O. Box 177), Taos, NM 87571. ℂ 505/758-0287. Fax 505/758-5895. www.taoshacienda delsol.com. 11 units. $125–$325 double. Rates include full breakfast and evening sweets. AE, DISC, MC, V. **Amenities:** Jacuzzi; concierge; in-room massage. *In room:* Wireless Internet, minibar, hair dryer, CD player.

Inn on La Loma Plaza 🏵🏵 Named by *American Historic Inns* as 1 of the 10 most romantic inns in America, the Inn on La Loma Plaza provides the comfortable intimacy of a B&B with the service and amenities of an inn. It's on a historic neighborhood plaza, complete with dirt streets and a tiny central park, which was once a 1796 neighborhood stronghold—adobe homes built around a square, with thick outer walls to fend off marauders. The building, a 10-minute walk from Taos Plaza, is a 200-year-old home, complete with aged vigas and maple floors, decorated tastefully with comfortable furniture and Middle Eastern rugs. Each room is unique, most with sponge-painted walls and Talavera tile in the bathrooms to provide an eclectic ambience. All have robes, slippers, lighted makeup mirrors, bottled water, and fireplaces, and most have balconies or terraces and views. Some have special touches, such as the Happy Trails Room, with knotty pine paneling, a brass bed, old chaps, and decorative hanging spurs. Some rooms have kitchenettes. Guests dine on such delights as breakfast burritos or green-chile strata (a casserole) in a plant-filled sunroom or on the patio. Internet connection is available on a courtesy computer.

315 Ranchitos Rd., Taos, NM 87571. (C) **800/530-3040** or 505/758-1717. Fax 505/751-0155. www.vacationtaos.com. 7 units. $135–$240 double; $265–$325 artist's studios; $480–$540 suite. Additional person $25. Children 12 and under stay free in parent's room. Discounts available. Rates include full breakfast. AE, DISC, MC, V. **Amenities:** Pool and spa privileges at nearby Taos Spa; Jacuzzi. *In room:* TV/VCR/DVD, wireless Internet, hair dryer, iron.

La Posada de Taos 🏵 This cozy inn just a few blocks from the plaza rests within thick and cozy adobe walls and is decorated with a combination of Mexican tile and country antiques. The three rooms off the common area are the coziest. All the rooms except one have fireplaces and private patios. El Solecito and the Beutler Room have Jacuzzi tubs. The place lights with special touches such as old Mexican doors opening onto a patio in the Lino, a view of Taos Mountain from the Taos room, and a skylight over the bed in La Casa de la Luna Miel, the honeymoon suite, which is set in a cottage separate from the rest of the inn. Expect such breakfast treats as baked apple French toast or spinach frittata. Special ski packages include a free pass to Taos Spa. A dataport is available for Internet connection in the sunroom.

309 Juanita Lane (P.O. Box 1118), Taos, NM 87571. (C) **800/645-4803** or 505/758-8164. www.laposadadetaos.com. 5 units, 1 cottage. $114–$219 double. Winter discounts available, except during holidays. Additional person $15. Rates include full breakfast and homemade afternoon snack. AE, DISC, MC, V. **Amenities:** In-room massage. *In room:* Hair dryer.

Little Tree Bed & Breakfast 🏵🏵 *(Finds)* Little Tree is one of my favorite Taos bed-and-breakfasts, partly because it's in a beautiful, secluded setting, and partly because it's constructed with real adobe that's been left in its raw state, lending the place an authentic hacienda feel. Two miles down a country road, about midway between Taos and the ski area, it's surrounded by sage and piñon. The charming and cozy rooms have radiant heat under the floors, queen-size beds (one with a king-size), nice medium-size baths (one with a Jacuzzi tub), and access to the portal and courtyard garden, at the center of which is the little tree for which the inn is named. The Piñon (my favorite) and Juniper rooms are equipped with fireplaces and private entrances. The Piñon and Aspen rooms offer sunset views. The Spruce Room, Victorian in ambience, is decorated with quilts. In the main building, the living room has a traditional viga-and-*latilla* ceiling and *tierra blanca* adobe (adobe that's naturally white; if you look closely at it, you can see little pieces of mica and straw). Visiting hummingbirds enchant guests as they enjoy a scrumptious breakfast on the portal during warmer months. On arrival, guests are treated to refreshments. A courtesy computer with Internet is available for guest use.

County Road B-143 (P.O. Box 509), Taos, NM 87513. © **800/334-8467** or 505/776-8467. www.littletreebandb.com. 4 units. $125–$185 double. Rates include breakfast and afternoon snack. MC, V. *In room:* TV/VCR.

Mabel Dodge Luhan House   This National Historic Landmark is also called "Las Palomas de Taos" because of the throngs of doves *(palomas)* that live in enchanting weathered birdhouses on the property. Like so many other free spirits, they were attracted by the flamboyant Mabel Dodge (1879–1962), who came to Taos in 1916. A familiar figure in these parts, she and her fourth husband, a full-blooded Pueblo named Tony Luhan, enlarged this 200-year-old home to its present size of 22 rooms in the 1920s. If you like history and don't mind the curves and undulations it brings to a building, this is a good choice, but it doesn't quite compete with the other B&Bs in town. The place has a mansion feel, evoking images of the glitterati of the 1920s—writers, artists, adventurers—sitting on the terrace under the cottonwoods, drinking margaritas. The entrance is marked by a Spanish colonial–style portal.

All rooms in the main house have thick vigas, arched pueblo-style doorways, hand-carved doors, kiva fireplaces, and dark hardwood floors. Most rooms have private bathrooms; others must share. Eight newer guest rooms are also equipped with fireplaces, but they lack character so I don't recommend them. Many educational workshops are held here throughout the year, the rooms often reserved for participants. Wireless Internet access is available in the living room.

240 Morada Lane, Taos, NM 87571. © **800/846-2235** or 505/751-9686. www.mabeldodgeluhan.com. 18 units, 16 with bathroom. $95–$220 double. Additional person $20. During holiday season add $35. Rates include full breakfast. AE, MC, V.

Salsa del Salto ✪   If you're seeking a secluded retreat equipped like a country club, Salsa del Salto—between Taos town and Taos Ski Valley—is a good choice. The main house, built in 1971, has the modernity of that era's architecture. The rooms here are tastefully decorated with a Southwestern motif but don't have the ambience of inns such as the Little Tree (p. 189) or Adobe & Pines (p. 186). Each room offers views of the mountains or mesas of Taos, and the bathrooms are modern and spacious. Three newer rooms (my favorites) are well designed, decorated in a whimsical Southwestern style, and each includes two queen-size beds, a minirefrigerator, fireplace, TV, VCR, and Jacuzzi tub. The focus here is on relaxation and outdoor activities. Salsa del Salto is the only bed-and-breakfast in Taos with a pool, Jacuzzi, and private tennis courts. The innkeepers, both with years of hospitality experience, serve guests' needs well and share information about favorite activities in the area. A courtesy computer with Internet is available for guest use.

543 State Hwy. 150 (Taos Ski Valley Rd.), Arroyo Seco, NM 87514. © **800/530-3097** or 505/776-2422. Fax 505/776-5734. www.bandbtaos.com. 10 units. $85–$180 double. Rates include full breakfast. Additional person $20. AE, DISC, MC, V. **Amenities:** Outdoor heated pool, open seasonally; tennis court; Jacuzzi; concierge; massage by arrangement. *In room:* TV, high-speed Internet, fridge, coffeemaker, hair dryer.

MODERATE
Old Taos Guesthouse Bed & Breakfast ✪   Once a farmer's home and later an artist's estate, this 180-year-old adobe hacienda has been restored by owners and incorrigible ski bums Tim and Leslie Reeves, who, for more than 18 years, have carefully maintained the country charm: Mexican tile in the bathrooms, vigas on the ceilings,

and kiva-style fireplaces in most of the rooms. Each room has an entrance from the outside, some off the broad portal that shades the front of the hacienda, some from a grassy lawn in the back, with a view toward the mountains. Some rooms are more utilitarian, some quainter, so make a request depending on your needs. One of my favorites is the Taos Suite, with a king-size bed, a big picture window, and a full kitchen that includes an oven, a stove, a minirefrigerator, and a microwave. Less than 2 miles from the plaza, this guesthouse sits on 7½ acres and provides a cozy northern New Mexico rural experience, complete with an *acequia* (irrigation system) and healthy breakfast. Dial-up Internet access is available on a courtesy computer.

1028 Witt Rd., Taos, NM 87571. (C) **800/758-5448** or 505/758-5448. www.oldtaos.com. 9 units. $85–$160 double. Rates include a full breakfast. DISC, MC, V. Pets accepted in some rooms with $25 fee. **Amenities:** Jacuzzi; concierge; tour desk; in-room massage; babysitting. *In room:* Hair dryer, iron.

San Geronimo Lodge   This lodge received a major renovation in 1994, but it could use some updating now. Built in 1925 in the style of a grand old lodge, it has high ceilings and a rambling veranda, all situated on 2½ acres of grounds with views of Taos Mountain, yet it's a 5-minute drive from the plaza. The interior is in good shape, the guest rooms cozy and comfortable, eight with kiva fireplaces, all with furniture hand-built by local craftspeople and some with Mexican tile in the bathrooms. Beds are comfortably firm and baths are medium size. The disrepair of the exterior and unkempt grounds reveal the commitment of the owners, which has waned in the past few years. Mornings bring a full breakfast attuned to diners' special needs in the grand dining room, which looks out on gardens. There's an outdoor swimming pool, unusual for a B&B. High-speed Internet access is available on a courtesy computer.

1101 Witt Rd., Taos, NM 87571. (C) **800/894-4119** or 505/751-3776. Fax 505/751-1493. www.sangeronimolodge.com. 18 units. $99–$175 double. Rates include full breakfast and afternoon snack. AE, DISC, MC, V. Pets accepted with prior arrangements. **Amenities:** Outdoor pool (summer only); Jacuzzi; concierge; massage. *In room:* TV, hair dryer.

2 Taos Ski Valley

For information on the skiing and the facilities offered at Taos Ski Valley, see "Skiing," in chapter 14.

LODGES
EXPENSIVE

The Bavarian Lodge ✦ *Kids*   At an elevation of 10,200 feet, this mountain-getaway lodge with interesting accommodations and excellent food offers the quintessence of Bavaria at the base of Taos Ski Valley's back bowls. The first-floor restaurant/reception area is crafted with aged pine paneling accented by an antler chandelier. Upstairs, the rooms combine antique and modern elements—not always successfully, but with good intent. All are fairly spacious, with large bathrooms, most with lofts to accommodate kids. The rooms aren't cozy, and some have odd configurations, but they all utilize faux painting to evoke old Europe; some have kitchenettes and balconies. The sun deck is the place to be on sunny ski days, and The Bavarian Restaurant (see chapter 13) is worth visiting even if you aren't a guest. The lodge offers nature hikes in summer. Wireless Internet connection is available in the lobby.

100 Kachina Rd. (P.O. Box 653), Taos Ski Valley, NM 87525. (C) **888/205-8020** or 505/776-8020. Fax 888/304-5301. www.thebavarian.com. 4 units. Dec 15–Jan 8 and Feb 10–Apr 6 $355–$425; late Nov–Dec 15 and Jan 9–Feb 9 $305–$355; summer $185–$205. AE, MC, V. Free parking. **Amenities:** Restaurant (p. 203); bar; courtesy shuttle to and from the ski area. *In room:* TV, coffeemaker, microwave, no phone.

Powderhorn Suites and Condominiums ★★ (Value) A cozy, homelike feel and Euro-Southwestern ambience make this inn one of the best buys in Taos Ski Valley, just a 2-minute walk from the lift. You'll find consistency and quality here, with impeccably clean medium-size rooms, mountain views, vaulted ceilings, spotless bathrooms, and comfortable beds. The larger suites have stoves, balconies, and fireplaces. Adjoining rooms are perfect for families. You can expect conscientious and expert service as well. There's no elevator, so if stairs are a problem for you, make sure to ask for a room on the ground floor.

5 Ernie Blake Rd. (P.O. Box 69), Taos Ski Valley, NM 87525. (C) **800/776-2346** or 505/776-2341. Fax 505/776-2341, ext. 103. www.taoswebb.com/powderhorn. 17 units. Ski season $99–$165 double, $130–$200 suite, $195–$400 condo; summer $69–$129 2- to 6-person occupancy. MC, V. Valet parking. **Amenities:** 2 Jacuzzis; massage. *In room:* TV, dataport, kitchenette.

MODERATE

Alpine Village Suites ★ Alpine Village is a small village within Taos Ski Valley, a few steps from the lift. Owned by John and Barbara Cottam, the complex also houses a ski shop and bar/restaurant. The Cottams began with seven rooms, still nice rentals, above their ski shop. Each has a sleeping loft for the agile who care to climb a ladder, as well as sunny windows. The newer section has nicely decorated rooms, with attractive touches such as Mexican furniture and inventive tile work done by locals. Like most other accommodations at Taos Ski Valley, the rooms are not especially soundproof. Fortunately, most skiers go to bed early. All rooms have VCRs and small kitchenettes equipped with stoves, microwaves, and minirefrigerators. In the newer building, rooms have fireplaces and private balconies. Request a south-facing room for a view of the slopes. The Jacuzzi has a fireplace and a view of the slopes. High-speed and wireless Internet access is available in all but two rooms.

100 Thunderbird Rd. (P.O. Box 98), Taos Ski Valley, NM 87525. (C) **800/576-2666** or 505/776-8540. Fax 505/776-8542. www.alpine-suites.com. 29 units. Ski season $70–$145 suite for 2, $265–$335 suite for up to 6; summer $80–$120 suite for 2 (includes continental breakfast). AE, DISC, MC, V. Covered valet parking $10 per night. **Amenities:** Jacuzzi; sauna; massage; business center. *In room:* TV/VCR, kitchenette.

Austing Haus Hotel This beautiful example of a timber-frame structure was hand-built by owner Paul Austing, who will gladly give you details of the process. Though an interesting structure, at times it feels a bit fragile. The medium-size guest rooms, about 1½ miles from the ski resort, have a cute mountain-inn feel, with comfortable beds and small but functional and clean baths. There are boot lockers available for skiers.

1282 State Hwy. 150. (P.O. Box 8), Taos Ski Valley, NM 87525. (C) **800/748-2932** or 505/776-2649. Fax 505/776-8751. www.austinghaus.net 23 units. $49–$170 double. Rates include lavish continental breakfast. AE, MC, V. Free parking. Pets stay free. **Amenities:** Jacuzzi. *In room:* TV, high-speed and wireless Internet.

CONDOMINIUMS
EXPENSIVE

Edelweiss Lodge & Spa ★★ Opened in 2005, this lodge at the base of the mountain took the place of a 1960s classic chalet. Now, it's a brand new condo-hotel. The condominiums are upscale, each with a flagstone fireplace and full kitchen with marble countertops, stainless steel appliances, and many with nice views of the slopes. All have luxury furnishings decorated in earth tones. For those looking for an upscale stay, this is your choice, though the service will be less personal than, say, the Powderhorn Suites and Condominiums. Hotel rooms follow with the same luxury as the condos. Rooms are medium size with comfortable beds and medium-size baths. Check the website for a glimpse of the rooms and other facilities. Underground parking, a full spa, an excellent restaurant, and—get this—valet service for your skis, add to the appeal. Wireless Internet access is available in the lobby.

106 Sutton Place, Taos Ski Valley, NM 87525. © **800/I-LUV-SKI** or 505/737-6900. Fax 505/737-6995. www.edelweiss lodgeandspa.com. 46 units. Hotel room winter $220–$440 double; summer $125 double; condo winter $275–$1,056 depending on the season; summer $198–$375 (ranges cover 1 bedroom/1 bath–3 bedrooms/3 baths). AE, DISC, MC, V. Free parking. **Amenities:** Restaurant; bar; health club and full spa; 2 Jacuzzis; sauna; concierge; massage; ski shop. *In room:* TV, high-speed Internet, fridge, coffeemaker, hair dryer.

Sierra del Sol Condominiums ⭐

I have wonderful memories of these condominiums, which are just a 2-minute walk from the lift; family friends used to invite me to stay with them when I was about 10. I was happy to see that the units, built in the 1960s, with additions through the years, have been well maintained. Though they're privately owned, and therefore decorated at the whim of the owners, management does inspect them every year and make suggestions. They're smartly built and come in a few sizes: studio, one-bedroom, and two-bedroom. The one- and two-bedroom units have big living rooms with fireplaces and porches that look out on the ski runs. The bedrooms are spacious, and some have sleeping lofts. Each has a full kitchen, with a dishwasher, stove, oven, and refrigerator. Most units also have microwaves and humidifiers. Two-bedroom units sleep up to six. Grills and picnic tables on the grounds sit near a mountain river. High-speed and wireless Internet access is available in a guest computer room.

13 Thunderbird Rd. (P.O. Box 84), Taos Ski Valley, NM 87525. © **800/523-3954** or 505/776-2981. Fax 505/776-2347. www.sierrataos.com. 32 units. Prices range from $70 for studio in summer to $395 for 2-bedroom condo in high season. AE, DISC, MC, V. Free parking. **Amenities:** 2 Jacuzzis; 2 saunas; massage; babysitting; coin-op laundry. *In room:* TV/VCR, kitchen, hair dryer upon request, iron upon request, safe.

Snakedance Condominiums and Spa ⭐⭐

A recent $3.5 million renovation has transformed the rooms of this once-hotel into comfortable condominiums. Skiers appreciate the inn's location, just steps from the lift, as well as amenities such as ski storage and boot dryers. The original structure that stood on this site (part of which has been restored for use today) was known as the Hondo Lodge. Before there was a Taos Ski Valley, Hondo Lodge served as a refuge for fishermen, hunters, and artists. Constructed from enormous pine timbers that had been cut for a copper-mining operation in the 1890s, it was literally nothing more than a place for the men to bed down for the night. The Snakedance Condominiums today are privately owned units, so each may differ some, though they seem consistent in quality. All have balconies with French doors and kitchens with granite counters and a range, fridge, dishwasher, and microwave. Many feature wood-burning fireplaces. The Hondo Restaurant and Bar, remodeled in 2006, offers dining and entertainment daily during the ski season (schedules vary off-season) and also sponsors wine tastings and wine dinners. Grilled items, salads, and snacks are available on an outdoor deck. The hotel also offers shuttle service to and from nearby shops and restaurants. Smoking is prohibited on the property.

110 Sutton Place (P.O. Box 89), Taos Ski Valley, NM 87525. © **800/322-9815** or 505/776-2277. Fax 505/776-1410. www.snakedancecondos.com. 33 units. 1 bedroom condo $225–$475 double in winter, in summer $95; 2-bedroom condo $285–$600 for 4 people in winter, $120 in summer; 2 bedroom loft condo $345–$725 for 6 people in winter, $150 in summer. Extra person $30 in winter, $10 in summer. AE, DC, DISC, MC, V. Free parking at Taos Ski Valley parking lot. Closed mid-Apr to Memorial Day and mid-Oct to mid-Nov. **Amenities:** Restaurant; bar; exercise room; spa; Jacuzzi; sauna; massage; convenience store (with food, sundries, video rental, and alcoholic beverages). *In room:* Satellite TV, wireless Internet, kitchen, coffeemaker, hair dryer.

MODERATE

Taos Mountain Lodge *Value*   These loft suites (which can each accommodate up to six) provide airy, comfortable lodging for a good price. Built in 1990, about a mile west of Taos Ski Valley on the road from Taos, the place has undergone some renovation over the years. Don't expect a lot of privacy in these condominiums, but they're good for a romping ski vacation. The beds are comfortable and the baths are small but functional. Each unit has a small bedroom downstairs and a loft bedroom upstairs, as well as a foldout or futon couch in the living room. Regular rooms have kitchenettes, with minirefrigerators and stoves, and deluxe rooms have full kitchens, with full refrigerators, stoves, and ovens.

Taos Ski Valley Rd. (P.O. Box 202), Taos Ski Valley, NM 87525. (C) **866/320-8267** or 505/776-2229. Fax 505/776-3982. www.taosmountainlodge.com. 10 units. Ski season $119–$280 suite; May–Oct $80–$100 suite. AE, DISC, MC, V. *In room:* Kitchen or kitchenette.

3 RV Parks & Campgrounds

Carson National Forest   There are nine national-forest camping areas within 20 miles of Taos; these developed areas are open from Memorial Day to Labor Day. They range from woodsy, streamside sites on the road to Taos Ski Valley to open lowlands with lots of sage. Call the Forest Service to discuss the best location for your needs.

208 Cruz Alta Rd., Taos, NM 87571. (C) **505/758-6200**. www.fs.fed.us/r3/carson. Fees range from $7–$15 per night. No credit cards.

Questa Lodge   On the banks of the Red River, this RV camp is just outside the small village of Questa. It's a nice pastoral setting. The cabins aren't in the best condition, but the RV and camping accommodations are pleasant—all with amazing mountain views.

Lower Embargo Rd. #8 (P.O. Box 155), Questa, NM 87556. (C) **505/586-9913**. 24 sites. Full RV hookup $20 per day, $200 per month. 4 cabins for rent in summer. AE, DISC, MC, V. Closed Nov–Apr.

Taos RV Park   This RV park, on the edge of town (and on a local bus line), offers a convenient location but a city atmosphere. It has very clean and nice bathrooms and showers. Two tepees rent for $25 each, but beware: They're right on the main drag and may be noisy. A better teepee bet is at the Abominable Snowmansion Skiers' Hostel (p. 186) north of town in Arroyo Seco, which is a quieter setting. Senior discounts are available. Wireless Internet access is available throughout most of the park, and there's a high-speed Internet connection in the lobby.

1802 NM 68, Taos, NM 87557. (C) **800/323-6009** or 505/758-1667. Fax 505/758-1989. www.taosbudgethost.com. 33 spaces. $17 without RV hookup; $25 with RV hookup. DISC, MC, V.

Taos Valley RV Park and Campground   Just 2½ miles south of the plaza, this campground is surrounded by sage and offers views of the surrounding mountains. Each site has a picnic table and grill. The place has a small store, a laundry room, a playground, and tent shelters, as well as a dump station and very clean restrooms. Pets are welcome. Wireless Internet access is available throughout the park.

120 Este Rd., off NM 68 (7204 NDCBU), Taos, NM 87571. (C) **800/999-7571** or 505/758-4469. Fax 505/758-4469. www.camptaos.com/rv. 92 spaces. $22 without RV hookup; $29–$35 with RV hookup. MC, V.

13

Where to Dine in Taos

Taos has some of the region's most inventive and fun restaurants. The creativity of the town flourishes in the flavors here. It's also a comfortable place to dine. Informality reigns; at a number of restaurants, you can eat world-class food while wearing jeans or even ski pants. Nowhere is a jacket and tie mandatory.

This informality doesn't extend to reservations, however; especially during the peak season, it's important to make reservations well in advance and keep them or else cancel. Also, be aware that Taos is not a late-night place; most restaurants finish serving at about 9pm.

1 Restaurants by Cuisine

AMERICAN
The Apple Tree ✸✸ ($$, p. 199)
Bravo ✸ ($$, p. 200)
Caffé Renato ✸✸ ($$, p. 200)
De La Tierra ✸✸✸ ($$$, p. 196)
Gypsy 360° ✸ ($, p. 204)
Michael's Kitchen ($, p. 203)
Old Blinking Light ✸ ($$, p. 200)

ASIAN
Gypsy 360° ✸ ($, p. 204)

BAVARIAN
The Bavarian Restaurant ✸ ($, p. 203)

CONTEMPORARY AMERICAN
Lambert's of Taos ✸✸ ($$$, p. 198)

CONTINENTAL
Stakeout Grill & Bar ✸✸ ($$$, p. 199)

DELI/CAFE
Bent Street Cafe & Deli ($$, p. 199)
Bravo ✸ ($$, p. 200)
Taos Cow ✸ ($, p. 204)

FRENCH/SPANISH FUSION
Gutiz ✸✸ ($, p. 203)

INTERNATIONAL
Bent Street Cafe & Deli ($$, p. 199)
La Folie ✸✸ ($$$, p. 198)
Gutiz ✸✸ ($, p. 203)
Ogelvie's Bar & Grille ($$, p. 200)
Trading Post Café ✸✸ ($$, p. 201)

ITALIAN
Caffé Renato ✸✸ ($$, p. 200)
Taos Pizza Out Back ✸ ($$, p. 201)
Trading Post Café ✸✸ ($$, p. 201)

MEDITERRANEAN
Gutiz ✸✸ ($, p. 203)
Joseph's Table ✸✸✸ ($$$, p. 196)

MEXICAN
Guadalajara Grill ✸ ($, p. 202)

NEW AMERICAN
Doc Martin's ✸ ($$$, p. 196)
Gutiz ✸✸ ($, p. 203)
Joseph's Table ✸✸✸ ($$$, p. 199)

NEW MEXICAN
Michael's Kitchen ($, p. 203)
Orlando's New Mexican Café ✸ ($, p. 203)

Key to Abbreviations: $$$$ = Very Expensive $$$ = Expensive $$ = Moderate $ = Inexpensive

PIZZA

Taos Pizza Out Back ✦ ($$, p. 201)

SOUTHWESTERN

The Apple Tree ✦✦ ($$, p. 199)
Eske's Brew Pub and Eatery ✦
($, p. 202)

STEAK/SEAFOOD

Stakeout Grill & Bar ✦✦ ($$$, p. 199)

2 Expensive

De La Tierra ✦✦✦ REGIONAL AMERICAN   Come here for artfully prepared American fare with an emphasis on wild game. Located in the eco-resort El Monte Sagrado (p. 181), this restaurant offers an old-world Orient ambience, with a high ceiling, comfortable black silk chairs, and notable contemporary art on the walls. Service is excellent, even down to the master sommelier overseeing the wine selections. The chef utilizes seasonal and local ingredients, including organic ones when he can. For starters, I recommend the Dungeness crab cake, or, for a more exotic treat, try the yak satay, the meat from the resort owner's high-mountain cattle-like animals. For a main course, I've enjoyed the venison medallions, served over garlic mashed potatoes and with roasted spring mushrooms. My mother likes the rosemary skewered shrimp, served with white-corn polenta and chard. Tasty food is served during the day at The Gardens, a more casual spot, with lots of exotic plants and a lovely patio (try the yak cheese frittata). Tapas are served at the Anaconda Bar.

In the El Monte Sagrado Hotel, 317 Kit Carson Rd. © **800/828-TAOS** or 505/758-3502. Reservations recommended. The Gardens breakfast $7–$12; lunch $8–$16; De La Tierra dinner $27–$39. AE, DC, DISC, MC, V. The Gardens daily 7–10am and 11am–2:30pm; De La Tierra daily 5:30–10pm.

Doc Martin's ✦ NEW AMERICAN   Doc Martin's serves innovative food in a historic setting. The restaurant comprises Dr. Thomas Paul Martin's former home, office, and delivery room. In 1912, painters Bert Philips (Doc's brother-in-law) and Ernest Blumenschein hatched the concept of the Taos Society of Artists in the dining room. Art still predominates here, in both the paintings that adorn the walls and the cuisine offered. The food is often good here, but it can be inconsistent.

The wine list has received numerous "Awards of Excellence" from *Wine Spectator* magazine. In the rich atmosphere of a thick-walled adobe home with a kiva fireplace, diners feast on Southwestern breakfast fare such as huevos rancheros (fried eggs on a blue-corn tortilla smothered with chile and Jack cheese). Lunch might include the house specialty, the Doc Chile relleno or chipolte shrimp on corn cake. For dinner, a good bet is the piñon-encrusted salmon or the Southwest lacquered duck served with *posole* and mango relish. If you still have room, there's always a nice selection of desserts—try the chocolate mousse cake or the *capirotada* (New Mexican bread pudding). The Adobe bar has live jazz with no cover charge. Brunch is served on Sundays from 7:30am to 2:30pm.

In the Historic Taos Inn, 125 Paseo del Pueblo Norte. © **505/758-1977.** www.taosinn.com. Reservations recommended. Breakfast $5–$9; lunch $5.50–$11; dinner $14–$28; fixed-price menu $33. AE, DISC, MC, V. Daily 7:30–11am, 11:30am–2:30pm, and 5:30–9pm.

Joseph's Table ✦✦✦ (Finds) NEW AMERICAN/MEDITERRANEAN   This notable eatery, in the Hotel La Fonda de Taos on the plaza, serves some of the most imaginative and precisely prepared food in northern New Mexico. The ambience is

Taos Area Dining

The Apple Tree **7**	Joseph's Table **9**
The Bavarian Restaurant **1**	La Folie **7**
Bent Street Cafe & Deli **8**	Lambert's of Taos **13**
Bravo **14**	Michael's Kitchen **5**
Caffé Renato **6**	Ogelvie's Bar & Grill **10**
De La Tierra **12**	Old Blinking Light **1**
Doc Martin's **6**	Orlando's New Mexican Café **2**
Eske's Brew Pub and Eatery **11**	Taos Pizza Out Back **4**
Guadalajara Grill **3, 15**	Stakeout Grill & Bar **15**
Gutiz **3**	Trading Post Café **15**
Gypsy 360° **1**	Taos Cow **1**

something like old-west saloon meets sophisticated artist's home. Hand-painted pastel flowers decorate the walls and pussy-willow-and-iron chandelliers hang between hand-hewn vigas (beams) on the ceiling. There are hardwood floors and some Asian-style tables with pillow seating along the back. Chef/owner Joseph Wrede (once selected as 1 of the 10 "Best New Chefs" in America by *Food and Wine Magazine*) creates such delicacies as a juicy green chile buffalo burger served with homemade sweet potato chips or Mediterranean mussels in a pesto broth and Tuscan bread for lunch. Dinner is equally inventive. It might start with tempura squash blossoms stuffed with goat cheese and green chiles, with fire-roasted tomato salsa, and move on to pepper-crusted elk tenderloin with creamed spinach, morel mushrooms, and truffle demi-glaze or the spice-rubbed grilled wild salmon with potato hash and sweet peas. There's typically a vegetarian option as well. Be aware that Wrede likes complex flavors, so those who prefer more conservative food might opt for the Stakeout (below). The friendly and attentive servers can help guide you through the complex menu, so be sure to ask. For dessert, try such delicacies as the mescal chocolate bar with lime sorbet or the buttermilk panna cotta with strawberry rose sauce. An eclectic selection of beers and wines by the bottle and glass is available.

In the Hotel La Fonda de Taos, 108-A South Taos Plaza. © 505/751-4512. www.josephstable.com. Reservations recommended. Main courses $8–$18 lunch, $18–$35 dinner. AE, DISC, MC, V. May–Aug Mon–Sat 11:30am–2:30pm and daily 5:30–10pm; Sun brunch 10:30am–2:30pm. Hours are abbreviated in winter; call first.

La Folie ★★ *Finds* FRENCH   An inventive menu and a casually imaginative atmosphere make this one of Taos's best new dining experiences. La Folie, "the folly," run by two brothers, serves complex flavors in a long, moodily lit dining room or, in summer, on a bright outdoor patio. Service is excellent. Lunch brings such options as an onion soup with burgundy wine or an endive salad on field greens with Roquefort, walnuts, and apples. Dinner is even more rich. I've enjoyed a seared scallops salad followed by grouper with a potato cake and a white sauce with caviar. The roasted tenderloin served with saffron polenta is also delicious. For dessert, the Aztec hot chocolate is legendary. Watch for the monthly beer dinners and cigar and wine dinners.

106-B Paseo del Pueblo Norte. © 505/751-7549. www.restaurantlafolie.com. Reservations recommended in summer. Main courses lunch $7.25–$9, dinner $18–$25. June–Aug daily noon–5pm and 6–10pm. Abbreviated hours in winter; call first.

Lambert's of Taos ★★ CONTEMPORARY AMERICAN   Zeke Lambert, once the head chef at Doc Martin's (p. 196), opened this fine dining establishment in late 1989 in the historic Randall Home near Los Pandos Road. It's a sparsely decorated hacienda with wood floors and lacy curtains—a nice spot for a romantic evening. The service ranges from good to begrudging. The food is well prepared and imaginative, though not quite of the caliber of Joseph's Table (above). You might start with a bowl of roasted corn chowder or duck dumplings. The spinach salad with sautéed mushrooms and bacon in a walnut raspberry dressing is excellent. For an entree, the pepper-crusted lamb—very peppery—served with garlic pasta is a signature dish, but you might opt for one of the fresh fish specials, such as seared ahi tuna, or a game special such as buffalo tenderloin. For dessert, try the warm apple and almond crisp with white chocolate ice cream or Zeke's chocolate mousse with raspberry sauce. A full bar, with an interesting wine and beer list and espresso coffee, is available. Recently, the restaurant opened a cozy lounge with its own bar menu.

309 Paseo del Pueblo Sur. © 505/758-1009. Reservations recommended. Main courses $15–$32. AE, DC, DISC, MC, V. Daily 5pm–closing, usually 9pm or so.

Stakeout Grill & Bar ✹✹ CONTINENTAL/STEAKS/SEAFOOD   This is one of northern New Mexico's most adventurous dining experiences. You drive about a mile up a dirt road toward the base of the Sangre de Cristo Mountains to reach the restaurant, and dine looking down on the Taos gorge while the sun sets over the Jemez Range. The warm, rustic decor of this sprawling hacienda with a broad patio (a great place to sit in summer) includes creaking hardwood floors—and a crackling fireplace in the winter. The fare, which focuses on steak and seafood, is fresh and thoughtfully prepared. Start with baked brie with sliced almonds and apples, or green chile crab cakes with citrus aioli. Move on to a filet mignon served with béarnaise sauce, or sample one of the chef's excellent pasta specials. Recently, I had shrimp over linguini with goat cheese that was a bowl of pure joy. This is also the place to come if you have a craving for lobster. Try to time your reservation so you can see the sunset. A full bar, an extensive wine list, and cigars are available.

101 Stakeout Dr. (9 miles south of Taos, just off Hwy. 68). ⓒ 505/758-2042. www.stakeoutrestaurant.com. Reservations recommended. Main courses $20–$50. AE, DC, DISC, MC, V. Daily 5–9:30pm.

3 Moderate

The Apple Tree ✹✹ SOUTHWESTERN/AMERICAN   Eclectic music pervades the four adobe rooms of this hacienda, a block north of the plaza. Original paintings by Taos masters watch over the candlelit service indoors. Outside, diners sit at wooden tables beneath a sprawling apple tree. If you like comfort, both in your food and ambience, this is your place. For starters, the Apple Tree salad (greens sprinkled with dried cranberries and walnuts, tossed with honey blue cheese dressing) is very good, as is the *calabasa* (squash) quesadilla. A local's favorite (and mine too) is mango chicken enchiladas (chicken simmered with onions and spices, layered between blue-corn tortillas with mango chutney, sour cream, and salsa fresca, and smothered with green chile). Less adventuresome diners might prefer fresh rainbow trout with a citrus-piñon butter sauce or roasted vegetable lasagna. The brunch offerings are worth sampling, even more so when eaten out on the lovely patio under the restaurant's namesake. Such standards as French toast and eggs Benedict are good, but the specials usually outshine them, especially the fresh fruit crepes, such as blueberry or peach, served with whipped cream. The Apple Tree has an award-winning wine list, and the desserts are prepared fresh daily.

123 Bent St. ⓒ 505/758-1900. Reservations recommended. Main courses $5–$11 brunch, $6–$12 lunch, $12–$30 dinner. AE, DC, DISC, MC, V. Mon–Sat 11:30am–3pm; daily 5:30–9pm; brunch Sun 10:30am–3pm.

Bent Street Cafe & Deli CAFE/INTERNATIONAL   This popular cafe, a short block north of the plaza, serves decent food in a country-home atmosphere. Outside, a flower box surrounds sidewalk seating that is heated in winter. Inside, wood floors and lots of windows provide a country diner feel. The menu features breakfast burritos and homemade granola in the morning; for lunch—the best meal to eat here—you can choose from 18 deli sandwiches, plus a "create-your-own" column, as well as a variety of salads. At dinner, choose from more elaborate offerings such as prawns sautéed with sun-dried tomatoes and artichoke hearts over fettuccine or sausage lasagna. Only negative: During a recent visit, the food lacked freshness. To grab a picnic to go, head for the deli, which offers carryout service.

120 Bent St. ⓒ 505/758-5787. Reservations accepted. Breakfast $2–$8; lunch $2.50–$8; dinner $11–$20. MC, V. Mon–Sat 8am–9pm.

Bravo ★ (Value) AMERICAN/CAFE   This bustling cafe on the south end of town offers a refreshing big-city mix of atmosphere and flavors. As well as a restaurant, it's a specialty wine and beer shop, package liquor store, and gourmet deli—a great place to stock your lunch basket. There's a large communal table at the restaurant's heart. Some tables are situated in a wine-cellar atmosphere that's a little heavy on the bottles for my taste. Those near the martini bar are more atmospheric. The menu is eclectic, offering good-size portions of very tasty food. With owner/chef Lionel Garnier's French background lending magic, the flavors are refined. Each day a unique pizza studs the menu—my favorite is the Bravo, with roasted vegetables. The Caesar salad with chicken is also popular, as is the elaborate salad bar, complete with pasta and bean concoctions. An assortment of sandwiches fills the menu as well. My mother, a reuben aficionado, found theirs one of the best she's ever had. In the evenings, you can order Continental dishes. The half roast chicken is perfectly seasoned, served au jus with fries and tossed salad. During busy hours, service is slow but congenial. There's also a martini and beer bar here with specials, such as a beer sampler and enough types of martinis to make you really wonder how many things you should mix with gin or vodka.

1353-A Paseo del Pueblo Sur, Ranchos de Taos. (C) 505/758-8100. Lunch $7–$12; dinner $9–$18. AE, DISC, MC, V. Mon–Sat 11am–9pm.

Caffé Renato ★★ (Moments) AMERICAN/ITALIAN   You can't miss this cafe decked out with bright red umbrellas on its patio. Diners enjoy the cool Taos air while feasting on tasty food prepared with fine ingredients. A back patio is quieter, and inside, sunporch- and kitchen-side dining rooms provide a comfortable ambience decorated with art—the restaurant shares space with the Farnsworth Gallery, which is fun to stroll through while you await your food. Service is friendly but may be understaffed. The lunch menu holds a variety of sandwiches (including create-your-own panini options) and salads. The angus burger is stellar, as is the turkey bacon ranch salad. For dinner, the old classic spaghetti with meatballs is easy on the wallet, while the grilled salmon with a lemon tarragon aioli is equally delicious. Finish with a chocolate truffle torte. A selection of beers and wines accompanies the menu.

133 Paseo del Pueblo North. (C) 505/758-0244. Reservations recommended on weekend nights. Main courses lunch $7–$13; dinner $10–$25. Daily 11am–9pm.

Ogelvie's Bar & Grille INTERNATIONAL   The only real reason to go to this restaurant is to have a cocktail on the plaza. In the warm months, there's a nice balcony where diners can sit and drink margaritas and indulge in chips or other appetizers, such as potato skins, or even burgers. Otherwise, the food here is not flavorful, and the atmosphere inside is dated.

103E. Plaza Suite I. (C) 505/758-8866. Lunch $6–$12; dinner $8.50–$25. AE, DC, DISC, MC, V. Daily 11am–9pm dining, 11am–10pm bar.

Old Blinking Light ★ AMERICAN   This restaurant on the Ski Valley Road provides tasty American food in a casual atmosphere. It's named for the blinking yellow light that was once the marker Taoseños used to give directions ("turn left at the blinking light," etc.), now replaced by a stoplight. Decorated with Spanish colonial furniture and an excellent art collection, this restaurant is a good place to stop after skiing or for a romping night of music. The service is friendly and efficient. To accompany the free chips and homemade salsa, order a margarita—preferably their standard, made with Sauza Gold Tequila—and sip it next to the patio bonfire, open evenings

Family-Friendly Restaurants

Michael's Kitchen (p. 203) With a broad menu, comfy booths, and a very casual, diner-type atmosphere, Michael's Kitchen makes both kids and their parents feel at home.

Orlando's New Mexican Café (p. 203) The relaxed atmosphere and playfully colorful walls will please the kids almost as much as the tacos and quesadillas made especially for them.

Taos Cow (p. 204) Pot pies and sandwiches will fill kids up before they dive into the all-natural ice cream at this cafe north of town.

Taos Pizza Out Back (below) The pizza will please both parents and kids, and so will all the odd decorations, such as the chain with foot-long links hanging over the front counter.

year-round. The menu is broad, ranging from salads and burgers to steaks, seafood, and Mexican food. I say head straight for the fajitas, especially the jumbo shrimp wrapped in bacon and stuffed with poblano peppers and jack cheese. Leave room for the Old Blinking Light mud pie, made with local Taos Cow Ice Cream. Live music plays on Monday and Friday nights.

US 150, mile marker 1. ℂ 505/776-8787. Reservations recommended weekends and Mon nights. Main courses $9–$26. AE, MC, V. Wine shop daily noon–10pm. Restaurant daily 5–10pm.

Taos Pizza Out Back ℛ 𝘒𝘪𝘥𝘴 PASTA AND GOURMET PIZZA My kayaking buddies always go here after a day on the river. That will give you an idea of the level of informality (very), as well as the quality of the food and beer (great), and the size of the portions (large). It's a raucous old hippie-decorated adobe restaurant, with a friendly and eager waitstaff. What to order? I have one big word here: PIZZA. Sure the spicy Greek pasta is good, as is the Veggie Zone (a calzone filled with stir-fried veggies and two cheeses)—but, why? The pizzas are incredible. All come with a delicious thin crust (no sogginess here) that's folded over on the edges and sprinkled with sesame seeds. The sauce is unthinkably tasty, and the variations are broad. There's Thai chicken pizza (pineapple, peanuts, and a spicy sauce); The Killer, with sun-dried tomatoes, Gorgonzola, green chile, and black olives; and my favorite, pizza Florentine (spinach, basil, sun-dried tomatoes, chicken breast, mushrooms, capers, and garlic, sautéed in white wine). Don't leave without trying either a Dalai Lama bar (coconut, chocolate, and caramel) or the Taos Yum (a "mongo" chocolate-chip cookie with ice cream, whipped cream, and chocolate sauce). Check out the small selection of wines and large selection of microbrews.

712 Paseo del Pueblo Norte (just north of Allsup's). ℂ 505/758-3112. Reservations recommended weekends and holidays. Pizzas $12–$26; pastas and calzones $7–$12. MC, V. Summer daily 11am–10pm; winter Sun–Thurs 11am–9pm, Fri–Sat 11am–10pm.

Trading Post Café ℛℛ 𝘍𝘪𝘯𝘥𝘴 NORTHERN ITALIAN/INTERNATIONAL One of my tastiest writing assignments was when I did a profile of this restaurant for the *New York Times*. Chef/owner René Mettler spent 3 hours serving course after course of dishes prepared especially for us. If you think this gastronomical orgy might color my opinion, just ask anyone in town where they most like to eat. Even notables such as Dennis Hopper and Gene Hackman will likely name the Trading Post. What draws the crowds here is a gallery atmosphere, where rough plastered walls washed with an orange hue are set off by sculptures, paintings, and photographs. The meals are also artistically served. "You eat with your eyes," says Mettler. If you show up without reservations, be prepared to wait for a table, and don't expect quiet romance here: The place bustles. A bar encloses an open-exhibition kitchen. If you're dining alone or just don't feel like waiting for a table, the bar is a fun place to sit. Although the focus is on the fine food, diners can feel comfortable here, even if trying three appetizers and skipping the main course. The outstanding Caesar salad has an interesting twist—garlic chips. If you like pasta, you'll find a nice variety on the menu. The fettuccine alla carbonara is tasty, as is the seafood pasta. Heartier appetites might like the New Zealand lamb chops with tomato-mint sauce. There's also a fresh fish of the day and usually some nice stews and soups at very reasonable prices. A good list of beers and wines rounds out the experience. For dessert, try the tarts.

4179 Paseo del Pueblo Sur, Ranchos de Taos. ⓒ **505/758-5089.** Reservations accepted. Menu items $6–$28. AE, DC, DISC, MC, V. Tues–Sat 11:30am–9:30pm; Sun 5–9pm.

4 Inexpensive

Eske's Brew Pub and Eatery ⊛ SOUTHWESTERN PUB FARE   I have a fondness for this place that one might have for an oasis in the desert. The first time I ate here, I'd been on assignment ice climbing and just spent 8 hours in the shadow of a canyon, hacking my way up an 80-foot frozen waterfall. I sat down at one of the high tables in the main room, dipped into a big bowl of Wanda's green-chile turkey stew, and felt the blood return to my extremities. My climbing buddies ordered The Fatty (a whole-wheat tortilla filled with beans, mashed potatoes, onions, and feta and cheddar cheeses, smothered in green-chile turkey stew). Eske's also serves bratwurst, burgers, and vegetarian dishes. With our meal, we enjoyed a tasty black and tan (a mixture of barley wine and stout, the heavier beer sinking to the bottom), and a Mesa pale ale. When I asked the owner, Steve "Eske" Eskeback, which was his favorite beer, he replied "the one in my hand," meaning he recommends all the beers, which are his own recipes. The service is friendly and informal. The crowd is local, a few people sitting at the bar, where they can visit and watch the beer-pouring and food preparation. At times it can be a rowdy place, but mostly it's just fun, with lots of ski patrollers and mountain guides showing up to swap stories. In summer, you can eat on picnic tables outside.

106 Des Georges Lane. ⓒ **505/758-1517.** All menu items under $10. MC, V. Mar–Sept and peak times such as spring and winter breaks daily 11:30am–10pm; rest of winter Fri–Sun 11:30am–10pm.

Guadalajara Grill ⊛ MEXICAN   My organic-lettuce-farmer friend Joe introduced me to this authentic Mexican restaurant; then he disappeared into Mexico, only communicating occasionally by e-mail. Did the incredible food lure him south? I wonder. The restaurant is in a plain building on the south side, but don't let that put you off; the food here is excellent. It's Mexican rather than New Mexican, a refreshing treat. I recommend the tacos, particularly pork or chicken, served in soft homemade corn tortillas, the meat artfully seasoned and grilled. The burritos are large and smothered in chile. *Platos* are served with rice and beans, and half orders are available for smaller appetites. There are also some seafood dishes available—try the *mojo de ajo* (shrimp cooked with garlic), served with rice, beans, and guacamole. Beer and wine are served.

1384 Paseo del Pueblo Sur. ℭ **505/751-0063.** Main courses $5–$15. MC, V. Mon–Sat 10:30am–9pm; Sun 11am–9pm. A second location, at 1822 Paseo del Pueblo Norte (ℭ **505/737-0816**), is open Mon–Sat 10:30am–9pm; Sun 11am–8:30pm.

Gutiz ↷↷ *Finds* FRENCH/LATIN FUSION   Between lavender walls hung with bright contemporary art, this new restaurant, the creation of chef Eduardo Gutiz, serves some of Taos's most unique and flavorful cuisine. Born in Spain, raised in France, he traveled in Peru and Bolivia. From these locales, he's combined flavors using organic greens and fresh meats and fish. Service is friendly and efficient. Breakfast brings delicacies such as a Tortilla Alicantina—a baked omelet with potatoes and onions, served with a green tapenade. The French toast is thick, made with home-baked bread, the best I've had since the old Super Chief days. Lunch might begin with fried calamari or chicken tenders served with an aji amarillo sauce. For an entree, the pork tenderloin with onion confit and garbanzo beans is delicious, as are the many sandwiches served on homemade bread. Alongside the great food, sip from a variety of coffees and chai tea. Eduardo hopes to open on weekend evenings; call to find out if he's done it yet.

812-B Paseo del Pueblo Norte. ℭ **505/758-1226.** Main courses $6.50–$15. Tues–Sun 7am–4pm.

Michael's Kitchen *Kids* NEW MEXICAN/AMERICAN   A couple blocks north of the plaza, this eatery provides big portions of rib-sticking food in a relaxed atmosphere. Between its hardwood floor and viga ceiling are various knickknacks: an antique wood stove here, a Tiffany lamp there. Seating is at booths and tables. Breakfast is the meal to eat here, with a large selection of pancakes and egg preparations (with names like the "Moofy" and "Omelette Extraordinaire") served all day. Lunch brings sandwiches, including a Philly cheese steak, a tuna melt, and a veggie option. Some people like the generically (and facetiously) titled "Health Food" meal, a double order of fries with red or green chile and cheese. Dinners range from stuffed sopaipillas to chopped sirloin steak. If you're in a hurry, try one of the excellent doughnuts served from Michael's bakery.

304 C Paseo del Pueblo Norte. ℭ **505/758-4178.** No reservations. Breakfast $3–$8; lunch $4–$9.50; dinner $6–$14. AE, DISC, MC, V. Daily 7am–8:30pm (except major holidays).

Orlando's New Mexican Café ↷ *Kids* NEW MEXICAN   Festivity reigns in this spicy little cafe on the north end of town. Serving some of northern New Mexico's best chile, this place has colorful tables set around a bustling open kitchen and airy patio dining during warmer months. Service is friendly but minimal. Try the Los Colores, their most popular dish, with three enchiladas (chicken, beef, and cheese) smothered in chile and served with beans and *posole*. The taco salad is another favorite. Portions are big here, and you can order a Mexican or microbrew beer, or a New Mexican or California wine.

114 Don Juan Valdez Lane. (1¾ miles north of the plaza, off Paseo del Pueblo Norte). ℭ **505/751-1450.** Reservations not accepted. Main courses under $10. No credit cards. Daily 10:30am–3pm and 5–9pm.

NORTH OF TOWN

The Bavarian Restaurant ↷ *Finds* BAVARIAN   Enter through 300-year-old castle doors into a high alpine world full of Bavaria. This restaurant, sitting high above Taos Ski Valley at an elevation of 10,200 feet, creates, with beamed ceilings, aged pine paneling, and an antler lamp all set around an authentic kachelofe, a Bavarian-style stove, a feel both rustic and elegant. Service is uneven but well intentioned. At lunch, the porch fills with sun-worshipers and menu choices include traditional foods such as goulash (a hearty beef and paprika stew) and spaetzle (Bavarian-style pasta). Dinner-time brings classic dishes such as Wiener schnitzel (Viennese veal cutlet) and sauerbraten (beef roast). Most entrees come with a potato dish and fresh vegetable. For dessert, try the apple strudel. Accompany your meal with a selection from the well-chosen European wine list or with a beer, served in an authentic stein. The road to The Bavarian is easily drivable in summer. In winter, most diners ski here or call to arrange for a shuttle to pick them up at the Taos Ski Valley parking lot. Proust!

In The Bavarian Lodge, Taos Ski Valley. ℂ **888/205-8020** or 505/776-8020. Reservations recommended at dinner. Lunch $7.50–$15; dinner $17–$35. AE, MC, V. Daily ski season 11:30am–3pm and 6–9pm; summer Thurs–Sun 11:30am–3:30pm and 5:30pm–closing.

Gypsy 360° ✦ *Finds* ASIAN/AMERICAN   This funky cafe on a side street is as cute as the village of Arroyo Seco where it resides. And the food is tasty and inventive. During the winter, diners sit in a sunny atrium or a more enclosed space, all casual with lawn-style furnishings and bright colors. In warm months, a sunny patio opens up the place. Service is accommodating though at times overworked. The food ranges from sushi to Thai to sandwiches. My Berkley Bowl salad had lots of spring greens and crisp goodies such as carrots and jicama, and the chef accommodated my request for grilled salmon on top. The pesto dressing is now my all-time favorite. My mother's angus burger was thick and juicy, topped with crisp bacon and bleu cheese; her potato salad had fresh dill. Other times I've enjoyed the noodle bowls, such as a Sri Lankan red curry or pad Thai. If you're staying in Taos, this spot makes for a great destination, with plenty of fun shops to peruse when your tummy's full.

480 NM 150, Seco Plaza, Arroyo Seco. ℂ **505/776-3166**. Main courses $7.50–$15. MC, V. Tues–Wed and Sat 8am–4pm; Thurs–Fri 8am–8pm; Sun 9am–3pm.

Taos Cow ✦ *Kids* DELI/ICE CREAM   Set in one of my favorite villages, Taos Cow offers fun breakfast and lunch fare in a relaxed atmosphere—and, of course, ice cream! Diners order and pick up at a counter. A unique item here is the pot pies in chicken, buffalo, beef, or veggie varieties, all with rich sauce and lots of vegetables. Village residents like to wake up to the breakfast tacos, made with fresh local eggs and lots of green chile. A different quiche special tops the menu each day such as a veggie with quinoa, and a variety of sandwiches are made with fresh ingredients ranging from black forest ham to portobello mushrooms. All that said, the real reason to come here is the ice cream in a variety of flavors. My favorite this week is the Cherry Ristra, with piñon nuts and chocolate chunks. Kids love their shakes. On chillier afternoons, there's espresso, cappuccino, and hot chocolate to warm you after a day on the slopes.

485 Highway 150, Arroyo Seco. ℂ **505/776-5640**. All menu items under $10. AE, DISC, MC, V. Daily 7am–7pm.

14

What to See & Do in Taos

With a history shaped by pre-Columbian civilization, Spanish colonialism, and the Wild West; outdoor activities that range from ballooning to world-class skiing; and a clustering of artists, writers, and musicians, Taos has something to offer almost everybody. Its pueblo is the most accessible in New Mexico, and its museums represent a world-class display of regional history and culture.

1 The Top Attractions

Millicent Rogers Museum of Northern New Mexico ✿ This museum will give you a glimpse of some of the finest Southwestern arts and crafts anywhere, but it's small enough to avoid being overwhelming. It was founded in 1953 by Millicent Rogers's family members after her death. Rogers was a wealthy Taos émigré who in 1947 began acquiring a magnificent collection of beautiful Native American arts and crafts. Included are Navajo and Pueblo jewelry, Navajo textiles, Pueblo pottery, Hopi and Zuni kachina dolls, paintings from the Rio Grande Pueblo people, and basketry from a wide variety of Southwestern tribes. The museum also presents exhibitions of Southwestern art, crafts, and design.

Since the 1970s, the scope of the museum's permanent collection has been expanded to include Anglo arts and crafts and Hispanic religious and secular arts and crafts, from Spanish and Mexican colonial to contemporary times. Included are *santos* (religious images), furniture, weavings, *colcha* embroideries, and decorative tinwork. Agricultural implements, domestic utensils, and craftspeople's tools dating from the 17th and 18th centuries are also displayed.

The museum gift shop has a fine collection of superior regional art. Classes and workshops, lectures, and field trips are held throughout the year.

Off US 64, 4 miles north of Taos Plaza, on Millicent Rogers Rd. ✆ 505/758-2462. www.millicentrogers.org. Admission $8 adults, $6 students, $7 seniors, $2 children 6–16, $18 family rate. Daily 10am–5pm. Closed Mon Nov–Mar, Easter, Thanksgiving, Christmas, New Year's Day.

San Francisco de Asis church ✿✿ On NM 68, about 4 miles south of Taos, this famous church appears as a modern adobe sculpture with no doors or windows, an image that has often been photographed and painted, most notably by Georgia O'Keeffe. Visitors must walk through the garden on the east side to enter the two-story church and get a full perspective of its massive walls, authentic adobe plaster, and beauty.

A video presentation is given in the church office every hour on the half-hour. Also, displayed on the wall is an unusual painting, *The Shadow of the Cross,* by Henri Ault (1896). Under ordinary light, it portrays a barefoot Christ at the Sea of Galilee; in

---

Tips **A Tip for Museumgoers**

If you'd like to visit five museums that comprise the Museum Association of Taos—Blumenschein Home, Martinez Hacienda, Harwood Museum, Millicent Rogers Museum, and Taos Art Museum—you'll save money by purchasing a combination ticket for $20. The ticket allows one-time entry to each museum during a 1-year period and is fully transferable. You may purchase the pass at any of the five museums. For more information, call ℂ **505/758-0505.**

---

darkness, however, the portrait becomes luminescent, and the perfect shadow of a cross forms over the left shoulder of Jesus' silhouette. The artist reportedly was as shocked as everyone else to see this. The reason for the illusion remains a mystery. A few crafts shops surround the square.

Ranchos de Taos Plaza. ℂ **505/758-2754.** Admission $3 for video and mystery painting. Mon–Sat 9am–4pm. Visitors may attend Mass Mon–Fri 5pm, Sat 6pm (Mass rotates from this church to the 3 mission chapels), Sun 7 (Spanish), 9, and 11:30am. Closed to the public 1st 2 weeks in June, when repairs are done; however, services still take place.

Taos Art Museum ✦ *Finds*   Set in the home of Russian artist Nicolai Fechin (*Feh-shin*), this collection displays works of the Taos Society of Artists, which give a sense of what Taos was like in the late 19th and early 20th centuries. The works are rich and varied, including panoramas and images of the Native American and Hispanic villagers. The setting in what was Fechin's home from 1927 until 1933 is truly unique. The historic building commemorates his career. Born in Russia in 1881, Fechin came to the United States in 1923, already acclaimed as a master of painting, drawing, sculpture, architecture, and woodwork. In Taos, he renovated the home and embellished it with hand-carved doors, windows, gates, posts, fireplaces, and other features of a Russian country home. Fechin died in 1955.

227 Paseo del Pueblo Norte. ℂ **505/758-2690.** www.taosmuseums.org. Admission $8 adults, $4 children 6–12, free for under 6. Summer Thurs–Sun 10am–5pm; call for winter hours.

Taos Historic Museums ✦✦   Two historical homes are operated as museums, affording visitors a glimpse of early Taos lifestyles. The Martinez Hacienda and Ernest Blumenschein home each has unique appeal.

The **Martinez Hacienda,** Lower Ranchitos Road, Highway 240 (ℂ **505/758-1000**), is the only Spanish colonial hacienda in the United States that's open to the public year-round. This was the home of the merchant, trader, and *alcalde* (mayor) Don Antonio Severino Martinez, who bought it in 1804 and lived here until his death in 1827. His eldest son was Padre Antonio José Martinez, northern New Mexico's controversial spiritual leader from 1826 to 1867. Located on the west bank of the Rio Pueblo de Taos, about 2 miles southwest of the plaza, the museum is remarkably beautiful, with thick, raw adobe walls. The hacienda has no exterior windows—this was to protect against raids by Plains tribes.

Twenty-one rooms were built around two *placitas,* or interior courtyards. They give you a glimpse of the austerity of frontier lives, with only a few pieces of modest period furniture in each. You'll see bedrooms, servants' quarters, stables, a kitchen, and a large fiesta room. Exhibits tell the story of the Martinez family and life in Spanish Taos between 1598 and 1821, when Mexico gained control.

Taos Attractions

Arroyo Seco **4**
D. H. Lawrence Ranch **1**
Ernest L. Blumenshein
  Home & Museum **12**
Governor Bent House
  Museum **10**
Harwood Museum
  of Art **11**
Martinez Hacienda **15**
Kit Carson Home &
  Museum **9**
Kit Carson Park &
  Cemetery **8**
Millicent Rogers Museum **3**
Plaza **13**
Rio Grande Gorge Bridge **2**
Rodeo **16**
San Francisco de Asis
  Church **17**
Taos Art Museum **7**
Taos Institute of Arts **14**
Taos Pueblo **6**
Taos Ski Valley **5**

CARSON
NATIONAL FOREST

Veterans

Highway

Hondo-Seco Rd.

Taos Ski Valley Rd.

Paseo del Pueblo Norte

Taos
Municipal
Airport

Millicent Rogers Rd.

Lucero Rd.

Blueberry Hill Rd.

**Taos
Mesa**

Pueblo Creek

Upper Ranchitos Rd.

Camino de la Placita

Town Hall
Civic Center

Paseo del Pueblo Norte
(North Santa Fe Rd.)

Kit Carson St.

Ranchitos Rd.

Siler Rd.

State Hwy. 240

Lower Ranchitos Rd.

Camino del Medio

Tewa Rd.

Paseo del Pueblo Sur
(South Santa Fe Rd.)

64

Los Pandos Rd.

Callejon

La Posta Rd.

Arroyo de los Coyotes

Herdner Rd.

Camino de la Merced

Salazar Rd.

Santa Fe Rd.

Cruz Alta Rd.

68

Chamisa Rd.

Sunshine Rd.

Camino de Abajo de la Lama

**Chamber of Commerce
& Information Center**

Paseo del Cañon

585

Roy Rd.

Gusdorf Rd.

Estes Rd.

Morgan Rd.

Weimer Rd.

240

Cordillera Rd.

To Santa Fe

**NEW
MEXICO**

Santa Fe • Taos
Albuquerque

0   1/2 mi
0   1/2 km

N

Airport   ✈
Church   ✝
Information   (i)
Post Office   ✉

Taos Historic Museums has developed the Martinez Hacienda into a living museum with weavers, blacksmiths, and wood carvers. Demonstrations are scheduled daily, and during the **Taos Trade Fair** (held in late Sept) they run virtually nonstop. The Trade Fair commemorates the era when Native Americans, Spanish settlers, and mountain men met here to trade with each other.

The **Ernest L. Blumenschein Home & Museum,** 222 Ledoux St. (© **505/758-0505**), 1½ blocks southwest of the plaza, re-creates the lifestyle of one of the founders of the Taos Society of Artists (founded 1915). An adobe home with garden walls and a courtyard, parts of which date from the 1790s, it became the home and studio of Blumenschein (1874–1960) and his family in 1919. Period furnishings include European antiques and handmade Taos furniture in Spanish colonial style.

Blumenschein was born and raised in Pittsburgh. In 1898, after training in New York and Paris, he and fellow painter Bert Phillips were on assignment for *Harper's* and *McClure's* magazines of New York when a wheel of their wagon broke 30 miles north of Taos. Blumenschein drew the short straw and thus was obliged to bring the wheel by horseback to Taos for repair. He later recounted his initial reaction to the valley he entered: "No artist had ever recorded the New Mexico I was now seeing. No writer had ever written down the smell of this air or the feel of that morning sky. I was receiving . . . the first great unforgettable inspiration of my life. My destiny was being decided."

That spark later led to the foundation of Taos as an art colony. An extensive collection of works by early-20th-century Taos artists, including some by Blumenschein's daughter, Helen, is on display in several rooms of the home.

222 Ledoux St. © **505/758-0505** (information for both museums can be obtained at this number). www.taos historicmuseums.com. Admission for each museum $7 adults, $3 children ages 6–16, free for children under 6, $15 families. Summer daily 9am–5pm; call for winter hours.

Taos Pueblo ⟨⟨⟨   It's amazing that in our frenetic world more than 100 Taos Pueblo residents still live much as their ancestors did 1,000 years ago. When you enter the pueblo, you'll see two large buildings, both with rooms piled on top of each other, forming structures that echo the shape of Taos Mountain (which sits to the northeast). Here, a portion of Taos residents lives without electricity and running water. The remaining 2,000 residents of Taos Pueblo live in conventional homes on the pueblo's 95,000 acres.

The main buildings' distinctive flowing lines of shaped mud, with a straw-and-mud exterior plaster, are typical of Pueblo architecture throughout the Southwest. It's architecture that blends in with the surrounding land. Bright blue doors are the same shade as the sky that frames the brown buildings.

The northernmost of New Mexico's 19 pueblos, Taos Pueblo has been home to the Tiwa tribes for more than 900 years. Many residents here still practice ancestral rituals. The center of their world is still nature; women use hornos to bake bread, and most still drink water that flows down from the sacred Blue Lake. Meanwhile, arts and crafts and other tourism-related businesses support the economy, along with government services, ranching, and farming.

The village looks much the same today as it did when a regiment from Coronado's expedition first came upon it in 1540. Though the Tiwa were essentially a peaceful agrarian people, they are perhaps best remembered for spearheading the only successful revolt by Native Americans in history. Launched by Pope (poh-*pay*) in 1680, the uprising drove the Spanish from Santa Fe until 1692 and from Taos until 1698.

As you explore the pueblo, you can visit the residents' studios, sample homemade bread, look into the **San Geronimo Chapel,** and wander past the fascinating ruins of the old church and cemetery. You're expected to ask permission from individuals before taking their photos; some will ask for a small payment. Do not trespass into kivas (ceremonial rooms) and other areas marked as restricted.

The **Feast of San Geronimo** (the patron saint of Taos Pueblo), on September 29 and 30, marks the end of the harvest season. The feast day is reminiscent of an ancient trade fair for the Taos Indians, when tribes from as far south as South America and as far north as the Arctic would come and trade for wares, hides, clothing, and harvested crops. The day is filled with foot races, pole climbing done by traditional Indian clowns, and artists and craftspeople mimicking the early traders. Dances are performed the evening of September 29. Other annual events include a **turtle dance** on New Year's Day, **deer or buffalo dances** on Three Kings Day (Jan 6), and **corn dances** on Santa Cruz Day (May 3), San Antonio Day (June 13), San Juan Day (June 24), Santiago Day (July 25), and Santa Ana Day (July 26). The annual **Taos Pueblo Powwow,** a dance competition and parade that brings together tribes from throughout North America, is held the second weekend of July on tribal lands off NM 522 (see "Northern New Mexico Calendar of Events," in chapter 2). The pueblo Christmas celebration begins on Christmas Eve, with bonfires and a procession with children's dances. On Christmas day, the deer or **Matachine dances** take place (p. 294).

During your visit to the pueblo you will have the opportunity to purchase traditional fried and oven-baked bread as well as a variety of arts and crafts. If you would like to try traditional feast-day meals, the **Tiwa Kitchen,** near the entrance to the pueblo, is a good place to stop. Close to Tiwa Kitchen is the **Oo-oonah Children's Art Center,** where you can see the creative works of pueblo children.

As with many of the other pueblos in New Mexico, Taos Pueblo has opened a casino. **Taos Mountain Casino** (© 888/WIN-TAOS) is on the main road to Taos Pueblo and features slot machines, blackjack, and poker.

Note: To learn more about the pueblo and its people, we highly recommend taking a 30-minute guided tour. Ask upon arrival when the next one will be given and where you should meet your guide.

Veterans Hwy. (P.O. Box 1846), Taos Pueblo. © 505/758-1028. www.taospueblo.com. Admission cost, as well as camera, video, and sketching fees, subject to change on a yearly basis; be sure to ask about telephoto lenses and digital cameras; photography not permitted on feast days. Daily 8am–4:30pm, with a few exceptions. Guided tours available. Closed for 45 consecutive days every year late winter or early spring (call ahead). Also, because this is a living community, you can expect periodic closures. From Paseo del Pueblo Norte, travel north 2 miles on Veterans Hwy.

2 More Attractions

D. H. Lawrence Ranch   A trip to this ranch north of Taos leads you into odd realms of devotion for the controversial early-20th-century author who lived and wrote in the area in the early '20s. A short uphill walk from the ranch home (not open to visitors), is the D. H. Lawrence Memorial, a shedlike structure that's a bit of a forgotten place, where people have left a few mementos such as juniper berries and sticks of gum. The guest book is also interesting: One couple wrote of trying for 24 years to get here from England.

Lawrence lived in Taos on and off between 1922 and 1925. The ranch was a gift to his wife, Frieda, from the art patron Mabel Dodge Luhan. Lawrence repaid Luhan the favor by giving her the manuscript of *Sons and Lovers.* When Lawrence died in southern

France in 1930 of tuberculosis, his ashes were returned here for burial. The grave of Frieda, who died in 1956, is outside the memorial. The memorial is the only public building at the ranch, which is operated today by the University of New Mexico as an educational and recreational retreat.

NM 522, San Cristobal. (✆ 505/776-2245. Free admission. Daily 8am–5pm. To reach the site, head north from Taos about 15 miles on NM 522, then another 6 miles east into the forested Sangre de Cristo Range via a well-marked dirt road.

Governor Bent House Museum *(Kids)*   This residence of Charles Bent, New Mexico Territory's first American governor, offers an interesting peek into the region's at-times brutal history. Bent, a former trader who established Fort Bent, Colorado, was murdered during the 1847 Native American and Hispanic rebellion, while his wife and children escaped by digging through an adobe wall into the house next door. The hole is still visible. Period art and artifacts are on display at the museum, just a short block north of the plaza.

117 Bent St. (✆ 505/758-2376. Admission $2 adults, $1 children 8–15, free for children under 8. MC, V. Summer daily 9:30am–5pm; winter daily 10am–5pm. Closed Easter, Thanksgiving, Christmas, New Year's Day. Street parking.

Harwood Museum of Art of the University of New Mexico *(✦)*   With its high ceilings and broad wood floors, this museum is a lovely place to wander among New Mexico–inspired images. A cultural and community center since 1923, the museum displays paintings, drawings, prints, sculpture, and photographs by Taos-area artists from 1800 to the present. Featured are paintings from the early days of the art colony by members of the Taos Society of Artists, including Oscar Berninghaus, Ernest Blumenschein, Herbert Dunton, Victor Higgins, Bert Phillips, and Walter Ufer. Also included are works by Emil Bisttram, Andrew Dasburg, Agnes Martin, Larry Bell, and Thomas Benrimo.

Upstairs are 19th-century pounded-tin pieces and *retablos,* religious paintings of saints that have traditionally been used for decoration and inspiration in the homes and churches of New Mexico. The permanent collection includes sculptures by Patrociño Barela, one of the leading Hispanic artists of 20th-century New Mexico—well worth seeing, especially his 3-foot-tall "Death Cart," a rendition of Doña Sebastiána, the bringer of death.

The museum also schedules more than eight changing exhibitions a year, many of which feature works by celebrated artists currently living in Taos.

238 Ledoux St. (✆ 505/758-9826. www.harwoodmuseum.org. Admission $7, $6 seniors, free for children under 12. Tues–Sat 10am–5pm; Sun noon–5pm.

Finds Art Classes

If you'd like to pursue an artistic adventure of your own in Taos, check out the week-long classes in such media as painting, Native American pottery making, and weaving offered by **Taos Art School** *(✦* (✆ **505/758-0350**; www.taosart school.org). This organization is especially known for its weaving and horse-back-riding creative "odyssey." Open since 1989, the school is a virtual campus in which classes go where they need to be. For instance, a painting class on Georgia O'Keeffe is held in Abiquiu, a Pueblo pottery class at Taos Pueblo, and a class on churches in New Mexico is held at five different churches in the region. The fees vary from class to class and usually don't include the cost of materials.

Kit Carson Home and Museum   If you want a glimpse into the modest lifestyle of Taos's frontiersmen, head to this 3-room adobe home, a block east of the plaza. Built in 1825 and purchased in 1843 by Carson—the famous mountain man, Indian agent, and scout—it was a wedding gift for his young bride, Josefa Jaramillo. It remained their home for 25 years, until both died (exactly a month apart) in 1868. Rooms have sparse displays such as buffalo hide and sheepskin bedding, a wooden chest, basic kitchen utensils, and a cooking fireplace. The treasure of the museum is interpreter Natívídad Mascarenas-Gallegos, a distant relative of Carson, who can tell you plenty about the family. The museum also includes a film on Carson produced by the History Channel. The price of a visit here is a bit steep for what you see, but if you decide to come, plan on spending about a half-hour. If you'd like to see more of Carson's possessions, visit the Martinez Hacienda (see above).

113 Kit Carson Rd. ℂ 505/758-4613. www.kitcarsonhome.com. Admission $5 adult, $4 seniors 65 years and older, $3 teens 13–18, $2 children 6–12. Daily 9am–6pm.

Kit Carson Park and Cemetery   Major community events are held in the park in summer. The cemetery, established in 1847, contains the graves of Carson, his wife, Governor Charles Bent, the Don Antonio Martinez family, Mabel Dodge Luhan, and many other noted historical figures and artists. Their lives are described briefly on plaques.

Paseo del Pueblo Norte. ℂ 505/758-8234. Free admission. Daily 24 hr.

Rio Grande Gorge Bridge ✹ (Kids)   This impressive bridge, west of the Taos airport, spans the Southwest's greatest river. At 650 feet above the canyon floor, it's one of America's highest bridges. If you can withstand the vertigo, it's interesting to come more than once, at different times of day, to observe how the changing light plays tricks with the colors of the cliff walls. A curious aside is that the wedding scene in the movie *Natural Born Killers* was filmed here.

US 64, 10 miles west of Taos. Admission free. Daily 24 hr.

3 Organized Tours

An excellent opportunity to explore the historic downtown area of Taos is offered by **Taos Historic Walking Tours** (ℂ 505/758-4020). Tours cost $10 and take 1½ to 2 hours, leaving from the Mabel Dodge Luhan house at 10am Monday to Saturday (June–Aug). Closed Sundays and holidays. Call to make an appointment during the off season.

If you'd really like a taste of Taos history and drama, call **Enchantment Dreams Walking Tours** ✹ (ℂ 505/776-2562). Roberta Courtney Meyers, a theater artist, dramatist, and composer, will tour you through Taos's history while performing a number of characters, such as Georgia O'Keeffe and Kit Carson. Walking tours cost $20 per person.

4 Skiing ✹✹✹
DOWNHILL

Five alpine resorts are within an hour's drive of Taos; all offer complete facilities, including equipment rentals. Although exact opening and closing dates vary according to snow conditions, the season usually begins around Thanksgiving and continues into early April.

Ski clothing can be purchased, and ski equipment can be rented or bought, from several Taos outlets. Among them are **Cottam's Ski & Outdoor Shops,** with four locations (call ✆ **800/322-8267** or 505/758-2822 for the one nearest you), and **Taos Ski Valley Sportswear, Ski & Boot Co.,** in Taos Ski Valley (✆ **505/776-2291**).

Taos Ski Valley ✪✪✪, P.O. Box 90, Taos Ski Valley, NM 87525 (✆ **505/776-2291;** www.skitaos.org), is the preeminent ski resort in the southern Rocky Mountains. It was founded in 1955 by a Swiss-German immigrant, Ernie Blake. According to local legend, Blake searched for 2 years in a small plane for the perfect location for a ski resort comparable to what he was accustomed to in the Alps. He found it at the abandoned mining site of Twining, high above Taos. Today, under the management of two younger generations of Blakes, the resort has become internationally renowned for its light, dry powder (as much as 320 in. annually), its superb ski school, and its personal, friendly service.

Taos Ski Valley can best be appreciated by the more experienced skier. It offers steep, high-alpine, high-adventure skiing. The mountain is more intricate than it might seem at first glance, and it holds many surprises and challenges—even for the expert. The *London Times* called the valley "without any argument the best ski resort in the world. Small, intimate, and endlessly challenging, Taos simply has no equal." And, if you're sick of dealing with yahoos on snowboards, you will be pleased to know that they're not permitted on the slopes of Taos Ski Valley. The quality of the snow here (light and dry) is believed to be due to the dry Southwestern air and abundant sunshine.

Between the 11,819-foot summit and the 9,207-foot base, there are 72 trails and bowls, more than half of them designated for expert and advanced skiers. Most of the remaining trails are suitable for advanced intermediates; there is little flat terrain for novices to gain experience and mileage. However, many beginning skiers find that after spending time in lessons they can enjoy the **Kachina Bowl,** which offers spectacular views as well as wide-open slopes.

The area has an uphill capacity of 15,000 skiers per hour on its five double chairs, one triple, four quads, and one surface tow. Full-day lift tickets, depending on the season, cost $33 to $57 for adults, $21 to $35 for children 12 and under, $22 to $45 for teens ages 13 to 17, $43 for seniors ages 65 to 79, and are free for seniors over 80 and for children 6 and under with an adult ticket purchase. Full rental packages are $20 for adults and $13 for children. Taos Ski Valley is open daily 9am to 4pm from Thanksgiving to around the second week of April. *Note:* Taos Ski Valley has one of the best ski schools in the country, specializing in teaching people how to negotiate steep and challenging runs.

Taos Ski Valley has many lodges and condominiums, with nearly 1,500 beds. (See "Taos Ski Valley," in chapter 12, for details on accommodations.) All offer ski-week packages; three of them have restaurants. There are three restaurants on the mountain in addition to the many facilities of Village Center at the base. For reservations, call the **Taos Valley Resort Association** (✆ **800/776-1111** or 505/776-2233).

Not far from Taos Ski Valley is **Red River Ski & Snowboard Area,** P.O. Box 900, Red River, NM 87558 (✆ **800/331-7669** for reservations; 505/754-2223 for information; www.redriverskiarea.com). One of the bonuses of this ski area is that lodgers at Red River can walk out their doors and be on the slopes. Two other factors make this 40-year-old, family-oriented area special: First, most of its 58 trails are geared toward the intermediate skier, though beginners and experts also have some trails, and second, good snow is guaranteed early and late in the year by snowmaking equipment

---

(Kids) **Skiing with Kids**

With its children's ski school, Taos Ski Valley has always been an excellent choice for skiing families, but with the 1994 addition of an 18,000-square-foot children's center (Kinderkäfig Center), skiing with your children in Taos is even better. Kinderkäfig offers every service imaginable, from equipment rental for children to babysitting services. Call ahead for more information.

---

that can work on 87% of the runs, more than any other in New Mexico. However, be aware that this human-made snow tends to be icy, and the mountain is full of inexperienced skiers, so you really have to watch your back. Locals in the area refer to this as "Little Texas" because it's so popular with Texans and other Southerners. A very friendly atmosphere, with a touch of redneck attitude, prevails.

There's a 1,600-foot vertical drop here to a base elevation of 8,750 feet. Lifts include four double chairs, two triple chairs, and a surface tow, with a capacity of 7,920 skiers per hour. The cost of a lift ticket for all lifts is $53 for adults for a full day, $39 half-day; $47 for teens 13 to 19 for a full day, $34 half-day; and $38 for children ages 4 to 12 and seniors 60 through 69 for a full day, $26 half-day. Free for seniors 70 and over. All rental packages start at $20 for adults, $13 for children. Lifts run daily 9am to 4pm Thanksgiving to about March 28. Ask about their lesson packages.

Also quite close to Taos is **Angel Fire Resort** ✾, P.O. Drawer B, Angel Fire, NM 87710 (© **800/633-7463** or 505/377-6401; www.angelfireresort.com). If you (or your kids) don't feel up to skiing steeper Taos Mountain, Angel Fire is a good choice. The 62 trails are heavily oriented to beginner and intermediate skiers and snowboarders, with a few runs for more advanced skiers and snowboarders. The mountain has received over $7 million in improvements in past years. This is not an old village like you'll find at Taos and Red River. Instead, it's a Vail-style resort, built in 1960, with a variety of activities other than skiing (see "Exploring Beyond Taos: A Driving Tour of the Enchanted Circle," later in this chapter). The snowmaking capabilities here are excellent, and the ski school is good, though I hear it's so crowded that it's difficult to get in during spring break. Two high-speed quad lifts whisk you to the top quickly. There are also three double lifts and one surface lift. A large snowboard park contains a banked slalom course, rails, jumps, and other obstacles. Cross-country skiing, snowshoeing, and snowbiking are also available. All-day lift tickets cost $48 for adults and $33 for children (ages 7–12). Kids 6 and under and seniors 70 and over ski free. Open from approximately Thanksgiving to March 29 (depending on the weather) daily 9am to 4pm.

The oldest ski area in the Taos region, founded in 1952, **Sipapu Ski and Summer Resort,** HC 65, Rte. Box 29, Vadito, NM 87579 (© **505/587-2240;** www.sipapu nm.com), is 25 miles southeast of Taos, on NM 518 in Tres Ritos Canyon. It prides itself on being a small local ski area, especially popular with schoolchildren. It has two triple chairs and two surface lifts, with a vertical drop of 1,025 feet to the 8,200-foot base elevation. There are 31 trails, half classified as intermediate, and two terrain park trails have been added. It's a nice little area, tucked way back in the mountains, with excellent lodging rates. Be aware that because the elevation is fairly low, runs get very icy. Lift tickets are $38 for adults for a full day, $26 half-day; $26 for children under 12 for a full day, $22 half-day; $22 for seniors (ages 60–69) for a half or full day; and free for seniors age 70 and over, as well as children 5 and under. A package including lift tickets, equipment rental, and a lesson costs $53 for adults and $42 for children. Sipapu is open from about the end of November to April 1, and lifts run daily from 9am to 4pm.

CROSS-COUNTRY

Numerous popular Nordic trails exist in **Carson National Forest.** If you call or write ahead, the ranger will send you a booklet titled *Where to Go in the Snow,* which gives cross-country skiers details about the maintained trails. One of the more popular trails is **Amole Canyon,** off NM 518 near the Sipapu Ski Area, where the Taos Nordic Ski Club maintains set tracks and signs along a 3-mile loop. It's closed to snowmobiles, a comfort to lovers of serenity.

Just east of Red River, with 16 miles of groomed trails (in addition to 6 miles of trails strictly for snowshoers) in 400 acres of forestlands atop Bobcat Pass, is the **Enchanted Forest Cross Country Ski Area** ⚡ (✆ **505/754-6112;** www.enchanted forestxc.com). Full-day trail passes, good 9am to 4:30pm, are $12 for adults, $9 for teens 13 to 17 and seniors 62 to 69, $5 for children age 7 to 12, and free for seniors age 70 and over, as well as for children 6 and under. In addition to cross-country ski and snowshoe rentals, the ski area also rents pulk sleds—high-tech devices in which children are pulled by their skiing parents. The ski area offers a full snack bar. Equipment rentals and lessons can be arranged either at Enchanted Forest or at **Miller's Crossing** ski shop at 417 W. Main St. in Red River (✆ **505/754-2374**). Nordic skiers can get instruction in cross-country classic as well as freestyle skating.

Taos Mountain Outfitters, 114 S. Plaza (✆ **505/758-9292**), offers telemark and cross-country sales, and rentals. **Southwest Nordic Center** ⚡ (✆ **505/758-4761;** www.southwestnordiccenter.com) offers rental of five *yurts* (Russian-style huts), four of which are in the Rio Grande National Forest near Chama. The fifth and newest addition is located outside the Taos Ski Valley (offering access to high-alpine terrain) and is twice as big as the others. These are insulated and fully equipped accommodations, each with a stove, pots, pans, dishes, silverware, mattresses, pillows, a table and benches, and wood-stove heating. Skiers trek into the huts, carrying their clothing and food in backpacks. Guide service is provided, or people can go in on their own, following directions on a map. The yurts are rented by the night and range from $65 to $125 per group. Call for reservations as much in advance as possible as they do book up. The season is mid-November through April, depending on snow conditions.

5 More Outdoor Activities

Taos County's 2,200 square miles embrace a great diversity of scenic beauty, from New Mexico's highest mountain, 13,161-foot **Wheeler Peak,** to the 650-foot-deep chasm of the **Rio Grande Gorge** ⚡⚡. Carson National Forest, which extends to the eastern city limits of Taos and cloaks a large part of the county, contains several major ski facilities as well as hundreds of miles of hiking trails through the Sangre de Cristo Range.

Recreation areas are mainly in the national forest, where pine and aspen provide refuge for abundant wildlife. Forty-eight areas are accessible by road, including 38 with campsites. There are also areas on the high desert mesa, carpeted by sagebrush, cactus, and, frequently, wildflowers. Two beautiful areas within a short drive of Taos are the **Valle Vidal Recreation Area,** north of Red River, and the **Wild Rivers**

Recreation Area, near Questa. For complete information, contact **Carson National Forest,** 208 Cruz Alta Rd. (© 505/758-6200), or the **Bureau of Land Management,** 226 Cruz Alta Rd. (© 505/758-8851).

BALLOONING

As in many other towns throughout New Mexico, hot-air ballooning is a top attraction. Recreational trips over the Taos Valley and Rio Grande Gorge are offered by **Paradise Hot Air Balloon Adventure** (© 505/751-6098). The company also offers ultralight rides.

The **Taos Mountain Balloon Rally,** P.O. Box 3096 (© 505/751-1000), is held each year in late October. (See "Northern New Mexico Calendar of Events," in chapter 2.)

BIKING

Even if you're not an avid cyclist, it won't take long for you to realize that getting around Taos by bike is preferable to driving. You won't have the usual parking problems, and you won't have to sit in the line of traffic as it snakes through the center of town. If you feel like exploring the surrounding area, Carson National Forest rangers recommend several biking trails in the greater Taos area. Head to the **West Rim Trail** for a scenic and easy ride. To reach the trail, travel US 64 to the Taos Gorge Bridge, cross it and find the trailhead on your left, or head south on NM 68 for 17 miles to Pilar; turn west onto NM 570. Travel along the river for 6¼ miles, cross the bridge, and drive to the top of the ridge. Watch for the trail marker on your right. For a more technical and challenging ride, go to **Devisadero Loop:** From Taos drive out of town on US 64 to your first pullout on the right, just as you enter the canyon at El Nogal Picnic Area. To ride the notorious **South Boundary Trail,** a 20-mile romp for advanced riders, contact Native Sons Adventures (below). Native Sons can arrange directions, a shuttle, and a guide, if necessary. The **U.S. Forest Service** office, 208 Cruz Alta Rd. (© 505/758-6200), has excellent trail information. Also look for the *Taos Trails* map (created jointly by Carson National Forest, Native Sons Adventures, and Trails Illustrated) at area bookstores.

Bicycle rentals are available from the **Gearing Up Bicycle Shop,** 129 Paseo del Pueblo Sur (© 505/751-0365); daily rentals run $35 for a mountain bike with front suspension.

Annual touring events include Red River's **Enchanted Circle Century Bike Tour** (© 505/754-2366) on the weekend following Labor Day.

FISHING

In many of New Mexico's waters, fishing is possible year-round, though, due to conditions, many high lakes and streams are fishable only during the warmer months. Overall, the best fishing is in the spring and fall. Naturally, the Rio Grande is a favorite fishing spot, but there is also excellent fishing in the streams around Taos. Taoseños favor the Rio Hondo, Rio Pueblo (near Tres Ritos), Rio Fernando (in Taos Canyon), Pot Creek, and Rio Chiquito. Rainbow, cutthroat, German brown trout, and kokanee (a freshwater salmon) are commonly stocked and caught. Pike and catfish have been caught in the Rio Grande as well. Jiggs, spinners, or woolly worms are recommended as lure, or worms, corn, or salmon eggs as bait; many experienced anglers prefer fly-fishing.

Licenses are required, of course, and are sold, along with tackle, at several Taos sporting-goods shops. For backcountry guides, try **Deep Creek Wilderness Outfitters and**

Guides, P.O. Box 721, El Prado, NM 87529 (© **505/776-8423** or 505/776-5901), or **Taylor Streit Flyfishing Service,** 405 Camino de la Placita (© **505/751-1312;** www.streitflyfishing.com).

FITNESS FACILITIES

The **Taos Spa and Tennis Club,** 111 Dona Ana Dr. (across from Sagebrush Inn; © **505/758-1980;** www.taosspa.com), is a fully equipped fitness center that rivals any you'd find in a big city. It has a variety of cardiovascular machines, bikes, and weight-training machines, as well as saunas, indoor and outdoor Jacuzzis, a steam room, and indoor and outdoor pools. Classes range from yoga to Pilates to water fitness. In addition, it has tennis and racquetball courts. Therapeutic massage, facials, and physical therapy are available daily by appointment. Children's programs include a tennis camp and swimming lessons, and babysitting programs are available in the morning and evening. The spa is open Monday to Friday 4am to 9pm; Saturday and Sunday 7am to 8pm. Monthly memberships are available for individuals and families, as are summer memberships and punchcards. For visitors, there's a daily rate of $12.

The **Northside Health and Fitness Center,** at 1307 Paseo del Pueblo Norte (© **505/751-1242**), is also a full-service facility, featuring top-of-the-line Cybex equipment, free weights, and cardiovascular equipment. Aerobics classes are scheduled daily (Jazzercise classes weekly), and there are indoor/outdoor pools and four tennis courts, as well as children's and seniors' programs. Open weekdays 6am to 9pm, weekends 8am to 8pm. The daily visitors' rate is $11.

GOLF

Since the summer of 1993, the 18-hole golf course at the **Taos Country Club,** 54 Golf Course Dr., Ranchos de Taos (© **800/758-7375** or 505/758-7300), has been open to the public. Located on Country Road 110, just 6 miles south of the plaza, it's a first-rate championship golf course designed for all levels of play. It has open fairways and no hidden greens. The club also features a driving range, practice putting and chipping green, and instruction by PGA professionals. Greens fees are seasonal and start at $49; cart and club rentals are available. The country club has also added a clubhouse, featuring a restaurant and full bar. It's always advisable to call ahead for tee times 1 week in advance, but it's not unusual for people to show up unannounced and still manage to find a time to tee off.

The par-72, 18-hole course at the **Angel Fire Resort Golf Course** (© **800/633-7463** or 505/377-3055) is PGA endorsed. Surrounded by stands of ponderosa pine, spruce, and aspen, at 8,500 feet, it's one of the highest regulation golf courses in the world. It also has a driving range and putting green. Carts and clubs can be rented at the course, and the club pro provides instruction. Greens fees range from $47 to $89.

HIKING

There are hundreds of miles of hiking trails in Taos County's mountain and high-mesa country. The trails are especially well traveled in the summer and fall, although nights turn chilly and mountain weather may be fickle by September.

Free materials and advice on all **Carson National Forest** trails and recreation areas can be obtained from the **Forest Service Building,** 208 Cruz Alta Rd. (© **505/758-6200**), open Monday to Friday 8am to 4:30pm. Detailed USGS topographical maps of backcountry areas can be purchased from **Taos Mountain Outfitters,** South Plaza (© **505/758-9292**).

Trail Closures

The drought that has spread across the Southwest in recent years has caused the U.S. Forest Service to close trails in many New Mexico mountains during the summer in order to reduce fire hazard. Before you head out in this area, contact the **Carson National Forest** (*©* **505/758-6200**).

One of the easiest hikes to access is the **West Rim Trail,** aptly named because it runs along the rim of the Rio Grande Gorge. Access this 9-mile-long trail by driving west from Taos on U.S. 64, crossing the Rio Grande Gorge Bridge and turning left into the picnic area. The 19,663-acre **Wheeler Peak Wilderness** is a wonderland of alpine tundra, encompassing New Mexico's highest peak (13,161 ft.). A favorite (though rigorous) hike to Wheeler Peak's summit (15 miles round-trip with a 3,700-ft. elevation gain) makes for a long but fun day. The trail head is at Taos Ski Valley. For year-round hiking, head to the **Wild Rivers Recreation Area** *©* (*©* **505/770-1600**), near Questa (see "Exploring Beyond Taos: A Driving Tour of the Enchanted Circle," later in this chapter).

The sage meadows and pine-covered mountains around Taos make it one of the West's most romantic places to ride. **Taos Indian Horse Ranch** *©©*, on Pueblo land off Ski Valley Road, just before **Arroyo Seco** (*©* **505/758-3212**), offers a variety of guided rides. Open by appointment, the ranch provides horses for all types of riders (English, Western, Australian, and bareback) and ability levels. Call ahead to reserve and for prices, which will likely run about $85 for a 2-hour trail ride.

Horseback riding is also offered by **Rio Grande Stables,** P.O. Box 2122, El Prado (*©* **505/776-5913;** www.lajitasstables.com/taos.htm), with rides taking place during the summer months at Taos Ski Valley. Most riding outfitters offer lunch trips and overnight trips. Call for prices and further details.

HUNTING

Hunters in **Carson National Forest** bag deer, turkey, grouse, band-tailed pigeons, and elk by special permit. Hunting seasons vary year to year, so it's important to inquire ahead with the New Mexico **Game and Fish Department** in Santa Fe (*©* **505/476-8000**).

ICE-SKATING AND SKATEBOARDING

If a latent Michelle Kwan or Brian Boitano dwells in you, try your blades at **Taos Youth Family Center,** 406 Paseo del Cañon, 2 miles south of the plaza and about ¾ mile off Paseo del Pueblo Sur (*©* **505/758-4160**). The rink is open daily from early November thorough mid-March. Call for hours. Skate rentals are available for adults and children. Admission is $4. Also at the center is an in-line-skate and skateboarding park, open when there's no snow or ice. Admission is free.

JOGGING

The paved paths and grass of Kit Carson Park (see "More Attractions," earlier in this chapter) provide a quiet place to stretch your legs.

LLAMA TREKKING

For a taste of the unusual, you might want to try letting a llama carry your gear and food while you walk and explore, free of any heavy burdens. They're friendly, gentle animals that have keen senses of sight and smell. Often, other animals, such as elk, deer, and mountain sheep, are attracted to the scent of the llamas and will venture closer to hikers if the llamas are present.

Wild Earth Llama Adventures 🐾🐾 (© **800/758-LAMA [5262]** or 505/586-0174; www.llamaadventures.com) offers a "Take a Llama to Llunch" day hike—a full day of hiking into the Sangre de Cristo Mountains, complete with a gourmet lunch for $89. Wild Earth also offers a variety of custom multiday wilderness adventures tailored to trekkers' needs and fitness levels for $125 per person per day. Children under 12 receive discounts. Camping gear and food are provided. On the trips, experienced guides provide information about native plants and local wildlife, as well as natural and regional history of the area. The head guide has doubled as a chef in the off season, so the meals on these treks are quite tasty. **El Paseo Llama Expeditions** 🐾 (© **800/455-2627** or 505/758-3111; www.elpaseollama.com) utilizes U.S. Forest Service–maintained trails that wind through canyons and over mountain ridges. The llama expeditions are scheduled May to mid-October, and day hikes are scheduled year-round. Gourmet meals are provided. Half-day hikes cost $64, day hikes $84, and 2- to 8-day hikes run $249 to $989.

RIVER RAFTING

Half- or full-day white-water rafting trips down the Rio Grande and Rio Chama originate in Taos and can be booked through a variety of outfitters in the area. The wild **Taos Box** 🐾🐾🐾, a steep-sided canyon south of the Wild Rivers Recreation Area, offers a series of class IV rapids that rarely let up for some 17 miles. The water drops up to 90 feet per mile, providing one of the most exciting 1-day white-water tours in the West. May and June, when the water is rising, is a good time to go. Experience is not required, but you will be required to wear a life jacket (provided), and you should be willing to get wet.

Most of the companies listed run the **Taos Box** ($99–$112 per person) and **Pilar Racecourse** ($40–$52 per person for a half-day) on a daily basis.

I highly recommend **Los Rios River Runners** 🐾 in Taos, P.O. Box 2734 (© **800/544-1181** or 505/776-8854; www.losriosriverrunners.com). Other safe bets are **Native Sons Adventures,** 1033-A Paseo del Pueblo Sur (© **800/753-7559** or 505/758-9342; www.nativesonsadventures.com), and **Far Flung Adventures,** P.O. Box 707, El Prado (© **800/359-2627** or 505/758-2628; www.farflung.com).

Safety warning: Taos is not the place to experiment if you're not an experienced rafter. Do yourself a favor and check with the **Bureau of Land Management** (© **505/758-8851**) to make sure that you're fully equipped to go white-water rafting without a guide. Have them check your gear to make sure that it's sturdy enough—this is serious rafting!

Getting Pampered: The Spa Scene

Taos doesn't have the spa scene that Tucson and Phoenix do, but you can get pampered at **Taos Spa and Tennis Club** (see "Fitness Facilities," above).

If you'd like to stay at a spa, **El Monte Sagrado,** 317 Kit Carson Rd. (© **800/828-TAOS** or 505/758-3502; www.elmontesagrado.com), and **Casa de las Chimeneas,** 405 Cordoba Rd. (© **877/758-4777** or 505/758-4777; www.visit taos.com), offer a variety of treatments to their guests (see chapter 12).

ROCK CLIMBING

Mountain Skills, P.O. Box 206, Arroyo Seco, NM 87514 (© **505/776-2222;** www.climbingschoolusa.com), offers rock-climbing instruction for all skill levels, from beginners to more advanced climbers who would like to fine-tune their skills or just find out about the best area climbs.

SNOWMOBILING AND ATV RIDING

Native Sons Adventures, 1033-A Paseo del Pueblo Sur (© **800/753-7559** or 505/758-9342), runs fully guided tours in the Sangre de Cristo Mountains. Rates run $64 to $150. Advanced reservations required.

SWIMMING

The **Don Fernando Pool,** Civic Plaza Drive at Camino de la Placita, opposite the Convention Center (© **505/737-2622**), admits swimmers over age 8 without adult supervision.

TENNIS

Taos Spa and Tennis Club (see "Fitness Facilities," above) has four courts, and the **Northside Health and Fitness Center** (see "Fitness Facilities," above) has three tennis courts. In addition, there are four free public courts in Taos, two at **Kit Carson Park,** on Paseo del Pueblo Norte, and two at **Fred Baca Memorial Park,** on Camino del Medio, south of Ranchitos Road.

6 Shopping

Given the town's historical associations with the arts, it isn't surprising that many visitors come to Taos to buy fine art. Some 50-odd galleries are within walking distance of the plaza, and a couple dozen more are just a short drive from downtown. Galleries and shops are generally open 7 days a week during summer and closed Sundays during winter. Hours vary but generally run from 10am to 5 or 6pm. Some artists show their work by appointment only.

The best-known artist in modern Taos is the late R. C. Gorman, a Navajo from Arizona who made his home in Taos for more than 2 decades. He was internationally acclaimed for his bright, somewhat surrealistic depictions of Navajo women. His **Navajo Gallery,** at 210 Ledoux St. (© **505/758-3250**), is a showcase for his widely varied work: acrylics, lithographs, silk screens, bronzes, tapestries, hand-cast ceramic vases, etched glass, and more.

My favorite new spot to shop is the village of **Arroyo Seco** ⚓ on NM 150, about 5 miles north of Taos en route to Taos Ski Valley. Not only is there a lovely 1834 church, La Santísima Trinidad, but there are a few cute little shops lining the winding lane through town. My favorites are the **Taos Sunflower** ⚓ (© **505/776-5644**), selling specialty yarns and fibers, just off the highway near the Gypsy 360° cafe and **Arroyo Seco Mercantile** ⚓ (© **505/776-8806**) at 488 NM 150, which is full of cowboy hats, antiques, and country home items.

ART

Act I Gallery This gallery has a broad range of works in a variety of media. You'll find watercolors, *retablos,* furniture, paintings, Hispanic folk art, pottery, jewelry, and sculpture. 218 Paseo del Pueblo Norte. © **800/666-2933** or 505/758-7831.

Farnsworth Gallery Taos Sharing space with Caffé Renato (see p. 200), this gallery sells works by painter John Farnsworth, known for his intimate images of horses often painted close up and at imaginative angles. Other painters are represented as well, all utilizing themes linked to nature. 133 Paseo del Pueblo Norte. ✆ 877/319-7698 or 505/758-0776.

Fenix Gallery The Fenix Gallery focuses on Taos artists with national and/or international collections and reputations who live and work in Taos. The work is primarily nonobjective and very contemporary. Some "historic" artists are represented as well. 228A Ranchitos Rd. ✆ 505/758-9120.

Gallery A The oldest gallery in town, Gallery A has contemporary and traditional paintings and sculpture, including Gene Kloss etchings, watercolors, and oils, as well as regional and national collections. 105–107 Kit Carson Rd. ✆ 505/758-2343.

Inger Jirby Gallery ✷ *(Finds* The word *expressionist* could have been created to define the work of internationally known artist Inger Jirby. Full of bold color and passionate brush strokes, Jirby's oils record the lives and landscapes of villages from the southwestern U.S. to Guatemala to Bali. This gallery, which meanders back through a 400-year-old adobe house, is a feast for the eyes and soul. 207 Ledoux St. ✆ **505/758-7333.**

Lumina Contemporary Art ✷✷ *(Finds* North of Taos (about 8 minutes) outside the village of Arroyo Seco, this gallery, a new version of the notable gallery that was in Taos, offers a tranquil museum-quality experience. Set within a 3-acre Japanese garden, it has a water cascade and Buddhist tea-house accented with large stone sculptures. Inside, works offer a refreshing look at the world. Watch for Chacha's gold- and copper-leaf works on metal, Elizabeth Rose's stone sculptures and Annell Livingston's geometric paintings on handmade paper. Open in summer Thursday to Monday 11am to 6:30pm; winter Friday to Monday 11am to 5pm. 11 NM 230, Arroyo Seco. ✆ **877/ 5LUMINA** or 505/758-7282.

Michael McCormick Gallery ✷ *(Finds* Nationally renowned artists dynamically play with Southwestern themes in the works hanging at this gallery, steps from the plaza. Especially notable are the bright portraits by Miguel Martinez. If the gallery's namesake is in, strike up a conversation about art or poetry. 106C Paseo del Pueblo Norte. ✆ 800/279-0879 or 505/758-1372.

Nichols Taos Fine Art Gallery Here you will find traditional works in all media, including Western and cowboy art. 403 Paseo del Pueblo Norte. ✆ **505/758-2475.**

Parks Gallery ✷ Some of the region's finest contemporary art decks the walls of this gallery just off the plaza. Some of the top artists here include Melissa Zink, Jim Wagner, Susan Contreres, and Erin Currier. 127 Bent St. ✆ **505/751-0343.**

Philip Bareiss Gallery The works of some 30 leading Taos artists, including sculptor and painter Ron Davis, sculptor Gray Mercer, and watercolorist Patricia Sanford, are exhibited here, along with early Taos modernists. 15 Rt. 150. ✆ **505/776-2284.** www.taos artappraisal.com.

R. B. Ravens A trader for many years, including 23 on the Ranchos Plaza, R. B. Ravens is skilled at finding incredible period artwork. Here, you'll see (and have the chance to buy) Navajo rugs, and pottery, all in the setting of an old home with raw pine floors and hand-sculpted adobe walls. 4146 NM 68 (across from the St. Francis Church Plaza), Ranchos de Taos. ✆ **505/758-7322.**

BOOKS

Brodsky Bookshop   Come here for the exceptional inventory of fiction, nonfiction, Southwestern and Native American–studies books, children's books, used books, cards, tapes, and CDs. 226 Paseo del Pueblo Norte. ℂ **888/223-8730** or 505/758-9468.

Moby Dickens Bookshop ✿   This is one of Taos's best bookstores, with comfortable places to sit and read. You'll find children's and adults' collections of Southwest, Native American, and out-of-print books. 124A Bent St. ℂ **888/442-9980** or 505/758-3050.

CRAFTS

Clay & Fiber Gallery   Clay & Fiber represents more than 150 artists from around the country. Merchandise changes frequently, but you should expect to see a variety of ceramics, fiber arts, jewelry, and wearables. 201 Paseo del Pueblo Sur. ℂ **505/758-8093**.

Taos Artisans Cooperative Gallery *(Value)*   This seven-member cooperative gallery, owned and operated by local artists, sells local handmade jewelry, wearables, clay work, glass, leather work, and garden sculpture. You'll always find an artist in the shop. 107C Bent St. ℂ **505/758-1558**.

Taos Blue   This gallery has fine Native American and contemporary handcrafts. 101A Bent St. ℂ **505/758-3561**.

Twining Weavers and Contemporary Crafts   Here, you'll find an interesting mix of hand-woven wool rugs and pillows by owner Sally Bachman, as well as creations by other gallery artists in fiber, basketry, and clay. 133 Kit Carson Rd. ℂ **505/758-9000**.

Weaving Southwest   Contemporary tapestries by New Mexico artists, as well as one-of-a-kind rugs, blankets, and pillows, are the woven specialties found here. 216B Paseo del Pueblo Norte. ℂ **505/758-0433**.

FASHIONS

Artemisia   Wearable art in bold colors defines this little shop a block from the plaza. Goods are pricey but unique, most hand-woven or hand-sewn, all for women. 115 Bent St. ℂ **505/737-9800**.

Mariposa Boutique   What first caught my eye in this little shop were bright chile-pepper-print overalls for kids. Closer scrutiny brought me to plenty of finds for myself, such as suede and rayon broomstick skirts and Mexican-style dresses, perfect for showing off turquoise jewelry. 120-F Bent St. ℂ **505/758-9028**.

Overland Sheepskin Company ✿ *(Finds)*   You can't miss the romantically weathered barn sitting on a meadow north of town. Inside, you'll find anything you can imagine in leather: coats, gloves, hats, slippers. The coats here are exquisite, from oversize ranch styles to tailored blazers in a variety of leathers from sheepskin to buffalo hide. NM 522 (a few miles north of town). ℂ **505/758-8820**.

FOOD

Cid's Food Market   This store has the best selection of natural and gourmet foods in Taos. It's a great place to stock your picnic basket with such items as roasted chicken and barbecued brisket, or with lighter fare, such as sushi, Purple Onion–brand sandwiches, black-bean salad, and fresh hummus and tabbouleh. 623 Paseo del Pueblo Norte. ℂ **505/758-1148**.

Xocoatl   Set in a cozy enclave that shares space with La Folie restaurant, this fun chocolate and wine shop offers some of the tastiest truffles I've had. Tim Van Rixel makes such delicacies as mango truffles and pineapple coconut truffles. 107-B Juan Largo Lane. ⓒ 505/751-7549.

FURNITURE
Country Furnishings of Taos   Here, you'll find unique hand-painted folk-art furniture. The pieces are as individual as the styles of the local folk artists who make them. There are also home accessories, unusual gifts, clothing, and jewelry. 534 Paseo del Pueblo Norte. ⓒ 505/758-4633.

Lo Fino ⚘   With a name meaning "the refined," you know that this expansive showroom is worth taking time to wander through. You'll find a variety of home furnishings, from driftwood lamps and finely painted *trasteros* (armoires) to hand-crafted traditional and contemporary Southwestern furniture. Lo Fino specializes in custom-built furniture. 201 Paseo del Pueblo Sur. ⓒ 505/758-0298. lofino@newmex.com.

The Taos Company   This interior-design showroom specializes in unique Southwestern and contemporary furniture and decorative accessories. Especially look for graceful stone fountains, iron-and-wood furniture, and custom jewelry. 124K John Dunn Plaza, Bent St. ⓒ 800/548-1141 or 505/758-1141.

GIFTS & SOUVENIRS
Chimayo Trading del Norte   Specializing in Navajo weavings, pueblo pottery, and other types of pottery, this is a fun spot to peruse on the Ranchos de Taos Plaza. Look especially for the Casas Grandes pottery from Mexico. #1 Ranchos de Taos Plaza. ⓒ 505/758-0504.

El Rincón Trading Post *(Finds*   This shop has a real trading-post feel. It's a wonderful place to find turquoise jewelry, whether you're looking for contemporary or antique. In the back of the store is a museum full of Native American and Western artifacts. 114 Kit Carson Rd. ⓒ 505/758-9188.

San Francisco de Asis Gift Shop   Local devotional art fills this funky little shop behind the San Francisco de Asis church. *Retablos* (altar paintings), rosary beads, and hand-carved wooden crosses appeal to a range of visitors, from the deeply religious to the pagan power shopper. Ranchos de Taos Plaza. ⓒ 505/758-2754.

Two Graces Gallery *(Finds*   For a wild range of devotional and kitschy art, don't miss this place on the Ranchos de Taos Plaza. You'll find glittery magnet shrines, Southwest collectibles, books, and antiques as well as a wall full of milagro crosses. 66 Saint Francis Church Plaza, Ranchos de Taos. ⓒ 505/758-4639.

JEWELRY
Artwares Contemporary Jewelry   The gallery owners here call their contemporary jewelry "a departure from the traditional." True to this slogan, each piece here offers a new twist on traditional Southwestern and Native American design, by artists such as John Hardy, Diane Malouf, Judith Ripka, and Alex Sepkus. 129 N. Plaza. ⓒ 800/527-8850 or 505/758-8850.

Taos Gems & Minerals   In business for over 30 years, Taos Gems & Minerals is a fine lapidary showroom. This is a great place to explore; you can buy jewelry, carvings, and antique pieces at reasonable prices. 637 Paseo del Pueblo Sur. ⓒ 505/758-3910.

MUSICAL INSTRUMENTS

Taos Drum Company ✦   Drum-making is an age-old tradition to which local artisans give continued life in Taos. The drums are made of hollowed-out logs stretched with rawhide, and they come in all different shapes, sizes, and styles. Taos Drums has the largest selection of Native American log and hand drums in the world. In addition to drums, the showroom displays Southwestern and wrought-iron furniture, cowboy art, and more than 60 styles of rawhide lampshades, as well as a constantly changing selection of South American imports, primitive folk art, ethnic crafts, Native American music tapes, books, and other information on drumming. To find Taos Drum Company, look for the tepees and drums off NM 68. Ask about the tour that demonstrates the drum-making process. 5 miles south of Taos Plaza (off NM 68). ℂ 505/758-3796.

POTTERY & TILES

Stephen Kilborn Pottery   Visiting this shop in town is a treat, but for a real adventure, go 17 miles south of Taos toward Santa Fe to Stephen Kilborn's studio in Pilar, open Monday to Saturday 11am to 5pm and noon to 4pm on Sunday. There, you'll see where the pottery is made. 136A Paseo del Pueblo Norte. ℂ 800/758-0136 or 505/758-5760. www.kilbornpottery.com.

Vargas Tile Co.   Vargas Tile has a great little collection of hand-painted Mexican tiles at good prices. You'll find beautiful pots with sunflowers on them and colorful cabinet doorknobs, as well as inventive sinks. South end of town on NM 68. ℂ 505/758-5986.

7 Taos After Dark

For a small town, Taos has its share of top entertainment. The resort atmosphere and the arts community attract performers, and the city enjoys annual programs in music and literary arts. State troupes, such as the New Mexico Repertory Theater and New Mexico Symphony Orchestra, make regular visits.

Many events are scheduled by the **Taos Center for the Arts (TCA),** 133 Paseo del Pueblo Norte (ℂ 505/758-2052; www.taoscenterforthearts.org), at the **Taos Community Auditorium** (ℂ 505/758-2052). The TCA imports local, regional, and national performers in theater, dance, and concerts (Robert Mirabal among others, has performed here, and *The Vagina Monologues* has been presented). Also, look for a weekly film series offered year-round.

You can obtain information on current events in the *Taos News,* published every Thursday. The **Taos County Chamber of Commerce** (ℂ 800/732-TAOS or

The Major Concert & Performance Halls

Taos Civic Plaza and Convention Center, 121 Civic Plaza Dr. (ℂ 505/758-5792). This convention space has an exhibit center where presentations, lectures, and concerts are held.

Taos Community Auditorium, Kit Carson Memorial State Park (ℂ 505/758-4677). A comfortable, small-town space, this community auditorium makes a nice venue for films, concerts, and lectures.

505/758-3873; www.taoschamber.com) publishes semiannual listings of *Taos County Events,* as well as the annual *Taos Country Vacation Guide* that also lists events and happenings around town.

THE PERFORMING ARTS

Fort Burgwin   This historic site (of the 1,000-year-old Pot Creek Pueblo), located about 10 miles south of Taos, is a summer campus of Dallas's Southern Methodist University. From mid-May through mid-August, the SMU-in-Taos curriculum (including studio arts, humanities, and sciences) includes courses in music and theater. There are regularly scheduled orchestral concerts, guitar and harpsichord recitals, and theater performances available to the community, without charge, throughout the summer. 6580 NM 518, Ranchos de Taos. ℂ **505/758-8322.**

Music from Angel Fire   This acclaimed program of chamber music begins in mid-August, with weekend concerts, and continues up to Labor Day. Based in the small resort community of Angel Fire (located about 21 miles east of US 64), it also presents numerous concerts in Taos, Las Vegas, and Raton. P.O. Box 502, Angel Fire. ℂ **505/377-3233** or 505/989-4772.

Taos School of Music   Founded in 1963, this music summer school located at the Hotel St. Bernard in Taos Ski Valley offers excellent concerts by notable artists. From mid-June to mid-August there is an intensive 8-week study and performance program for advanced students of violin, viola, cello, and piano. The 8-week **Chamber Music Festival,** an important adjunct of the school, offers 16 concerts and seminars for the public; performances are given by pianist Robert McDonald, the Miami Quartet, the Brentano String Quartet, Michael Tree, and the international young student artists. Performances are held at the Taos Community Auditorium and the Hotel St. Bernard. P.O. Box 1879. ℂ **505/776-2388.** www.taosschoolofmusic.com. Tickets for chamber music concerts $15 for adults, $10 for children under 16.

THE CLUB & MUSIC SCENE

Adobe Bar ⋆ A favorite gathering place for locals and visitors, the Adobe Bar is known for its live music series (nights vary) devoted to the eclectic talents of Taos musicians. The schedule offers a little of everything—classical, jazz, folk, Hispanic, and acoustic. The Adobe Bar features a wide selection of international beers, wines by the glass, light New Mexican dining, desserts, and an espresso menu. In the Historic Taos Inn, 125 Paseo del Pueblo Norte. ℂ **505/758-2233.** Noon–10:30pm.

Alley Cantina ⋆ *(Moments*   This bar that touts its location as the oldest house in Taos has become the hot late-night spot. The focus is on interaction, as well as TV sports, but there's also a cozy outdoor patio. Patrons playing shuffleboard, pool, chess, and backgammon listen to live music 4 to 5 nights a week. Burgers, fish and chips, and other informal dishes are served until 11pm. 121 Teresina Lane. ℂ **505/758-2121.** Cover for live music only.

Anaconda Bar ⋆⋆   Set in the new eco-resort El Monte Sagrado, this is Taos's most happening nightspot, with live entertainment—jazz, blues, Native American flute, or country—playing nightly. An anaconda sculpture snaking across the ceiling and an 11,000-gallon fish tank set the contemporary tone of the place, where a variety of delectable tapas are served. In the El Monte Sagrado hotel, 317 Kit Carson Rd. ℂ **505/ 758-3502.**

Caffe Tazza 🖈   This cozy three-room cafe, with a summer patio, attracts local community groups, artists, performers, and poets. Plays, films, comedy, and musical performances are given here on weekends (and some weeknights in summer). You can read one of the assorted periodicals available (including the *New York Times*) while sipping a cappuccino or *cafe Mexicano* (espresso with steamed milk and Mexican chocolate), made from organic coffee beans. The food—soups and sandwiches—is quite good. Pastries, which are imported from many bakeries around the region, are almost as big a draw here as the Taos Cow ice cream. Choose from 15 flavors. 122 Kit Carson Rd. ✆ **505/758-8706.**

Hideaway Lounge   This hotel lounge, built around a large adobe fireplace, offers live entertainment and an extensive hors d'oeuvre buffet. Call for schedule. Don Fernando de Taos, 1005 Paseo del Pueblo Sur. ✆ **505/758-4444.**

Sagebrush Inn 🖈   This is a real hot spot for locals. The atmosphere is Old West, with a rustic wooden dance floor and plenty of smoke. Dancers generally two-step to country music nightly, year-round, starting at 9pm. Paseo del Pueblo Sur (P.O. Box 557). ✆ **505/758-2254.**

8 Exploring Beyond Taos: A Driving Tour of the Enchanted Circle 🖈🖈

If you're in the mood to explore, take this 90-mile loop north of Taos, through the old Hispanic villages of Arroyo Hondo and Questa, into a pass that the Apaches, Kiowas, and Comanches once used to cross the mountains to trade with the Taos Indians. You'll come to the Wild West mining town of Red River, pass through the expansive Moreno Valley, and travel along the base of some of New Mexico's tallest peaks. Then, you'll skim the shores of a high mountain lake at Eagle Nest, pass through the resort village of Angel Fire, and head back to Taos along the meandering Rio Fernando de Taos. Although one can drive the entire loop in 2 hours from Taos, most folks prefer to take a full day, and many take several days.

ARROYO HONDO

Traveling north from Taos via NM 522, it's a 9-mile drive to this village, the remains of an 1815 land grant along the Rio Hondo. Along the dirt roads that lead off NM 522, you may find a windowless *morada* or two, marked by plain crosses in front—places of worship for the still-active Penitentes, a religious order known for self-flagellation. This is also the turnoff point for trips to the Rio Grande Box, an awesome 1-day, 17-mile white-water run for which you can book trips in Santa Fe, Taos, Red River, and Angel Fire. (See the "Outdoor Activities" sections in chapter 7 and earlier in this chapter for booking agents in Santa Fe and Taos, respectively.)

Arroyo Hondo was also the site of the New Buffalo commune in the 1960s. Hippies flocked here, looking to escape the mores of modern society. Over the years, the commune members have dispersed throughout northern New Mexico, bringing an interesting creative element to the food, architecture, and philosophy of the state. En route north, the highway passes near **San Cristobal,** where a side road turns off to the **D. H. Lawrence Ranch** (see "More Attractions," earlier in this chapter) and **Lama,** site of an isolated spiritual retreat.

QUESTA

Next, NM 522 passes through Questa, most of whose residents are employed at a molybdenum mine about 5 miles east of town. Mining molybdenum (an ingredient

Along a Green Shore

A sweet spot en route to Taos from Santa Fe, the **Orilla Verde** (green shore) **Recreation Area,** offers just what its name implies: lovely green shores along the Rio Grande. It's an excellent place to camp or to simply have a picnic. If you're adventurous, the flat water in this section of the river makes for scenic canoeing, kayaking, rafting, and fishing. Hiking trails thread through the area as well. Along them, you may come across ancient cultural artifacts, but be sure to leave them as you find them.

While traveling to the area, you'll encounter two places of note. The village of **Pilar** ⚔ is a charming farming village, home to apple orchards, corn fields, and artists. The **Rio Grande Gorge Visitor Center** (at the intersection of NM 570 and NM 68; ℂ **505/751-4899**) provides information about the gorge and has very clean restrooms. It's open daily during business hours from Memorial Day to Labor Day.

The day use fee for Orilla Verde is $3 per day, camping is $7 per night, and RV camping is $15 per night. All campsites have picnic tables, grills, and restrooms. For information contact the **Orilla Verde Visitor Station** (ℂ **505/758-4060;** www.nm.blm.gov/tafo/rafting/rio_grande/ovra/ovra_info.html), at the campground. To reach the recreation area, travel north from Santa Fe 50 miles or southwest from Taos 15 miles on NM 68; turn north on NM 570 and travel 1 mile.

in lightbulbs, television tubes, and missile systems) in the area has not been without controversy. The process has raked across hillsides along the Red River, and though Molycorp, the mine's owner, treats the water it uses before returning it to the river, studies show that it has adversely affected the fish life. Still, the mine is a major employer in the area, and locals are grateful for the income it generates. Stop in at **Paloma Blanca Coffee House**, a new bright spot at 2322 NM 522 (ℂ **505/586-2261**). You'll find a variety of coffees and teas as well as homemade pies, cookies, and ice cream. Also for sale are weavings, earrings, and paintings.

If you turn west off NM 522 onto NM 378 about 3 miles north of Questa, you'll travel 8 miles on a paved road to the Bureau of Land Management–administered **Wild Rivers Recreation Area** ⚔ (ℂ **505/770-1600**). Here, where the Red River enters the gorge, you'll find 22 miles of trails, some suited for biking and some for hiking, a few trails traveling 800 feet down into the gorge to the banks of the Rio Grande. Forty-eight miles of the Rio Grande, which extend south from the Colorado border, are protected under the national Wild and Scenic River Act of 1968. Information on geology and wildlife, as well as hikers' trail maps, can be obtained at the visitor center here.

The village of **Costilla,** near the Colorado border, is 20 miles north of Questa. This is the turnoff point for four-wheel-drive jaunts and hiking trips into **Valle Vidal,** a huge U.S. Forest Service–administered reserve with 42 miles of roads and many hiking trails. A day hike in this area can bring you sightings of hundreds of elk.

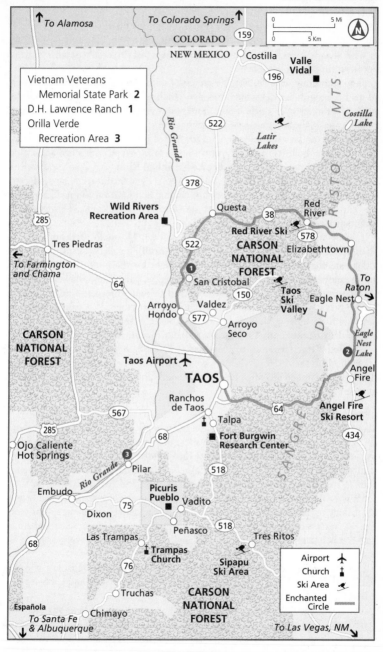

To Alamosa

To Colorado Springs

COLORADO

NEW MEXICO

159

Costilla

Valle
Vidal

196

0   5 Mi
0   5 Km

Rio Grande

522

Latir
Lakes

Costilla
Lake

MTS.

Vietnam Veterans
    Memorial State Park 2
D.H. Lawrence Ranch 1
Orilla Verde
    Recreation Area 3

378

285

Wild Rivers
Recreation Area

Questa

38

Red
River

CRISTO

Tres Piedras

522

Red River Ski

578

CARSON
NATIONAL
FOREST

Elizabethtown

To Farmington
and Chama

64

1

San Cristobal

150

Taos
Ski
Valley

To
Raton

Eagle Nest

CARSON
NATIONAL
FOREST

Arroyo
Hondo

Valdez

577

Arroyo
Seco

DE

Eagle
Nest
Lake

2

Taos Airport

TAOS

Angel
Fire

Ranchos
de Taos

Talpa

64

Angel Fire
Ski Resort

285

567

68

Fort Burgwin
Research Center

SANGRE

434

Ojo Caliente
Hot Springs

3

Pilar

518

Embudo

Rio Grande

Picuris
Pueblo

Vadito

Airport

Dixon

75

Church

Las Trampas

Peñasco

518

Tres Ritos

Ski Area

68

Trampas
Church

Sipapu
Ski Area

Enchanted
Circle

76

Truchas

CARSON
NATIONAL
FOREST

Española

Chimayo

To Santa Fe
& Albuquerque

To Las Vegas, NM

RED RIVER

To continue on the Enchanted Circle loop, turn east at Questa onto NM 38 for a 12-mile climb to Red River, a rough-and-ready 1890s gold-mining town that has parlayed its Wild West ambience into a pleasant resort village that's especially popular with families from Texas and Oklahoma.

This community, at 8,750 feet, is a center for skiing, snowmobiling, fishing, hiking, off-road driving, horseback riding, mountain biking, river rafting, and other outdoor pursuits. Frontier-style celebrations, honky-tonk entertainment, and even staged shootouts on Main Street are held throughout the year.

Though it can be a charming and fun town, Red River's food and accommodations are mediocre at best. Its patrons are down-home folks, happy with a bed and a diner-style meal. If you decide to stay, try **The Lodge at Red River,** P.O. Box 189, Red River, NM 87558 (© 800/91-LODGE or 505/754-6280; www.redrivernm.com/lodgeatrr), in the center of town. It offers hotel rooms ranging in price from $84 to $225. Knotty pine throughout, the accommodations are clean and comfortable. Downstairs, the restaurant serves three home-style meals daily.

If you're passing through and want a quick meal, **Mountain Treasures** (212 W. Main St., Red River, NM 87558, © 505/754-2700), a gallery, bistro, and espresso coffee bar offers excellent sandwiches. Go straight for the muffulettas or "muffys," Italian sandwiches made popular in New Orleans. Salami, turkey, provolone, cheddar, and olive spread are set within homemade Sicilian round bread and heated until the outside is crusty, the inside gooey rich. For dessert, try the Czech pastry *kolache* in a variety of fruits ranging from peach to cherry. Summer and winter ski season, the cafe is open daily 6am to 6pm. Other times Monday to Saturday 7am to 1pm.

The **Red River Chamber of Commerce,** P.O. Box 870, Red River, NM 87558 (© 800/348-6444 or 505/754-2366; www.redrivernewmexico.com), lists more than 40 accommodations, including lodges and condominiums. Some are open winters or summers only.

EAGLE NEST

About 16 miles southeast of Red River, on the other side of 9,850-foot Bobcat Pass, is the village of Eagle Nest, resting on the shore of Eagle Nest Lake in the Moreno Valley. Gold was mined in this area as early as 1866, starting in what is now the ghost town of **Elizabethtown** about 5 miles north; Eagle Nest itself (pop. 200) wasn't incorporated until 1976. The 4-square-mile **Eagle Nest Lake** (© 888-NM-PARKS or 505/476-3355; www.nmparks.com) recently became a New Mexico state park. Currently facilities include restrooms and a boat ramp, with plans underway to build a visitor center. The lake is considered one of the top trout producers in the United States and attracts ice fishermen in winter as well as summer anglers. It's too cold for swimming, but sailboaters and windsurfers ply the waters.

If you're heading to Cimarron or Denver, proceed east on US 64 from Eagle Nest. But if you're circling back to Taos, continue southwest on NM 38 and US 64 to Agua Fría and Angel Fire.

Shortly before the Agua Fría junction, you'll see the **Vietnam Veterans Memorial State Park** (County Rd., B-4, Angel Fire, © 505/377-6900). It's a stunning structure with curved white walls soaring high against the backdrop of the Sangre de Cristo Range. Consisting of a chapel and an underground visitor center, it was built by Dr. Victor Westphall in memory of his son, David, a marine lieutenant killed in Vietnam

> **Fun Fact   Ghosts of Elizabethtown**
>
> Although only a few trodden clues remain, the gold-mining town Elizabeth-town once boasted 7,000 residents and was the first seat of Colfax County. It was called Virginia City when founded in 1865, but the name was changed to honor Elizabeth Moore, daughter of a leading citizen. What has become known as E-town had plenty of gold-town perks: five stores, two hotels, seven saloons, and three dance halls. By the early 1900s, much of the gold had run out, and in 1903 fire blazed through the town, leveling much of it. Today, visitors can still see a few foundations and remnants of a cemetery. It's on the west side of NM 38, about 10 miles east of Red River.

in 1968. The 6,000-square-foot memorial houses exhibits, videos, and memorabilia. It also has a changing gallery of photographs of Vietnam veterans who lost their lives in the Southeast Asian war, but no photo is as poignant as this inscription written by young David Westphall, a promising poet:

> *Greed plowed cities desolate.*
> *Lusts ran snorting through the streets.*
> *Pride reared up to desecrate*
> *Shrines, and there were no retreats.*
> *So man learned to shed the tears*
> *With which he measures out his years.*

ANGEL FIRE

If you like the clean efficiency of a resort complex, you may want to plan a night or two here—at any time of year. Angel Fire is approximately 150 miles north of Albuquerque and 21 miles east of Taos. Opened in the late 1960s, this resort offers a hotel with spacious, comfortable rooms, as well as condominiums and cabins. Winter is the biggest season. This medium-size beginner and intermediate mountain is an excellent place for families to roam about (see "Skiing," earlier in this chapter). Two high-speed quad lifts zip skiers to the top quickly while allowing them a long ski down. The views of the Moreno Valley are awe inspiring. Fourteen miles of Nordic trail have been added at the top of the mountain; visitors can also snowmobile and take sleigh rides, including one out to a sheepherder's tent with a plank floor and a wood stove where you can eat dinner cooked over an open fire. Contact **Roadrunner Tours** (© **505/377-6416** or 505/377-1811).

During spring, summer, and fall, **Angel Fire Resort** offers golf, tennis, hiking, mountain biking (you can take your bike up on the quad lift), fly-fishing, river rafting, and horseback riding. There are other fun family activities, such as the Human Maze, 5,200 square feet of wooden passageway within which you can let loose your inner rat. There are a video arcade, a miniature golf course, theater performances, and, throughout the year, a variety of festivals, including a hot-air balloon festival, Winterfest, and concerts of both classical and popular music.

The unofficial community center is the **Angel Fire Resort,** North Angel Fire Road (P.O. Drawer B), Angel Fire, NM 87710 (© **800/633-7463** or 505/377-6401;

www.angelfireresort.com), a 155-unit hotel with spacious, comfortable rooms, some with fireplaces and some with balconies. Rates range from $90 to $200.

For more information on the Moreno Valley, including full accommodations listings, contact the **Angel Fire Chamber of Commerce,** P.O. Box 547, Angel Fire, NM 87710 (© **800/446-8117** or 505/377-6661; fax 505/377-3034; www.angelfirechamber.org).

A fascinating adventure you may want to try here is a 1-hour, 1-day, or overnight horseback trip with **Roadrunner Tours,** P.O. Box 274, Angel Fire, NM 87710 (© **505/377-6416;** www.rtours.com). One-hour rides run year-round for $35, but if you'd like a little more adventure, try an overnight. From Angel Fire, Nancy and Bill Burch guide adventurers on horseback through private ranchland of ponderosa forests and meadows of asters and sunflowers, often including wildlife sightings. Once at camp, riders bed down in an authentic mountain cowboy cabin. Call for prices.

15

Albuquerque

Albuquerque is the gateway to northern New Mexico, the portal through which most domestic and international visitors pass before traveling on to Santa Fe and Taos. But it's worth stopping in Albuquerque for a day or two in order to get a feel for the history of this area.

From the rocky crest of Sandia Peak at sunset, one can see the lights of this city of almost half a million people spread out across 16 miles of high desert grassland. As the sun drops beyond the western horizon, it reflects off the Rio Grande, flowing through Albuquerque more than a mile below.

This waterway is the bloodline for the area, what allowed a city to spring up in this vast desert, and it continues to be at the center of the area's growth. Farming villages that line its banks are being stampeded by expansion. As the west side of the city sprawls, more means for transporting traffic across the river have been built, breaking up the pastoral valley area.

The railroad, which set up a major stop here in 1880, prompted much of Albuquerque's initial growth, but that economic explosion was nothing compared with what happened since World War II. Designated a major national center for military research and production,

Albuquerque became a trading center for New Mexico, whose populace is spread widely across the land. That's why the city may strike visitors as nothing more than one big strip mall. Look closely, and you'll see ranchers, Native Americans, and Hispanic villagers stocking up on goods to take back to the New Mexico boot heel or the Texas panhandle.

Climbing out of the valley is **Route 66,** well worth a drive, if only to see the rust that time has left. Old court motels still line the street, many with their funky '50s signage. One enclave on this route is the **University of New Mexico and Nob Hill district,** with a number of hippie-ish cafes and shops.

Farther downhill, you come to **downtown Albuquerque.** During the day, this area is all suits and heels, but at night it boasts a hip nightlife scene. People from all over the state come to Albuquerque to check out the live music and dance clubs, most within walking distance from each other.

The section called **Old Town** is worth a visit. Though it's the most touristy part of town, it's also a unique Southwest village with a beautiful and intact plaza. Also in this area are Albuquerque's aquarium and botanical gardens, as well as its zoo.

1 Orientation

ARRIVING

Albuquerque is the transportation hub for New Mexico, so getting in and out of town is easy. For more detailed information, see "Getting There," in chapter 2.

BY PLANE The **Albuquerque International Sunport** (© **505/842-4366;** www. cabq.gov/airport) is in the south-central part of the city, between I-25 on the west and

Kirtland Air Force Base on the east, just south of Gibson Boulevard. Sleek and efficient, the airport is served by most national airlines and two local ones.

Most hotels have courtesy vans to meet their guests and take them to their respective destinations. In addition, **Checker Airport Express** (© **505/765-1234;** www. airportshuttleabq.com) runs services to and from city hotels. **ABQ Ride** (© **505/243-7433;** www.cabq.gov/transit/index.html), Albuquerque's public bus system, also makes airport stops. There is efficient taxi service to and from the airport, and there are numerous car-rental agencies.

BY TRAIN   **Amtrak's** "Southwest Chief" arrives and departs daily to and from Los Angeles and Chicago. The station is at 214 First St. SW, 2 blocks south of Central Avenue (© **800/USA-RAIL** or 505/842-9650; www.amtrak.com).

BY BUS   **Greyhound/Trailways** (© **800/231-2222;** www.greyhound.com) and **TNM&O** (© **505/243-4435;** www.tnmo.com) arrive and depart from the Albuquerque Bus Transportation Center, 300 Second St. SW (at the corner of Lead and Second, near the train station).

BY CAR   If you're driving, you'll probably arrive via either the east–west I-40 or the north–south I-25. Exits are well marked. For information and advice on driving in New Mexico, see "Getting There," in chapter 2.

VISITOR INFORMATION

The main office of the **Albuquerque Convention and Visitors Bureau** is at 20 First Plaza NW (© **800/284-2282** or 505/842-9918; www.itsatrip.org). It's open Monday to Friday 8am to 5pm. There are information centers at the airport, on the lower level at the bottom of the escalator, open daily 9:30am to 8pm; and in Old Town at 303 Romero St. NW (Suite 107), open daily 9am to 5pm. Tape-recorded information about current local events is available from the bureau after 5pm weekdays and all day Saturday and Sunday. Call © **800/284-2282.**

CITY LAYOUT

The city's sprawl takes awhile to get used to. A visitor's first impression is of a grid of arteries lined with shopping malls and fast-food eateries, with residences tucked behind on side streets.

If you look at a map of Albuquerque, you'll notice that it lies at the crossroads of I-25 north–south and I-40 east–west. Focus your attention on the southwest quadrant: Here, you'll find both downtown Albuquerque and Old Town, site of many tourist attractions. Lomas Boulevard and Central Avenue, the old Route 66 (US 66), flank downtown on the north and south. They come together 2 miles west of downtown near Old Town Plaza, the historical and spiritual heart of the city. Lomas and Central continue east across I-25, staying about half a mile apart as they pass by the University of New Mexico and the New Mexico State Fairgrounds. The airport is directly south of the UNM campus, about 3 miles via Yale Boulevard. Kirtland Air Force Base—site of Sandia National Laboratories—is an equal distance south of the fairgrounds, on Louisiana Boulevard.

Roughly paralleling I-40 to the north is Menaul Boulevard, the focus of midtown and uptown shopping, as well as the hotel districts. As Albuquerque expands northward, the Journal Center business park area, about 4½ miles north of the freeway interchange, is expanding. Near there is home to the Albuquerque International Balloon Fiesta and the new Balloon Museum. East of Eubank Boulevard lie the Sandia Foothills, where the alluvial plain slants a bit more steeply toward the mountains.

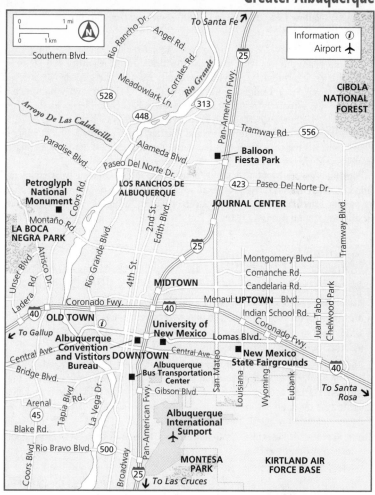

When looking for an address, it is helpful to know that Central Avenue divides the city into north and south, and the railroad tracks—which run just east of First Street downtown—comprise the dividing line between east and west. Street names are followed by a directional: NE, NW, SE, or SW.

MAPS The most comprehensive Albuquerque street map is distributed by the Convention and Visitors Bureau, 20 First Plaza NW (℅ **800/284-2282** or 505/842-9918).

2 Getting Around

Albuquerque is easy to get around, thanks to its wide thoroughfares and grid layout, combined with its efficient transportation systems.

BY PUBLIC TRANSPORTATION **ABQ Ride** (℅ **505/243-7433**) cloaks the arterials with its city bus network. Call for information on routes and fares.

BY TAXI   Yellow Cab (℡ **505/247-8888**) serves the city and surrounding area 24 hours a day.

BY CAR   The Yellow Pages list more than 30 car-rental agencies in Albuquerque. Among them are the following well-known national firms: **Alamo,** 3400 University Blvd. SE (℡ 505/842-4057; www.alamo.com); **Avis,** at the airport (℡ 505/842-4080; www.avis.com); **Budget,** at the airport (℡ 505/247-3443; www.budget.com); **Dollar,** at the airport (℡ 505/842-4224; www.dollar.com); **Hertz,** at the airport (℡ 505/842-4235; www.hertz.com); **Rent-A-Wreck,** 500 Yale Blvd. SE (℡ 505/232-7552; www.rentawreck.com/nm.htm); and **Thrifty,** 2039 Yale Blvd. SE (℡ 505/842-8733; www.thrifty.com). Those not located at the airport itself are close by and can provide rapid airport pickup and delivery service.

Parking is generally not difficult in Albuquerque. Meters operate weekdays 8am to 6pm and are not monitored at other times. Only the large downtown hotels charge for parking. Traffic is a problem only at certain hours. Avoid I-25 and I-40 at the center of town around 5pm.

FAST FACTS: Albuquerque

Airport   See "Orientation," above.

Area Code   The telephone area code for all of New Mexico is **505,** though at press time plans were rumbling to add new ones in the state.

ATMs   You can find ATMs (also known as *cash pueblos*) all over town, at supermarkets, banks, and drive-throughs.

Business Hours   **Offices** and **stores** are generally open Monday to Friday, 9am to 5pm, with many stores also open Friday night, Saturday, and Sunday in the summer season. Most **banks** are also open Monday to Friday, 9am to 5pm. Some may be open Saturday morning. Most branches have ATMs available 24 hours. Call establishments for specific hours.

Car Rentals   See "Getting Around Northern New Mexico," in chapter 2, or "Getting Around," above.

Climate   See "When to Go," in chapter 2.

Currency Exchange   Foreign currency can be exchanged at any of the branches of **Bank of America** (its main office is at 303 Roma NW; ℡ **505/282-2450**).

Dentists   Call the **Albuquerque District Dental Society,** at ℡ **505/237-1412,** for emergency service.

Doctors   Call the **Greater Albuquerque Medical Association,** at ℡ **505/821-4583,** for information.

Embassies & Consulates   See "Fast Facts: For the International Traveler," in chapter 2.

Emergencies   For police, fire, or ambulance, dial ℡ **911.**

Hospitals   The major hospital facilities are **Presbyterian Hospital,** 1100 Central Ave. SE (℡ **505/841-1234,** or 505/841-1111 for emergency services), and **University of New Mexico Hospital,** 2211 Lomas Blvd. NE (℡ **505/272-2111,** or 505/272-2411 for emergency services).

Hot Lines The following hot lines are available in Albuquerque: rape crisis (© **505/266-7711**), poison control (© **800/432-6866**), suicide (© **505/247-1121**), and UNM Children's Hospital emergency crisis (© **505/272-2920**).

Information See "Visitor Information," under "Orientation," above.

Internet Access **Fedex Kinko's** provides high-speed Internet access at five locations throughout the city. Two convenient ones are 6220 San Mateo Blvd. NE at Academy Boulevard (© **505/821-2222**) and 2706 Central Ave. SE at Princeton Boulevard (© **505/255-9673**).

Library The Albuquerque/Bernalillo County Public Library's **main branch** is at 501 Copper Ave. NW, between Fifth and Sixth streets (© **505/768-5140**). You can find the locations of the 17 other library facilities in the area by checking online at **www.cabq.gov/library**.

Liquor Laws The legal drinking age is 21 throughout New Mexico. Bars may remain open until 2am Monday to Saturday and until midnight on Sunday. Wine, beer, and spirits are sold at licensed supermarkets and liquor stores. It is illegal to transport liquor through most Native American reservations.

Lost Property Contact the city police at © **505/242-COPS**.

Newspapers & Magazines The two daily newspapers are the *Albuquerque Tribune* (© **505/823-7777**; www.abqtrib.com) and the *Albuquerque Journal* (© **505/823-7777**; www.abqjournal.com). You can pick up the *Alibi* (© **505/346-0660**; www.alibi.com), Albuquerque's alternative weekly, for free at newsstands all over town, especially around the University of New Mexico. It offers entertainment listings and alternative views on a variety of subjects.

Pharmacies **Walgreens** (www.walgreens.com) has many locations throughout Albuquerque. To find one near you, call © **800-WALGREENS.** Two centrally located ones that are open 24 hours are 8011 Harper Dr. NE at Wyoming (© **505/858-3134**) and 5001 Montgomery Blvd. NE at San Mateo (© **505/881-5210**).

Police For emergencies, call © **911.** For other business, contact the **Albuquerque City Police** (© **505/242-COPS**) or the **New Mexico State Police** (© **505/841-9256**).

Post Offices To find the nearest U.S. Post Office, dial © **800/275-8777.** The service will ask for your zip code and give you the closest post office address and hours.

Radio The local AM station **KKOB** (770) broadcasts news and events. FM band stations include **KUNM** (89.9), the University of New Mexico station, which broadcasts Public Radio programming and a variety of music, **KPEK** (100.3), which plays alternative rock music, and **KHFM** (95.5), which broadcasts classical music.

Taxes In Albuquerque, the sales tax is 6.75%. An additional hotel tax of 6% will be added to your bill.

Taxis See "Getting Around," above.

Television There are five Albuquerque network affiliates: **KOB-TV** (Channel 4, NBC), **KOAT-TV** (Channel 7, ABC), **KQRE-TV** (Channel 13, CBS), **KASA-TV** (Channel 2, FOX), and **KNME-TV** (Channel 5, PBS).

Time As is true throughout New Mexico, Albuquerque is on **Mountain Standard Time.** It's 2 hours earlier than New York, 1 hour earlier than Chicago, and 1 hour later than Los Angeles. Starting in 2007, daylight saving time will be observed from the second Sunday in March to the first Sunday in November.

Transit Information **ABQ Ride** is the public bus system. Call © **505/243-7433** for schedules and information.

Useful Telephone Numbers For **road information,** call © **800/432-4269** and for **emergency road service** (AAA), call © **505/291-6600.**

Weather For **time** and **temperature,** call © **505/821-1111.** To get **weather forecasts** on the Internet, check **www.accuweather.com** and use the Albuquerque zip code, 87104.

3 Where to Stay

Albuquerque's hotel glut is good news for travelers looking for quality rooms at a reasonable cost. Except during peak periods—specifically, the New Mexico Arts and Crafts Fair (late June), the New Mexico State Fair (Sept), and the Albuquerque International Balloon Fiesta (early Oct)—most of the city's hotels have vacant rooms, so guests can frequently request and get lower room rates than the ones posted.

A tax of nearly 12.75% is added to every hotel bill. All hotels and bed-and-breakfasts listed offer rooms for nonsmokers and travelers with disabilities.

HOTELS/MOTELS
EXPENSIVE
Albuquerque Marriott Pyramid North 🐾 About a 15-minute drive from Old Town and downtown, this Aztec pyramid–shaped structure provides well-appointed rooms in an interesting environment. The 10 guest floors are grouped around a hollow skylit atrium. Vines drape from planter boxes on the balconies, and water falls five stories to a pool between the two glass elevators. The rooms are spacious, though not extraordinary, all with picture windows and ample views. The third stage of a $10-million renovation was completed in 2005. With lots of convention space at the hotel, you're likely to encounter name-tagged conventioneers here. Overall, the service seems to be good enough to handle the crowds, but there are only two elevators, so guests often must wait. Wireless Internet connection is offered in the lobby atrium.

5151 San Francisco Rd. NE, Albuquerque, NM 87109. © **800/262-2043** or 505/821-3333. Fax 505/822-8115. www. marriott.com/abqmc. 310 units. $159–$184 double; $169–$275 suite. Ask about special weekend and package rates. AE, DC, DISC, MC, V. Free parking. **Amenities:** Restaurant; lounge; indoor/outdoor pool; medium-size health club; Jacuzzi; concierge; business center; room service; valet laundry. *In room:* A/C, TV, high-speed Internet, coffeemaker, hair dryer, iron.

Hyatt Regency Albuquerque 🐾🐾 If you're looking for luxury and want to be right downtown, this is the place to stay. This $60-million hotel, which opened in 1990, is pure shiny gloss and Art Deco. The lobby features a palm-shaded fountain beneath a pyramidal skylight, and throughout the hotel's public areas is an extensive art collection, including original Frederic Remington sculptures. The spacious guest rooms enhance the feeling of richness with mahogany furnishings, full-length mirrors, and views of the mountains. The hotel is right next door to the Galeria, a shopping

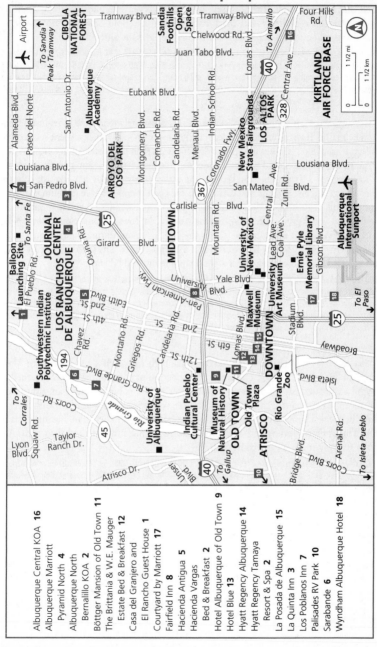

Albuquerque Central KOA **16**
Albuquerque Marriott
Pyramid North **4**
Albuquerque North
Bernalillo KOA **2**
Böttger Mansion of Old Town **11**
The Brittania & W.E. Mauger
  Estate Bed & Breakfast **12**
Casa del Granjero and
  El Rancho Guest House **1**
Courtyard by Marriott **17**
Fairfield Inn **8**
Hacienda Antigua **5**
Hacienda Vargas
  Bed & Breakfast **2**
Hotel Albuquerque of Old Town **9**
Hotel Blue **13**
Hyatt Regency Albuquerque **14**
Hyatt Regency Tamaya
  Resort & Spa **2**
La Posada de Albuquerque **15**
La Quinta Inn **3**
Los Poblanos Inn **7**
Palisades RV Park **10**
Sarabande **6**
Wyndham Albuquerque Hotel **18**

area, and has a number of shops itself. McGrath's serves three meals daily in a setting of forest-green upholstery and black-cherry furniture. Bolo Saloon is noted for its whimsical oil paintings depicting "where the deer and the antelope play."

330 Tijeras Ave. NW, Albuquerque, NM 87102. © **800/233-1234** or 505/842-1234. Fax 505/843-2710. www.hyatt. com. 395 units. Weekdays $225 double; weekends $105 double; $350–$700 suite. AE, DC, DISC, MC, V. Self-parking $12, valet $16. **Amenities:** Restaurant; bar; outdoor pool; health club; sauna; concierge; car-rental desk; business center and secretarial services; salon; room service; babysitting; laundry service; dry cleaning. *In room:* A/C, TV, wireless Internet, coffeemaker, hair dryer.

Hotel Albuquerque at Old Town ✦✦   This completely renovated hotel just 5 minutes from Old Town offers artfully decorated rooms with views and excellent service. No Albuquerque hotel is closer to top tourist attractions than the Hotel Albuquerque. Constructed in 1975, it existed for years under the Sheraton banner. Now a Heritage Hotel, it has received a $16 million makeover. The cathedral-style lobby has Spanish colonial furnishings and art, a theme that carries into the guest rooms. They're medium size, with comfortable beds and medium-size baths with outer vanities. Request a south-side room, and you'll get a balcony with a view over Old Town. A north-side room yields mountain views but no balconies (this is the side to request during the Balloon Fiesta). The lovely grounds have a long portal and a quaint chapel. The Q Bar is one of Albuquerque's chicest night spots, with a good tapas menu and billiards.

800 Rio Grande Blvd. NW, Albuquerque, NM 87104. © **800/237-2133** reservations only, or 505/843-6300. Fax 505/ 842-8426. www.hotelabq.com. 188 units. $99–$209 double, $149–$350 Jr. suite double. Children stay free in parent's room. AE, DC, DISC, MC, V. Free parking. **Amenities:** 2 restaurants; lounge; outdoor pool open in summer; Jacuzzi; concierge; business center; limited room service; valet laundry; same-day dry cleaning; executive-level rooms. *In room:* A/C, TV, pay movies, wireless Internet, coffeemaker, hair dryer, iron.

MODERATE
Courtyard by Marriott ✦   If you don't like high-rises such as the Wyndham Albuquerque Hotel (see below), this is the best selection of airport-area hotels. Opened in 1990, this four-story member of the Marriott family is built around an attractively landscaped courtyard. Families appreciate the security system—access is only by key card between 11pm and 6am—though most of the hotel's clients are business travelers. The units are roomy and comfortable, with walnut furniture and firm beds. Ask for a balcony room on the courtyard.

1920 Yale Blvd. SE, Albuquerque, NM 87106. © **800/321-2211** or 505/843-6600. Fax 505/843-8740. www.marriott. com. 150 units. $139 double week days. Weekend rates $89–$99. AE, DC, DISC, MC, V. Free parking. **Amenities:** Restaurant; lounge; indoor pool; exercise room; Jacuzzi; valet and coin-op laundry. *In room:* A/C, TV, high-speed Internet, coffeemaker, hair dryer, iron.

Wyndham Albuquerque Hotel ✦✦   This 15-story hotel right at the airport provides spacious rooms with a touch of elegance. The lobby, grill, and lounge areas employ a lot of sandstone, wood, copper, and tile to lend an Anasazi feel, which carries into the rooms, each with a broad view from a balcony. Air travelers enjoy this hotel's location, but because it has good access to freeways and excellent views, it could also be a wise choice for a few days of browsing around Albuquerque. Of course, you will hear some jet noise. The Rojo Grill serves a variety of American and Southwestern dishes.

2910 Yale Blvd. SE, Albuquerque, NM 87106. © **800/227-1117** or 505/843-7000. Fax 505/843-6307. www.wyndham. com. 276 units. $99–$179 double. AE, DC, DISC, MC, V. Free parking. Small pets welcome with prior approval. **Amenities:** Restaurant; outdoor pool; access to golf club; 2 tennis courts; concierge; business center; coin-op laundry. *In room:* A/C, TV, dataport and wireless Internet, coffeemaker, hair dryer, iron.

Renovation of a Classic

Built in 1939 by Conrad Hilton, **La Posada de Albuquerque,** 125 Second St., NW, at Copper Ave. (© **800/777-5732** or 505/242-9090; www.laposada-abq.com), was the famed hotelier's first inn in his home state of New Mexico. It's currently receiving a major makeover, with a hoped-for completion date of spring 2007. The $12-million restoration to this hotel on the National Register of Historic Places will completely remake the guest rooms, lobby, and meeting spaces, including installation of state-of-the-art energy management systems. When it's finished, the hotel will have a solar heating system and other environmentally conscious elements. The hotel will also have two restaurants and room for live musical performances and art shows. Call to see if they'll be booking rooms to coincide with your travel plans.

INEXPENSIVE

Fairfield Inn ⟨*Value*⟩   Owned by Marriott, this hotel has exceptionally clean rooms and easy access to freeways that can quickly get you to Old Town, downtown, or the heights. Ask for an east-facing room to avoid the noise and a view of the highway. Rooms are medium-size and have medium-size bathrooms. Each has a balcony or terrace. You probably couldn't get more for your money (in a chain hotel) anywhere else.

1760 Menaul Blvd. NE, Albuquerque, NM 87102. © **800/228-2800** or 505/889-4000. Fax 505/872-3094. www.fairfieldinn.com. 188 units. $72 double. Additional person $10. Children 18 and under stay free in parent's room. Free continental breakfast. AE, DC, DISC, MC, V. Free parking. **Amenities:** Indoor/outdoor pool; health club; Jacuzzi; sauna; laundry service. *In room:* A/C, TV, wireless Internet.

Hotel Blue   If you like the bustle of a city stay but your bank balance prohibits the Hyatt or La Posada, this is your place. A total remodel in 2001 turned this five-story 1960s hotel into a comfortable Art Deco inn with the color blue as a theme. It's nothing fancy but neither are the prices. Rooms are medium size with a small bath that has a two-sink outer vanity. Beds are awesomely comfortable. A hot breakfast greets you in the mornings. Street noise from busy Central Avenue carries into the rooms but quiets down at bedtime. Old Town is a brisk 20-minute walk away. A lovely and large pool with grass makes for a great cool-off spot in summer. Note that at press time, this hotel was moving to the Clarion banner so a name change may occur.

717 Central Ave., NW. © **877/878-4868** or 505/924-2400. Fax 505/924-2465. www.thehotelblue.com. 134 units. $69 double; $99 suite. Price includes hot breakfast. AE, DC, DISC, MC, V. Free parking. **Amenities:** Outdoor pool open in summer; small fitness room; laundry service; shuttle. *In room:* A/C, TV, high-speed Ethernet and wireless Internet, hair dryer, iron.

La Quinta Inn   La Quinta offers reliable, clean rooms at a decent price. Rooms are tastefully decorated, fairly spacious, and comfortable, each with a table and chairs and a shower-only bathroom big enough to move around in. Each king room has a recliner, and two-room suites are available. If you're headed to the Balloon Fiesta, this is a good choice because it's not far from the launch site, though you'll have to reserve as much as a year in advance.

There's another La Quinta near the airport (La Quinta Airport Inn, 2116 Yale Blvd. SE); you can make reservations for either branch at the toll-free number.

5241 San Antonio Dr. NE, Albuquerque, NM 87109. © **800/531-5900** or 505/821-9000. Fax 505/821-2399. www.lq.com. 130 units. $70–$76 double (higher during Balloon Fiesta). Children stay free in parent's room. AE, DC, DISC,

MC, V. Free parking. Pets welcome. **Amenities:** Heated outdoor pool open May–Oct. *In room:* A/C, TV, dataport and wireless Internet, coffeemaker, hair dryer, iron.

BED & BREAKFASTS

The Böttger Mansion of Old Town ⍟⍟   Decorated with antiques but not over-done with chintz, this Victorian inn situated right in Old Town is an excellent choice. It offers a sweet taste of a past era. My favorite room is the Carole Rose, with a canopy bed and lots of sun; also lovely is the Rebecca Leah, with pink marble tile and a Jacuzzi tub. All rooms are medium-size and have excellent beds; most have small bathrooms. The rooms facing south let in the most sun but pick up a bit of street noise from nearby Central Avenue and a nearby elementary school (both quiet down at night). Breakfast (such as green-chile quiche) is elaborate enough to keep you going through the day, at the end of which you can enjoy treats from the guest snack bar (try the chocolate cookies with a little chile in them). During warm months, the patio is lovely.

110 San Felipe NW, Albuquerque, NM 87104. © **800/758-3639** or 505/243-3639. www.bottger.com. 8 units. $110–$169 double. Rates include full breakfast and snack bar. AE, DISC, MC, V. *In room:* A/C, TV/VCR, wireless Internet, hair dryer.

The Brittania & W. E. Mauger Estate Bed & Breakfast ⍟   A restored Queen Anne–style home constructed in 1897, this former residence of wool baron William Mauger is listed on the National Register of Historic Places. Today, it is a wonderfully atmospheric bed-and-breakfast, with high ceilings and elegant decor that ranges from Tuscany to Africa in its sensibility. It's close to downtown and Old Town, just 5 blocks from the convention center and only 5 miles from the airport. All rooms feature period furnishings and private bathrooms with showers, and one has a balcony. Treats of cheese, wine, and other beverages are offered in the evenings, and a full breakfast is served each morning in indoor and outdoor dining rooms.

701 Roma Ave. NW, Albuquerque, NM 87102. © **800/719-9189** or 505/242-8755. Fax 505/842-8835. www.mauger bb.com. 10 units. $89–$109 double. Additional person $25. Rates include full breakfast and evening refreshments. AE, DC, DISC, MC, V. Free parking. Dogs welcome with prior arrangement for a $30 fee. *In room:* A/C, TV/VCR, wireless Internet, fridge, coffeemaker, hair dryer, iron.

Casa del Granjero and El Rancho Guest House ⍟   From the pygmy goats to the old restored wagon out front, Casa del Granjero (The Farmer's House) is true to its name. About a 20-minute drive north from Old Town, it's quiet and has a rich, homey feeling. Butch and Victoria Farmer have transformed this residence—the original part of which is 120 years old—into a fine bed-and-breakfast. The great room has an enormous sculptured adobe fireplace, comfortable *bancos* (benches) for lounging, a library, and many Southwestern artifacts. There's a 52-inch TV in the den. The guest rooms are beautifully furnished and decorated. Most have fireplaces. The Cuarto del Rey room features Mexican furnishings and handmade quilts and comforters. The Cuarto de Flores has French doors that open onto a portal. The guesthouse has com-fortable rooms and access to a kitchen, but a less luxurious and Southwestern feel. A full breakfast is served every morning. Catered lunches and dinners are also available by arrangement. Smoking is permitted outdoors only.

414 C de Baca Lane NW, Albuquerque, NM 87114. © **800/701-4144** or 505/897-4144. Fax 505/897-9788. 7 units. $79–$179 double. Additional person $20. Rates include full breakfast. DISC, MC, V. Free parking. Pets accepted with extra fee. **Amenities:** Jacuzzi; sauna; business center with courtesy computer; in-room massage; babysitting; laundry service. *In room:* A/C.

Hacienda Antigua _(kids) (Finds)_   This 200-year-old adobe home was once the first stagecoach stop out of Old Town in Albuquerque. Now, it's one of Albuquerque's most elegant inns. The artistically landscaped courtyard, with its large cottonwood tree and abundance of greenery, offers a welcome respite for tired travelers. The rooms are gracefully and comfortably furnished with antiques. La Capilla, the home's former chapel, is furnished with a queen-size bed, a fireplace, and a carving of St. Francis (the patron saint of the garden). La Sala has a king-size bed and a large Jacuzzi with a view of the Sandia Mountains. All the rooms are equipped with fireplaces and signature soaps. A gourmet breakfast is served in the garden during warm weather and by the fire in winter. The inn is a 20-minute drive from the airport. Light sleepers beware— the Santa Fe Railroad runs by this inn, with one to three trains passing by each night. High-speed Internet access is available in the lobby.

6708 Tierra Dr. NW, Albuquerque, NM 87107. (C) **800/201-2986** or 505/345-5399. Fax 505/345-3855. www. haciendantigua.com. 8 units. $129–$209 double. Additional person $25. Rates include gourmet breakfast. AE, MC, V. Free parking. Pets welcome with $30 fee. **Amenities:** Outdoor pool; Jacuzzi. _In room:_ A/C, TV/VCR, coffeemaker, hair dryer.

Los Poblanos Inn _(kids)_   Lushness in the desert city of Albuquerque? It's no mirage. Nestled among century-old cottonwoods, this bed-and-breakfast sits on 25 acres of European-style gardens and peasant-like vegetable and lavender fields. Notable architect John Gaw Meem built the structure in the 1930s. Each of the six guest rooms, most arranged around a poetically planted courtyard, has unique touches such as hand-carved doors, traditional tin fixtures, fireplaces, and views across the lushly landscaped grounds. The rooms vary in size. All are comfortable and offer organic shampoo and soap scented with lavender from the inn's garden. At breakfast, you might feast on eggs Florentine made with eggs from the inn's chickens, spinach from the garden, and artisanal bread made locally, while watching peacocks preen outside the windows of the very Mexican-feeling, boldly decorated cantina. Light sleepers should be aware that the peacocks can be noisy at night. A copy of the _New York Times_ arrives on each doorstep in the morning.

4803 Rio Grande Blvd. NW, Albuquerque, NM 87107. (C) **866/344-9297** or 505/344-9297. Fax 505/342-1302. www. lospoblanos.com. 6 units. $145–$250 double. Rates include full breakfast. AE, MC, V. Free parking. _In room:_ A/C, wireless Internet, hair dryer, iron.

Sarabande _(kids)_   You'll find home-style comfort mixed with elegance at this bed-and-breakfast in the North Valley, a 10-minute drive from Old Town. Once you pass through the front gate and into the well-tended courtyard gardens with fountains, you'll forget that you're staying on the fringes of a big city. With cut-glass windows, lots of pastels, traditional antiques, and thick carpet (in all but the pool-side room), you'll be well pampered here. Innkeepers Janie and Scott Eggers have filled the home with fine art as well as comfortable modern furniture. The Rose Room has a Japanese soaking tub and kiva fireplace. The Iris Room has a stained-glass window depicting irises and a king-size bed. Both rooms open onto a wisteria-shaded patio where you can eat breakfast in the morning. Out back are a 50-foot lap pool and a Jacuzzi, and some great walking paths are accessible from the inn. Janie serves a full breakfast either in the courtyard or the dining room.

5637 Rio Grande Blvd. NW, Albuquerque, NM 87107. (C) **888/506-4923** or 505/345-4923. Fax 505/341-0654. www. sarabandebb.com. 6 units. $99–$179 double. Rates include full breakfast. AE, DISC, MC, V. Free parking. **Amenities:** Outdoor pool; Jacuzzi; bike rental; massage by appointment; library; walking paths. _In room:_ A/C, TV, wireless Internet.

NEAR ALBUQUERQUE

Hacienda Vargas Bed and Breakfast Inn *✦*   Unassuming in its elegance, this bed-and-breakfast feels like an old Mexican hacienda. It sits within the small town of Algodones (about 20 miles from Albuquerque), which is a good place to stay if you're planning to visit both Santa Fe and Albuquerque but don't want to stay in one of the downtown hotels in either city. There's a real Mexican feel to the decor, with brightly woven place mats in the breakfast room and Spanish suits of armor hanging in the common area. Each guest room has a private entrance; many opening onto a court-yard. All rooms are furnished with New Mexico antiques, are individually decorated, and have handmade kiva fireplaces. Each of the four suites has a Jacuzzi tub, fireplace, and private patio. A full breakfast is served every morning in the dining room. Light sleepers take note: A train passes near the inn a few times most nights. Dial-up Inter-net connection is available in the lobby.

El Camino Real (P.O. Box 307), Algodones/Santa Fe, NM 87001. ⓒ **800/261-0006** or 505/867-9115. Fax 505/867-0640. www.haciendavargas.com. 7 units. $89–$179 double. Additional person $15. Rates include full breakfast. AE, MC, V. Free parking. Some pets accepted with prior arrangement. **Amenities:** Jacuzzi; room service; in-room massage. *In room:* A/C, hair dryer, iron.

Hyatt Regency Tamaya Resort and Spa *✦✦✦*   This is the spot for a get-away-from-it-all luxury vacation. Set in the hills above the lush Rio Grande Valley on the Santa Ana Pueblo, this pueblo-style resort offers a 16,000-square-foot full-service spa and fitness center, an 18-hole Twin Warriors Championship Golf Course designed by Gary Panks, and views of the Sandia Mountains. Rooms are spacious, with large tile bathrooms. Request one that faces the mountains for one of the state's more spectac-ular vistas. Other rooms look out across a large courtyard, where the pools and hot tub are. Though the resort is surrounded by acres of quiet countryside, it's only 20

Finds   **Cruising Corrales**

If you'd like to travel along meadows and apple orchards into a place where life is a little slower and sweeter, head 20 minutes north of Albuquerque to the village of Corrales. Home to farmers, artists, and affluent land owners, this is a fun place to roam through shops and galleries, and, in the fall, sam-ple vegetables from roadside vendors. Two excellent restaurants, both serving imaginative new American cuisine, sit on the main street. **Indigo Crow** *✦*, 4515 Corrales Rd. (ⓒ **505/898-7000**), serves lunch and dinner Tues-day to Saturday and brunch on Sunday, and Jim White's **Casa Vieja** *✦✦*, 4541 Corrales Rd. (ⓒ **505/898-7489**), serves dinner nightly. If you'd like to stay in the village, contact the **Sandhill Crane Bed-and-Breakfast,** 389 Camino Her-mosa (ⓒ **800/375-2445** or 505/898-2445; www.sandhillcranebandb.com).

The town also has a nature preserve and a historic church. In September, the Harvest Festival is well worth the trip. For more information about Cor-rales, contact Corrales Village (ⓒ **505/897-0502**; www.corrales-nm.org).

To get to the village, head north on either I-25 or Rio Grande Boulevard, turn west on Alameda Boulevard, cross the Rio Grande, and turn north on Corrales Road (NM 448). The village is just a few minutes up the road.

minutes from Albuquerque and 50 minutes from Santa Fe. The concierge offers trips to attractions daily, as well as on-site activities such as hot-air balloon rides, horseback rides, and nature/cultural walks or carriage rides by the river. Plan at least one dinner at the innovative Corn Maiden (see "Where to Dine," below).

1300 Tuyuna Trail, Santa Ana Pueblo, NM 87004. ✆ **800/55-HYATT** or 505/867-1234. www.tamaya.hyatt.com. 350 units. May–Oct $245–$415; Nov–Apr $199–$305, depending on the type of room. Suite rates available upon request. Inquire about spa, horseback riding, golf, and family packages. AE, DC, DISC, MC, V. Free parking. From I-25 take exit 242, following US 550 west to Tamaya Blvd.; drive 1½ miles to the resort. **Amenities:** 2 restaurants (p. ###); 2 snack bars; lounge; 3 pools (heated year-round); golf course; 2 tennis courts; health club and spa; children's programs; concierge; tour desk; elaborate business center; room service; laundry; basketball court. *In room:* A/C, TV, high-speed Ethernet and wireless Internet, fridge, coffeemaker, hair dryer, iron, safe.

RV PARKS
Albuquerque Central KOA   This RV park in the foothills east of Albuquerque is a good choice for those who want to be close to town. It offers lots of amenities and convenient freeway access. Cabins are available.

12400 Skyline Rd. NE, Albuquerque, NM 87123. ✆ **800/562-7781** or 505/296-2729. www.koa.com. $20–$36 tent site; $35–$51 RV site, depending on hook-up; $38–$55 1-room cabin; $48–$65 2-room cabin. All prices valid for up to 2 people. Additional adult $5, child $3. AE, DISC, MC, V. Free parking. Pets welcome. **Amenities:** Outdoor pool (summer only); Jacuzzi; bike rentals; store; coin-op laundry; bathhouse; miniature golf; playground; accessible restroom; wireless Internet access throughout the park.

Albuquerque North Bernalillo KOA ⌘   More than 1,000 cottonwood and pine trees shade this park, and you'll see many flowers in the warm months. At the foot of the mountains, 14 miles from Albuquerque, this campground has plenty of amenities. Guests enjoy a free pancake breakfast daily. Reservations are recommended. Six camping cabins are also available.

555 Hill Rd., Bernalillo, NM 87004. ✆ **800/562-3616** or 505/867-5227. www.koa.com. $20–$23 tent site; $30–$36 RV site, depending on hook-up; $38 1-bedroom cabin; $48 2-bedroom cabin. Rates include pancake breakfast and are valid for up to 2 people. Additional person $4. Children 5 and under free with parent. AE, DISC, MC, V. Free parking. Pets welcome. **Amenities:** Restaurant; outdoor pool (summer only); store; coin-op laundry; playground; free outdoor movies; wireless Internet access throughout the park.

Palisades RV Park   Sitting out on the barren west mesa, this RV park has nice views of the Sandia Mountains and is the closest RV park to Old Town and the Biological Park (10-min. drive; see "Especially for Kids," later in this chapter); however, it is also in a fairly desolate setting, with only a few trees about. In midsummer, it's hot.

9201 Central Ave. NW, Albuquerque, NM 87121. ✆ **888/922-9595** or 505/831-5000. Fax 505/352-9599. www. palisadesrvpark.com. 110 sites. $29 per day; $128 per week; $295 per month plus electricity. MC, V. Free parking. Pets welcome. **Amenities:** Store; coin-op laundry; reception room; bathhouse; propane; wireless Internet access throughout the park.

4 Where to Dine

RESTAURANTS BY CUISINE
AMERICAN
La Hacienda (Old Town, $$, p. 247)
Range Café ⌘ (Bernalillo, $$, p. 252)
66 Diner (University/Nob Hill, $, p. 251)

BAKERY
Flying Star Cafe (University/Nob Hill, $, p. 250)

CONTEMPORARY AMERICAN
Seasons Grill ⌘⌘ (Old Town, $$$, p. 246)

Key to Abbreviations: $$$$ = Very Expensive $$$ = Expensive $$ = Moderate $ = Inexpensive

CONTINENTAL

Artichoke Cafe ✹✹ (Downtown, $$, p. 248)

High Finance Restaurant and Tavern ✹ (Northeast, $$$, p. 248)

DELI/CAFE

Flying Star Cafe (University/Nob Hill, $, p. 250)

Gold Street Caffè ✹ (Downtown, $$, p. 246)

ECLECTIC

AmbroZia Café & Wine Bar ✹✹ (Old Town, $$$, p. 244)

Chef du Jour ✹ (Old Town, $, p. 247)

FRENCH

La Crêpe Michel ✹✹ (Old Town, $$, p. 246)

GREEK

Olympia Cafe (University/Nob Hill, $, p. 250)

INTERNATIONAL

AmbroZia Café & Wine Bar ✹✹ (Old Town, $$$, p. 244)

Scalo ✹ (University/Nob Hill, $$, p. 250)

ITALIAN

Scalo ✹ (University/Nob Hill, $$, p. 250)

NEW AMERICAN

Corn Maiden ✹✹ (Santa Ana Pueblo, $$$, p. 252)

Graze ✹✹ (University/Nob Hill, $$, p. 249)

Prairie Star ✹✹ (Santa Ana Pueblo, $$$, p. 252)

Terra ✹ (Old Town, $$$, p. 246)

Zinc Wine Bar and Bistro ✹✹ (University/Nob Hill, $$$, p. 249)

NEW MEXICAN

Duran Central Pharmacy ✹ (Old Town, $, p. 247)

La Hacienda (Old Town, $$, p. 247)

Range Café ✹ (Bernalillo, $$, p. 252)

Sadie's ✹ (Old Town, $, p. 248)

STEAK/SEAFOOD

Corn Maiden ✹✹ (Santa Ana Pueblo, $$$, p. 252)

Seasons Grill ✹✹ (Old Town, $$$, p. 246)

IN OR NEAR OLD TOWN
EXPENSIVE

AmbroZia Café & Wine Bar ✹✹ *Finds* CONTEMPORARY GLOBAL   Those who like a worldly culinary adventure will enjoy this Old Town restaurant. Set in a series of small rooms with artfully carved pine tables, it's an intimate and inviting spot. During warm months, the back patio sparkles with white Christmas lights. The wine bar has a Southwest Art Deco theme. Service is excellent. The food here is inspired and bold, which might mean for some, overwhelming. More conservative palates would be better suited to Seasons. The brunch has offerings such as a smoked salmon and asparagus crepe or huevos rancheros made with pork on crispy tortillas with green chile. Dinner might start with roasted tomato bisque with a brie cheese sandwich. For an entree, I can't recommend enough the grilled duck burger (I know it sounds weird) topped with house-made duck bacon and served with polenta corn fries. The crab crusted sea bass with artichoke and asparagus ragu over red chile gnocchi is also delicious. For dessert, try the "S'mores"—milk chocolate crème brûlée on homemade graham crackers. A lovely wine list accompanies the menu.

108 Rio Grande Blvd. NE (at the corner of Rio Grande and Central). ✆ **505/242-6560.** Brunch fixed-price four-course $20–$30; dinner main courses $20–$30. AE, DC, DISC, MC, V. Reservations recommended. Tues–Thurs 5:30–9pm; Fri–Sat 5:30–10:30pm; Sun brunch 11am–3pm.

Central Albuquerque Dining

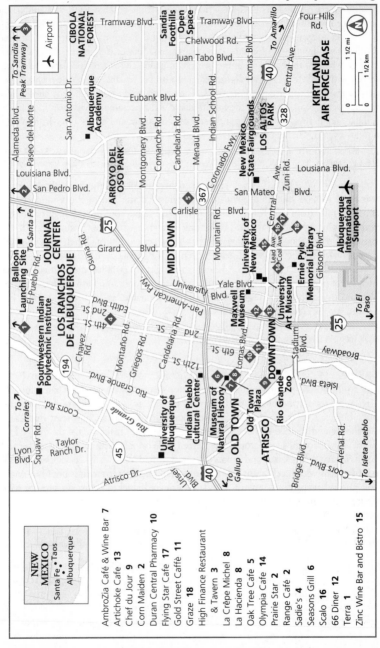

Tramway Blvd.
Tramway Blvd.

CIBOLA NATIONAL FOREST

Sandia Foothills Open Space

Chelwood Rd.

Juan Tabo Blvd.

Four Hills Rd.

To Amarillo

Airport

To Sandia Peak Tramway

Alameda Blvd.
Paseo del Norte

San Antonio Dr.

Albuquerque Academy

Eubank Blvd.

Lomas Blvd.

KIRTLAND AIR FORCE BASE

Central Ave.

Montgomery Blvd.

Comanche Rd.

Candelaria Rd.

Menaul Blvd.

Indian School Rd.

New Mexico State Fairgrounds

LOS ALTOS PARK

328

ARROYO DEL OSO PARK

Louisiana Blvd.

San Pedro Blvd.

Coronado Fwy.

Carlisle

367

San Mateo Blvd.

Mountain Rd.

Lousiana Blvd.

Zuni Rd.

Albuquerque International Sunport

To Santa Fe
To Sandia

JOURNAL CENTER

El Pueblo Rd.

Balloon Launching Site

Southwestern Indian Polytechnic Institute

LOS RANCHOS DE ALBUQUERQUE

Osuna Rd.

Girard Blvd.

MIDTOWN

University Blvd.

Central Ave.
Lead Ave.
Coal Ave.

University of New Mexico

Ernie Pyle Memorial Library

Gibson Blvd.

Yale Blvd.

Maxwell Museum

University Art Museum

To El Paso

25

2nd St.
4th St.
Edith Blvd.

Chavez Rd.

Montaño Rd.

Griegos Rd.

Candelaria Rd.

Pan-American Fwy.

12th St.

6th St.

Lomas Blvd.

DOWNTOWN

Stadium Blvd.

Broadway

To Corrales

Coors Rd.

194

Rio Grande Blvd.

University of Albuquerque

Indian Pueblo Cultural Center

Museum of Natural History

OLD TOWN

Old Town Plaza

Rio Grande Zoo

ATRISCO

Isleta Blvd.

Lyon Blvd.
Squaw Rd.

Taylor Ranch Dr.

45

Rio Grande

Unser Blvd.

Atrisco Dr.

40

To Gallup

Bridge Blvd.

Coors Blvd.

Arenal Rd.

To Isleta Pueblo

245

NEW MEXICO
Santa Fe • Taos
• Albuquerque

AmbroZia Café & Wine Bar **7**
Artichoke Cafe **13**
Chef du Jour **9**
Corn Maiden **2**
Duran Central Pharmacy **10**
Flying Star Cafe **17**
Gold Street Caffè **11**
Graze **18**
High Finance Restaurant & Tavern **3**
La Crêpe Michel **8**
La Hacienda **8**
Oak Tree Cafe **5**
Olympia Cafe **14**
Prairie Star **2**
Range Café **2**
Sadie's **4**
Seasons Grill **6**
Scalo **16**
66 Diner **12**
Terra **1**
Zinc Wine Bar and Bistro **15**

Seasons Grill ✶✶ AMERICAN   Between sunshine-colored walls and under an arched ceiling, this restaurant serves sophisticated flavors just steps from Old Town. It's a sweet oasis at midday and a romantic spot in the evening. The upstairs cantina bustles at sundown, with folks drinking margaritas. Service is excellent. At lunch you can't go wrong with the Angus burger with lemon aioli and roasted poblano chiles and served with herb fries. For the lighter eater, a number of salads head the menu. Dinner brings more sophisticated offerings. The grilled pork chop with goat cheese and roasted potatoes is tasty, as is the hoisin-glazed Atlantic salmon with jasmine rice. A full bar and an imaginative wine and beer list accompany the menu. On Saturday and Sunday evenings in summer, live jazz plays.

2031 Mountain Rd. NW. ✆ 505/766-5100. Reservations recommended at dinner. Main courses $7–$14 lunch, $16–$40 dinner. AE, DC, DISC, MC, V. Mon–Fri 11:30am–2:30pm; daily 5–10:30pm. Cantina daily 4pm–midnight.

Terra ✶ NEW AMERICAN   Those who live in Albuquerque's north valley are overjoyed to have fine dining within their midst (at the end of Rio Grande Blvd., about 15 min. from Old Town). Owner/chef Peter Lukes combines thoughtful flavors with imaginative presentation. The setting is comfortable, quiet, and relaxed. An exposed kitchen allows diners to watch the chef in action. During lunch you can select from sandwiches such as grilled jerk chicken with Fontana cheese, as well as a variety of salads and heartier entrees. For dinner, you might try griddled crab and corn cakes with sweet-pepper sauce, then move on to pan-seared pork loin with aromatic vegetables and dill corn bread. Vegetarian entrees are available, as are beer and wine. For dessert, try the chocolate Appaloosa cake.

1119 Alameda NW. ✆ 505/792-1700. Reservations recommended. Lunch $9.50–$11; dinner $14–$23. AE, DISC, MC, V. Tues–Fri 11am–1:30pm; Tues–Sat 5:30–9 or 10pm.

MODERATE

Gold Street Caffè ✶ *Finds* CONTEMPORARY AMERICAN   Opened in 1996, this hip little spot in the popular Gold Avenue district offers finely prepared food in a relaxed urban atmosphere. With its marble table tops and hardwood floors, this place bustles at all hours. Service is courteous. Nice touches such as toast from Sage Bakehouse and upscale versions of classics greet you at breakfast. Try the "Eggs Eleganza"—two poached eggs atop toasted green chile brioche with local goat cheese and herbs. Lunch offers salads and sandwiches and some New Mexico specialties, including fish tacos with black beans and coconut rice. The dinner menu is brief but good. You might have seafood stew or a grilled marinated chicken breast on spinach with raisins and pine nuts. An imaginative coffee, wine, and beer list accompanies the menu. Finish with a dessert special such as chocolate mousse pie.

218 Gold Ave. SW. ✆ 505/765-1633. Reservations recommended at dinner. Breakfast $3–$11; lunch $7–$11; dinner $12–$20. AE, DC, DISC, MC, V. Tues–Fri 7am–10pm; Sat 8am–10pm; Sun 8am–2pm; Mon 7am–2pm.

La Crêpe Michel ✶✶ FRENCH   Locals love this small cafe tucked away in a secluded walkway not far from the plaza, where the food is fun and imaginatively prepared. Run by chef Claudie Zamet-Wilcox from France, it has a cozy, informal European feel, with checked table coverings and simple furnishings. Service is friendly and calm, which makes this a good place for a romantic meal. You can't miss with any of the crepes. The *crêpe aux fruits de mer* (blend of sea scallops, bay scallops, and shrimp in a velouté sauce with mushrooms) is especially nice, as is the *crêpe à la volaille* (chunks of chicken in a cream sauce with mushrooms and Madeira wine). For a heartier meal, try one of the specials listed on the board on the wall, such as the beef filet (tenderloin finished with either black peppercorn–brandy cream sauce or Roquefort-brandy cream sauce) or the *saumon au poivre vert* (filet of salmon with green peppercorn–brandy sauce). Both are served with vegetables cooked just enough to leave them crisp and tasty. For dessert, don't leave without having a *crêpe aux fraises* (strawberry crepe). To accompany your meal, choose from a carefully planned beer and wine menu.

400 San Felipe C2. © 505/242-1251. Main courses $6–$24. MC, V. Tues–Sun 11:30am–2pm; Tues–Sat 6–9pm.

La Hacienda NEW MEXICAN/AMERICAN This restaurant, which appeals mostly to tourist traffic, offers more atmosphere than flavor. The food is a muted version of real northern New Mexican cuisine. If you want the real thing, I suggest Duran Central Pharmacy or Sadie's (p. below and 248). Still, this place is full of history. It's set in a 100-year-old adobe structure and has been in business for over 70 years. A mural on La Hacienda's outer wall depicts the construction of this Villa de Albuquerque at the turn of the 18th century, and President Clinton ate here during a 1998 visit. Diners enter through a large gift shop. The interior, which has an intimate, laid-back atmosphere, has brightly painted tables and chairs set very close together. In summer, choose the sidewalk dining with a view of the plaza. Most like to start with one of the big margaritas in a variety of flavors, from strawberry to pineapple. The specialty here is the chimichanga, a fried burrito stuffed with *carne adovada* and topped with guacamole and sour cream, tasty but *muy rico* (very rich). The chicken enchilada is also a nice choice. Meals come with chips and salsa and good *sopaipillas*. The servers are friendly but elusive.

302 San Felipe St. NW (at N. Plaza). © 505/243-3131. Reservations recommended for large parties. Lunch $5–$10; dinner $10–$16. AE, DC, DISC, MC, V. Sun–Thurs 11am–9pm; Fri–Sat 11am–9:30pm.

INEXPENSIVE

Chef du Jour ✦ ECLECTIC This small, quiet, and informal one-room cafe (with a few outdoor tables) serves elegantly prepared food at very reasonable prices. There's an open kitchen along one side and oddly matched tables. Once you get a taste of what's on the menu (which changes every week), you'll be coming back for more. Take special note of the condiments, all of which—from the ketchup to the salsa—are homemade. Recent menu offerings included a smoked chicken quesadilla with barbecue drizzle and a garden burger with smoked gouda cheese. There is also a salad du jour. If you call in advance, the restaurant will fax you a copy of its current menu. Microbrewed beers and hard ciders are available. The restaurant is a little difficult to find; travel south from the plaza, cross Lomas, and find San Pasquale.

119 San Pasquale SW. © 505/247-8998. Reservations recommended. Lunch $3–$9; dinner $6–$20. AE, DISC, MC, V. Tues–Fri 11am–2pm; Wed–Sat 5:30–10pm. Closed Christmas to New Year's Day.

Duran Central Pharmacy ✦ *Finds* NEW MEXICAN Sounds like an odd place to eat, I know. You could go to one of the touristy New Mexican restaurants in the middle of Old Town and have lots of atmosphere and mediocre food—or you could come here, where locals eat, and feast on better, more authentic fare. It's a few blocks up Central, east of Old Town. On your way through the pharmacy, you may want to stock up on specialty soaps; there's a pretty good variety here. The restaurant itself is plain, with a red tile floor and small tables, as well as a counter. For years, I used to come here for a bowl of green-chile stew and a homemade tortilla, which is still an excellent choice. Now I go for the full meals, such as the blue-corn enchilada plate or the huevos rancheros (eggs over corn tortillas, smothered with chile). The menu is short, but you can count on authentic northern New Mexican food.

1815 Central Ave. NW. ☎ 505/247-4141. Menu items $5–$9. No credit cards. Mon–Fri 9am–6:30pm; Sat 9am–2pm.

Oak Tree Café DELI   If you're in the northeast part of town, at the mall or State Fair maybe, and get a craving for a good sandwich, head to this little oasis amid the strip-mall madness of Menaul. With yellow walls, it's a bright little cafe with a friendly atmosphere presided over by New Yorker Robert Carson. These are true deli-style creations. Breakfast brings a breakfast burrito or bagels and cream cheese. For lunch, try the "Extreme," a roast beef sandwich with green chile and melted provolone, or the "Monte Hall," with turkey breast, green chile, and pepper jack cheese. Wash it all down with a cappuccino or Italian sparkling water.

5504 Menaul Ave., N.E., Suite G. ☎ 505/830-2233. Menu items under $7. MC, V. Mon–Fri 8am–3pm.

Sadie's 🖈 🄺ids NEW MEXICAN   Many New Mexicans lament the lost days when this restaurant was in a bowling alley. It's true that you can no longer hear the pins fall, and the main dining room is a little too big and the atmosphere a little too bright, but something is still drawing crowds: It's the food—simply some of the best in New Mexico, with tasty sauces and large portions. I recommend the enchilada, either chicken or beef. The stuffed *sopaipilla* dinner is also delicious and is one of the signature dishes. All meals come with chips and salsa, beans, and *sopaipillas*. There's a full bar, with excellent margaritas (and TV screens for you sports lovers). A casual atmosphere where kids can be themselves makes this a nice spot for families.

6230 4th St. NW. ☎ 505/345-5339. Main courses $7–$15. AE, DC, DISC, MC, V. Mon–Sat 11am–10pm; Sun 10am–9pm.

DOWNTOWN
MODERATE
Artichoke Cafe 🖈🖈 CONTINENTAL   An art gallery as well as a restaurant, this popular spot has modern paintings and sculptures set against azure walls, a hint at the innovative dining experience offered here. Set in three rooms, with dim lighting, this is a nice romantic place. The staff is friendly and efficient, though a little slow on busy nights. I was impressed by the list of special drinks available: a variety of interesting waters that included my favorite, Ame, as well as ginger beer, Jamaican iced coffee, microbrews, and an excellent list of California and French wines. You might start with an artichoke, steamed with three dipping sauces, or have roasted garlic with Montrachet goat cheese. For lunch, there are a number of salads and gourmet sandwiches, as well as dishes such as garlic and lime prawns with orzo. Check out the fresh fish specials; my favorite is wahoo on glass noodles with miso broth. From the menu, try the pumpkin ravioli with butternut squash, spinach, and ricotta filling with hazelnut-sage butter sauce.

424 Central Ave. SE. ☎ 505/243-0200. Reservations recommended. Main courses $7–$12 lunch, $13–$24 dinner. AE, DC, DISC, MC, V. Mon–Fri 11am–2:30pm; Mon 5:30–9pm; Tues–Sat 5:30–10pm; Sun 5–9 pm.

THE NORTHEAST HEIGHTS
EXPENSIVE
High Finance Restaurant and Tavern 🖈 CONTINENTAL   People don't rave about the food at this restaurant, but they do rave about the experience of eating here. Set high above Albuquerque, at the top of the Sandia Peak Tramway, it offers a fun and romantic adventure. The decor includes lots of shiny brass and comfortable furniture,

Family-Friendly Restaurants

Range Café (p. 252)   The fun and funky decor and Taos Cow ice cream make this a good spot for kids.

Sadie's (p. 248)   Kids like the quesadillas, tacos, and *sopaipillas* drizzled with honey; parents like the casual atmosphere where kid noise isn't scorned.

66 Diner (p. 251)   A full range of burgers and treats such as root beer floats and hot fudge sundaes will make any youngster happy.

and the service is decent. You might start with the sesame-fried calamari, served with greens and Thai dipping sauce. There are a number of pasta dishes, or you can try skillet-roasted ahi tuna served with spicy curry glaze. For meat lovers, there's prime rib or a filet. High Finance has a full bar. The restaurant recommends that you arrive at the Tramway base 45 minutes before your reservation.

40 Tramway Rd. NE (atop Sandia Peak). ☎ **505/243-9742.** www.highfinancerestaurant.com. Reservations requested. Main courses $9–$13 lunch, $15–$45 dinner. Tramway $10 with dinner reservations ($15 without). AE, DC, DISC, MC, V. Summer daily 11am–9pm; winter daily 11am–8pm.

UNIVERSITY & NOB HILL
EXPENSIVE

Zinc Wine Bar and Bistro 🐾🐾 NEW AMERICAN   In a moody, urban atmosphere with wood floors and a high ceiling, this newest in-place serves imaginative food meticulously prepared. The bi-level dining room with well-spaced tables can get crowded and noisy at peak hours (especially under the balcony, so avoid sitting there then). Service is congenial but inconsistent. Business people and others fill the seats here, dining on such treats as a blackened flank steak over a Greek salad at lunch (my favorite), or portobello-crusted Alaskan halibut with chorizo sausage polenta at dinner. The restaurant offers other inventive elements, such as "wine flights," in which diners may sample a variety of wines from a particular region for a set and fairly reasonable price. Or, you may simply opt for an excellent martini from the full bar. In the lower level, a lounge serves less formally in a wine cellar atmosphere with live music playing 2 to 3 nights a week (open Mon–Sat 5pm–1am; food served to midnight).

3009 Central Ave. NE. ☎ **505/254-ZINC.** Reservations recommended. Main courses $8–$14 lunch, $17–$26 dinner. AE, DC, DISC, MC, V. Mon–Fri 11am–2:30pm; Mon–Thurs 5–10pm; Fri–Sat 5–11pm.

MODERATE

Graze 🐾🐾 *Finds* NEW AMERICAN   My first trip to this new restaurant not far from the university was with a relative from a small Texas town. The place offers a chance to sample the divine creations of chef Jennifer James. My relative looked at the menu and then looked at me with consternation. Be aware that this isn't a chicken-fried-steak kind of place, though I wouldn't be surprised to see some refined version of that on this inventive menu. Set in a minimalist room, with hardwood floors and sunny colored walls, it's a fun spot for a culinary adventure, even for a small-town Texas girl, it turned out. Service is excellent. The portion sizes here are intentionally small, with the notion that diners will order many and share, though they're larger than tapas, so will suffice for a meal for a medium-size appetite. You might try the "piccolo frito," flash-fried calamari, with baby tomatoes, garbanzo beans, and basil, or the grilled tuna, with nori, daikon salad, and nicely sweet ponzu sauce. My relative loved the traditional French country pâté and fried chick peas. A nice selection of beers and wines accompanies the menu, and delectable desserts appear daily.

3128 Central Ave. SE. ℂ 505/268-4729. Reservations recommended on weekend nights. Individual plates $2–$25. AE, DISC, MC, V. Mon–Thurs 11am–10pm; Fri–Sat 11am–11pm; Sun noon–9pm.

Scalo ✦ INTERNATIONAL/ITALIAN   This Italian restaurant is a local favorite, so it's usually crowded, a good sign of the food's quality. The place has a simple, bistro-style elegance, with white-linen-clothed tables indoors, plus outdoor tables in a covered, temperature-controlled patio. Service is decent. The kitchen, which makes its own pasta and breads, offers an international menu with meals in small, medium, and large portions. Seasonal menus focus on New Mexico–grown produce. One signature dish is a risotto-fried calamari with a spicy marinara sauce. A hearty main dish is the double-cut pork chop with champagne-roasted peaches, kale, and fried shallots. The daily specials are big hits. Dessert selections change daily. There's a good wine list, from which you can sample 30 wines by the glass; or you may order from the full bar.

3500 Central Ave. SE. ℂ 505/255-8781. Reservations recommended. Lunch $6–$10; dinner $8–$29. AE, DC, DISC, MC, V. Mon–Thurs 11:30am–10pm; Fri 11:30am–11pm; Sat 5–11pm; Sun 5–10pm.

INEXPENSIVE
Flying Star Cafe CAFE/BAKERY   The Flying Star Cafe makes good on its promise of uptown food with down-home ingredients. It's a hip and urban restaurant with excellent contemporary international food. But beware: During mealtime, the university location on Central Avenue gets packed and rowdy. The selections range broadly, from 16 different breakfast options to homemade soups and salads to sandwiches and pasta (and pizza at the Juan Tabo and Rio Grande locations). Try the Rancher's melt (New Zealand sirloin sautéed with green chile, provolone, and horseradish on sourdough) or the Buddha's bowl (sautéed vegetables in ginger sauce with tofu over jasmine rice). Flying Star also has locations at 4501 Juan Tabo Blvd. NE (ℂ **505/275-8311**); 8001 Menaul Blvd. NE (ℂ **505/293-6911**); and 4026 Rio Grande Blvd. NW (ℂ **505/344-6714**). They don't serve alcohol, but they do brew up plenty of espresso and cappuccino. Though hours vary for each location, they are all open daily for breakfast, lunch, and dinner.

3416 Central Ave. SE. ℂ 505/255-6633. Reservations not accepted. All menu items under $10. AE, DISC, MC, V. Daily 6am–11:30pm.

Olympia Cafe GREEK   Run by a boisterous Mediterranean family, this cafe is where many New Mexico residents go for authentic Greek food. It's very informal (you order at a counter), it's right across from the university, and diners eat there at all times of day. It has a lively atmosphere, with bursts of enthusiastic Greek chatter emanating from the kitchen. With a full carryout menu, it's also a great place to grab a meal on the run. I like to get the Greek salad, served with fresh pita bread, and white-bean soup. A standard is the falafel sandwich with tahini, though my most recent one was light on falafel. The restaurant is well known for its gyros, and the moussaka is excellent. For dessert, try the baklava.

2210 Central Ave. SE. ℂ 505/266-5222. Menu items $3–$12. DISC, MC, V. Mon–Fri 11am–10pm.

Moments   **Route 66 Revisited: Rediscovering New Mexico's Stretch of the Mother Road**

As the old Bobby Troupe hit suggests: Get your kicks on Route 66. The highway that once stretched from Chicago to California was hailed as the road to freedom. During the Great Depression, it was the way west for farmers escaping Dust Bowl poverty out on the plains. If you found yourself in a rut in the late 1940s and 1950s, all you had to do was hop in the car and head west on Route 66.

Of course, the road existed long before it gained such widespread fascination. Built in the late 1920s and paved in 1937, it was the lifeblood of communities in eight states. Nowadays, however, US 66 is as elusive as the fantasies that once carried hundreds of thousands west in search of a better life. Replaced by other roads, covered up by interstates (mostly I-40), and just plain out of use, Route 66 still exists in New Mexico, but you'll have to do a little searching and take some extra time to find it.

Motorists driving west from Texas can take a spin (make that a slow spin) on a 20-mile gravel stretch of the original highway running from Glenrio (Texas) to San Jon. From San Jon to Tucumcari, you can enjoy nearly 24 continuous paved miles of vintage 66. In Tucumcari, the historic route sliced through the center of town along what is now Tucumcari Boulevard. Santa Rosa's Will Rogers Drive is that city's 4-mile claim to the Mother Road. In Albuquerque, US 66 follows Central Avenue for 18 miles, from the 1936 State Fairgrounds, past original 1930s motels and the historic Nob Hill district, on west through downtown.

One of the best spots to pretend you're a 1950s road warrior crossing the desert—whizzing past rattlesnakes, tepees, and tumbleweeds—is along NM 124, which winds 25 miles from Mesita to Acoma in northwestern New Mexico. You can next pick up old Route 66 in Grants, along the 6-mile Santa Fe Avenue. In Gallup, a 9-mile segment of US 66 is lined with restaurants and hotels reminiscent of the city's days as a western film capital from 1929 to 1964. Just outside Gallup, the historic route continues west to the Arizona border as NM 118.

For more information about Route 66, contact the **Grants/Cíbola County Chamber of Commerce** (🕜 **800/748-2142;** www.grants.org) or the **New Mexico Department of Tourism** (🕜 **800/545-2040;** www.newmexico.org).

66 Diner *Kids* AMERICAN   Like a trip back in time to the days when Martin Milner and George Maharis got "their kicks on Route 66," this thoroughly 1950s-style diner comes complete with Seeburg jukebox and full-service soda fountain. The white caps make great green-chile cheeseburgers, along with meatloaf sandwiches, grilled liver and onions, and chicken-fried steaks. Ham-and-egg and pancake breakfasts are served on weekends. Beer and wine are available. Comfy booths and their own menu will please the kids.

1405 Central Ave. NE. 🕜 **505/247-1421.** Menu items $3–$9. AE, DC, DISC, MC, V. Mon–Thurs 11am–11pm; Fri 11am–midnight; Sat 8am–midnight; Sun 8am–10pm.

OUTSIDE ALBUQUERQUE

Corn Maiden 🌟🌟 NEW AMERICAN   Plan a sunset dinner at this restaurant at the Hyatt Tamaya, north of town. You'll feast not only on delicious innovative cuisine but also on one of the best views in New Mexico. Set in the Rio Grande valley, with banks of windows looking out on the Sandia Mountains, this restaurant has a comfortably subdued decor wrapped around an open kitchen. The offerings will likely please conventional as well as adventurous palates. Served with your bread is a tasty Southwestern tapenade made with napolito cactus. For an appetizer, you might try the seared blue lump crab cake. For an entree, the big favorite is the rotisserie—an interesting combination of meats and seafood. You'll also find an excellent filet mignon with sautéed mushrooms or a veal tenderloin with white asparagus. Dessert brings a dazzling display of confections as lively to look at as to taste. Wine lovers have their pick of a broad range of labels.

In the Hyatt Regency Tamaya Resort and Spa, 1300 Tuyana Trail, Santa Ana Pueblo. 🕐 **505/867-1234.** Reservations recommended. Main courses $30–$40. AE, DC, DISC, MC, V. Tues–Sat 5:30–10pm. From I-25 take exit 242, following US 550 west to Tamaya Blvd.; drive 1½ miles to the resort.

Prairie Star 🌟🌟 NEW AMERICAN   On the Santa Ana Pueblo, about 25 minutes north of Albuquerque, and set in a sprawling adobe home with a marvelous view across the high plains and a golf course, this restaurant offers an interesting blend of old and new, both in terms of atmosphere and flavor. It was built in the 1940s in Mission architectural style. Exposed vigas and full *latilla* ceilings, as well as hand-carved fireplaces and *bancos,* complement the thick adobe walls. There is a lounge at the top of the circular stairway. Diners can start with wild-mushroom bruschetta, with kalamata-olive tapenade and goat chevre. Signature dishes include Chama Valley lamb chops with caramelized apple torte and white asparagus (delicious), and soy-grilled quail with wasabi potatoes and Asian shrimp mousse. An extensive wine list with more than 30 flavors by the glass tops out the menu, as do special desserts, which vary nightly.

288 Prairie Star Rd., Santa Ana Pueblo. 🕐 **505/867-3327.** Reservations recommended. Main courses $17–$33. AE, DC, DISC, MC, V. Sun–Thurs 5–9pm (lounge opens at 4:30pm); Fri–Sat 5-10pm.

Range Café 🌟 *Kids* NEW MEXICAN/AMERICAN   This cafe on the main drag of Bernalillo, about 20 minutes north of Albuquerque, is a perfect place to stop on your way out of town. Housed in what was once an old drugstore, the restaurant has a pressed tin ceiling and is decorated with western touches, such as cowboy boots and whimsical art. The food ranges from enchiladas and burritos to chicken-fried steak to more elegantly prepared meals. The proprietors and chef here have come from such notable restaurants as Scalo in Albuquerque (p. 250) and Prairie Star at Santa Ana Pueblo (p. 252), so you can count on great food. For breakfast, try the pancakes or the breakfast burrito. For lunch or dinner, I recommend Tom's meatloaf, served with roasted-garlic mashed potatoes, mushroom gravy, and sautéed vegetables. For dinner, you might try pan-seared trout with sun-dried tomato and caper butter sauce. Taos Cow ice cream is the order for dessert, or try the baked goods and specialty drinks from the full bar. In the same locale, the Range has opened the Lizard Rodeo Lounge, a smoke-free, hoppin' place with Wild West decor that offers live music many nights a week. There's also a retail space that sells local art and New Mexico wines. Two other branches of the restaurant in Albuquerque have similar food offerings (4200 Wyoming Blvd., NE, 🕐 **505/293-2633,** and 2200 Menaul Blvd., NE 🕐 **505/888-1660**).

925 Camino del Pueblo (P.O. Box 1780), Bernalillo. (C) **505/867-1700.** Reservations accepted for 8 or more. Breakfast and lunch $5–$10; dinner $9–$25. AE, DISC, MC, V. Summer Sun–Thurs 7:30am–10pm; winter Sun–Thurs 7:30am–9:30pm; a half-hour later on Fri and Sat. Closed Thanksgiving and Christmas.

5 What to See & Do

Albuquerque's original town site, known today as Old Town, is the central point of interest for visitors. Here, grouped around the plaza, are the venerable Church of San Felipe de Neri and numerous restaurants, art galleries, and crafts shops. Several important museums are close by. Within a few blocks are the 25,000-square-foot Albuquerque Aquarium and the 50-acre Rio Grande Botanic Garden (near Central Ave. and Tingley Dr. NW), both well worth a visit.

But don't get stuck in Old Town. Elsewhere, you'll find the Sandia Peak Tramway, the new Balloon Museum, and a number of natural attractions. Within day-trip range are several pueblos and significant monuments (see "Exploring Nearby Pueblos & Monuments," later in this chapter).

THE TOP ATTRACTIONS

Albuquerque Museum of Art and History *Finds* *Kids*   Take an interesting journey down into the caverns of New Mexico's past in this museum on the outskirts of Old Town. Drawing on the largest U.S. collection of Spanish colonial artifacts, displays here include Don Quixote–style helmets, swords, and horse armor. You can wander through an 18th-century house compound with adobe floor and walls, and see gear used by *vaqueros,* the original cowboys who came to the area in the 16th century. A weaving exhibition allows kids to try spinning wool, and a trapping section provides them with pelts to touch. In an old-style theater, two films on Albuquerque history are shown. In the History Hopscotch area, kids can explore an old trunk or play with antique blocks and other toys. An Old Town walking tour originates here at 11am Tuesday to Sunday during spring, summer, and fall. The upper floors house permanent art collections and, best of all, a huge exhibit space (recently expanded), where you'll find some extraordinary shows. A gift shop sells books and jewelry and has a nice selection of Navajo dolls. Plan to spend 1 to 2 hours.

2000 Mountain Rd. NW. (C) 505/243-7255. www.albuquerquemuseum.com. Admission $4 adults, $2 seniors 65 and older, $ 1 children 4–12. Tues–Sun 9am–5pm. Closed major holidays.

Balloon Museum *Finds Finds* *Kids*   The Anderson-Abruzzo Albuquerque International Balloon Museum holds special significance for me, as my parents owned part of the first hot air balloon in Albuquerque over 30 years ago. Today, with the Albuquerque International Balloon Fiesta drawing hundreds of brilliantly colored and imaginatively shaped balloons to the city each October (see p. 19), this museum's time has come. It tells the history of ballooning, from the first flight in France in 1783, with a rooster, sheep, and duck as passengers, to the use of balloons in military, science, and aerospace research. Most poignant are displays of Albuquerque balloonists Maxie Anderson and Ben Abruzzo, who, with Larry Newman, completed the first manned crossing of the Atlantic Ocean in 1978. Originals and replicas of various historic crafts dot the three-story-tall space, and windows look out at the Sandia Mountains and Rio Grande Valley. Kids will enjoy the flight simulator, which tests their ability to fly and land a balloon on target. Plan on spending at least an hour here.

9201 Balloon Museum Dr., NE. (C) 505/768-6020. www.balloonmuseum.com. Admission $4 adults, $2 seniors 65 and older, $1 children 4–12, free for children 3 and under. Tues–Sun 9am–5pm.

Indian Pueblo Cultural Center ✦ *Kids*   Owned and operated as a nonprofit organization by the 19 pueblos of New Mexico, this is a fine place to begin an exploration of Native American culture. About a mile northeast of Old Town, this museum—modeled after Pueblo Bonito, a spectacular 9th-century ruin in Chaco Culture National Historic Park—consists of several parts.

You'll want to spend 1 to 2 hours here. Begin in the basement, where a permanent exhibit depicts the **evolution of the various pueblos** from prehistory to present, including displays of the distinctive handicrafts of each community. Note especially how pottery differs in concept and design from pueblo to pueblo. The **Pueblo House Children's Museum,** in a separate building, is a hands-on experience that gives children the opportunity to learn about and understand the evolution of Pueblo culture. There they can touch pot shards, play with *heishi* (shell) drills, and even don fox tails and dance.

Upstairs in the main building is an enormous (10,000-sq.-ft.) **gift shop** featuring fine pottery, rugs, sand paintings, kachinas, drums, and jewelry, among other things. Southwestern clothing and souvenirs are also available. Prices here are quite reasonable.

Every weekend throughout the year, **Native American dancers** perform at 11am and 2pm in an outdoor arena surrounded by original murals. Often, artisans demonstrate their crafts there as well. During certain weeks of the year, such as the Balloon Fiesta, dances are performed daily.

A restaurant serves traditional Native American foods. It's a good place for some Indian fry bread and a bowl of *posole.*

2401 12th St. NW. ℂ 800/766-4405 or 505/843-7270. www.indianpueblo.org. Admission $6 adults, $5 seniors, $3 students, free for children 4 and under. AE, DISC, MC, V. Daily 9am–5:30pm; restaurant 8am–3pm. Closed New Year's Day, Memorial Day, July 4, Labor Day, Thanksgiving, and Christmas.

National Hispanic Cultural Center ✦   In the historic Barelas neighborhood on the Camino Real, this gem of Albuquerque museums offers a rich cultural journey through hundreds of years of history and across the globe. It explores Hispanic arts and lifeways with visual arts, drama, music, dance, and other programs. I most enjoyed the 11,000-square-foot gallery space, which exhibits exciting contemporary and traditional works. Look for photographs by Miguel Gandert. A restaurant offers New Mexican and American food. It's a good spot to sample authentic regional dishes such as tacos and enchiladas either from a buffet or by ordering from the menu. My favorite is the tortilla burger (a burger served in a flour tortilla, with all the fixin's). Plans are to incorporate a cultural cooking component into the center, which would allow visitors to sample Hispanic foods from all over the world. Plan to spend 1 to 2 hours here.

1701 4th St. SW (corner of 4th St. and Avenida Cesar Chavez). ℂ 505/246-2261. Fax 505/246-2613. www.nhccnm. org. Admission Tues–Sat $3 adults, $2 seniors 60 and over, free for children 16 and under; Sun $1 adults and seniors. AE, DISC, MC, V. Tues–Sun 10am–5pm; restaurant 8am–3pm. Closed New Year's Day, Easter, Memorial Day, Labor Day, and Christmas.

Old Town ✦✦   A maze of cobbled courtyard walkways leads to hidden patios and gardens, where many of Old Town's 150 galleries and shops are located. Adobe buildings, many refurbished in the pueblo revival style of the 1950s, are grouped around the tree-shaded plaza, created in 1780. Pueblo and Navajo artisans often display their pottery, blankets, and silver jewelry on the sidewalks lining the plaza.

The buildings of Old Town once served as mercantile shops, grocery stores, and government offices, but the importance of Old Town as Albuquerque's commercial center declined after 1880, when the railroad came through 1¼ miles east of the plaza

Central Albuquerque Attractions

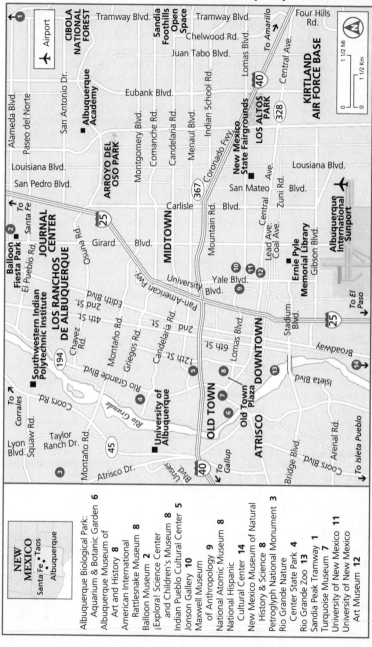

NEW MEXICO

Santa Fe • Taos
Albuquerque

Albuquerque Biological Park: Aquarium & Botanic Garden **6**
Albuquerque Museum of Art and History **8**
American International Rattlesnake Museum **8**
Balloon Museum **2**
¡Explora! Science Center and Children's Museum **8**
Indian Pueblo Cultural Center **5**
Jonson Gallery **10**
Maxwell Museum of Anthropology **9**
National Atomic Museum **8**
National Hispanic Cultural Center **14**
New Mexico Museum of Natural History & Science **8**
Petroglyph National Monument **3**
Rio Grande Nature Center State Park **4**
Rio Grande Zoo **13**
Sandia Peak Tramway **1**
Turquoise Museum **7**
University of New Mexico **11**
University of New Mexico Art Museum **12**

and businesses relocated to be closer to the trains. Old Town clung to its historical and sentimental roots, but the quarter fell into disrepair until the 1930s and 1940s, when artisans and other shop owners rediscovered it and the tourism industry burgeoned.

When Albuquerque was established in 1706, the first building erected by the settlers was the **Church of San Felipe de Neri,** which faces the plaza on its north side. It's a cozy church with wonderful stained-glass windows and vivid *retablos* (religious paintings). This house of worship has been in almost continuous use for nearly 300 years.

Though you'll wade through a few trinket and T-shirt shops on the plaza, don't be fooled: Old Town is an excellent place to shop. Look for good buys from the Native Americans selling jewelry on the plaza, especially silver bracelets and strung turquoise. If you want to take something fun home and spend very little, buy a dyed corn necklace. Your best bet when wandering around Old Town is to just peek into shops, but there are a few places you'll definitely want to spend time. See "Shopping," later in this chapter, for a list of recommendations. An excellent Old Town historic walking tour originates at the Albuquerque Museum of Art and History (see above) at 11am Tuesday to Sunday during spring, summer, and fall. Plan to spend 2 to 3 hours strolling around.

Northeast of Central Ave. and Rio Grande Blvd. NW. Old Town Visitor Center: 303 Romero St. NW, Albuquerque, NM 87104 (across the street from the Church of San Felipe de Neri). © **505/243-3215.** Visitor Center daily 9am–5pm summer; daily 9:30am–4:30pm rest of the year.

Sandia Peak Tramway (Kids) (★★)   This fun and exciting half-day or evening outing allows incredible views of the Albuquerque landscape and wildlife. The Sandia Peak Tram is a "jigback"; in other words, as one car approaches the top, the other nears the bottom. The two pass halfway through the trip, in the midst of a 1½-mile "clear span" of unsupported cable between the second tower and the upper terminal.

Several hiking trails are available on Sandia Peak, and one of them—La Luz Trail— takes you on a steep and rigorous trek from the base to the summit. The views in all directions are extraordinary. *Note:* The trails on Sandia may not be suitable for children. There's a popular and expensive restaurant, High Finance Restaurant and Tavern (see p. 248), at Sandia's summit. Special tram rates apply with dinner reservations. Be aware that the tram does not operate on very windy days.

10 Tramway Loop NE. © **505/856-7325.** Fax 505/856-6335. www.sandiapeak.com. Admission $15 adults, $13 seniors, $10 children 5–12, free for children under 5. Memorial Day to Labor Day daily 9am–9pm; spring and fall Thurs–Tues 9am–8pm, Wed 5–8pm; ski season Thurs–Tues 9am–8pm, Wed noon–8pm. Closed 2 weeks each spring and fall for maintenance; check the website for details. Parking $1 daily. AE, DISC, MC, V. To reach the base of the tram, take I-25 north to Tramway Rd. (exit 234), then proceed east about 5 miles on Tramway Rd. (NM 556); or take Tramway Blvd., exit 167 (NM 556), north of I-40 approximately 8½ miles.

OTHER ATTRACTIONS

National Atomic Museum (★)   "I am become death, the shatterer of worlds." Shortly after the successful detonation of the first atomic bomb, Robert Oppenheimer, who headed the Manhattan Project, said this, quoting from ancient Hindu texts. This and other valuable information highlight the 51-minute film *Ten Seconds That Shook the World,* which is shown daily (throughout the day) at this museum, an experience worth fitting into a busy schedule. The museum itself offers the next-best introduction to the nuclear age after the Bradbury Science Museum in Los Alamos, making for an interesting 1- to 2-hour perusal. It traces the history of nuclear-weapons development, beginning with the top-secret Manhattan Project of the 1940s, including a copy of the letter Albert Einstein wrote to President Franklin D. Roosevelt suggesting the possible need to beat the Germans at creating an atomic bomb—a letter that surprisingly went ignored for nearly 2 years. You'll find a permanent Marie Curie exhibit in the lobby and full-scale models of the "Fat Man" and "Little Boy" bombs, as well as displays and films on the peaceful application of nuclear technology—including nuclear medicine—and other alternative energy sources.

1905 Mountain Rd. NW. (C) 505/245-2137. Fax 505/242-4537. www.atomicmuseum.com. Admission $5 adults, $4 seniors and children 7–18, free for children 6 and under. Children under 12 not admitted without adult. Group rates available. Daily 9am–5pm. Closed New Year's Day, Easter, Thanksgiving, and Christmas.

Petroglyph National Monument 🔆 *Kids* These lava flows were once a hunting and gathering area for prehistoric Native Americans, who left a chronicle of their beliefs etched on the dark basalt boulders. Some 25,000 petroglyphs provide a nice outdoor adventure after a morning in a museum. You'll want to stop at the visitor center to get a map, check out the interactive computer, and, in summer, hook up with a ranger-led tour. From there, you can drive north to the Boca Negra area, where you'll have a choice of three trails. Take the Mesa Point Trail (30 min.) that climbs quickly up the side of a hill, offering many petroglyph sightings as well as an outstanding view of the Sandia Mountains. If you're traveling with your dog, you can bring her along on the Rinconada Trail. Hikers can have fun searching the rocks for more petroglyphs; there are many yet to be found. This trail (a few miles south of the visitor center) runs for miles around a huge *rincon* (corner) at the base of the lava flow. Camping is not permitted in the park; it's strictly for day use, with picnic areas, drinking water, and restrooms provided.

6001 Unser Blvd. NW (3 miles north of I-40 at Unser and Western Trail). (C) 505/899-0205. Fax 505/899-0207. www. nps.gov/petr. Admission $1 per vehicle weekdays, $2 weekends. DISC, MC, V. Visitor Center and Boca Negra area daily 8am–5pm. Closed New Year's Day, Thanksgiving, and Christmas.

Turquoise Museum *Kids* Don't be put off by the setting of this little gem of a museum in a strip mall west of Old Town. For those with curiosity, it's a real find that's been featured in *Smithsonian Magazine* and on *60 Minutes*. The passion of father and son Joe P. Lowry and Joe Dan Lowry, it contains "the world's largest collection of turquoise"—from 60 mines around the world. You start through a tunnel, where turquoise is embedded in the walls, and move on to exhibits that present the blue stone's geology, history, and mythology. You'll see maps showing where turquoise is mined, ranging from Egypt to Kingman, Arizona, and find out how to determine whether the turquoise you're hoping to buy is quality or not. Lowry, Sr., will fill in any details and even tell you more about turquoise you're wearing. There's also a real lapidary shop; jewelry made there is sold in a gift shop that's open until 5pm. If you're lucky, one of Lowry's grandkids will tell a joke like this one she told me: What do you call a sleeping bull? A bulldozer. Plan to spend about 1 hour here.

2107 Central Ave. NW. (C) 505/247-8650. Admission $4 adults, $3 children 7–17 and seniors 60 and over, free for children 6 and under, $10 family rate. AE, DISC, MC, V. Mon–Sat 9:30am–4pm.

University of New Mexico The state's largest institution of higher learning stretches across an attractive 70-acre campus about 2 miles east of downtown Albuquerque, north of Central Avenue and east of University Boulevard. The five campus museums, none of which charges admission, are constructed (like other UNM buildings) in a modified pueblo style. Popejoy Hall, in the south-central part of the campus, hosts many performing-arts presentations, including those of the New Mexico

Symphony Orchestra; other public events are held in nearby Keller Hall and Wood-ward Hall.

I've found the best way to see the museums and campus is on a walking tour, which can make for a nice 2- to 3-hour morning or afternoon outing. Begin on the west side of campus at the Maxwell Museum of Anthropology. You'll find parking meters there, as well as Maxwell Museum parking, for which you can get a permit inside.

The **Maxwell Museum of Anthropology,** situated on the west side of the campus on Redondo Drive, south of Las Lomas Road (© 505/277-4405; www.unm.edu/maxwell), is an internationally acclaimed repository of Southwestern anthropological finds. What's really intriguing here is not just the ancient pottery, tools, and yucca weavings, but the anthropological context within which these items are set. You'll see a reconstruction of an archaeological site, complete with string markers, brushes, and field notes, as well as microscope lenses you can examine to see how archaeologists perform temper analysis to find out where pots were made, and pollen analysis to help reconstruct past environments. There are two permanent exhibits: *Ancestors,* which looks at human evolution, and *People of the Southwest,* a look at the history of the Southwest from 10,000 years ago to the 16th century from an archaeological perspective. It's open Tuesday to Friday 9am to 4pm, and Saturday 10am to 4pm; the museum is closed Sundays, Mondays, and holidays. From the Maxwell, walk east into the campus until you come to the Duck Pond and pass Mitchell Hall; then turn south (right) and walk down a lane until you reach Northrup Hall.

In **Northrup Hall** (© 505/277-4204), about halfway between the Maxwell Museum and Popejoy Hall in the southern part of the campus, the adjacent **Geology Museum** (© 505/277-4204) and **Meteorite Museum** (© 505/277-1644) cover the gamut of recorded time from dinosaur bones to moon rocks. Within the Geology Museum, you'll see stones that create spectacular works of art, from black-on-white orbicular granite to brilliant blue dioptase. In the Meteorite Museum, 550 meteorite specimens comprise the sixth-largest collection in the United States. You'll see and touch a sink-size piece of a meteorite that weighs as much as a car, as well as samples of the many variations of stones that fall from the sky. Both museums are open Monday to Friday 9am to 4pm.

From here, you walk east, straight through a mall that takes you by the art building to the Fine Arts Center. The **University of New Mexico Art Museum** (© 505/277-4001; http://unmartmuseum.unm.edu) is located here, just north of Central Avenue and Cornell Street. The museum features changing exhibitions of 19th- and 20th-century art. Its permanent collection includes Old Masters paintings and sculpture, significant New Mexico artists, Spanish-colonial artwork, the Tamarind Lithography Archives, and one of the largest university-owned photography collections in the country. This is my favorite part. You'll see modern and contemporary works, and some striking images that you'll remember for years. It's open Tuesday to Friday 9am to 4pm, Tuesday evening 5 to 8pm, and Sunday 1 to 4pm; the museum is closed holidays. A gift shop offers a variety of gifts and posters. Admission is free.

By now you'll probably want a break. Across the mall to the north is the Student Union Building, where you can get treats from muffins to pizza. Campus maps can be obtained here, along with directions. Once you're refreshed, head out the north door of the Student Union Building and walk west through Smith Plaza, then turn north by the bus stop and walk to Las Lomas Road, where you'll turn right and walk a half-block to the intimate **Jonson Gallery,** at 1909 Las Lomas Rd. NE (© 505/277-4967; www.unm.edu/jonsong), on the north side of the central campus. This museum

Taking Home a Southwest Kitchen

If you've fallen in love with New Mexican and Southwestern cooking during your stay (or if you did even before you arrived), you might like to sign up for cooking classes with Jane Butel, a leading Southwest cooking authority, author of 18 cookbooks, and host of the national TV show *Jane Butel's Southwestern Kitchen.* At **Jane Butel Cooking School** ☆ 2655 Pan American NE Suite F; ℂ **800/473-8226** or 505/243-2622; fax 505/243-8296; www.jane butel.com or www.pecosvalley.com), you'll learn the history and techniques of Southwestern cuisine and have ample opportunity for hands-on preparation. If you choose the weeklong session, you'll start by learning about chiles and move on to native breads and dishes, appetizers, beverages, and desserts. Weekend sessions and special vegetarian sessions are also available, as are some sessions that include "culinary tours," including trips to Santa Fe. Call, fax, or visit Jane's website for current schedules and fees.

displays more than 2,000 works by the late Raymond Jonson, a leading modernist painter in early-20th-century New Mexico, as well as works by contemporary artists. This is my least favorite of the campus museums; if you're going to miss one, make it this one. The gallery is open Tuesday to Friday 9am to 4pm and Tuesday evening 5 to 8pm. From the Jonson you can walk west on Las Lomas Road to Redondo Road, where you'll turn south and arrive back at the Maxwell Museum, where your car is parked. Touring these museums takes a full morning or afternoon.

1 University Hill NE (north of Central Ave.). ℂ **505/277-0111.** www.unm.edu.

6 Especially for Kids

Albuquerque Biological Park: Aquarium and Botanic Garden ☆ *Kids* For those of us born and raised in the desert, this attraction quenches years of soul thirst. The self-guided aquarium tour begins with a beautifully produced 9-minute film that describes the course of the Rio Grande from its origin to the Gulf Coast. Then, you'll move on to the touch pool, where at certain times of day you can gently touch hermit crabs and starfish. Next comes the eel tank, an arched aquarium you get to walk through and a colorful coral-reef exhibit, and finally the culminating show, in a 285,000-gallon shark tank.

Within a state-of-the-art 10,000-square-foot conservatory, you'll find the botanical garden, split into two sections. The smaller one houses the desert collection and features plants from the lower Chihuahuan and Sonoran deserts, including unique species from Baja, California. The larger pavilion exhibits the Mediterranean collection and includes many exotic species native to the Mediterranean climates of southern California, South Africa, Australia, and the Mediterranean Basin. Allow at least 2 hours to see both parks. There is a restaurant on the premises. May to September, the new PNM Butterfly Pavilion fills with the colors of several hundred North American butterflies.

In December, you can see the "River of Lights Holiday Light Display" Tuesday through Sunday; and June through August you can attend Thursday evening concerts.

2601 Central Ave. NW. ✆ **505/764-6200**. www.cabq.gov/biopark. Admission $7 adults ($12 with Rio Grande Zoo admission), $3 seniors 65 and over and children 12 and under ($5 with Rio Grande Zoo admission). Ticket sales stop a half-hour before closing. MC, V. Tues–Sun 9am–5pm (June–Aug Sat–Sun until 6pm) Closed New Year's Day, Thanksgiving, and Christmas.

American International Rattlesnake Museum *Finds* *Kids*   This unique museum, just off Old Town Plaza, has living specimens of common, uncommon, and very rare rattlesnakes of North, Central, and South America in naturally landscaped habitats. Oddities such as albino and patternless rattlesnakes are included, as is a display popular with youngsters: baby rattlesnakes. More than 30 species can be seen, followed by a 7-minute film on this contributor to the ecological balance of our hemisphere. Throughout the museum are rattlesnake artifacts from early American history, Native American culture, medicine, the arts, and advertising. You'll also find a gift shop that specializes in Native American jewelry, T-shirts, and other memorabilia related to the natural world and the Southwest, all with an emphasis on rattlesnakes.

202 San Felipe St. NW. ✆ **505/242-6569**. www.rattlesnakes.com. Admission $3.50 adults, $3 seniors, $2.50 children. AE, DISC, MC, V. Mon–Sat 10am–6pm; Sun noon–5pm.

¡Explora! Science Center and Children's Museum ✦ *Kids*   As a center for lifelong learning, ¡Explora! houses more than 250 hands-on scientific exhibits for visitors of all ages on topics as diverse as water, the Rio Grande, light and optics, biological perception, and energy. It features exhibits utilizing technology that is creatively accessible to the public and exhibits that engage visitors in creating all kinds of art. You could spend an hour and a half to a full day here.

1701 Mountain Rd. NW. ✆ **505/224-8300**. Fax 505/224-8325. www.explora.mus.nm.us. Admission $7 adults ages 12–64, $5 seniors 65 and over, $3 children 1–11, free for children under 1. Mon–Sat 10am–6pm; Sun noon–6pm.

New Mexico Museum of Natural History and Science ✦✦ *Kids*   A trip through this museum will take you through 12 billion years of natural history, from the formation of the universe to the present day. Begin by looking at a display of stones and gems, then stroll through the "Age of Giants" display, where you'll find dinosaur skeletons cast from the real bones. You can ride the Evolator (kids love this!), a simulated time-travel experience that moves and rumbles, taking you 1¼ miles (2km) up (or down) and through 38 million years of history. Soon, you'll find yourself in the age of the mammoths and moving through the Ice Age. Other stops along the way include the Naturalist Center, where kids can peek through microscopes and make their own bear or raccoon footprints in sand, and FossilWorks, where paleontologists work behind glass, excavating bones of a seismosaurus. Be sure to check out

Kids **In Search of Disneyland**

If you want to occupy the kids for a day, there's a fun option, though don't expect Disneyland. **Cliff's Amusement Park**, 4800 Osuna Rd. NE (✆ **505/881-9373**; www.cliffs.net), has roller coasters, including the daring "Galaxy," a waterpark with some fun get-wet rides, and an arcade. Gate entrance is $2.50; ride passes run $19 for kids 48 inches tall and under and $22 for those over 48 inches; individual ride tickets $2.

the newest addition to the museum, the LodeStar Astronomy Center, a sophisticated planetarium with the Virtual Voyages Simulation theater. Those exhibits, as well as the DynaTheater, which surrounds you with images and sound, cost an additional fee. A gift shop on the ground floor sells imaginative nature games and other curios. This museum has good access for people with disabilities, including scripts for people with impaired hearing and exhibit text written in Braille. Plan to spend 1 to 2 hours here, more if you take in extra attractions.

1801 Mountain Rd. NW. ℂ 505/841-2800. www.nmnaturalhistory.org. Admission $6 adults, $5 seniors, $3 children 3–12, free for children under 3. DynaTheater, Planetarium, and Virtual Voyages cost extra, with prices in the $6 range adults and $3 range children. Buying ticket combinations qualifies you for discounts. Daily 9am–5pm. Jan and Sept closed Mon except major holidays, when it's open Mon; also closed Thanksgiving and Christmas.

Rio Grande Nature Center State Park *(Kids)*   This center, just a few miles north of Old Town, spans 270 acres of riverside forest and meadows that include stands of 100-year-old cottonwoods and a 3-acre pond. On the Rio Grande Flyway, an important migratory route for many birds, it's an excellent place to see sandhill cranes, Canadian geese, and quail—more than 260 bird species have made this their temporary or permanent home. In a protected area where dogs aren't allowed (you can bring dogs on most of the 2 miles of trails), you'll find exhibits of native grasses, wildflowers, and herbs. Inside a building built half above and half below ground, you can sit next to the pond in a glassed-in viewing area and comfortably watch ducks and other birds in their avian antics. There are 21 self-guided interpretive exhibits as well as photo exhibits, a library, a small nature store, and a children's resource room. On Saturday mornings, you can join a guided nature walk. Other weekend programs are available for adults and children, including nature photography and bird- and wildflower-identification classes. Call for a schedule.

2901 Candelaria Rd. NW. ℂ 505/344-7240. Fax 505/344-4505. www.rgnc.org. Admission $3 per vehicle. DISC, MC, V. Daily 10am–5pm; store Mon–Fri 11am–3pm, Sat–Sun 10am–4pm. Closed New Year's Day, Thanksgiving, and Christmas.

Rio Grande Zoo *(Kids)*   More than 1,200 animals from 300 species live on 60 acres of riverside bosque among ancient cottonwoods. Open-moat exhibits with animals in naturalized habitats are a treat for zoo-goers. Major exhibits include polar bears, giraffes, sea lions (with underwater viewing), the cat walk, the bird show, and ape country, with gorillas and orangutans. The zoo has an especially fine collection of elephants, mountain lions, koalas, reptiles, and native Southwestern species. A children's petting zoo is open during the summer. There are numerous snack bars on the zoo grounds, and La Ventana Gift Shop carries film and souvenirs. Also check out the seal and sea lion feeding at 10:30am and 3:30pm daily and the summer Zoo Music Concert Series.

903 10th St. SW. ℂ 505/764-6200. www.cabq.gov/biopark/zoo. Admission $7 adults ($10 with Aquarium and Botanic Garden admission), $3 seniors and children 3–12 ($5 with Aquarium and Botanic Garden admission), free for children 2 and under. Daily 9am–5pm (6pm summer weekends). Closed New Year's Day, Thanksgiving, and Christmas.

7 Outdoor Activities

BALLOONING

Visitors have a choice of several hot air balloon operators; rates start at about $150 per person per hour. Call **Rainbow Ryders,** 11520 San Bernardino NE (ℂ **505/823-1111**), or **World Balloon Corporation,** 1103 La Poblana NW (ℂ **505/293-6800**).

If you'd rather just watch, go to the annual **Albuquerque International Balloon Fiesta** ✿✿, which is held the first through second weekends of October (see "The

Most Unforgettable Northern New Mexico Experiences," in chapter 1, and "Northern New Mexico Calendar of Events," in chapter 2, for details).

BIKING

Albuquerque is a major bicycling hub in the summer, for both road racers and mountain bikers. For an excellent map of Albuquerque bicycle routes, call the **Albuquerque Parks & Recreation Department** at ⒸⒸ 505/768-3550 or visit www.cabq.gov, click on "Interactive Maps (GIS)," and then click on "Bike Paths." You can also find links to many recreation opportunities for adults and kids at www.cabq.gov/visiting.htm. A great place to bike is **Sandia Peak** (ⒸⒸ 505/242-9133; www.sandiapeak.com) in Cíbola National Forest. You can't take your bike on the tram, but chairlift no. 1 is available for up- or downhill transportation with a bike. Bike rentals are available at the top and bottom of the chairlift. They cost $40 for adult bikes and $30 for junior ones. The lift costs $16 and runs on Saturday and Sunday, with Friday added in July and August, though you'll want to call to be sure. Helmets are mandatory. Bike maps are available; the clearly marked trails range from easy to very difficult.

Down in the valley, there's a **bosque trail** that runs along the Rio Grande, accessed through the Rio Grande Nature Center (see "Especially for Kids," above). To the east, the **Foothills Trail** runs along the base of the mountains. It's a fun 7-mile-long trail that offers excellent views. Access it by driving east from downtown on Montgomery Boulevard, past the intersection with Tramway Boulevard. Go left on Glenwood Hills Drive and head north about ½ mile before turning right onto a short road that leads to the Embudito trail head.

Northeast Cyclery, 8305 Menaul Blvd. NE (ⒸⒸ 505/299-1210) rents bikes at the rate of $25 per day for front-suspension mountain bikes and $35 per day for road bikes. Multiday discounts are available. Unfortunately, the shop doesn't rent children's bikes. Rentals come with helmets.

BIRD-WATCHING

Bosque del Apache National Wildlife Refuge ⭐⭐ (ⒸⒸ 505/835-1828) is a haven for migratory waterfowl such as snow geese and cranes. It's 90 miles south of Albuquerque on I-25, and it's well worth the drive. You'll find 7,000 acres of carefully managed riparian habitat, which include marshlands, meadows, agricultural fields, and old-growth cottonwood forests lining the Rio Grande. Particularly if you're here from November through March, the experience is thrilling, not only because of the variety of birds—more than 300 species—but for the sheer numbers of them. Huge clouds of snow geese and sandhill cranes take flight at dawn and dusk, the air filling with the sounds of their calls and wing flaps. In early December, the refuge may harbor as many as 45,000 snow geese, 57,000 ducks of many different species, and 18,000 sandhill cranes. You may even be fortunate enough—as I was on my last visit—to see a whooping crane or two. There are also plenty of raptors about, including numerous red-tailed hawks and northern harriers (or marsh hawks), Cooper's hawks and kestrels, and even bald and golden eagles. The refuge has a 15-mile auto-tour loop, which you should drive very slowly. Closer to town, check out the **Rio Grande Nature Center State Park** (see "Especially for Kids," above).

FISHING

There are no real fishing opportunities in Albuquerque as such, but there is a nearby fishing area known as **Shady Lakes** (ⒸⒸ 505/898-2568). Nestled among cottonwood trees, it's near I-25 on Albuquerque's north side. The most common catches are rainbow trout, black bass, bluegill, and channel catfish. To reach Shady Lakes, take I-25 north to the Tramway exit. Follow Tramway Road west for a mile and then go right on NM 313 for ½ mile. **Sandia Lakes Recreational Area** (℗ **505/897-3971**), also on NM 313, is another popular fishing spot. There is a bait and tackle shop there.

GOLF

There are quite a few public courses in the Albuquerque area. The **Championship Golf Course at the University of New Mexico,** 3601 University Blvd. SE (℗ **505/ 277-4546**), is one of the best in the Southwest and was rated one of the country's top 25 public links by *Golf Digest.* **Paradise Hills Golf Course,** 10035 Country Club Lane NW (℗ **505/898-7001**), is a popular 18-hole golf course on the west side of town.

Other Albuquerque courses to check with for tee times are **Ladera,** 3401 Ladera Dr. NW (℗ **505/836-4449**); **Los Altos,** 9717 Copper Ave. NE (℗ **505/298-1897**); **Puerto del Sol,** 1800 Girard Blvd. SE (℗ **505/265-5636**); and **Arroyo del Oso,** 7001 Osuna Rd. NE (℗ **505/884-7505**).

If you're willing to drive a short distance just outside Albuquerque, you can play at the **Santa Ana Golf Club at Santa Ana Pueblo,** 288 Prairie Star Rd., Bernalillo, NM 87004 (℗ **505/867-9464**), which was rated by the *New York Times* as one of the best public golf courses in the country. Club rentals are available (call for information). In addition, **Isleta Pueblo,** 4001 Hwy. 47 (℗ **505/869-0950**), south of Albuquerque, has an 18-hole course.

HIKING

The 1½-million-acre **Cíbola National Forest** offers ample hiking opportunities. Within town, the best hike is the **Embudito Trail,** which heads up into the foothills, with spectacular views down across Albuquerque. The 5.5-mile one-way hike is moderate to difficult. Allow 1 to 8 hours, depending on how far you want to go. Access it by driving east from downtown on Montgomery Boulevard past the intersection with Tramway Boulevard. Go left on Glenwood Hills Drive and head north about a half mile before turning right onto a short road that leads to the trail head. The premier Sandia Mountain hike is **La Luz Trail,** a very strenuous journey from the Sandia foothills to the top of the Crest. It's a 15-mile round-trip jaunt, and it's half that if you take the Sandia Peak Tramway (see "The Top Attractions," earlier in this chapter) either up or down. Allow a full day for this hike. Access is off Tramway Boulevard and Forest Service Road 333. For more details contact **Sandia Ranger Station,** Highway 337 south toward Tijeras (℗ **505/281-3304**).

HORSEBACK RIDING

Sometimes I just have to get in a saddle and eat some trail dust. If you get similar hankerings, call the **Hyatt Regency Tamaya Resort and Spa,** 1300 Tuyuna Trail, Santa Ana Pueblo (℗ **505/771-6037**). The resort offers 2½-hour-long rides near the Rio Grande for $75 per person. Children must be over 7 years of age and over 4 feet tall.

Trail Closures

The drought that has spread across the Southwest in recent years has caused the U.S. Forest Service to close trails in many New Mexico mountains during the summer in order to reduce fire hazard. Before you head out in this area, contact the **Sandia Ranger Station** at (℗ **505/281-3304**).

Getting Pampered: The Spa Scene

If you're looking to get pampered, you have a few options. **Mark Prado Salon & Spa** (© 800/363-7115) offers treatments at four locations: 1100 Juan Tabo Blvd. NE (© **505/298-2983**), 8001 Wyoming Blvd. NE (© **505/856-7700**), 3500 Central Ave. SE 7-B (© **505/266-2400**), and Cottonwood Mall, 10,000 Coors Blvd. NE (© **505/897-2288**).

Albuquerque's most luxurious spa experience is at the **Hyatt Regency Tamaya Resort & Spa,** 1300 Tuyuna Trail, Santa Ana Pueblo (© **505/867-1234**). A vast array of treatments, as well as a sauna and a steam room, are available in a refined atmosphere set near the Rio Grande, 15 minutes north of Albuquerque, near the village of Bernalillo.

The resort is about 15 miles north of Albuquerque. From I-25 take exit 242, following US 550 west to Tamaya Boulevard, and drive 1½ miles to the resort.

SKIING

The **Sandia Peak Ski Area** is a good place for family skiing. There are plenty of beginner and intermediate runs. (However, if you're looking for more challenge or more variety, you'd better head north to Santa Fe or Taos.) The ski area has twin base-to-summit chairlifts to its upper slopes at 10,360 feet and a 1,700-foot vertical drop. There are 30 runs (35% beginner, 55% intermediate, 10% advanced) above the day lodge and ski-rental shop. Four chairs and two pomas accommodate 3,400 skiers an hour. All-day lift tickets are $38 for adults, $33 for teens ages 13 to 20, $29 for children ages 6 to 12 and seniors (ages 62–71), and free for children 46 inches tall or less in ski boots and seniors ages 72 and over; rental packages are available. The season runs mid-December to mid-March. Contact the ski area, 10 Tramway Loop NE (© **505/242-9133**), for more information, or call the hot line for ski conditions (© **505/857-8977**).

Cross-country skiers can enjoy the trails of the Sandia Wilderness from the ski area, or they can go an hour north to the remote Jemez Wilderness and its hot springs.

TENNIS

Albuquerque has 29 public parks with tennis courts. Because of the city's size, your best bet is to call the **Albuquerque Convention and Visitors Bureau** (© **800/284-2282**) to find out which park is closest to your hotel.

8 Spectator Sports

BASEBALL

The **Albuquerque Isotopes** play 72 home games as part of the Pacific Coast League in their new stadium, Isotopes Park. Tickets range in price from $5 to $10. For information, contact © **505/924-2255;** www.albuquerquebaseball.com. Isotopes Park is at 1601 Avenida Cesar Chavez SE. Take I-25 south of town to Avenida Cesar Chavez and go east; the stadium is at the intersection of Avenida Cesar Chavez and University Boulevard.

BASKETBALL

The University of New Mexico team, **"The Lobos,"** plays an average of 16 home games from late November to early March. Capacity crowds cheer the team at the 17,121-seat University Arena (fondly called "The Pit") at University and Stadium boulevards. For tickets and information, call © **505/925-Lobo** (www.golobos.com).

FOOTBALL

The **UNM Lobos** football team plays a September-to-November season, usually with five home games, at the 30,000-seat University of New Mexico Stadium, opposite both Albuquerque Sports Stadium and University Arena at University and Stadium boulevards. For tickets and information, call © **505/925-Lobo** (www.golobos.com).

HOCKEY

The **New Mexico Scorpions** play in the Western Professional Hockey League. Their home is at the **Rio Rancho Events Center,** Rio Rancho (© **505/881-7825;** www. scorpionshockey.com).

HORSE RACING

The **Downs at Albuquerque Racetrack and Casino,** New Mexico State Fairgrounds (© **505/266-5555** for post times; www.abqdowns.com), is near Lomas and Louisiana boulevards NE. Racing and betting—on thoroughbreds and quarter horses—take place on weekends from April to July and during the State Fair in September. The Downs has a glass-enclosed grandstand and exclusive club seating. General admission is free. Seasonal live horse racing takes place March through June and during the New Mexico State Fair. Simulcast racing happens year-round daily. The 300-slot casino is open daily noon to 2 am, with a buffet for $10.

9 Shopping

Visitors seeking regional specialties will find many **local artists** and **galleries** of interest in Albuquerque, although not as many as in Santa Fe and Taos. The galleries and regional fashion designers around the plaza in Old Town comprise a kind of a shopping center for travelers, with more than 40 merchants represented. The Sandia Pueblo runs its own **crafts market** at the reservation, off I-25 at Tramway Road, just beyond Albuquerque's northern city limits.

Albuquerque has three of the largest **shopping malls** in New Mexico, two within 2 blocks of each other on Louisiana Boulevard just north of I-40—Coronado Center and Winrock Center. The other is the Cottonwood Mall on the west mesa, at 10000 Coors Blvd. NW (© **505/899-SHOP**).

Business hours vary, but shops are generally open Monday to Saturday 10am to 6pm; many have extended hours; some have reduced hours; and a few, especially in shopping malls or during the high tourist season, are open on Sunday.

In Albuquerque the sales tax is 6.75%.

BEST BUYS

The best buys in Albuquerque are Southwestern regional items, including **arts and crafts** of all kinds—traditional Native American and Hispanic as well as contemporary works. In local Native American art, look for silver and turquoise jewelry, pottery, weavings, baskets, sand paintings, and Hopi kachina dolls. Hispanic folk art—handcrafted furniture, tinwork and *retablos,* and religious paintings—is worth seeking out.

Shopping en Route

While cruising the remote desert lands between Albuquerque and Santa Fe, you may want to stop in at **Traditions! A Festival Marketplace,** on I-25, exit 257 (© 505/867-9700). The open-air mall offers shoppers the chance to sample many forms of New Mexico culture, from art to jewelry to food to entertainment. It's open 10am to 5pm; closed Tuesday and Wednesday.

The best contemporary art is in paintings, sculpture, jewelry, ceramics, and fiber art, including weaving.

Other items of potential interest are Southwestern fashions, gourmet foods, and unique local Native American and Hispanic creations.

By far, the most **galleries** are in Old Town; others are spread around the city, with smaller groupings in the university district and the northeast heights. Consult the brochure published by the **Albuquerque Gallery Association,** *A Select Guide to Albuquerque Galleries,* or Wingspread Communications's annual *The Collector's Guide to Albuquerque,* widely distributed at shops. Once a month, usually from 5 to 9pm on the third Friday, the **Albuquerque Art Business Association** (© **505/244-0362** for information) sponsors an ArtsCrawl to dozens of galleries and studios. It's a great way to meet the artists.

You'll find some interesting shops in the Nob Hill area, which is just west of the University of New Mexico and has an Art Deco feel.

Following are some shopping recommendations for the greater Albuquerque area.

ARTS & CRAFTS

Amapola Gallery ✴ Fifty artists and craftspeople show their talents at this lovely cooperative gallery off a cobbled courtyard. You'll find pottery, paintings, textiles, carvings, baskets, jewelry, and other items. 205 Romero St. © 505/242-4311.

Bien Mur Indian Market Center ✴ Sandia Pueblo's crafts market, on the reservation, sells turquoise and silver jewelry, pottery, baskets, kachina dolls, hand-woven rugs, sand paintings, and other arts and crafts. The market is open Monday through Saturday from 9am to 5:30pm and Sunday from 11am to 5pm. I-25 at Tramway Rd. NE. © 800/365-5400 or 505/821-5400.

Dartmouth Street Gallery ✴ This gallery features vapor mirage works of Larry Bell, tapestries by Nancy Kozikowski, and a variety of work by 40 other contemporary artists, most from New Mexico. 3011 Monte Vista NE. © 800/474-7751 or 505/266-7751. www.dsg-art.com.

Gallery One This gallery features folk art, jewelry, contemporary crafts, cards and paper, and natural-fiber clothing. In the Nob Hill Shopping Center, 3500 Central Ave. SE. © 505/268-7449.

Hispaniae in Old Town ✴ *Finds* Day of the Dead people and Frida Kahlo faces greet you at this wild shop with everything from kitschy Mexican tableware to fine Oaxacan woodcarvings. 410 Romero St. NW. © 505/244-1533.

La Piñata This shop features—what else?—piñatas, in shapes from dinosaurs to parrots to pigs, as well as paper flowers, puppets, toys, and crushable bolero hats decorated with ribbons. No. 2 Patio Market (Old Town). © 505/242-2400.

Mariposa Gallery ⭐⭐ 𝘝𝘢𝘭𝘶𝘦 Eclectic contemporary art, jewelry, blown glass, and sculpture fill this Nob Hill shop, with prices that even a travel writer can afford. In the Nob Hill Shopping Center, 3500 Central Ave. SE. ℂ 505/268-6828.

Ortega's Indian Arts and Crafts An institution in Gallup, adjacent to the Navajo Reservation, Ortega's now has this Albuquerque store. It sells, repairs, and appraises silver and turquoise jewelry. 6600 Menaul Blvd. NE, no. 359. ℂ 505/881-1231.

The Pueblo Loft (at Gallery One) Owner Kitty Trask takes pride in the fact that all items featured at The Pueblo Loft are crafted by Native Americans. For almost 15 years, her slogan has been "Every purchase is an American Indian work of art." In the Nob Hill Shopping Center, 3500 Central Ave. SE. ℂ 505/268-8764.

R. C. Gorman Nizhoni Gallery Old Town ⭐ The painting and sculpture of the late Navajo artist Gorman, who was a resident of Taos, are shown here. Most works are available in limited-edition lithographs. 323 Romero NW, Suite 1. ℂ 505/843-7666.

Schelu Gallery ⭐⭐ Inventive pottery you'll want to use in your kitchen as well as bold textiles present a sojourn in color in this Old Town shop. 306 San Felipe NW. ℂ 800/234-7985 or 505/765-5869.

Skip Maisel's 𝘝𝘢𝘭𝘶𝘦 If you want a real bargain in Native American arts and crafts, this is the place to shop. You'll find a broad range of quality and price here in goods such as pottery, weavings, and kachinas. *Take note:* Adorning the outside of the store are murals painted in 1933 by notable Navajo painter Harrison Begay and Pueblo painter Pablita Velarde. 510 Central Ave. SW. ℂ 505/242-6526.

Tanner Chaney Galleries ⭐ In business since 1875, this gallery has fine jewelry, pottery, rugs, and more. 323 Romero NW, no. 4 (Old Town). ℂ 800/444-2242 or 505/247-2242.

Weyrich Gallery (Rare Vision Art Galerie) Contemporary paintings, sculpture, textiles, jewelry, and ceramics by regional and nonregional artists are exhibited at this spacious midtown gallery. 2935-D Louisiana Blvd. at Candelaria Rd. ℂ 505/883-7410.

Wright's Collection of Indian Art This gallery, first opened in 1907, features a free private museum and carries fine handmade Native American arts and crafts, both contemporary and traditional. 1100 San Mateo Blvd. NE. ℂ 505/266-0120.

BOOKS

Barnes & Noble On the west side, just north of Cottonwood Mall, this huge bookstore offers plenty of browsing room and a Starbucks Cafe for lounging. The store is

A Taste of the Grape

In addition to everything else New Mexico has to offer, wineries seem to be springing up all over the state. Call to find out about their wine-tasting hours. Wineries in Albuquerque or within a short driving distance of the city include **Anderson Valley Vineyards**, 4920 Rio Grande Blvd. NW, Albuquerque, NM 87107 (ℂ 505/344-7266); **Sandia Shadows Vineyard and Winery**, 11704 Coronado NE, Albuquerque 87122 (ℂ 505/856-1006; www.sandiawines.com); and **Gruet Winery**, 8400 Pan-American Hwy. NE, Albuquerque, NM 87113 (ℂ 505/821-0055; www.gruetwinery.com).

⟮*Moments* All That Glitters Is on Gold

For years, downtown Albuquerque has been reinventing itself and nowhere is the luster more brilliant than on Gold Avenue. A funky boutique street, it's the home of many unique shops and restaurants, well worth a morning or afternoon perusal. Look for "fine, fun, and funky" functional art at **Patrician Design**, 216 Gold Ave., SW (📞 505/242-7646). Nearby, you'll find kitschy shoes and clothing at **Ruby Shoesday**, 228 Gold Ave. SW (📞 505/848-RUBY). Down the street, step into **Ooh! Aah! Jewelry**, 311 Gold Ave., SW (📞 505/242-7101), to find a wide selection of contemporary jewelry and handbags. If you work up an appetite, head to **Gold Street Caffè** (see p. 246), or for a creamy snack try **Cold Stone Creamery**, 101 Gold Ave., SW (📞 505/843-9456), for a serious selection of ice cream flavors made in-house.

---

known for its large children's section and weekly story-time readings. 3701 Ellison Dr. NW #A. 📞 505/792-4234. Or at the Coronado Center, 6600 Menaul Blvd. NE. 📞 **505/883-8200**.

Bookworks ⭐ Selling both new and used books, Bookworks has one of the most complete Southwestern nonfiction and fiction sections in the region. A good place to linger, the store has a coffee bar and a stage area for readings. It also carries CDs, cassettes, and books on tape. 4022 Rio Grande Blvd. NW. 📞 **505/344-8139**.

Borders This branch of the popular chain provides a broad range of books, music, and videos, and hosts in-store appearances by authors, musicians, and artists. Winrock Center, 2100 Louisiana Blvd. NE. 📞 **505/884-7711**.

FOOD

The Candy Lady Having made chocolate for over 20 years, The Candy Lady is especially known for 21 varieties of fudge, including jalapeño flavor. 524 Romero NW (Old Town). 📞 **800/214-7731** or 505/243-6239.

La Mexicana This is a great place to go shopping if you're a diehard fan of Mexican food. Many items at La Mexicana are imported directly from Mexico, and others, such as tortillas, tamales, and Mexican pastries, are made fresh daily. 423 Atlantic Ave. SW. 📞 **505/243-0391**.

Rocky Mountain Chocolate Factory Old-fashioned candy is made right before your eyes. All chocolates are handmade. 380 Coronado Center. 📞 **800/658-6151** or 505/888-3399.

FURNITURE

Ernest Thompson Furniture ⭐ Original-design, handcrafted furniture is exhibited in the factory showroom. Thompson is a fifth-generation furniture maker who still uses traditional production techniques. 4531 Osuna Rd. NE (¼ block west of I-25 and ½ block north of Osuna Rd.). 📞 **800/568-2344** or 505/344-1994.

Strictly Southwestern You'll find nice, solid pine and oak Southwestern-style furniture here. Lighting, art, pottery, and other interior items are also available. 1321 Eubank Blvd. NE. 📞 **505/292-7337**.

GIFTS/SOUVENIRS

Jackalope International ✦✦ Wandering through this vast shopping area is like an adventure to another land—to many lands, really. You'll find Mexican *trasteros* (armoires) next to Balinese puppets. The store sells sculpture, pottery, and Christmas ornaments as well. 834 US 550, Bernalillo. ✆ **505/867-9813**.

MARKETS

Flea Market Every Saturday and Sunday, year-round, the fairgrounds host this market from 8am to 5pm. It's a great place to browse for turquoise and silver jewelry and locally made crafts, as well as newly manufactured inexpensive goods such as socks and T-shirts. The place takes on a fair atmosphere, with the smell of cotton candy filling the air. There's no admission charge. New Mexico State Fairgrounds. For information, call the Albuquerque Convention and Visitors Bureau, ✆ **800/284-2282**.

SOUTHWESTERN APPAREL

Albuquerque Pendleton Cuddle up in a large selection of blankets and shawls, and haul them away in a handbag. 1100 San Mateo NE, Suites 2 and 4. ✆ **505/255-6444**.

Western Warehouse Family Western wear, including an enormous collection of boots, is retailed here. This store claims to have the largest selection of work wear and work boots in New Mexico (8,000 pairs of boots altogether). 6210 San Mateo Blvd. NE. ✆ **505/883-7161**.

10 Albuquerque After Dark

Albuquerque has an active performing-arts and nightlife scene, as befits a city of half a million people. As also befits this area, the performing arts are multicultural, with Hispanic and (to a lesser extent) Native American productions sharing stage space with Anglo works, including theater, opera, symphony, and dance. Albuquerque also attracts many national touring companies. Nightclubs cover the gamut, with rock, jazz, and country predominant.

Complete information on all major cultural events can be obtained from the **Albuquerque Convention and Visitors Bureau** (✆ **800/284-2282** for recorded information after 5pm). Current listings appear in the two daily newspapers; detailed weekend arts calendars can be found in the Thursday evening *Tribune* and the Friday morning *Journal*. The monthly *On the Scene* also carries entertainment listings.

Tickets for nearly all major entertainment and sporting events can be obtained from **Ticketmaster**, 4004 Carlisle Blvd. NE (✆ **505/883-7800**). Discount tickets are often available for midweek and matinee performances; check with individual theater or concert hall box offices.

THE PERFORMING ARTS

CLASSICAL MUSIC

Chamber Orchestra of Albuquerque This 32-member professional orchestra performs from October to June, primarily at St. John's United Methodist Church, 2626 Arizona St. NE. There's a subscription series of seven classical concerts. The orchestra features guest artists of national and international renown. 2730 San Pedro Dr. NE, Suite H-23. ✆ **505/881-0844**. http://coa.aosys.com. Tickets $19–$28; $2 discount for students and seniors (62 and over).

New Mexico Ballet Company Founded in 1972, the state's oldest ballet company holds most of its performances at Popejoy Hall. Typically there's a fall production such

The Major Concert & Performance Halls

Journal Pavilion, 5601 University Blvd. NE (© **505/452-5100**).

Keller Hall, University of New Mexico, Cornell Street at Redondo Drive South NE (© **505/277-4569**).

KiMo Theatre, 423 Central Ave. NW (© **505/768-3544**).

Popejoy Hall, University of New Mexico, Cornell Street at Redondo Drive South NE (© **505/277-3824**).

South Broadway Cultural Center, 1025 Broadway Blvd. SE (© **505/848-1320**).

as *Dracula,* a holiday one such as *The Nutcracker* or *A Christmas Carol,* and a contemporary spring production. 4200 Wyoming Blvd. NE, Suite B2 Albuquerque, NM 87154-1518. © 505/292-4245. www.nmballet.org. Tickets $20–$25 adults, $10–$20 children 12 and under.

New Mexico Symphony Orchestra ☞   My first introduction to symphony was with the NMSO. Although I was so young that I didn't quite understand the novelty of hearing live symphony, I loved picking out the distinct sounds and following as they melded together. The NMSO first played in 1932 (long before I attended, thank you) and has continued as a strong cultural force throughout the state. The symphony performs classics and pops, as well as family and neighborhood concerts. It plays for more than 20,000 grade-school students and visits communities throughout the state in its annual tour program. Concert venues are generally Popejoy Hall on the University of New Mexico campus and the Rio Grande Zoo, both of which are accessible to people with disabilities. Each season a few notable artists visit; recent years have included such guests as Yo Yo Ma and Guillermo and Ivonne Figueroa. I recommend going to one of the outdoor concerts at the band shell at the Rio Grande Zoo. 3301 Menaul Blvd. NE, Suite 4. © 800/251-6676 for tickets and information, or 505/881-9590. www.nmso. org. Ticket prices vary with concert; call for details.

THEATER

Albuquerque Little Theatre   The Albuquerque Little Theatre has been offering a variety of productions ranging from comedies to dramas to musicals since 1930. Seven plays are presented here annually during an August-to-May season. Located across from Old Town, Albuquerque Little Theatre offers plenty of free parking. 224 San Pasquale Ave. SW. © 505/242-4750. www.swcp.com/alt. Tickets $18, $16 for students, $13 seniors. Box office Mon–Fri noon–6pm.

La Compañía de Teatro de Albuquerque *Finds*   Productions given by the company can provide a focused view into New Mexico culture. One of the few major professional Hispanic companies in the United States and Puerto Rico, La Compañía stages a series of bilingual productions (most original New Mexican works) every year, late September to May. Comedies, dramas, and musicals are offered, along with an occasional Spanish-language play. Performances take place in the National Hispanic Cultural Center, the South Broadway Cultural Center (1025 Broadway Blvd. SE), and other venues regionally. P.O. Box 884. © 505/242-7929. Tickets $12 adults, $8 students ages 18 and above and seniors, $7 children under 18.

Musical Theatre Southwest   From February to January, this theater presents six major Broadway musicals, in addition to several smaller productions, at either Pope-joy Hall or the MTS's own 890-seat Hiland Theater. Most productions are staged for three consecutive weekends, including some Sunday matinees. 2401 Ross. SE. ✆ 505/262-9301. www.musicaltheatresw.com. Tickets $15–$30 adults; students and seniors receive a $2 discount.

Vortex Theatre ✦   A 30-year-old community theater known for its innovative productions, the Vortex is Albuquerque's "Off-Broadway" theater, presenting a range of plays from classic to original. You'll see such plays as *One Flew Over the Cuckoo's Nest* and *Wait Until Dark* by Frederick Knott. Performances take place on Friday and Saturday at 8pm and on Sunday at 6pm. The black-box theater seats 90. 2004½ Central Ave. SE. ✆ 505/247-8600. Tickets $10 adults, $8 students and seniors, $8 for everyone on Sun.

THE CLUB & MUSIC SCENE
COMEDY CLUBS/DINNER THEATER

Laffs Comedy Cafe   This club offers top acts from each coast, including comedians who have appeared on *The Late Show with David Letterman* and HBO. San Mateo Blvd. and Osuna Rd., in the Fiesta del Norte Shopping Center. ✆ 505/296-5653. www.laffscomedy.com. Shows Wed–Sun nights. $8 per person, with a two-item minimum purchase. Call for show times.

Mystery Cafe *Finds*   If you're in the mood for a little interactive dinner theater, the Mystery Cafe might be just the ticket. You'll help the characters in this ever-popular, delightfully funny show solve the mystery as they serve you a four-course meal. Reservations are a must. P.O. Box 11433. Performances held at Sheraton Uptown (at Menaul Blvd. and Louisiana Blvd.). ✆ 505/237-1385. www.abqmystery.com. Approximately $39. Performances Fri and Sat evenings at 7:30pm; doors open at 7pm.

ROCK/JAZZ

Burt's Tiki Lounge   This club won the weekly paper *Alibi's* award for the best variety of drinks. The club offers live music Thursday to Sunday and charges no cover. 313 Gold Ave. ✆ 505/243-BURT.

Kelly's BYOB   Near the university, Kelly's is a local brewpub, set in a renovated auto-body shop. The place has tasty pub fare, excellent brew specials, and live music Thursday to Saturday, usually with no cover. 3222 Central SE. ✆ 505/262-2739.

Martini Grille ✦   On the eastern side of the Nob Hill district, this is the place for young professionals, who lush out on more than 30 flavors of martinis within a seductive Batman cave atmosphere. Live entertainment plays most weekends and some weeknights. 4200 Central SE. ✆ 505/255-4111.

O'Niell's Pub, Inc.   A favorite club in the University of New Mexico area, this Irish bar serves up good pub fare as well as live local music on Saturday nights and Celtic and bluegrass on Sunday evenings. 4310 Central Ave. S E, ✆ 505/255-6782.

MORE ENTERTAINMENT

Albuquerque's best nighttime attraction is the **Sandia Peak Tramway,** with the restaurant High Finance at the summit (see "What to See & Do" and "Where to Dine," earlier in this chapter). Here, you can enjoy a view nonpareil of the Rio Grande Valley and the city lights.

The best place to catch foreign films, art films, and limited-release productions is the **Guild Cinema,** 3405 Central Ave. NE (✆ 505/255-1848). For film classics, check out the **Southwest Film Center,** on the UNM campus (✆ 505/277-5608), which has double features, changing nightly (when classes are in session). In addition, Albuquerque has a number of first-run movie theaters whose numbers you can find in the local telephone directory.

Many travelers like to include a little dice-throw and slot-machine play in their trip to New Mexico. Those who do are in luck, with the expansive **Sandia Casino,** north of I-25 and a quarter-mile east on Tramway Boulevard (© **800/526-9366;** www. sandiacasino.com). The $80-million structure sits on Sandia Pueblo land and has outstanding views of the Sandia Mountains. Built in pueblo architectural style, the graceful casino has a 3,650-seat outdoor amphitheater, three restaurants (one, **Bien Shur,** has excellent food), a lounge, more than 1,350 slot and video poker machines, the largest poker room in the state, and blackjack, roulette, and craps tables. It's open from 8am to 4am Sunday to Wednesday and 24 hours Thursday to Saturday. The **Isleta Gaming Palace,** 11,000 Broadway SE (© **800/460-5686** or 505/724-3800; www. isletacasinoresort.com), is a luxurious, air-conditioned casino (featuring blackjack, poker, slots, bingo, and keno) with a full-service restaurant, nonsmoking section, and free bus transportation on request. Open Monday to Thursday 8am to 4am, Friday to Sunday 24 hours a day.

11 Exploring Nearby Pueblos & Monuments

Ten Native American pueblos are within an hour's drive of central Albuquerque. One national and two state monuments preserve another five ancient pueblo ruins.

The active pueblos nearby include Acoma, Cochiti, Isleta, Jemez, Laguna, Sandia, San Felipe, Santa Ana, Santo Domingo, and Zia. Of these, Acoma is the most prominent.

ACOMA PUEBLO ✿✿✿

This spectacular "Sky City," a walled adobe village perched high atop a sheer rock mesa 365 feet above the 6,600-foot valley floor, is believed to have been inhabited at least since the 11th century—the longest continuously occupied community in the United States. Native legend claims that it has been inhabited since before the time of Christ. Both the pueblo and **San Estevan del Rey Mission** are National Historic Landmarks. In 2006, the Sky City Cultural Center and Haak'u Museum opened below Acoma, showcasing pottery, textiles, baskets and other art from the tribe.

The Keresan-speaking Acoma (*Ack*-oo-mah) Pueblo boasts 6,005 inhabitants, but only about 50 people reside year-round on the 70-acre mesa top. They make their living from tourists who come to see the large church containing examples of Spanish colonial art and to purchase the pueblo's thin-walled white pottery with polychrome designs.

To reach Acoma from Albuquerque, drive west on I-40 approximately 52 miles to the Acoma–Sky City exit, then travel about 12 miles southwest.

Pueblo Etiquette

When you visit pueblos, it's important to observe certain rules of etiquette: Remember to respect the pueblos as people's homes; don't peek into doors and windows or climb on top of the buildings. Stay out of cemeteries and ceremonial rooms (such as kivas), since these are sacred grounds. Don't speak during dances or ceremonies or applaud after their conclusion; silence is mandatory. Most pueblos require a permit to carry a camera or to sketch or paint on location. Several pueblos prohibit photography at any time.

Taos Ski Valley
Wheeler Peak
Taos Pueblo
84
285
68
Taos
Angel Fire
JICARILLA
APACHE
RESERVATION
Picuris Pueblo
64
550
Okhay Owingeh
Sipapu
Chaco Culture
National Historic Park
Española
Los Alamos
Nambe
Pueblo
Santa Fe
Ski Area
25
Jemez State
Monument
Bandelier National
Monument
Tesuque Pueblo
Fort Union
National
Monument
Jemez Pueblo
Jemez
Springs
4
Cochiti
Pueblo
Santa Fe
84
Zia Pueblo
Los Cerrillos
Pecos
National
Monument
Las Vegas
Coronado State
Monument
Madrid
14
84
Grants
Laguna
Pueblo
Rio Rancho
Golden
Turquoise Trail
Pecos River
40
ALBUQUERQUE
40
Santa Rosa
El Malpais
National
Monument
Acoma
Pueblo
Isleta
Pueblo
337
ALAMO
NAVAJO
RESERVATION
Salinas National
Monument: Quarai
Mountainair
54
25
60
Salinas National
Monument: Abo
60
Very Large Array
Radio Telescope
Socorro
Salinas National
Monument:
Gran Quivera
285
380
Bosque del Apache
National Wildlife Refuge
25
Lincoln State
Monument
Rio Grande
Ski Apache
Ruidoso
70
Roswell
Truth or
Consequences
MESCALERO
APACHE
RESERVATION
Alamogordo
White Sands
National Monument
Cloudcroft
NEW
MEXICO
Fort Selden
State Monument
54
Santa Fe
Taos
Albuquerque
Rio Grande
70
Las Cruces
Ski Area
Mountain
Carlsbad Caverns
National Park
Deming
180
10
70
180
NEW MEXICO
0   40 mi
0   40 km
N
10
TEXAS
El Paso
Guadalupe Mtns.
National Park

You absolutely cannot wander freely around Acoma Pueblo, but you can start your tour at the new 40,000-square-foot museum, which gives a good look into this culture, and peruse their gallery, offering art and crafts for sale. You can even have a meal at the new Yaak'a Café. Then board the **tour bus,** which climbs through a rock garden of 50-foot sandstone monoliths and past precipitously dangling outhouses to the mesa's summit. There's no running water or electricity in this medieval-looking village; a small reservoir collects rainwater for most purposes, but drinking water is transported up from below. Wood-hole ladders and mica windows are prevalent among the 300-odd adobe structures. As you tour the village, you'll have many opportunities to buy pottery and other pueblo treasures. Pottery is expensive here, but you're not going to find it any cheaper anywhere else, and you'll be guaranteed that it's authentic if you buy it directly from the craftsperson. Along the way, be sure to sample some Indian fry bread topped with honey.

The annual San Esteban del Rey feast day is September 2, when the pueblo's patron saint is honored with a midmorning Mass, a procession, an afternoon corn dance, and an arts-and-crafts fair. A Governor's Feast is held annually in February, and 4 days of Christmas festivals run from December 25 to 28. Still cameras are allowed for a $10 fee, and guided tours do not operate on the mesa during feast days.

Other celebrations are held in low-lying pueblo villages at Easter (in Acomita), the first weekend in May (Santa Maria feast at McCartys), and August 10 (San Lorenzo Day in Acomita).

The **Acoma Pueblo's** address is P.O. Box 309, Acoma, NM 87034 (© **800/747-0181** or 505/ 552-6604; www.skycity.com). Admission for the tour is $8 for adults, $7 for seniors (60 and over), $6 for children 6 to 17, and free for children under 6. Group discounts apply to parties of 15 or more, and there's also a discount for students and Native American visitors. The charge to take still photographs is $10; digital cameras and tripods are prohibited, telephoto lenses are restricted, and no video cameras are allowed. Generally, the pueblo is open daily in the summer 8am to 6pm; daily in the spring, fall, and winter 8am to 4pm. One-hour tours begin every 30 minutes, depending on the demand; the last tour is scheduled 1 hour before closing. The pueblo is closed to visitors on Easter weekend (some years), June 24 and 29, July 10 to 13, and the first or second weekend in October. It's best to call ahead to make sure that the tour is available when you're visiting.

Coronado State Monument ⊛   When the Spanish explorer Coronado traveled through this region in 1540–41 while searching for the Seven Cities of Cíbola, he wintered at a village on the west bank of the Rio Grande—probably one on the ruins of the ancient Anasazi Pueblo known as Kuaua. Those excavated ruins have been preserved in this state monument.

Hundreds of rooms can be seen, and a kiva has been restored so that visitors can descend a ladder into the enclosed space, once the site of sacred rites. Unique multicolored murals, depicting human and animal forms, were found on successive layers of wall plaster in this and other kivas here; some examples are displayed in the monument's small archaeological museum.

485 Kuana Rd., Bernalillo. © **505/867-5351.** Admission $3 adults, free for children 16 and under. Wed–Mon 8am–5pm. Closed Easter, Thanksgiving, Christmas, New Year's. To get to the site (20 miles north of Albuquerque), take I-25 to Bernalillo and US 550 west for 1 mile.

Salinas Pueblo Missions National Monument ⊛ *(Finds)*   These rarely visited ruins provide a unique glimpse into history. The Spanish conquistadors' Salinas Jurisdiction,

Traditional Native American Bread Baking

While visiting the pueblos in New Mexico, you'll probably notice outdoor ovens (they look a bit like giant ant hills), known as *hornos,* which Native Americans have used to bake bread for hundreds of years. For Native Americans, making bread is a tradition that links them directly to their ancestors. The long process of mixing and baking also brings mothers and daughters together for what today we might call "quality time."

Usually in the evening, the bread dough (made of white flour, lard, salt, yeast, and water) is made and kneaded, and the loaves are shaped. They are then allowed to rise overnight. In the morning, the oven is stocked with wood and a fire lighted. After the fire burns down to ashes and embers, the oven is cleared, and the ashes are shoveled away. These primitive ovens don't have thermometers, so the baker has to rely on experience to judge when the temperature is right. At that point, the loaves are placed into the oven with a long-handled wooden paddle. They bake for about an hour.

If you would like to try a traditional loaf, you can buy one at the **Indian Pueblo Cultural Center** in Albuquerque (see "What to See & Do," earlier in the chapter), among other places.

on the east side of the Manzano Mountains (southeast of Albuquerque), was an important 17th-century trade center because of the salt extracted by the Native Americans from the salt lakes. Franciscan priests, utilizing native labor, constructed missions of Abo red sandstone and blue-gray limestone for the native converts. The ruins of some of the most durable missions—along with evidence of preexisting Anasazi and Mogollon cultures—are the highlights of a visit to Salinas Pueblo Missions National Monument. The monument consists of three separate units: the ruins of Abo, Quarai, and Gran Quivira. They are situated around the quiet town of Mountainair, 75 miles southeast of Albuquerque at the junction of US 60 and NM 55.

Abo (© **505/847-2400**) boasts the 40-foot-high ruins of the **Mission of San Gregorio de Abo,** a rare example of medieval architecture in the United States. **Quarai** (© **505/847-2290**) preserves the largely intact remains of the **Mission of La Purísima Concepción de Cuarac** (1630). Its vast size, 100 feet long and 40 feet high, contrasts with the modest size of the pueblo mounds. A small museum in the visitor center has a scale model of the original church, along with a selection of artifacts found at the site. **Gran Quivira** (© **505/847-2770**) once had a population of 1,500. The pueblo has 300 rooms and seven kivas. Rooms dating back to 1300 can be seen. There are indications that an older village, dating to 800, may have previously stood here. Ruins of two churches (one almost 140 ft. long) and a *convento* (convent) have been preserved. The visitor center includes a museum with many artifacts from the site and shows a 40-minute movie about the excavation of some 200 rooms, plus a short history video of the pueblo.

All three pueblos and the churches that were constructed above them are believed to have been abandoned in the 1670s. Self-guided tour pamphlets can be obtained at the units' respective visitor centers and at the **Salinas Pueblo Missions National Monument Visitor Center** in Mountainair, on US 60, 1 block west of the intersection of US

Historic Culture with a Hint of Honey

Jemez Pueblo, home to more than 3,000, no longer welcomes visitors except on selected days. However, visitors can get a taste of the Jemez culture at the **Walatowa Visitor Center,** on NM 4, 8 miles north of the junction with US 550 (✆ 877/733-5687 or 505/834-7235; www.jemezpueblo.org). A museum and shop highlight the center, which also offers information about hiking and scenic tour routes. While in the area, you may encounter Jemez people sitting under *ramadas* (thatch-roofed lean-tos) selling home-baked bread, cookies, and pies. If you're lucky, they may also be making fry bread, which you can smother with honey for one of New Mexico's more delectable treats.

60 and NM 55. The visitor center offers an audiovisual presentation on the region's history, a bookstore, and an art exhibit.

P.O. Box 517, Mountainair. ✆ 505/847-2585. www.nps.gov/sapu. Free admission. Sites summer daily 9am–6pm, rest of year 9am–5pm; visitor center in Mountainair daily 8am–5pm. Closed New Year's Day, Thanksgiving, and Christmas. Abo is 9 miles west of Mountainair on US 60. Quarai is 8 miles north of Mountainair on NM 55. Gran Quivira is 25 miles south of Mountainair on NM 55. All roads are paved.

JEMEZ SPRINGS

Getting to this village along the Jemez River is half the fun. You'll drive the **Jemez Mountain Trail** ✮ into the Jemez Mountains, a trip that can provide a relaxing retreat and/or an exhilarating adventure. In the area are historic sites and relaxing hot springs, as well as excellent stream fishing, hiking, and cross-country skiing. You may want to combine a drive through this area with a visit to Los Alamos and Bandelier National Monument (see chapter 10).

North of town you'll come to the **Soda Dam,** a strange and beautiful mineral mass formed by travertine deposits—minerals that precipitate out of geothermal springs. Considered a sacred site by Native Americans, it has a gushing waterfall and caves. During the warm months it's a popular swimming hole.

Jemez State Monument ✮ A stop at this small monument takes you on a journey through the history of the Jemez people. The journey begins in the museum, which tells the tale of Giusewa, "place of boiling waters," the original Tewa name of the area. Then it moves out into the mission ruins, whose story is told on small plaques that juxtapose the first impressions of the missionaries against the reality of the Jemez life. The missionaries saw the Jemez people as barbaric and set out to settle them. Part of the process involved hauling up river stones and erecting 6-foot-thick walls of the Mission of San José de los Jemez (founded in 1621) in the early 17th century. Excavations in 1921–22 and 1935–37 unearthed this massive complex through which you may wander. You enter through a broad doorway to a room that once held elaborate fresco paintings, the room tapering back to the nave, with a giant bell tower above. The setting is startling next to a creek, with steep mountains rising behind.

18160 NM 4 (P.O. Box 143), Jemez Springs. ✆ 505/829-3530. Admission $3 adults, free for children 17 and under. Wed–Mon 8:30am–5pm. Closed New Year's Day, Easter, Thanksgiving, and Christmas. From Albuquerque, take NM 550 (NM 44) to NM 4 and then continue on NM 4 for about 18 miles.

WHERE TO STAY AND DINE

Cañon del Rio–Riverside Inn ✮ "Eventually the watcher joined the river, and there was only one of us. I believe it was the river," wrote Norman Maclean in *A River*

Runs Through It. That was my experience while sitting on a cottonwood-shaded bench at Cañon del Rio, on a long bow of the Jemez River, a small, fast-flowing stream lined with cottonwoods. Built in 1994, the inn has clean lines and comfortable rooms, each named after a Native American tribe. I stayed in the Hopi room, a queen room that wasn't large but was well planned, with built-in drawers and many amenities. Each room has a sliding glass door that opens out to a patio where there's a fountain. The beds are comfortably firm, with good reading lights. The suites have private Jacuzzis and kitchens. The Great Room has a cozy, welcoming feel, with a big-screen TV, as well as a large table where breakfast is served family style. A separate house is available for rent, the only option for children at the inn. Also, smoking is not allowed.

16445 (Scenic) NM 4, Jemez Springs, NM 87025. (℃ **505/829-4377.** www.canondelrio.com. 7 units. $99–$150 double, depending on the season; house $125–$150. Rates include full breakfast with inn room. AE, DISC, MC, V. **Amenities:** Jacuzzi. *In room:* A/C, wireless Internet, hair dryer.

Moments **Sampling Nature's Nectars**

When I was young, people often used to head out from Albuquerque to "the Jemez." That meant they were going to the hot springs. Back then, it was the place where the hippies hung out, naked, and it held a kind of foreboding allure for me. Today, the allure is one of comfort and beauty. My choice is to go to the naturally running springs (ask locally for directions), but if you prefer the more controlled environment of a bathhouse, that option is available, too. The waters running through the Jemez area are high in mineral content. In fact, the owner of **Jemez Springs Bath House,** 62 NM 4, on the Jemez Springs Plaza (℃ **505/829-3303;** www.jemezspringsbathhouse.com) says they are so healing, more than once she's had to run after visitors who walked off without their canes. This bathhouse was one of the first structures to be built in what is now Jemez Springs. Built in 1870 and 1878 of river rock and mud, it has thick walls and a richly herbal scent. You soak in individual tubs in either the men's side or the women's side. In back are a series of massage rooms, and outside is a hot tub within a wooden fence—not the most romantic setting. In front is a gift shop packed with interesting soaps and soulful gifts. Jemez Springs Bath House is open daily 10am to 8pm.

At **Ponderosa Valley Vineyard & Winery,** 3171 Hwy. 290, Ponderosa, NM 87044 (℃ **800/WINE-MAKER** or 505/834-7487; www.ponderosawinery.com), 3 miles off NM 4 south of Jemez Springs, you'll find a quaint country store with some of New Mexico's best wines. If you're lucky, the vintners will be presiding over the small curved bar and will pour you delectable tastes while telling stories of the history of wine in New Mexico and of the Jemez area, where they have lived and grown grapes for 30 years. Be sure to try the dry Vidal Blanc and the full-bodied Cabernet Sauvignon, both excellent, and both award winners at the New Mexico State Fair. The fruity zinfandel is like nothing you've ever tasted. This is the oldest wine-growing region in the United States, and the product definitely has its own spirit. A 10- to 15-minute tour will take you through the cellar and vineyards. You'll likely want to take a bottle with you. They range in price from $8 to $20.

The Laughing Lizard Inn & Cafe ⊛ AMERICAN   This is the kind of small-town cafe that doesn't have to try to have a personality. It already has thick adobe walls, wood floors, and a wood-burning stove for its innate charm. Added touches are the brightly painted walls and funky old tables. If there were a Western version of the Whistle Stop Cafe, this would be it. The menu is somewhat eclectic—most dishes have a bit of an imaginative flair. The burritos come in a variety of types, such as fresh spinach with black beans, mushrooms, jack cheese, salsa, and guacamole. The home-made pizzas, made with blue-corn crusts, feature ingredients such as pesto, sun-dried tomatoes, and feta, or more basic ones with red sauce as well. Beer and wine are served, and there are daily dessert treats such as piñon pie, chocolate mousse, and berry cobbler. The staff is friendly and accommodating. A small inn attached to the cafe provides inexpensive rooms that are clean but a bit timeworn.

17526 NM 4, Jemez Springs, NM 87025. © **505/829-3108.** www.thelaughinglizard.com. Main courses lunch $5–$10 and dinner $6–$13. DISC, MC, V. May–Nov Tues–Sat 11am–8pm, Sun 11am–6pm; Dec–April Thurs–Sat 11–8pm, Sun 11am–6pm.

THE TURQUOISE TRAIL ⊛⊛

Known as "The Turquoise Trail," NM 14 begins about 16 miles east of downtown Albuquerque, at I-40's Cedar Crest exit, and winds some 46 miles to Santa Fe along the east side of the Sandia Mountains. This state-designated scenic and historic route traverses the revived ghost towns of Golden, Madrid, and Cerrillos, where gold, silver, coal, and turquoise were once mined in great quantities. Modern-day settlers, mostly artists and craftspeople, have brought a renewed frontier spirit to the old mining towns.

GOLDEN   Golden is approximately 10 miles north of the Sandia Park junction on NM 14. Its sagging houses, with their missing boards and the wind whistling through the broken eaves, make it a purist's ghost town. There's a general store widely known for its large selection of well-priced jewelry, as well as, across the street, a bottle seller's "glass garden." Be sure to slow down and look for the village church, a great photo opportunity, on the east side of the road. Nearby are the ruins of a pueblo called **Paako,** abandoned around 1670.

MADRID   Madrid (pronounced *mah*-drid) is about 12 miles north of Golden. This town and neighboring Cerrillos were in a fabled turquoise-mining area dating back to prehistory. Gold and silver mines followed, and when they faltered, there was coal. The Turquoise Trail towns supplied fuel for the locomotives of the Santa Fe Railroad until the 1950s, when the railroad converted to diesel fuel. Madrid used to produce 100,000 tons of coal a year, and was a true "company town" but the mine closed in 1956. Today, this is a village of artists and craftspeople seemingly stuck in the 1960s: Its funky, ramshackle houses have many counterculture residents who operate several crafts stores and import shops.

The **Old Coal Mine Museum and Old West Photography** (© **505/438-3780**) invites visitors to peek into a mine that was saved when the town was abandoned. You can see the old mine's offices, steam engines, machines, and tools. It's open daily; admission is $4 for adults, $3 for seniors, $1 for children 6 to 12, and free for children under 6. You might want to have a picture taken in one of the 1,000 costumes at Old West Photography, $3 per person, $25 for one 8 by 10 or two 5 by 7s.

Next door, the **Mine Shaft Tavern** (© **505/473-0743**) continues its colorful career by offering a variety of burgers (try the green chile cheeseburger) and presenting live

There's Art in Them Thar Hills

Once a fabled mining town, now Madrid has become a notable arts village, a great place to wander on a sunny day. Start on the south end of town at **Al Lee-dom Studio,** 2485 NM 14 (📞 505/473-2054), where the studio's namesake blows inventive glassware (on weekends, you can watch). Around the corner, step into the **Painted Horse Gallery,** 2850 NM 14, (📞 505/473-5900), an intimate place showing modern landscape paintings by Dean Dovey, as well as jewelry and gifts. **Jezebel,** 2860 NM 14 (📞 505/866-JEZEBEL), just down the street has lamps with dazzling pressed-glass shades. Next door, **Indigo Gallery** ⭐, 2584 NM 14 (📞 505/438-6202), represents 20 artists who live in New Mexico, their colorful work ranging from realism to abstract. Stop for coffee and pastries at **Java Junction,** 2855 NM 14 (📞 505/438-2772), where you'll want to gawk over their vast hot sauce collection, including brands named "Scorned Woman," "Cowboy Cayenne," and "Original Death Sauce." If you'd like to stay the night, inquire about their Victorian suite upstairs. On the north end of town, check out **Seppanen & Daughters Fine Textiles** ⭐, 2879 NM 14 (📞 505/242-7470), a quaint house draped floor to ceiling with weavings from lands as near as Navajo and as distant as Tibet.

music Saturday nights and Sunday afternoons; it's open for meals in summer Monday to Thursday 11am to 6pm and Friday to Sunday 11am to 8pm. In winter, meals are served Monday to Thursday from noon to 4pm and Friday to Sunday noon to 8pm. The bar is open in summer Sunday to Thursday 11am to 11pm and Friday to Saturday 11am to 1am. In winter the bar is open from Sunday to Thursday noon to 10pm and Friday to Saturday noon to 1am. Next door is the **Madrid Engine House Theater** (📞 **505/438-3780**), offering melodrama during the summer. Its back doors open out so a steam locomotive can take center stage. The place to eat is **Mama Lisa's Café** ⭐, 2859 NM 14 (📞 **505/471-5769**). You'll find salads, sandwiches, and New Mexican specialties, all prepared with fresh ingredients. During the summer, it's open Wednesday to Monday, from 11am to 4:30pm. In winter, it's open intermittently, so call ahead.

CERRILLOS AND GALISTEO Cerrillos, about 3 miles north of Madrid, is a village of dirt roads that sprawls along Galisteo Creek. It appears to have changed very little since it was founded during a lead strike in 1879; the old hotel, the saloon, and even the sheriff's office look very much like parts of an Old West movie set. You may want to stop in at **Casa Grande Trading Post,** 17 Waldo St. (📞 **505/436-3005**), a shop that was featured on PBS's *Antiques Roadshow.* You'll find lots of jewelry and rocks, as well as the **Cerrillos Turquoise Mining Museum,** full of artifacts from this region's mining era.

It's another 15 miles to Santa Fe and I-25. If, like me, you're enchanted by the Galisteo Basin, you might want to stay a night or two in nearby Galisteo at the **Galisteo Inn** ⭐⭐ (📞 **866/404-8200** or 505/466-4000; www.galisteoinn.com). Set on grassy grounds under towering cottonwood trees, this 300-year-old hacienda has thick adobe walls and all the quiet a person could want. Rooms, all remodeled in 2004, are decorated with brightly painted walls and fun, bold-colored art. In their La Mancha restaurant, May through October, the inn serves Sunday brunch and lunch Friday and Saturday and dinner Tuesday to Saturday; some nights live music plays on the lovely patio; in winter, hours are more limited. There's a lovely pool large enough to swim laps, a hot tub, and guided horseback riding with **Galarosa Stables** (© 505/466-465; www.galarosastables.com). The inn is on NM 41, 15 miles from Cerrillos via the dirt County Road 42. For another good horseback-riding outfitter in this beautiful area, try **Broken Saddle Riding Company**. A 1½-hour ride is $55 a person, and riders are grouped according to skill level. For more information, call © 505/424-7774 and listen to the recorded message, or go to www.brokensaddle.com.

If you're getting hungry on the way back to Santa Fe, stop by the **San Marcos Café** ⊛, 3877 NM 14, near Lone Butte (© 505/471-9298). Set next to a feed store in a curvaceous old adobe with wood plank floors and lots of Southwest ambience, this cafe serves creative fare such as cinnamon rolls and their special eggs San Marcos—tortillas stuffed with scrambled eggs and topped with guacamole, pinto beans, Jack cheese, and red chile. Open daily 8am to 1:50pm.

Appendix:
Northern New Mexico in Depth

When I was a child in New Mexico, we'd sing a song while driving the dusty roads en route to such ruins as Chaco Canyon or Puye Cliff Dwellings. Sung to the tune of "Oh Christmas Tree," it went like this:

New Mexico, New Mexico
Don't know why we love you so.
It never rains
It never snows
The winds and sand
They always blow.
And how we live
God only knows
New Mexico, we love you so.

Although this song exaggerates the conditions here, the truth remains that in many ways New Mexico has an inhospitable environment. So why are so many people drawn here, and why do so many of us stay?

Ironically, the very extremes that this song presents are the reason. From the moment you set foot in this 121,666-square-mile state, you're met with wildly varied terrain, temperature, and temperament. On a single day, you might experience temperatures from 25° to 75°F (–4°–24°C). From the vast heat and dryness of White Sands in the summer to the 13,161-foot subzero, snow-encrusted Wheeler Peak in the winter, New Mexico's beauty is carved by extremes.

Culturally, this is also the case. Pueblo, Navajo, and Apache tribes occupy much of the state's lands, many of them still speaking their native languages and living within the traditions of their people. Some even live without running water and electricity. Meanwhile, the Hispanic culture remains deeply linked to its Spanish roots, practicing a devout Catholicism, and speaking a centuries-old Spanish dialect; some still live by subsistence farming in tiny mountain villages.

New Mexico has its very own sense of time and its own social mores. The pace is slow, the objectives of life less defined. People rarely arrive on time for appointments, and businesses don't always hold to their posted hours. In most cases, people wear whatever they want here. You'll see men dressed for formal occasions in a buttoned collar with a bolo tie and women in cowboy boots and skirts. The other day I saw a man wearing a broad-brimmed bull-rider's hat and lemon-yellow cowboy boots.

All this leads to a certain lost-and-not-caring-to-be-found spell the place casts on visitors that's akin to some kind of voodoo magic. We find ourselves standing amid the dust or sparkling light, within the extreme heat or cold, not sure whether to speak Spanish or English. That's when we let go completely of society's common goals, its pace, and social mores. We slip into a kayak and let the river take us, or hike a peak and look at the world from a new perspective. Or we climb into a car and drive past ancient ruins being excavated at that instant, past ghost mining towns, and under hot air balloons, by chile fields, and around hand-smoothed *santuarios,* all on the road to nowhere, New Mexico's best destination. At some point in your travels, you'll likely find yourself on this road, and you'll realize that there's no destination so fine.

And after that surrender, you may find yourself looking about with a new clarity. Having experienced the slower pace, you may question your own life's speediness. Having tasted New Mexico's relaxed style, you may look askance at those nylon stockings and heels or that suit and tie. And the next time you climb in the car in your own state or country, you might just head down a road you've never been on and hope that it goes nowhere.

1 How New Mexico Was Won—And Lost

The Pueblo tribes of the upper Rio Grande Valley are descendants of the Anasazi, better known today as the ancestral Puebloans, who from the mid-9th to the 13th centuries lived in the Four Corners Region—where the states of New Mexico, Arizona, Colorado, and Utah now meet. The ancestral Puebloans built spectacular structures; you get an idea of their scale and intricacy at the ruins at **Chaco Canyon** and **Mesa Verde.** It isn't known exactly why they abandoned their homes (some archaeologists suggest it was due to drought; others claim social unrest), but most theories suggest that they moved from these sites to areas like Frijoles Canyon **(Bandelier National Monument)** and **Puye,** where they built villages resembling the ones they had left. Then several hundred years later, for reasons not yet understood, they moved down from the canyons onto the flat plain next to the Rio Grande. By the time the Spaniards arrived in the 1500s, the Pueblo culture was well established throughout what would become northern and western New Mexico.

Architectural style was a unifying mark of the otherwise diverse ancestral Puebloan and today's Pueblo cultures. Both built condominium-style communities of stone and mud adobe bricks, three and four stories high. Grouped around central plazas, the villages incorporate circular spiritual chambers called kivas. As farmers, the ancestral Puebloan and Pueblo peoples used the waters of the Rio Grande and its tributaries to irrigate fields of corn, beans, and squash. They were also the creators of elaborate works of pottery.

THE SPANISH OCCUPATION

The Spanish ventured into the upper Rio Grande after conquering Mexico's Aztecs from 1519 to 1521. In 1540, Francisco Vásquez de Coronado led an expedition in search of the fabled Seven Cities of Cíbola, coincidentally introducing horses and sheep to the region. Neither Coronado nor a succession of fortune-seeking conquistadors could locate the legendary cities of gold, so the Spanish concentrated their efforts on exploiting the Native Americans.

Franciscan priests attempted to turn the Pueblo people into model peasants. Their churches became the focal points of every pueblo, with Catholic schools an essential adjunct. By 1625, there were approximately 50 churches in the Rio Grande Valley. (Two of the Pueblo missions, at Isleta and Acoma, are still in use today.) The Pueblos, however, weren't enthused about doing "God's work" for the Spanish—building new adobe missions, tilling fields, and weaving garments for export to Mexico—so Spanish soldiers came north to back the padres in extracting labor. In effect, the Pueblo people were forced into slavery.

Santa Fe was founded in 1610 as the seat of Spanish government in the upper Rio Grande. Governor Don Pedro de

Spots of Regional Historic Interest

TRAILS AND EXPLORATION ROUTES
Chihuahua Trail **7**
Cimarron Cutoff **3**
Coronado Route (1540-42) **5**
Esteban and Niza (1549) **4**
Goodnight-Loving Trail **1**
Jornada del Muerto **8**
Onate Expedition Route (1598) **6**
Santa Fe Trail **2**

Peralta named the settlement La Villa Real de la Santa Fe de San Francisco de Asis (The Royal City of the Holy Faith of St. Francis of Assisi). The **Palace of the Governors** has been used continuously as a public building ever since—by the Spanish, Pueblos (1680–92), Mexicans, and Americans. Today it stands as the flagship of the state museum system.

Decades of oppression by the Spanish colonials led to Pueblo unrest. Uprisings in the 1630s at Taos and Jemez left village priests dead and triggered even more repression. In 1680, a unified Pueblo rebellion, orchestrated from Taos, succeeded in driving the Spaniards from the upper Rio Grande. The leaders of the revolt defiled or destroyed the churches, just as the Spanish had destroyed the religious symbols of the native people. Revolutionaries took the Palace of the Governors, where they burned archives and prayer books, and converted the chapel into a kiva. They also burned much of the property in Santa Fe that had been built by the Europeans and laid siege to Spanish settlements up and down the Rio Grande Valley. Forced to retreat to Mexico, the colonists were not able to retake Santa Fe until 12 years later. Bloody battles raged for the next several years, but by the beginning of the 18th century, Nuevo Mexico was firmly in Spanish hands.

It remained so until Mexico gained its independence from Spain in 1821. The most notable event in the intervening years was the mid-1700s departure of the Franciscans, exasperated by their failure to wipe out all vestiges of traditional Pueblo religion. Throughout the Spanish occupation, eight generations of Pueblos had clung tenaciously to their way of life. However, by the 1750s, the number of Pueblo villages had shrunk by half.

THE ARRIVAL OF THE ANGLOS

The first Anglos to spend time in the upper Rio Grande Valley were mountain men: itinerant hunters, trappers, and traders. Trailblazers of the U.S. westward expansion, they began settling in New Mexico in the first decade of the 19th century. Many married into Pueblo or Hispanic families. Perhaps the best known was **Kit Carson,** a sometime federal agent, sometime scout, whose legend is inextricably interwoven with that of early Taos. Though he seldom stayed in one place for long, he considered the Taos area his home. He married Josepha Jaramillo, the daughter of a leading Taos citizen. Later he became a prime force in the final subjugation of the Plains Indians. The Taos home where he lived off and on for 40 years, until his death in 1868, is now a museum.

Wagon trains and eastern merchants followed Carson and the other early settlers. Santa Fe, Taos, and Albuquerque, already major trading and commercial centers at the end of the **Chihuahua Trail** (the Camino Real from Veracruz, Mexico, 1,000 miles south), became the western terminals of the new **Santa Fe Trail** (from Independence, Missouri, 800 miles east).

Even though independent Mexico granted the Pueblo people full citizenship and abandoned restrictive trade laws instituted by their former Spanish rulers, the subsequent 25 years of direct rule from Mexico City were not peaceful in the upper Rio Grande. Instead, they were marked by ongoing rebellion against severe taxation, especially in Taos. Neither did things quiet down when the United States assumed control of the territory during the U.S.–Mexican War. Shortly after General Stephen Kearney occupied Santa Fe (in a bloodless takeover) on orders of President James Polk in 1846, a revolt in Taos in 1847 led to the slaying of the new governor of New Mexico, Charles Bent. In 1848, the Treaty of Guadalupe Hidalgo officially transferred title of New Mexico, along with Texas, Arizona, and California, to the United States.

Aside from Kit Carson, perhaps the two most notable personalities of 19th-century New Mexico were priests. **Father José Martinez** (1793–1867) was one of the first native-born priests to serve his people. Ordained in Durango, Mexico, he jolted the Catholic church after assuming control of the Taos parish: Martinez abolished the obligatory church tithe because it was a hardship on poor parishioners, published the first newspaper in the territory (in 1835), and fought large land acquisitions by Anglos after the United States annexed the territory.

On all these issues Martinez was at loggerheads with **Bishop Jean-Baptiste Lamy** (1814–88), a Frenchman appointed in 1851 to supervise the affairs of the first independent New Mexican diocese. Lamy, on whose life Willa Cather based her novel *Death Comes for the Archbishop,* served the diocese for 37 years. Lamy didn't take kindly to Martinez's independent streak and, after repeated conflicts, excommunicated the maverick priest in 1857. But Martinez was steadfast in his preaching. He established an independent church and continued as northern New Mexico's spiritual leader until his death.

Nevertheless, Lamy made many positive contributions to New Mexico, especially in the fields of education and architecture. Santa Fe's Romanesque **Cathedral of St. Francis** and the nearby Gothic-style **Loretto Chapel,** for instance, were constructed under his aegis. But he was adamant about adhering to strict Catholic religious tenets. Martinez, on the other hand, embraced the folk tradition, including the craft of *santero* (religious icon) carving and a tolerance of the Penitentes, a flagellant sect that flourished after the departure of the Franciscans in the mid–18th century.

With the advent of the **Atchison, Topeka & Santa Fe Railway** in 1879, New Mexico began to boom. Albuquerque in particular blossomed in the wake of a series of major gold strikes in the Madrid Valley, close to ancient Native American turquoise mines. By the time the gold lodes began to shrink in the 1890s, cattle and sheep ranching had become well entrenched. The territory's growth culminated in statehood in 1912.

Territorial governor Lew Wallace, who served from 1878 to 1881, was instrumental in promoting interest in the arts, which today flourish in northern New Mexico. While occupying the Palace of the Governors, Wallace penned the great biblical novel *Ben-Hur.* In the 1890s, Ernest Blumenschein, Bert Phillips, and Joseph Sharp launched the Taos art colony; it boomed in the decade following World War I when Mabel Dodge Luhan, D. H. Lawrence, Georgia O'Keeffe, Willa Cather, and many others visited or established residence in the area.

During World War II, the federal government purchased an isolated boys' camp west of Santa Fe and turned it into the **Los Alamos National Laboratory,** where the Manhattan Project and other top-secret atomic experiments were developed and perfected. The science and military legacies continue today; Albuquerque is among the nation's leaders in attracting defense contracts and high technology.

2 Life Today—From Flamenco to Craps

On rock faces throughout northern New Mexico, you'll find circular symbols carved in sandstone, the wavy mark of Avanu the river serpent, or the ubiquitous Kokopelli playing his magic flute. These petroglyphs are constant reminders of the enigmatic history of the ancestral Puebloans (Anasazi), the Indians who inhabited this area from A.D. 1100 until the arrival of the Spanish conquistadors, around 1550.

The Spanish conquistadors, in their inimitable fashion, imposed a new, foreign order on the resident Native Americans and their land. As an inevitable component of conquest, they changed most Native American names—today, you'll find a number of Native Americans with Hispanic names—and renamed the villages "pueblos." The Spaniards' most far-reaching legacy, however, was the

forceful conversion of Indian populations to Catholicism, a religion that many Indians still practice today. In each of the pueblos you'll see a large, often beautiful, Catholic church, usually made with sculpted adobe; during the holiday seasons, Pueblo people perform ritual dances outside their local Catholic churches. The churches, set against the ancient adobe dwellings, are symbolic of the melding of two cultures.

This mix of cultures is apparent in today's northern New Mexican cuisine. When the Spaniards came to the New World, they brought cows and sheep. They quickly learned to appreciate the indigenous foods here, most notably corn, beans, squash, and chiles, and also more rare foods such as the thin-layered blue *piki* bread, or *chauquehue,* a thick corn pudding similar to polenta.

GROWING PAINS

Northern New Mexico is experiencing a reconquest of sorts, as the Anglo population soars and outside money and values again make their way in. The process continues to transform New Mexico's three distinct cultures and their unique ways of life, albeit in a less violent manner than during the Spanish conquest.

Certainly, the Anglos—many of them from large cities—add a cosmopolitan flavor to life here. The variety of restaurants has greatly improved, as have entertainment options. For their small size, towns such as Taos and Santa Fe offer a broad variety of restaurants and cultural events. Santa Fe has developed a strong dance and drama scene, with treats such as flamenco and opera that you'd expect to find in New York or Los Angeles. And Albuquerque has an exciting nightlife scene downtown; you can walk from club to club and hear a wealth of jazz, rock, country, and alternative music.

Yet many newcomers, attracted by the adobe houses and exotic feel of the place, often bring only a loose appreciation for the area. Some tend to romanticize the lifestyle of the other cultures and trivialize their beliefs. Native American symbology, for example, is employed in ever-popular Southwestern decorative motifs; New Age groups appropriate valued rituals, such as sweats (in which believers sit encamped in a very hot, enclosed space to cleanse their spirits). The effects of cultural and economic change are even apparent throughout the countryside, where land is being developed at an alarming rate.

Transformation of the local way of life and landscape is also apparent in the stores continually springing up in the area. For some of us, these are a welcome relief from Western clothing stores and provincial dress shops. The downside is that city plazas, which once contained pharmacies and grocery stores frequented by residents, are now crowded with T-shirt shops and galleries appealing to tourists. Many locals in these cities now rarely visit their plazas except during special events such as fiestas.

Environmental threats are another regional reality. Nuclear-waste issues form part of an ongoing conflict affecting the entire Southwest, and a section of southern New Mexico has been designated a nuclear-waste site. Because much of the waste must pass through Santa Fe, the U.S. government, along with the New Mexico state government, constructed a bypass that directs some transit traffic around the west side of the city.

Still, new ways of thinking have also brought positive changes to the life here, and many locals have directly benefited from New Mexico's influx of wealthy newcomers and popularity as a tourist destination. Businesses and industries large and small have come to the area. In Albuquerque, Intel Corporation now employs more than 5,500 workers, and in Santa Fe, the nationally renowned *Outside* magazine publishes monthly. Local artists and artisans also benefit from growth. Many craftspeople—furniture makers, tin workers, and weavers—have expanded their businesses. The influx of people has broadened the sensibility of a fairly provincial state. The area has become a refuge for many gays and lesbians, as well as for political exiles, such as Tibetans. With them has developed a level of creativity and tolerance you would generally find only in very large cities.

CULTURAL QUESTIONS

Faced with new challenges to their ways of life, both Native Americans and Hispanics are marshaling forces to protect their cultural identities. A prime concern is language. Through the years, many Pueblo people have begun to speak more and more English, with their children getting little exposure to their native tongue. In a number of the pueblos, elders are working with school children in language classes. Some of the pueblos have even developed written dictionaries, the first time their languages have been presented in this form.

Many pueblos have introduced programs to conserve the environment, preserve ancient seed strains, and protect religious rites. Because their religion is tied closely to nature, a loss of natural resources would threaten the entire culture. Certain rituals have been closed off to outsiders, the most notable being some of the rituals of Shalako at Zuni, a popular and elaborate series of year-end ceremonies.

Hispanics, through art and observance of cultural traditions, are also embracing their roots. In northern New Mexico, murals depicting important historic events, such as the Treaty of Guadalupe Hidalgo of 1848, adorn many walls. The **Spanish Market** in Santa Fe has expanded into a grand celebration of traditional arts—from tin working to *santo* carving. Public schools in the area have bilingual education programs, allowing students to embrace their Spanish-speaking roots.

Hispanics are also making their voices heard, insisting on more conscientious development of their neighborhoods and rising to positions of power in government. When she was in office, former Santa Fe Mayor Debbie Jaramillo made national news as an advocate of the Hispanic people, and Congressman Bill Richardson, Hispanic despite his Anglo surname, was appointed U.S. ambassador to the United Nations and then left that post to become energy secretary in President Clinton's cabinet. Currently, he is governor of New Mexico.

GAMBLING WINS & LOSSES

Gambling, a fact of life and source of much-needed revenue for Native American populations across the country, has been a center of controversy in northern New Mexico for a number of years. In 1994, Governor Gary Johnson signed a compact with tribes in New Mexico, ratified by the U.S. Department of the Interior, to allow full-scale gambling. **Tesuque Pueblo** was one of the first to begin a massive expansion, and many other pueblos followed suit.

Many New Mexicans are concerned about the tone gambling sets in the state. The casinos are for the most part large, neon-bedecked buildings that stand out sorely on some of New Mexico's most picturesque land. Though most residents appreciate the boost that gambling can ultimately bring to the Native American economies, many critics wonder where gambling profits actually go—and if the casinos can possibly be a good thing for the pueblos and tribes. Some detractors suspect that profits go directly into the pockets of outside backers.

A number of pueblos and tribes, however, are showing signs of prosperity, and they are using newfound revenues to buy firefighting and medical equipment and to invest in local schools. Isleta Pueblo built a $3½-million youth center, and the lieutenant governor says the money for it came from gambling revenues. Sandia Pueblo built a $2-million medical and dental clinic and, most recently, provided a computer for every tribal home. Its governor said these projects were "totally funded by gaming revenues." Some of the pueblos have built hotels on their property, most notable of them the Hyatt Regency Tamaya Resort at Santa Ana.

SANTA FE

Santa Fe is where the splendor of diverse cultures really shines, and it does so in a setting that's unsurpassed. There's a magic in Santa Fe that's difficult to explain, but you'll sense it when you glimpse an old adobe building set against blue mountains and giant billowing thunderheads, or when you hear a ranchero song come from a low-rider's radio and you smell chicken and chile grilling at a roadside vending booth. Although it's quickening, the pace of life here is still a few steps slower than that in the rest of the country. We use the word *mañana* to describe the pace—which doesn't mean "tomorrow" exactly, it just means "not today." There's also a level of creativity here that you'll find in few other places in the world. Artists who have fled big-city jobs are here to follow their passions, as are locals who grew up making crafts and continue to do so. Conversations often center on how to structure one's day so as to take advantage of the incredible outdoors while still making enough money to survive.

Meanwhile, Santa Fe's precipitous growth and enduring popularity with tourists have been a source of conflict and squabbling. Outsiders have bought up land in the hills around the city, building housing developments and sprawling single-family homes. The hills that local populations claimed for centuries as their own are being overrun, while property taxes for all have skyrocketed. Local outcry has prompted the city to implement zoning restrictions on where and how development can proceed. Some of the restrictions include banning building on ridge tops and on steep slopes and limiting the size of homes built.

Only in recent years have Santa Fe's politicians become conscientious about the city's growth. Mayor Debbie Jaramillo was one of the first local politicians to take a strong stand against growth. A fiery native of Santa Fe, she came into office as a representative of *la gente* (the people) and set about discouraging tourism and rapid development. Subsequent mayors have taken a middle-of-the-road approach to the issue, which has resulted in a calmer community and an increase in tourism and development.

TAOS

A funky town in the middle of a beautiful, sage-covered valley, Taos is full of narrow streets dotted with galleries and artisan shops. You might find an artist's studio tucked into a century-old church or a furniture maker working at the back of his own small shop.

More than any other major northern New Mexico community, Taos has successfully opposed much of the heavy development slated for the area. In the 1980s, locals stalled indefinitely plans to expand their airport; in the 1990s, they blocked plans for a $40-million golf course and housing development; and in 2003, they prevented a Super Wal-Mart from opening. It's hard to say where Taos gets its rebellious strength; the roots may lie in the hippie community that settled here in the '60s, or possibly the Pueblo community around which the city formed. After all, Taos Pueblo was at the center of the 17th-century Pueblo revolt.

Still, changes are upon Taoseños. The blinking light that for years residents used as a reference point has given way to a real traffic light. You'll also see the main route through town becoming more and more like Cerrillos Road in Santa Fe, as fast-food restaurants and service businesses set up shop. Though the town is working on alternate routes to channel through-traffic around downtown, there's no feasible way of widening the main drag because the street—which started out as a wagon trail—is bordered closely by historic buildings.

ALBUQUERQUE

The largest city in New Mexico, Albuquerque has borne the brunt of the state's most massive growth. Currently, the city sprawls more than 16 miles, from the lava-crested mesas on the west side of the Rio Grande to the steep alluvial slopes of the Sandia Mountains on the east, and north and south through the Rio Grande Valley. New subdivisions sprout up constantly.

Despite the growth, this town is most prized by New Mexicans for its genuineness. You'll find none of the self-conscious artsy atmosphere of Santa Fe here. Instead, there's a traditional New Mexico feel that's evident when you spend some time in the heart of the city. It centers around downtown, a place of shiny skyscrapers built around the original Route 66, which still maintains some of its 1950s charm.

The most emblematic growth problem concerns the **Petroglyph National Monument** on the west side. The area is characterized by five extinct volcanoes. Adjacent lava flows became a hunting and gathering place for prehistoric Native Americans, who left a chronicle of their beliefs etched in the dark basalt boulders. Over 25,000 petroglyphs have been found in the preserve. Now, a highway is being constructed through the center of the monument. Opponents fought it for more than a decade, with Native American groups likening the highway to building a road through a church.

Northern New Mexico's extreme popularity as a tourist destination has leveled out in the 21st century. Though many artists and other businesspeople lament the loss of the crowds we had back in the '80s, most people are glad that the wave has subsided. It's good news for travelers, too; they longer have to compete so heavily for restaurant seats or space when hiking through ruins. Though parts of northern New Mexico have lost some of the unique charm that attracted so many to the area, the overall feeling is still one of mystery and a cultural depth unmatched in the world.

3 Land of Art

It's all in the light—or at least that's what many artists claim drew them to northern New Mexico. In truth, the light is only part of the attraction: Nature in this part of the country, with its awe-inspiring thunderheads, endless expanse of blue skies, and rugged desert, is itself a canvas. To record the wonders of earth and sky, the Anasazi imprinted images—in the form of **petroglyphs** and **pictographs**—on the sides of caves and on stones, as well as on the sides of pots they shaped from clay dug in the hills.

Today's Native American tribes carry on that legacy, as do the other cultures that have settled here. Life in northern New Mexico is shaped by the arts. Everywhere you turn, you see pottery, paintings, jewelry, and weavings. You're liable to meet an artist whether you're having coffee in a Taos cafe or walking along Canyon Road in Santa Fe.

The area is full of little villages that maintain their own artistic specialties. Each Indian pueblo has a trademark design, such as Santa Clara's and San Ildefonso's black pottery and Zuni's needlepoint silver work. Bear in mind that the images used often have deep symbolic meaning. When purchasing art or an artifact, you may want to talk to its maker about what the symbols mean.

Hispanic villages are also distinguished by their artistic identities. Chimayo has become a center for Hispanic weaving, while the village of Cordova is known for its *santo* (icon) carving. *Santos, retablos* (paintings), and *bultos* (sculptures), as well as works in tin, are traditional devotional arts tied to the Roman Catholic faith. Often, these works are sold out of artists' homes in these villages, allowing you to glimpse the lives of the artists and the surroundings that inspire them.

Hispanic and Native American villagers take their goods to the cities, where for centuries people have bought and traded. Under the portals along the plazas of Santa Fe, Taos, and Albuquerque, you'll find a variety of works in silver, stone, and pottery for sale. In the cities, you'll find streets lined with galleries, some very slick, some more modest. At major markets, such as the Spanish Market and Indian Market in Santa Fe, some of the top artists from the area sell their works. Smaller shows at the pueblos also attract artists and artisans. The **Northern Pueblo Artists and Craftsman Show,** revolving each July to a different pueblo, continues to grow.

Drawn by the beauty of the local landscape and respect for indigenous art, artists from all over have flocked here, particularly during the 20th and 21st centuries. They have established locally important art societies; one of the most notable is the **Taos Society of Artists.** An oft-repeated tale explains the roots of this society. The artists **Bert Phillips** and **Ernest L. Blumenschein** were traveling through the area from Colorado on a mission to sketch the Southwest when their wagon broke down north of Taos. The scenery so overwhelmed them that they abandoned their journey and stayed. Joseph Sharp joined them, and still later came Oscar Berninghaus, Walter Ufner, Herbert Dunton, and others. You can see a brilliant collection of some of their romantically lit portraits and landscapes at the **Taos Art Museum.** The 100th anniversary marking the artists' broken wheel was celebrated in 1998.

A major player in the development of Taos as an artists' community was the arts patron **Mabel Dodge Luhan.** A writer who financed the work of many an artist, in the 1920s Luhan held court for many notables, including Georgia O'Keeffe, Willa Cather, and D. H. Lawrence. This illustrious history goes a long way to explaining how it is that Taos—a town of about 5,000 inhabitants—has more than 100 arts-and-crafts galleries and many resident painters.

Santa Fe has its own art society, begun in the 1920s by a nucleus of five painters who became known as **Los Cinco Pintores.** Jozef Bakos, Fremont Ellis, Walter Mruk, Willard Nash, and Will Shuster lived in the area of dusty Canyon Road (now the arts center of Santa Fe, with countless artists, approximately 100 galleries, and many museums). Despite its small size, Santa Fe is, remarkably, considered one of the top three art markets in the United States.

Perhaps the most celebrated artist associated with northern New Mexico is **Georgia O'Keeffe** (1887–1986), a painter who worked and lived most of her later years in the region. O'Keeffe's first sojourn to New Mexico in 1929 inspired her sensuous paintings of the area's desert landscape and bleached animal skulls. The house where she lived in Abiquiu (42 miles northwest of Santa Fe on US 84) is now open for limited public tours (see "Along the High Road to Taos," in chapter 10 for details). The **Georgia O'Keeffe Museum,** the largest museum in the United States dedicated entirely to a woman artist, opened in Santa Fe in 1997.

Santa Fe is also home to the **Institute of American Indian Arts,** where many of today's leading Native American artists have studied, including the Apache sculptor Allan Houser (whose works you can see near the State Capitol building and in other public areas in Santa Fe). The best-known Native American painter is R. C. Gorman, an Arizona Navajo who made his home in Taos for more than 2 decades. Recently deceased, Gorman is internationally acclaimed for his bright, somewhat surrealistic depictions of Navajo women. Also in the spotlight is Dan Namingha, a Hopi artist who weaves native symbology into contemporary concerns.

If you look closely, you'll find notable works from a number of local artists. There's Tammy Garcia, a young Taos potter who year after year continues to sweep the awards at Indian Market with her intricately shaped and carved pots. Cippy Crazyhorse, a Cochiti, has acquired a steady following of patrons for his silver jewelry. All around the area you'll see the frescoes of Frederico Vigil, a noted muralist and Santa Fe native. From the village of Santa Cruz comes a new rising star named Andrés Martinez, noted for his Picassoesque portraits of Hispanic village life.

For the visitor interested in art, however, some caution should be exercised; there's a lot of schlock out there, targeting the tourist trade. Yet if you persist, you're likely to find much inspiring work as well. The museums and many of the galleries are excellent repositories of local art. Their offerings range from small-town folk art to works by major artists who show internationally.

4 Architecture: A Rich Melting Pot

Northern New Mexico's distinctive architecture reflects the diversity of cultures that have left their imprint on the region. The first people in the area were the ancestral Puebloans or Anasazi, who built stone and mud homes at the bottom of canyons and inside caves (which look rather like condominiums to the modern urban eye). **Pueblo-style adobe architecture** evolved and became the basis for traditional New Mexican homes: sun-dried clay bricks mixed with grass for strength, mud-mortared, and covered with additional protective layers of mud. Roofs are supported by a network of vigas—long beams whose ends protrude through the outer facades—and *latillas,* smaller stripped branches layered between the vigas. Other adapted Pueblo architectural elements include plastered adobe-brick kiva fireplaces, *bancos* (adobe benches that protrude from walls), and *nichos* (small indentations within a wall in which religious icons are placed). These adobe homes are characterized by flat roofs and soft, rounded contours.

Spaniards wedded many elements to Pueblo style, such as portals (porches held up with posts, often running the length of a home) and enclosed patios, as well as the simple, dramatic sculptural shapes of Spanish mission arches and bell towers. They also brought elements from the Moorish architecture found in southern Spain: heavy wooden doors and elaborate *corbels*—carved wooden supports for vertical posts.

With the opening of the Santa Fe Trail in 1821 and later the 1860s gold boom, both of which brought more Anglo settlers, came the next wave of building. New arrivals contributed architectural elements such as neo-Grecian and Victorian influences popular in the middle part of the United States at the time. Distinguishing features of what came to be known as **Territorial-style** architecture can be seen today; they include brick facades and cornices as well as porches, often placed on the second story. You'll also note millwork on doors and wood trim around windows and doorways, double-hung windows, and Victorian bric-a-brac.

Santa Fe Plaza is an excellent example of the convergence of these early architectural styles. On the west side is a Territorial-style balcony, while the Palace of the Governors is marked by Pueblo-style vigas and oversize Spanish/Moorish doors.

Nowhere else in the United States are you likely to see such extremes of architectural style as in northern New Mexico. In Santa Fe, you'll see the Romanesque architecture of the **St. Francis Cathedral** and the Gothic-style **Loretto Chapel,** brought by Archbishop Lamy from France, as well as the railroad station built in the **Spanish Mission style**—popular in the early part of the 20th century.

Since 1957, strict city building codes have required that all new structures within the circumference of the Paseo de

Peralta conform to one of two revival styles: Pueblo or Territorial. The regulation also limits the height of the buildings and restricts the types of signs permitted, and it requires buildings to be topped by flat roofs.

Albuquerque also has a broad array of styles, most evident in a visit to **Old Town.** There, you'll find the large Italianate brick house known as the **Herman Blueher home,** built in 1898; throughout Old Town you'll find little *placitas,* homes, and haciendas built around courtyards, a strategy developed not only for defense purposes but also as a way to accommodate several generations of the same family in different wings of a single dwelling. **The Church of San Felipe de Neri** at the center of Old Town is centered between two folk Gothic towers. This building was begun in a cruciform plan in 1793; subsequent architectural changes resulted in an interesting mixture of styles.

Most notable architecturally in Taos is the **Taos Pueblo,** the site of two structures emulated in homes and business buildings throughout the Southwest. Built to resemble Taos Mountain, which stands behind it, the two structures are pyramidal in form, with the different levels reached by ladders. Also quite prevalent is architecture echoing colonial hacienda style. What's nice about Taos is that you can see historic homes inside and out. You can wander through artist **Ernest Blumenschein's home.** Built in 1797 and restored by Blumenschein in 1919, it represents another New Mexico architectural phenomenon: homes that were added onto year after year. Doorways are typically low, and floors rise and fall at the whim of the earth beneath them. The **Martinez Hacienda** is an example of a hacienda stronghold. Built without windows facing outward, it originally had 20 small rooms, many with doors opening out to the courtyard. One

of the few refurbished examples of colonial New Mexico architecture and life, the hacienda is on the National Historic Registry.

As you head into villages in the north, you'll see steep-pitched roofs on most homes. This is because the common flat-roof style doesn't shed snow; the water builds up and causes roof problems. In just about any town in northern New Mexico, you may detect the strong smell of tar, a sure sign that another resident is laying out thousands to fix his enchanting but frustratingly flat roof.

Today, very few new homes are built of adobe. Instead, most are constructed with wood frames and plasterboard, and then stuccoed over. Several local architects are currently employing innovative architecture to create a Pueblo-style feel. They incorporate straw bails, pumice-crete, rammed earth, old tires, even aluminum cans in the construction of homes. Most of these elements are used in the same way bricks are used, stacked and layered, and then covered over with plaster and made to look like adobe. Often it's difficult to distinguish homes built with these materials from those built with wood-frame construction. West of Taos, a number of "earthships" have been built. Many of these homes are constructed with alternative materials, most bermed into the sides of hills, utilizing the earth as insulation and the sun as an energy source.

A visitor could spend an entire trip to New Mexico focusing on the architecture. As well as relishing the wealth of architectural styles, you'll find more subtle elements everywhere. You may encounter an ox-blood floor, for example. An old Spanish tradition, ox blood is spread in layers and left to dry, hardening into a glossy finish that's known to last centuries. You're also likely to see coyote fences—narrow cedar posts lined up side by side—a system early settlers devised to ensure safety of their animals. Winding around homes and buildings you'll see *acequias,* ancient irrigation canals still maintained by locals for watering crops and trees. Throughout the area you'll notice that old walls are whimsically bowed, and windows and floors are often crooked, constant reminders of the effects time has had on even these stalwart structures.

5 Anthropology 101: Beliefs & Rituals

Religion has always been a central, defining element in the life of the Pueblo people. Within the cosmos, which they view as a single whole, all living creatures are mutually dependent. Thus, every relationship a human being may have, whether with a person, an animal, or a plant, has spiritual significance. A hunter prays before killing a deer, asking the creature to sacrifice itself to the tribe. A slain deer is treated as a guest of honor, and the hunter performs a ritual in which he sends the animal's soul back to its community, so that it may be reborn. Even the harvesting of plants requires prayer, thanks, and ritual.

The Pueblo people believe that their ancestors originally lived under the ground, which, as the place from which plants spring, is the source of all life. According to their beliefs, the original Pueblos, encouraged by burrowing animals, entered the world of humans—the so-called "fourth" world—through a hole, a *sipapu.* The ways in which this came about and the deities that the Pueblo people revere vary from tribe to tribe. Most, however, believe this world is enclosed by four sacred mountains, where four sacred colors—coral, black, turquoise, and yellow or white—predominate.

There is no single great spirit ruling over this world; instead, it is watched over by a number of spiritual elements. Most common are Mother Earth and Father Sun. In this desert land, the sun is an element of both life and death. The tribes watch the skies closely, tracking solstices and planetary movements, to determine the optimal time for crop planting.

Ritualistic dances are occasions of great symbolic importance. Usually held in conjunction with the feast days of Catholic saints (including Christmas Eve), Pueblo ceremonies demonstrate the parallel absorption of Christian elements without the surrendering of traditional beliefs. To this day, communities enact medicine dances, fertility rites, and prayers for rain and for good harvests. The spring and summer corn, or *tablita,* dances are among the most impressive. Ceremonies begin with an early-morning Mass and procession to the plaza; the image of the saint is honored at the forefront. The rest of the day is devoted to song, dance, and feasting, with performers masked and clad as deer, buffalo, eagles, or other creatures.

Visitors are usually welcome to attend Pueblo dances, but they should respect the tribe's requests not to be photographed or recorded. It was exactly this lack of respect that led the Zunis to ban outsiders from attending many of their famous Shalako ceremonies.

Catholicism, imposed by the Spaniards, has infused northern New Mexico with an elaborate set of beliefs. This is a Catholicism heavy with iconography, expressed in carved *santos* (statues) and beautiful *retablos* (paintings) that adorn the altars of many cathedrals. Catholic churches are the focal points of most northern New Mexico villages. If you take the high road to Taos, be sure to note the church in **Las Trampas,** as well as the one in **Ranchos de Taos;** both have 3- to 4-foot-thick walls sculpted from adobe and inside have old-world charm, with beautiful *retablos* decorating the walls and vigas supporting the ceiling.

Hispanics in northern New Mexico, in particular, maintain strong family and

Moments   Danse Macabre

The **Dance of the Matachines,** a ritualistic dance performed at northern New Mexico pueblos and in many Hispanic communities, reveals the cultural miscegenation, identities, and conflicts that characterize northern New Mexico. It's a dark and vivid ritual in which a little girl, Malinche, is wedded to the church. The dance, depicting the taming of the native spirit, is difficult even for historians to decipher.

Brought to the New World by the Spaniards, the dance has its roots in the painful period during which the Moors were driven out of Spain. However, some symbols seem obvious: At one point, men bearing whips tame "El Toro," a small boy dressed as a bull who has been charging about rebelliously. The whip-men symbolically castrate him and then stroll through the crowd, pretending to display the dismembered body parts, as if to warn villagers of the consequences of disobedience. At another point, a hunched woman-figure births a small troll-like doll, perhaps representative of the union between Indian and Hispanic cultures.

The Dance of the Matachines ends when two *abuelo* (grandparent) figures dance across the dirt, holding up the just-born baby, while the Matachines, adorned with bishop-like headdresses, follow them away in a recessional march. The Matachines' dance, often performed in the early mornings, is so dark and mystical that every time I see it, my passion for this area deepens. The image of that baby always stays with me, and in a way represents New Mexico itself: a place born of disparate beliefs that have melded with the sand, sage, and sun and produced incredible richness.

Catholic ties, and they continue to honor traditions associated with both. Communities plan elaborate celebrations such as the *quinciniera* for young girls reaching womanhood, and weddings with big feasts and dances in which well-wishers pin money to the bride's elaborately laced gown.

If you happen to be in the area during a holiday, you may even get to see a religious procession or pilgrimage. Most notable is the **pilgrimage to the Santuario de Chimayo,** an hour's drive north of the state capital. Constructed in 1816, the sanctuary has long been a pilgrimage site for Catholics who attribute miraculous healing powers to the earth found in the chapel's anteroom. Several days before Easter, fervent believers begin walking the highway headed north or south to Chimayo, some carrying large crosses, others carrying nothing but small bottles of water, most praying for a miracle.

In recent years, New Mexico has become known (and in some circles, ridiculed) for **New Age pilgrims and celebrations.** The roots of the local movement are hard to trace. It may have something to do with northern New Mexico's centuries-old reputation as a place where rebel thinkers come to enjoy the freedom to believe what they want. Pueblo spirituality and deeply felt connection to the land are also factors that have drawn New Agers. At any rate, the liberated atmosphere here has given rise to a thriving New Age network, one that now includes alternative churches, healing centers, and healing schools. You'll find all sorts of alternative medicine and fringe practices here, from aromatherapy to rolfing (a form of massage that realigns the muscles and bones in the body) and chelation therapy (in which an IV drips ethylene diamine tetra-acetic acid into the blood to remove heavy metals). If those sound too invasive, you can always try psychic surgery.

New Age practices and beliefs have given rise to a great deal of local humor targeting their supposed psychobabble. One pointed joke asks: "How many New Agers does it take to change a light bulb?" Answer: "None. They just form a support group and learn to live in the dark." For many, however, there's much good to be found in the movement. The Dalai Lama visited Santa Fe because the city is seen as a healing center and has become a refuge for Tibetans. Notable speakers such as Ram Dass and Thomas Moore have also come to the area. Many practitioners find the alternatives—healing resources and spiritual paths—they are looking for in the receptive northern New Mexico desert and mountains.

6 Chiles, *Sopaipillas* & Other New Mexican Specialties

Northern New Mexicans are serious about eating, and the area's cuisine reflects the amalgam of cultural influences found here. Locals have given their unique blend of Hispanic and Pueblo recipes a rather prosaic, but direct, label: "Northern New Mexico Cuisine."

Food here isn't the same as Mexican cuisine or even variations like Tex-Mex and Cal-Mex. New Mexican cooking is a product of Southwestern history: Native Americans taught the Spanish conquerors about corn—how to roast it and how to make corn pudding, stewed corn, cornbread, cornmeal, and *posole* (hominy)—and they also taught the Spanish how to use chile peppers, a crop indigenous to the New World, having been first harvested in the Andean highlands as early as 4000 B.C. The Spaniards brought the practice of eating beef to the area.

Waves of newcomers have introduced other elements to the food here. From Mexico came the interest in seafood. You'll find fish tacos on many menus as well as shrimp enchiladas and ceviche (or seviche; chilled fish marinated in lime juice). New Southwestern cuisine combines elements from various parts of Mexico, such as sauces from the Yucatán Peninsula, and fried bananas served with bean dishes, typical of Costa Rica and other Central American locales. You'll also find Asian elements mixed in, such as pot stickers in a tortilla soup.

The basic ingredients of northern New Mexican cooking are three indispensable, locally grown foods: **chile, beans,** and **corn.** Of these, perhaps the most crucial is the chile, whether brilliant red or green and with various levels of spicy bite. Chiles form the base for the red and green sauces that top most northern New Mexico dishes such as enchiladas and burritos. One is not necessarily hotter than the other; spiciness depends on the type and where and during what kind of season (dry or wet) the chiles were grown. You'll also find salsas, generally made with jalapeños, tomatoes, onions, and garlic, used for chip dipping and as a spice on tacos.

Beans—spotted or painted pinto beans with a nutty taste—are simmered with garlic, onion, cumin, and red chile powder and served as a side dish. When mashed and refried in oil, they become *frijoles refritos*. **Corn** supplies the vital dough for tortillas and tamales called *masa*. New Mexican corn comes in six colors, of which yellow, white, and blue are the most common.

Fun Fact You Say Chili, We Say Chile

You'll never see "chili" on a menu in New Mexico. New Mexicans are adamant that chile, the Spanish spelling of the word, is the only way to spell it—no matter what your dictionary might say.

In fact, we have such a personal attachment to this small agricultural gem that in 1983, we directed our senior U.S. senator Pete Domenici to enter New Mexico's official position on the spelling of chile into the Congressional Record. That's taking your chiles seriously.

Chiles are grown throughout the state, in a perfect climate for cultivating and drying the small but powerful red and green varieties. But it is the town of Hatch, in southern New Mexico, that bills itself as the "Chile Capital of the World." Regardless of where you travel in the state, chiles appear on the menu. Usually you'll be asked whether you prefer red or green. Your best bet is to inquire which, on that particular day in that particular restaurant, is hottest and tastiest and make your decision based on the answer. If you can't decide, just say, "Christmas," and you'll get both.

Virtually anything you order in a restaurant is likely to be topped with a chile sauce. If you're not accustomed to spicy foods, certain varieties will make your eyes water, your sinuses drain, and your palate feel as if it's on fire—all after just one forkful. *Warning:* No amount of water or beer will alleviate the sting. (Drink milk or eat a *sopaipilla* drizzled with honey.)

But don't let these words of caution scare you away from genuine New Mexico chiles. The pleasure of eating them far outweighs the pain. Start slow, with salsas and chile sauces first, perhaps rellenos (stuffed peppers) next. Before long, you'll be buying chile ristras (chiles strung on rope) and hanging them up for decoration. Perhaps you'll be so smitten that you'll purchase bags of chile powder or a chile plant to take home.

If you happen to be in New Mexico in the fall, you'll find chile roasting in tumblers in the parking lots of most grocery stores and at some roadside stands, the sweet, singed scent filling the air. If you have a means of freezing the chile before transporting it home, you can sample the delicacy throughout the year. This will certainly make you an expert on the difference between chile and chili.

Even if you're familiar with Mexican cooking, the dishes you know and love are likely to be prepared differently here. The following is a rundown of some regional dishes, a number of which aren't widely known outside the Southwest:

biscochito A cookie made with anise.

carne adovada Tender pork marinated in red chile sauce, herbs, and spices, and then baked.

chile rellenos Peppers stuffed with cheese, deep-fried, and then covered with green chile sauce.

chorizo burrito (also called a "breakfast burrito") Mexican sausage, scrambled eggs, potatoes, and scallions wrapped in a flour tortilla with red or green chile sauce and melted Jack cheese.

empañada A fried pie with nuts and currants.

enchiladas   Tortillas either rolled or layered with chicken, beef, or cheese, topped with chile sauce.

fajitas   Strips of beef or chicken sautéed with onions, green peppers, and other vegetables and served on a sizzling platter.

green chile stew   Locally grown chiles cooked in a stew with chunks of meat, beans, and potatoes.

huevos rancheros   Fried eggs on corn tortillas, topped with cheese and red or green chile, served with pinto beans.

pan dulce   A sweet Native American bread.

posole   A corn soup or stew (called *hominy* in other parts of the South), sometimes prepared with pork and chile.

sopaipilla   A lightly fried puff pastry served with honey as a dessert or stuffed with meat and vegetables as a main dish. *Sopaipillas* with honey have a cooling effect on your palate after you've eaten a spicy dish.

tacos   Spiced chicken or beef served either in soft tortillas or crispy shells.

tamales   A dish made from cornmeal mush, wrapped in husks and steamed.

vegetables and nuts   Unusual local ingredients, such as piñon nuts, jicama, and prickly pear cactus, will often be a part of your meals.

Index

See also Accommodations and Restaurant indexes, below.

ACCOMMODATIONS

THE NEW TRAVELOCITY GUARANTEE

EVERYTHING YOU BOOK WILL BE RIGHT, OR WE'LL WORK WITH OUR TRAVEL PARTNERS TO MAKE IT RIGHT, RIGHT AWAY.

*To drive home the point,
we're going to use the word "right" in every single sentence.*

Let's get right to it. Right to the meat! Only Travelocity guarantees everything about your booking will be right, or we'll work with our travel partners to make it right, right away. Right on!

Here's a picture taken smack dab right in the middle of Antigua, where the guarantee also covers you.

The guarantee covers all but one of the items pictured to the right.

Now, you may be thinking, "Yeah, right, I'm so sure." That's OK; you have the right to remain skeptical. That is until we mention help is always right around the corner. Call us right off the bat, knowing that our customer service reps are there for you 24/7. Righting wrongs. Left and right.

For example, what if the ocean view you booked actually looks out at a downright ugly parking lot? You'd be right to call – we're there for you. And no one in their right mind would be pleased to learn the rental car place has closed and left them stranded. Call Travelocity and we'll help get you back on the right track.

Now if you're guessing there are some things we can't control, like the weather, well you're right. But we can help you with most things – to get all the details in righting,* visit **travelocity.com/guarantee**.

*Sorry, spelling things right is one of the few things not covered under the guarantee.

You'll never roam alone.

IF YOU BOOK IT, IT SHOULD BE THERE.

Only Travelocity guarantees it will be, or we'll work with our travel partners to make it right, right away. So if you're missing a balcony or anything else you booked, just call us 24/7. 1-888-TRAVELOCITY.

travelocity
You'll never roam alone